Human Development:
The Adult Years
and Aging

carroll e. kennedy

KANSAS STATE UNIVERSITY

Human Development: The Adult Years and Aging

Macmillan Publishing Co., Inc.

NEW YORK

Collier Macmillan Publishers

LONDON

Macmillan Publishing Co., Inc.
866 Third Avenue, New York, New York 10022

Collier Macmillan Canada, Ltd.

Library of Congress Cataloging in Publication Data

Kennedy, Carroll E
Human development.

Bibliography: p.
Includes index.

   1.   Adulthood.   2.   Family—United States.
3.   Maturation (Psychology)   4.   Aging.
5.   Old age.   I.   Title.
QH1064.U5K47   301.43   77-617
ISBN 0-02-362450-7

Printing: 1 2 3 4 5 6 7 8   Year: 8 9 0 1 2 3 4

Preface

This text is designed for the adult development course in a human development curriculum. Its approach is to extend for the adult years the consideration of developmental experiences that other courses direct to childhood and adolescence.

An increasingly large proportion of our population is in middle and later adult life. This change is resulting in a new interest in the behavior, characteristics, and patterns of development of people throughout the adult years. New programs in education, health, recreation, and other human services are being developed, drawing on the expanding research in adult development and aging.

This text begins by providing an orientation to the study of human development and the processes of behavior change. These processes—social, self, physiological, and transpersonal—are considered from the perspective of adult years. The beginning chapters identify the significant issues necessary for understanding growth and development through the life-span. They include the factor of continuity and change in the individual personality, the effect of stress and environment, the voluntary and involuntary control of behavior, and the influence of norms and roles. Family life—including singlehood, widowhood, and divorce—and the world of work feature strongly in this consideration of adult developmental processes.

Part Two examines the successive stages of young adult years, middle adult years, maturity, and old age. In this section the reader—whether general education student or student in preparatory courses in human services—begins to formulate an understanding of motivations, satisfactions, needs, and perceptions of persons in different stages of adulthood.

Numerous vignettes from case material and popular literature help the student experience the concepts of development from the perspective of observing individual lives. Suggested activities at the end of each chapter direct attention to application of concepts and further study. Implications of the data in terms of programs to facilitate optimum development for persons of all ages are considered throughout the book and are a special focus of the final chapter.

The phenomenon of aging and the special concerns of old people are considered extensively in this text. The discussion differs from some other books on old age in that it views these issues from the perspective of developmental processes of learning, motivation, self-awareness, and physiological change; aging is seen as the continuation of lifelong patterns of development. The text recognizes the considerable diversity of competencies among people at all ages and sees individual functioning as the product of the interaction of multiple determinants and contingencies, many of which are not related to chronological age.

Many people have contributed to the development of this book, especially the students with whom I have talked in counseling and research interviews and the students who have provided feedback on preliminary drafts of the material in classes in human development and adult life. Although the responsibility for the specific content of the book is my own, I am appreciative of the many substantive suggestions offered in the critical reading of the text by Vern L. Bengtson, Sally L. VanZandt, and two anonymous readers.

I am grateful to my colleagues in the Department of Family and Child Development who shouldered extra burdens to allow me the opportunity of sabbatical leave for visiting gerontological centers and for writing. I wish also to acknowledge the contribution that my research time with the Kansas Agricultural Experiment Station has made to this study through the years. I am greatly appreciative of the dedication of Kitzel Thomas, Gayla Brown, Ruth Spiker, and JoAnn Driggers in the typing and retyping of the manuscript. Marilou Huxman helped with editing and with library work, as well as with the typing, and Kathleen Ward was of assistance with the photographs.

Preparing this book has afforded me special opportunities in family relations. Some of the chapters were written while we "house sat" the homes of vacationing relatives during our sabbatical leave. More especially significant has been the opportunity to share with my wife, Lois, in a new area of partnership as she worked consistently as research associate with me throughout the preparation of this book. Our relationship has been deepened by the experiences we shared and by the common body of knowledge that is now imprinted in our respective nervous systems.

In examples 3-7, 3-14, 8-2, 8-3, 8-4, 8-5, 8-6, and 8-7, the names and places have been changed to protect the privacy of individuals involved.

C. E. K.

Contents

chapter 3   *Adult Development through Family and Work Relationships*   46

chapter 4   *Physiological Processes*   114

Part TWO

STAGES OF ADULT DEVELOPMENT

chapter 7 *The Study of Adult Development: An Overview*   187

Part ONE

FOUNDATIONS OF HUMAN DEVELOPMENT AND AGING

chapter 1

Introduction

The chances are that if asked to do so, you could place yourself within one of the stages of adult development. Intuitively, you probably think of yourself as a young adult, middle-aged, in the preretirement period, or old-aged. Associated with each of these periods are certain family and community relationships, certain expectations you and others have about your behavior and your identity. You are one of nearly 134 million adults in America. Americans under 18 years of age number approximately 70 million.[1] Nearly two thirds of our people are adults.

Although the tenor of advertisements and much of the media presentations still maintain a youth orientation, the large majority of our population is clearly in the adult phase of the life-span. There is an increasing proportion of our population at all points along the adult life-span, whereas the portion of our population who are children and adolescents is decreasing.

As you think of your adult status, you are probably aware that your experiences and characteristics are much different from other persons of various age groups, and to plan services for different groups, we need to understand the similarities and differences among adults. We need to know what attitudes and activities are characteristic of young adults and of those in old age. We need to know what changes are going on in the emotions and physiology of those in middle age.

---

[1] U.S. Bureau of Census, *Statistical Abstracts of the United States: 1970* (Washington, D.C.: U.S. Government Printing Office, 1974), p. 31.

1–1 *The study of human development seeks to identify the reoccurring themes that form the score to the song of life.* (Manhattan Mercury photo)

Our Changing Population

As the percentage of older persons in our society increases, the experience of being older is also changing. These changes come about through new technologies and values charactcristic of a new historical period; and they come about also as the formula changes in the mix of young and old, resulting in a different social milieu. We can observe this as we follow through the social ripples accompanying the population wave of the "baby boom" following World War II.

The baby boom following World War II swelled the proportion of children in our population during the 1950s and of college students in the 1960s and 1970s. These war babies have caused bulges in the youth portions of our population profile and the bulge will shift toward middle-aged and older groups in the years ahead. The large number of births in the 1940s and 1950s, coupled with a decreasing rate of births in the following years, has caused this group of persons to be a focus of national planning throughout their life-

1–2 The baby boom swelled our population during the 1950s and caused bulges in the proportion of youth and college students in the 1960s. The bulge will shift toward middle age and older groups in the next decades. (Kansas State University Student Publications photos)

time. Combined with change in rate of births were improved health conditions that also contributed to a change in our population profile. The reduction in deaths from contagious diseases has helped to keep a large proportion of the war babies alive and well into adult life. The influences of improved health conditions have not been confined to those in the growing years of

5

childhood, however. Parents of the war babies also benefited. So now, as the war babies approach middle age, there will be many more of their parents (than in previous generations) alive and able to lead healthy, vigorous lives. This extends the size of the adult portion of our national profile further, and together these factors significantly alter our national picture.

Age-appropriate Human Services

Programs concerned with the quality of life must relate to the changing profile of a community or nation. The climate of a community—its values, interests, and commitment, its style of life—changes as the community's ratio of people with differing characteristics changes. Thus we have seen the psychosocial tones of our nation modulate as the proportion of old and young groups in our population has changed through the years. Needs of individuals vary as they move through entry into work and family life, as they reach new career plateaus and changes in community responsibilities, and as they make new commitments at midpoints in life. Adults will seek services appropriate to their different stages. The professional and community groups who plan community services will increasingly look to the field of human development for perspective with which to plan for changes throughout the life-span.

Life-span Perspective

The objective of this book is to put the periods of adult life within a framework of developmental processes; it is to extend the picture of human growth beyond infancy and childhood to encompass the whole life-span. Such a perspective needs to be built into the lenses society uses if we are to plan creatively for the new energies and resources that accompany the developmental stages in adult life.

The multitude of factors we have recognized as contributing to the individual differences in children and youth are also present in considering individual growth patterns of adults. The complexity of adult personality and behavior allows for even greater individuality in adult years because of the longer and more varied range of experiences combined with physiological changes. We cannot say that all old people are alike, or even that all 70-year-old people are alike. Some people at 70 are more like people 50 years old, and vice versa.

As the individual develops through the years, there is both *continuity* and *change* in his personality. The study of adult development seeks to understand what factors contribute to each aspect of growth. There is an orderliness through the changing years of adulthood that reflects certain sequences in development. But the kinds of factors that influenced sequence during childhood—such as the physical changes enabling the child to speak or crawl—are different from the kinds of factors that enable an individual to choose a career or a marriage partner.

There are certain attitudes, behaviors, and desires typically experienced by people at certain periods of their lives, people who have lived through common periods of history and experience. However, each person deals with the common experiences in an individual fashion. Thus, our study of adult development seeks to understand factors contributing to continuity and change and to commonality and uniqueness in the patterns of adult development. For example, we have learned that social class may alter the pace but not greatly change the pattern of developmental steps; and we have also learned that personality-change patterns often seem to differ for men and for women in their fifties.

Timing and pattern are important factors in considering personality development. A well-known student of human development at Harvard University[2] has pointed out that some of the personality characteristics of Winston Churchill that enabled him to unify, inspire, and lead his people in England's hour of peril were characteristics that had caused his career up to that time to be spotty and often unsuccessful. Each individual is developing his own unique pattern of life. "Strengths and weaknesses, maturities and immaturities, have to be judged according to their relevance to the individual pattern, recognizing that no person can be everything and that not all good qualities are necessarily compatible."[3] As we consider growth during adult years, we ask what are the interests and competencies of the individual in relation to the life pattern and goals he is projecting. Rather than specifying a certain list of attitudes and behaviors and measuring adult growth in terms of how many of those an individual possesses, we look instead at an individual's life plan.

[2] R. W. White, "The Healthy Personality," *The Counseling Psychologist* 4 (1973), 2:7–8.
[3] Ibid., p. 8.

Individuals do continue to change markedly throughout life—contrary to society's seeming assumption that all growth stops at age 18. Individuals continue to grow, to change through time, influenced by the circumstances about them, by their innate capacities and health, and by the self-image, hopes, and aspirations arising from their experiences. The issues with which adults are concerned are different from those of earlier life, and so the study of adult development and aging is different from the study of child development.

A Word About Old Age

This is a textbook on human development through adult years and aging. Unfortunately, there is a good chance that for most people who read the title of this book the phrase that will most register in their minds will be *old age*. Our society is experiencing a rising focus on old age and the impact of the shift in the distribution of our population. The reason I suggested that the heightened sensitivity to old age is unfortunate is that to adequately appreciate the qualities and meaning of that period of life, it must be put within the developmental context of the adult life spectrum.

Without a developmental basis for viewing old age, there is a tendency for individuals and social planners to focus on weaknesses and problems experienced by some elderly individuals and to think of these as characteristic of old age. However, many concerns that people associate with old age are the product of disease or poverty and not of old age itself. Disease and poverty are not confined to any one age group and their product is society's concern for all age groups.

Some physical decline does occur with old age; however, the following comments from the summary of a longitudinal study of normal aging point to the important place of individual differences and to the interrelated influences of physical, social, and psychological functioning.

The process of physical aging is not necessarily an irresistible and irreversible force. Health and functioning can and do improve for some older persons just as they do for younger persons . . . [There is] little or no decline in social and psychological functioning [in healthy old people] . . . It is impressive how many of the normal aged are able to compensate for their growing physical handicaps and maintain fairly stable levels of social and psychological functioning . . . The aged usually show more individual variability than the young . . . Thus, even when there are significant mean differences between old and young, there is usually considerable overlap between the two distributions. This means that many older persons have better functioning and better scores than many younger persons.[4]

Old age is the product of the interaction of multiple influences, as are all earlier stages. For example, the experience of old age will be different for the 20 million persons now over 65 than it was for people of similar age a few years ago. The new status that their rising influence will bring, the new modes of communication, and the multitude of other technological and cultural changes taking place will make old age different for old people in the 1980s.

[4] E. Palmore, ed., *Normal Aging II* (Durham: Duke University Press, 1974), pp. 289–290.

1–3 *To appreciate the qualities and meaning of old age, we must put it within the developmental context of the adult life-span.* (The Hiding Place, press photo)

Old age is but one of several periods in adult life. For years the study of human development was directed toward childhood and adolescence; but our changing population has brought about a change in research interest. In preparing a bibliography of biomedical and social science research on aging conducted during the period 1954–1974, one research center listed approximately 50,000 titles.[5] Old age is a rapidly growing area both in research and in program development.

The Writer's Lenses

For more than twenty years I have been—in varying combinations—a member of a counseling center staff, a college teacher, and a director of research projects engaged in the study of human development. It has been a happy ordering of life's fortunes that has allowed me to serve in these capacities, which in turn have enabled me to pursue lines of inquiry, hunches, and questions that began much earlier in life as a youth and as an undergraduate student of literature.

Literature was, of course, a provocative introduction to the study of human development. The artist, writer, or philosopher is to some extent simply charting his own progress through the developmental stages of life. His works reflect his interactions with life's flow—humorous or tragic. The novelist, the poet, and the researcher in human development—each in his own way—attempt to respond to man's self-conscious need to understand and make sense of "who he is" and "where he is going." The function of scholarship is to provide some integrative assembly of the interpretations and reflections men have made as, throughout history, they have examined the life they were encountering. Books or other products of scholarship are simply tools against which other students may try their life experiences.

In the analysis of individual experiences, we create some artificial categories and separate into segments the experience of life, which is in reality a seamless fabric. We talk about individuals and we talk about groups and we talk about families. We talk about physical processes and social processes, self-processes and spiritual processes. We talk about roles and traits, and abilities, interests, and values. These are simply conveniences. They help us stop the action for a moment and look at it from different perspectives. Certain

[5] D. S. Woodruff, "Introduction: Multidisciplinary Perspectives of Aging," in *Aging,* eds. D. S. Woodruff and J. E. Birren (New York: Van Nostrand, 1975), p. 3.

1–4 *The works of writers, philosophers, or students of human development simply reflect their interaction with life's flow—humorous or tragic. (Photo, University for Man, Manhattan, Kansas)*

1–5 *Our theories and scholarly terms are simply conveniences. They help us stop the action and look for a moment at life from different perspectives. (Photo, University for Man, Manhattan, Kansas)*

literary or scholarly conveniences have more popularity at one time than another, reflecting prevailing preoccupations of that particular period of history. They are the characters and words people put together to try to express how they are interacting with the world at that time.

The conveniences I will use reflect the period of history in which I grew up and in which I have been living during my professional life. They reflect the encouragement and the reinforcement I had to select certain ideas and vocabulary from a wide range of concepts and terms included in the long history of man's study of human experiences. The next few paragraphs suggest some of the value judgments I have developed, which influence my treatment of data and interpretation of events. Although later in the book some of these issues may be presented as ideas being debated by scholars in the field, and in that context alternative points of view will be included. Yet, it is important for the reader to know (and to keep in mind) the predispositions I have that in some way or other will have influenced my selection of issues and my way of treating them. This is simply to say that there is no writing and there are no research experiences that are without the subjective element of the person performing the task.

This is one in a series of texts on human development offered by this publisher. Others in the series deal with different stages in childhood. As we use the term *human,* we have begun a process of categorizing. The human being has life, self-consciousness, awareness of experience. This means that the human being can know himself to be active at this moment; at the same time he can remember himself in past activity and he can look forward to seeing himself in activities in the future. These are characteristics that distinguish him from other forms of life. Although having characteristics different from other forms of life, the human being is not totally separated from other influences of the universe.

Research has given us some understanding of the influence of our social environment—that is, our families, our neighbors, our employers. We are less sure at this time about how much we are influenced by the thought processes or the emotional feelings of other persons more distant from us. In the section of the book dealing with our bodies and our physical functioning, we will spend some time considering ways in which research in contemporary physics has opened the doors for us to be aware of energy systems that tend to create a closer unity between the individual and the physical universe. The rhythms of the body may well coincide with rhythms of the tides and of the universe.

There is an orderliness about the behavior of individuals that causes us at times to describe them as predictable. We can say that certain events are associated consistently with certain behaviors in a given individual. Much of our research has been to understand the meaning of events in the life of an individual or group so as to be able to make predictions about behavior. Man, however, is a creature of paradox. Whereas we need to underscore the predictable nature of man, we also need to recognize that each is a unique individual given to some aspects of choice and performance that cannot be explained on the basis of prior conditioning. These performances require some further concept such as will or hope or faith. Such references to paradox will appear time and again in the pages to follow. Paradox is at the core of human experience. We seek form and pattern; these create norms for daily activity and outlines for a theory of human development. However, "individuality" and "choice" force us to see norms only as background that help us anticipate and interpret personal experience.

The Plan of the Book

The tasks of various stages of adulthood have supplied the material for most of the outstanding fiction throughout time. The scientific data have equally exciting stories to tell—such as new awareness of and for women, medical and psychological studies of body rhythms, new technology for mastering body language, brain waves, and muscle tension.

Foundations of Human Development   To achieve an interdisciplinary perspective of human development from which to view the succeeding stages in adult life, the beginning chapters of this book review social, physical, psychological, and transpersonal aspects of human development. These chapters are intended to stimulate an appreciation for the complexity of interacting influences forming the basis of growth and development. An awareness of principles and issues present in human-development literature is necessary for the student to sense the dimensions of change in the various stages and to begin to work toward formulating a theory for adult development. Data concerning adult life are beginning to be collected and theories of various aspects of human behavior are present in sociology, psychology, and biology. We still have before us the challenge of formulating an integrated theory of adult development. An eminent scholar has made the following observation concerning the work of theory building in the field of gerontology.

> A psychology of the human life-cycle has been slow in making its appearance. From one point of view, biological and sociological perspectives have not yet been integrated into an overarching theory of human behavior, nor have they been combined even in describing a meaningful context against which to view psychological change over the life-cycle. From a different point of view, the primary problem is that we lack a developmental psychology of adulthood in the sense that we have a developmental psychology of childhood.[6]

Stages of Adult Development

In the last half of the book we will take a chronological view and consider characteristics of the various periods of adult life. We will begin with the young adult and move through middle adulthood, through the years of maturity and into old age. Somewhat more space will be devoted to the chapter on old age. This is in part because more research has been done on the old-age period, and in part because this is an area where social planning and the development of new services are most active.

As I have brought together this mosaic of the interweaving strands forming the human organism as the individual moves through adult years, I am humbled and made reverent at the beauty of the intricate design of life in a single being. The central concerns of adults are different from those of children and adolescents. Reflected in the differences are the ways in which the individual experiences time; how he organizes his social world, and how he balances work and love relationships. Throughout adult life a series of role commitments, including marriage, parenthood, and career choices, provide the means through which the self is shaped and afforded expression. As you proceed through this book, I hope you will come to have

—an increased understanding of developmental theory and of aging;
—an appreciation of the significant stages of adulthood;
—an awareness of the provocative issues associated with social changes as these relate to life during the adult years;

---

[6] B. L. Neugarten, "Adult Personality: Toward a Psychology of the Life Cycle," in *Middle Age and Aging,* ed. B. L. Neugarten (Chicago: University of Chicago Press, 1968), p. 137.

—an awareness of the coming together of biological, psychological, and spiritual research dealing with psychosomatic experiences;

—an ability to relate principles of human development in adults to human service programs and techniques.

There exists for the student of gerontology, or adult development, the challenging task of seeing patterns in the information from adult lives. Familiarity with theory and research in various aspects of behavioral science will help you conceptualize ways of explaining the changes occurring during adult years. Introspection and openness to one's own experiences can also assist in understanding and in raising questions concerning those processes of change.

Suggested Activities and Further Reading

1. Examine novels to see how adults of different age levels are presented. Do the behaviors and characteristics of various ages seem different in novels written in the 1800s and novels written today? That is, were young adults or old people pictured differently by James Fennimore Cooper and Philip Roth?

2. To prepare yourself for thinking about adult development, write a brief autobiography. Note the significant experiences you have had with persons of different ages.

3. Examine letters you wrote as a child and compare them with your more recent writings. What is there about them that is similar, perhaps representing the continuity in your personality? What are some of the indications of growth and change that you have experienced?

4. Jot down ways in which you think the attitudes of young adults, middle-aged persons, and people in old age are similar. Suggest issues or attitudes or interests in which you would expect them to differ.

5. Do you agree with the statement that older persons have greater individuality than children? Can you defend or illustrate your opinion?

6. What are some human services available to adults of different age levels today that were not available in 1900?

7. For a cross-cultural perspective and further background on the impact of aging on society, see D. O. Cowgill, "The Aging Populations and Societies," *The Annals of the American Academy of Political and Social Sciences* 415 (September 1974), pp. 1–18.
   N. E. Cutler and R. A. Harootyan present an informative collection of demo-

graphic data on the place of older persons in our society in "Demography of the Aged," in *Aging,* eds. Woodruff and Birren.

8. For a review of the literature of different methodological approaches to the study of adult development, see K. W. Schaie and K. Gribbin, "Adult Development and Aging," in *Annual Review of Psychology,* vol. 26, eds. M. R. Rosenzweig and L. W. Porter (Palo Alto, Calif., Annual Reviews, 1975).

chapter 2

Social Processes

What Does It Mean to Be Human?

There are some questions that at first seem hardly worth discussing, the answers seem so obvious. The more we consider them, however, the more we are aware of their complexity. "How to describe humanness" is one such question. Another is, "What is life?" At first we would think that all of us know the difference between life and death—until we begin to consider an individual in a coma,[1] for example, or a fetus 36 weeks old. Another such question is sanity: "What is sane and what is insane behavior?"

There are many characteristics that come to mind when we begin to think of the nature of humanness. Some of these characteristics are the ability to do problem solving, the ability to remember, the ability to speak and answer questions. However, we also recall that there are computers that can be programed to answer questions much more complex and with more efficiency than what humans can handle. They also store information. They also respond to questions with prerecorded answers on tape.

What picture comes to your mind when you are asked how man differs from *other* animals? In Chapter 4 we will consider some of the biological characteristics of man. It can be said that the biological inheritance provides the basic ingredients and sets the limit of human potential. The way in which other people, institutions, climate, and other environmental conditions treat the individual determine how much of that potential will be

[1] See the cover story "A Right to Die," by Matt Clark, *Newsweek* 86 (November 3, 1975), pp. 58–69.

2–1 *The way in which other people, institutions, and environment treat the individual will determine how much of his potential will be realized. (Photo, RSVP, Manhattan, Kansas)*

achieved. This will be the focus of Chapter 2. We will consider ways in which the social environment's treatment of the individual moves him along the continuum of humanness—from primitive animal-like forms to the higher levels of creativity and idealism.

Our Social Inheritance

What we will experience in the world around us will be largely determined by the continuing set of expectations, values, and roles that constitute the social milieu in which we live. Given the same physiological inheritance, I will experience a somewhat different social inheritance if I live in the city rather than in the country, in the north rather than in the south, in the midwest rather than on the coast. Differences will be greater between my social world and that of an island tribe in the South Seas.

To understand aging, I must understand what the expectations of a community are regarding different events. In this chapter we will consider some factors that have a part in forming the social "ocean" around me. And we will begin to look at how expectations are created and give meaning to my day-by-day activities. As we see how "reality" and "normality" are constructed by the values ascribed to certain events in the environment, we will also see the way in which my own inner world begins to "accummulate" and to take on form. This is the uniqueness of identity and life-style I will carry forward into each new stage of life that, to a greater or lesser degree, modifies but never totally changes it.

INDIVIDUAL CONTINUITY AND CHANGE.   Although Grandma Moses took up a new type of activity when she began to paint at the age of 78, her farm life continued and the paintings reflected the experiences and values accummulated while rearing children and grandchildren in rural New York and Virginia. Each of us continues to grow throughout our lifetime, and growth is change. However, as we enter each new role in life, we bring with us a way of viewing our experiences, a life-style that is uniquely our own theme of living. As we have stated, there is both continuity and change, and these are in continual tension.

AGING AND SOCIALIZATION.   As we prepare to review the general processes of socialization that form the context for adult development, there are a few observations concerning the concept of aging we may keep in mind. These will help us to touch land periodically with our theme of adult development even as we sail somewhat out to sea, inspecting the tides and eddies and streams flowing into the social ocean forming our cultural environment.

First, age is not absolute. The way in which I recognize and react to what the calendar tells me is conditioned by what my society has designated to be the meaning of my particular chronological period. Society has several schemes, or "computers," for making these designations, and the "printouts" from the different schemes do not always jibe.

Different segments of society use different definitions for various developmental categories. Some groups describe a person as an adult when she is 18 or 21, or when she is able to conceive a baby, or when she actually gives birth to a child, or when she leaves home, or when she is employed full-time. Some describe a person as old when he is 65, or when he retires, becomes a grandparent, or enters a nursing home.

We can note several things about the definition of age.[2] First, my perception is the determining factor in my response to each period of life; it is how I

[2] A helpful in-depth discussion can be found in V. L. Bengtson, P. L. Kasschau and P. K. Ragen, "The Impact of Social Structure and Aging Individuals," in *Handbook of Psychology of Aging,* vol. 2, eds. J. E. Birren and K. W. Schaie (New York: Van Nostrand, 1977), pp. 327–353.

know my age. I am the one who tells myself how old I am, but my view is based also on the *concensus* view of those other people who are important to me. Second, the defining process is influenced by my characteristics and by the characteristics of the group with whom I identify. My age will be defined differently because I am male rather than female. It will be defined differently in black and white communities. It will be defined one way by people who are 20 and another way by people who are over 65.

A third observation is that the events we have experienced, and not just the number of days we have lived, are bench marks in defining a person's age. And we need to remember that the meanings of those events are significantly influenced by the meaning our immediate social group gives to those events. It is our social group, reflecting the larger environment, that provides the meaning and milieu that shape our person and formulate the opportunities for the achievements that mark our progress through adult life. Communities provide different opportunities for people of different ages, different roles, different religions, different sexes, different levels of education, and different occupations.

The following pages in this chapter are intended to raise our level of awareness concerning the subtle ways in which we are shaped by our environment and how we, in turn, shape our environment.

The Shaping Process

Assisting individuals to develop their human potential is termed *socialization.* It involves interaction with others. It involves interaction with the customs and ideas of the community around the individual. To understand how treatment influences the emergence of human potential, we can imagine what sort of creature might emerge if a newborn child were treated like a young dog. Children who have been deprived of human contact have often died of marasmus.[3] Decline in mental functioning in some old people has been

---

[3] A "disease" that results from a lack of personal interaction and affection. R. Spitz, "Hospitalism: An Inquiry into the Genesis of Psychiatric Conditions in Early Childhood," *The Psychoanalytic Study of the Child* 1 (New York: International Press, 1945), pp. 53–74.

2–2 *Continuity and change: youthful interests in farms or books or sports can be recognized in the life-style of the older adult. (Kansas State University Student Publications photos)*

2–3 *Helping individuals develop new skills is an important part of the socialization process. (a, Manhattan Mercury photo; b, Kansas State University Student Publications photo)*

found to be the result of a lack of meaningful feedback from people around them.[4]

Our environment continues to assist or retard developmental processes throughout the life-span. The levels of interaction and the types of involvement are progressive. They involve both the development of new skills and attitudes and the maintenance of those human traits already achieved. Care for emotionally or physically handicapped individuals sometimes fails to provide the socialization resources necessary to maintain the human capacities those persons had already achieved.[5]

The attitudes of staff in nursing homes toward the possibility of continued growth and/or rehabilitation of persons living in long-term-care institutions may be placed on a continuum. One extreme views the elderly as "too far gone" and senile to respond to any restorative activities, whether medical, psychological, or social. It places a premium upon the needs of the institution

[4] G. Bellucci and W. J. Hoyer, "Feedback Effects on the Performance and Self-Reinforcing Behavior of Elderly and Young Adult Women," *Journal of Gerontology* 30 (July 1975), 4:456–460.

[5] What happens in a society if we say individuals are only human if they achieve a certain level of social or intellectual competence?

to provide efficient maintenance of the institutionalized population. The other view holds that although the institutionalized aged are ill, they are nonetheless capable of some level of improved functioning and that proper care and stimulation ought to be provided.[6]

It may be difficult to know when the physiological condition causes the loss of human functioning and when the loss results from inadequate treatment. For example, some nursing home residents benefit by being transferred to new environments, whereas such transfers hasten the death of others.

Some Human Characteristics

Every society, every community, and every family have some characteristics that they look for and hope to maintain in their members. These are their criteria for humanness. These differ in some specifics from community to community. The number of definitions of humanness and the lists of human characteristics are endless. They reflect our eternal quest for life's meaning.

It is difficult for us—even in our imagination—to put ourselves in a situation where some of our basic values are nonexistent. Whereas we may think of loyalty as a basic character trait, Don Richardson[7] tells of his experience of living with a people who honor betrayal of their enemies in place of forgiveness and treachery in place of love. His account of how these practices are changing among the headhunters of New Guinea helps us more clearly recognize underlying values within our own experience.

Although some writers question whether there are any universal characteristics, a definition of humanness requires some specification of traits. Even though they differ in specific behavior and reflect the relativity of values, some common characteristics appear, with varied emphasis of course, in almost all societies. Example 2–1 presents a list of characteristics that a Princeton University study reported finding in varying degrees in each student. To what extent do you think the list describes characteristics of the typical American adult?

Occasionally we may encounter an individual or group of people who does not seem to possess any of the traits common to most enduring so-

[6] J. I. Kosberg and J. F. Gorman, "Perceptions Toward the Rehabilitation Potential of Institutionalized Aged," *The Gerontologist* 15 (October 1975, Part I), 5:398–403.

[7] D. Richardson, *Peace Child* (Glendale, Calif.: Regal Books, 1974).

Example 2–1.
Some Human
Characteristics

1. Future orientation but in a sense of life as a game rather than as a struggle.
2. Intrinsic interest or involvement in his liberal-arts subjects.
3. Formation and maintenance of close friendships among his peers.
4. Self-objectification seen not only in his reflective interview behavior but also in the way he would create lively challenges, ones that had little to do with status or other security operation.
5. Possession of values and convictions that stemmed primarily from the authority of his own experience.
6. Tolerance of ambiguity. He could maintain a state of indecision until a basis for making the decision was at hand.
7. He was not easily bored. A wide range of matters and objects seemed to fascinate him.
8. A lively but benign sense of humor.

Adapted from S. R. Heath, "The Reasonable Adventurer and Others," *Journal of Counseling Psychology* 6 (1959), 1:3–14.

cieties.[8] We will also discuss factors influencing the realization of human potential when we discuss Maslow's theory of need hierarchy and self-actualization in the chapter on Self. In our study of adult development we will observe individuals with high levels of creativity and imagination, and we will also see individuals whose ability to solve problems and communicate is scarcely sufficient for survival. A part of our purpose will be to understand how the shaping influences of their environment have interacted with their inherited potentialities to either enhance or inhibit their human development through the course of their adult lives.

Foundations for Adult Life

Before we proceed with a discussion of the means by which various socialization processes shape people, we need to consider the unique differences

[8] The Alorese society near Java in the South Seas is one group that raises a problem to a definition of human qualities. The people seemed to have no sense of tenure or future. Anthropologists found it difficult to identify any heroes who personified their values, or to find anything that was valued other than food. Skill, affection, government, folk wisdom, or religion, at least as recognized by the anthropologist, did not seem to be a part of their existence. A. Kardiner, *Psychological Frontiers of Society* (New York: Columbia University Press, 1945); see also C. Du Bois' chapter in *In the Company of Man,* ed. J. B. Casagrande (New York: Harper & Row, 1960).

with which individuals enter life. Biological inheritance and differences in place of birth have a formative influence predisposing individuals to different adult life-styles.

Biological Influences

Studies of twins[9] are useful in helping us look at the effect of inheritance, both physical and social, on human development. For example, a study of the frequency of tuberculosis revealed that in New York City a little more than one person in 100 had the disease. Twenty-five times out of 100 a brother or sister of a tuberculosis patient also had the disease. In the case of identical twins, 87 times out of 100 when one twin had the disease the other had it also.

Prison records often reflect the effect of inheritance. Would you describe the effects in the following study as biological or environmental inheritance? The study showed that when one fraternal twin was in prison, at least one third of the time the other twin also had a prison record. In the case of identical twins, 70 times out of 100 both twins had prison records, usually for similar crimes often conducted in different parts of the country after the twins were separated.

Adults throughout their lives will continue to approach opportunities bringing with them both the predispositions of their inherited physiology and their past social experiences.

Geographical Influences

There are some parts of the country where the mortality rates are higher than in other parts. For example, one analysis of vital statistics indicated that "The risk of dying for white males in middle age (45–64 years) in the United States tends to be greatest among residents of East Coast states and least among residents of West Coast and mountainous states."[10] Studies suggest that the differences in mortality may come from differences in rate of aging in different environments.

It has been suggested that the chances of contracting multiple sclerosis are considerably greater if we are living in a cold rather than in a warm climate. In a comparison of two Atlantic seacoast towns, the prevalence of this disease was 2.4 times greater in Halifax County, Nova Scotia, than in Charles-

[9] C. Auerbach, *The Science of Genetics* (New York: Harper & Row, 1961).

[10] S. Watthana-Kasetr and P. S. Spiers, "Geographic Mortality Rates and Rates of Aging—A Possible Relationship?" *Journal of Gerontology* 28 (July 1973), 3:374–379.

ton County, South Carolina. Whether the environmental conditions contributing to this difference in human development is the temperature or other factors has yet to be fully documented. The fact that there are differences in the effects on human development in different geographic centers at different times seems well established.[11] We might note also the increasing number of retirement villages in the warmer regions of our country.

The interaction between the geography of our environment and our genetic inheritance is subtle but extremely important. Land with an overabundance or a deficit of some minerals needed by certain glands of our bodies will stimulate different kinds of personality development and behavior. For example, at one time in our history, an individual whose thyroid at birth was slightly less active than normal might function well on the seacoast but be less energetic when the person moved to a midwest state. Diseases of the thyroid gland caused by insufficient iodine in the diet are almost unknown where seafoods are plentiful. In the early part of the twentieth century, iodine deficiency existed in the central part of the United States and in the Swiss Alps, but this problem has been solved by the use of iodized salt.

Balance of Interaction

There is a principle in the study of human development that refers to certain factors as the "necessary but not sufficient cause" for the development of specific conditions. The size and efficiency of functioning of each gland and muscle in each of us is slightly different from that of anyone else in the world. Our bodies accommodate considerable variation and still operate with amazing efficiency. There are, however, for most of us some sectors of our body that are marginal. They function well when all the related elements maintain an optimum balance. Their marginal nature causes them to be described as predisposing toward certain behaviors or conditions. For example, a 19-year-old girl experienced a stressful period in a romance. Following that, within a matter of days, she developed a heavy beard. Biochemical studies revealed that she had a slight abnormality in the corticoandrogen ratio of adrenocortical secretion. The stress from her frustration and anxiety was sufficient to upset the balance in the normal functioning of her adrenal gland and the body began to produce hair growth usually associated with males.[12] We will be discussing further the effect of stress and hormonal balance in Chapter 4.

---

[11] M. Alter, "Multiple Sclerosis and Climate," *World Neurology* 1 (1960), pp. 55–70.

[12] I. E. Bush and V. B. Mahesh, "Hirsuitism and Emotional Tension," *Journal of Endocrinology* 18 (1959), 1.

Although human behavior is much more complex than that of animals in the farmyard, a study of the pecking order of hens illustrates how differences in hormonal balance influence behavior. A newcomer to a group of chickens has to fight each of the other residents to establish its status. Winning chickens in order of hierarchy are able to peck losing chickens without being pecked in return. They have first choice of foods, roosts, and nests. Treatment of hens with a dosage of male hormone increased aggressiveness, and hens so treated fought their way "up the social ladder." Hens that ranked below certain males in the pecking order mated with them readily; hens that outranked those males rejected them and drove them wildly about the pen.[13] Do you think that popular references to pecking order in industrial and social groups have such biological influences in mind?

In the Longitudinal Study of Aging at Duke University, long-lived men were compared with short-lived men and long-lived women with short-lived women on a variety of health and sociopsychological factors. The study found that there was no single factor that distinguished the long-lived from the short-lived. However, it did find a definite cluster of factors that together distinguished the two groups. Persons with high intelligence, sound financial status, well-maintained health, intact marriages, and a positive view of the contribution they were making to their community lived significantly longer.[14]

Individual Differences and Interdependence

In the provocative little book *Animal Farm*[15] there is the suggestion that all animals are equal, only some are "more equal." Recognition of individual differences has always been difficult to reconcile with an understanding of the concept of equal rights. Provision for equal opportunity sometimes gets confused with universal sameness for all persons. Whether we speak of the superrace that Hitler proclaimed or refer to women's liberation or to differences between ethnic groups, it is difficult to acknowledge differences without ascribing privilege. Lack of equality in characteristics is usually associated with lack of equality in opportunity.[16]

---

[13] A. M. Guhl, "Pecking Order of Hens," *Scientific American* (October 1954).

[14] E. Palmore, "Predicting Longevity: A New Method," in *Normal Aging II,* ed. E. Palmore (Durham: Duke University Press, 1975), pp. 281–285.

[15] G. Orwell, *Animal Farm* (New York: Harcourt Brace Jovanovich, 1946), p. 148.

[16] E. B. Palmore and K. Manton, "Agism Compared to Racism and Sexism," *Journal of Gerontology* 28 (July 1973), 3:363–369.

Our study of human development must underscore, nevertheless, that an appreciation of individual differences is central to an understanding of human development. We are each different, but we are also more similar to certain groups than to other groups of people. Our differences and our similarities also generate the interdependence we have on one another. Interdependence is a fundamental fact of life at all levels.

To illustrate the importance of such interdependence, we should note its presence in our biological functioning. There exists a multitude of germs and parasites that incapacitate or kill their animal or human hosts. But some germs and parasites also exist, such as those living in the intestines of every human being, that not only cause no appreciable harm but are even useful by manufacturing some of the vitamins needed by the human body. Some animals and plants have become so completely dependent upon such associated organisms that they die when the association is broken. This condition of mutual aid between members of different species is so widespread in both animal and plant kingdoms that the word *symbiosis* (living together) has been coined for it.

Mankind is a biological species and a part of nature. But man is also a unique being, the creator and possessor of a social organization and culture. In the next section we will consider a further dimension of our inheritance, that is, our social endowment.

The Social Environment of Adult Years

Family   Each of us began life in a climate that reflected the feelings of several significant persons toward our arrival. My family's expectation of joy or dread is part of my legacy.

How the members of my family felt about each other also contributed to the social atmosphere into which I was immersed at birth. As I "swam" about in the social flux of my family, that "fluid" enveloped and permeated my being. Not only the interpersonal attitude of the family but also the pace of action, time-rhythms, schedules, and tensions were absorbed by osmosis. They mingled with some early intuitions formed in my nervous system during my before-birth sojourn. The "lenses" with which I as an adult would come to view the world, the antenna with which I now feel and sound out each new circumstance, were being manufactured from the milieu of my birth and early years.

My race, religion, language, social class, prejudice, concepts of reality and

Example 2–2.
The Honorable
Elders

> The status of Japanese elders is substantially higher than that of the aged in other industrialized countries . . . The Japanese elders are much more integrated in their families . . . The employment status of the elders is much higher than in other industrialized countries . . .
>
> The main explanation for their relatively high status and integration is the tradition of respect for elders which has its roots in the vertical society and in religious doctrines of filial piety. Respect and affection for the elders are shown on a daily basis by honorific language; bowing; priority for the elders in seating, serving, bathing, and going through doors. It is also reflected in popular sayings, special celebrations of the sixty-first birthday, the national observance of Respect for Elders Day, and the National Law for Welfare of the Aged.
>
> E. Palmore, *The Honorable Elders: A Cross-Cultural Analysis of Aging in Japan* (Durham, N.C.: Duke University Press, 1975), pp. 127–128.

unreality were a part of my social inheritance. I was born into them. They, in turn, influenced the way in which I reacted to other socializing experiences through the years. Because of my race or my language I responded to certain stimuli but ignored or did not hear or see others. (See Example 2–2 for an illustration of language and custom.) Even as I was being formed by the influences of my family and community, I was also influencing them. My family and my community were different because of my presence, because of my interaction with various individuals, because of my contributions in work, creativity, love, and play. In Chapter 3 we will consider at greater length adult development in relation to family.

Place and Time

Being born in a pretelevision era and in a period of economic depression, I interpret certain situations differently than do younger persons whose views of events are more instantaneous. I think of things as progressing, moving forward step by step, whereas persons reared with television and in a more affluent society think more in terms of full-blown happenings changing the scenery overnight.[17]

The world is experienced differently by persons born in the 1900s, 1930s, and 1950s. Not only were different conditions prevailing in the early forma-

[17] M. McLuhan and Q. Fiore, *The Medium Is the Massage* (New York: Bantam Books, 1967).

tive years of their lives, but also the interraction of subsequent events through the course of their lives will have a different composite effect for each generational group. This will be referred to as *cohort* differences. "A cohort refers to those who were born during the same period of specific calendar time or who enter into a specific social institution, such as school or work, during the same precisely demarcated intervals. A generation refers to a group of people who are conscious of having shared similar sociocultural experiences, sometimes regardless of chronological time boundaries."[18]

Forming the Pattern   Studies suggest typical personalities or behavior for various groups. More than forty years ago, in a classic book, *Patterns of Culture,*[19] an anthropologist described three different primitive cultures. She said the people of one were sober, moderate, and ritualistic; those of another were high-strung, inclined toward rivalry and ecstacies; the third group was secretive, dour, and prudish. We make somewhat similar broad generalizations today when we refer to the generation of youth reared in the 1950s, the wild 1920s, or the rebellious 1960s. There is truth and value in identifying influences predominating in a group or an era. They are a part of the social inheritance for individuals entering a formative period of their lives. We need also to be aware of the dangers and errors of such stereotyping. The broad social milieu is only a part of what contributes to an individual's development. Not all blacks are good musicians or athletes, nor are all Kansans Republicans. We need to remember that there is a circular effect in human development. The individual influences his environment at the same time as he is being influenced by it.

Stereotypes influence the way we treat other people. For example, the popular stereotype is seen as intellectual ability increasing up to middle age. The tendency is to think of the mental ability of old people as being on the level of children and preadolescents. As a matter of fact, people are inclined to use simplified language with the elderly similar to the way they would talk with children.[20]

Other things, such as emotions and relationships, also influence the effects of stereotypes. We may hold a stereotype of people as a group but set that

[18] V. L. Bengtson and D. Haber, "Sociological Approaches to Aging," in *Aging,* eds. D. S. Woodruff and J. E. Birren (New York: Van Nostrand, 1975), p. 77.

[19] R. Benedict, *Patterns of Culture* (New York: Mentor Books, 1934).

[20] K. H. Rubin and I. D. R. Brown, "A Life-Span Look at Person Perception and Its Relationship to Communications Interaction," *Journal of Gerontology* 30 (July 1975), 4:461–468.

stereotype aside in the case of an individual. For example, college students[21] viewed old people in general as much less interesting and effective than they viewed 25-year-olds. However, when responding to a photograph and an autobiographical sketch—thus making the people more personal—students responded to the older individuals as more interesting and effective than the 25-year-olds.

PREDICTION AND CHOICE.   Both the individual and society develop patterns of organization. These are norms, roles, attitudes, and values. This structure helps individuals to make choices in behavior; it also helps individuals understand what others are thinking and doing. Social structure helps individuals and groups to predict behavior. However, prediction is not totally accurate; if it were, we would be robots operating with machinelike conformity.

THE CONTEXT OF LIVES.   Each individual life has a context—a continuing framework of values, motives, physiological propensities, and cultural opportunities. These factors flow together to form a whole, and the creativity and potentiality forming the total is greater than the sum of its parts. To understand an individual life requires cognizance of its many dimensions and an awareness of the integral life-style and identity being expressed. Thus there are behaviors and directions that can be anticipated as we study patterns of an individual life, but there is also the creative element of choice through which new elements and unpredictable combinations of motives may emerge.

Even with individuals whose life-styles undergo dramatic reorientations the theme of continuity and change can be observed, along with the novelty of unpredicted choice. When Charles Colson[22] was "converted," many doubted his sincerity because they were unable to see a predictable pattern in his behavior. As we read an account of his life (Example 2–3), we can see a pattern of certain continuing drives growing out of early needs and embarrassments. We can also see the imprinting of early values and parental identification. And although a strong predictability is present in his various life choices, there is also a creativity or unpredictability in the choices that brought about his new way of life. The example of Colson demonstrates

---

[21] L. E. Weinbergen and J. Milham, "A Multi-Dimensional, Multiple Method Analysis of Attitudes Toward the Elderly," *Journal of Gerontology* 30 (May 1975), 3:343–348.

[22] C. W. Colson, *Born Again* (Lincoln, Va.: Chosen Books, 1976).

Example 2–3.

A Case of
Character
Reversal

Charles Colson, whose character "reversal" was much in the limelight during the Watergate hearings of 1974–75, traces many of the later events of his life, including his role as "hatchet man" in the Nixon Administration, back to Boston's caste system that denied social acceptance to his low-income family during his youth. His father went to night school for twelve years and earned his law degree when Charles was eight years old. Equally indelible in his memory were the words and model of his father, "Work hard—tell the truth always—lies destroy." Colson himself was never sure he would have enough money for each semester's tuition at prep school. However, when he was offered a scholarship to Harvard, his long pent-up resentment of the Beacon Hill establishment found expression. His overwhelming sense of pride—formed out of years of being snubbed—soared in vindication when he turned down the scholarship and told the Harvard dean he had decided to accept a scholarship at another, less prestigious, institution.

Upon graduation from college in a naval ROTC program he was faced again with a status challenge. He wanted to take his commission in the Marines, but the Marine officer wanted proof that Colson was "good enough" for the Marines. That put-down only fired Colson's determination; spit and polish flourished night and day until he was accepted into the Marines. And so he continued through later years in law practice and politics to prove he was "good enough" to handle any task that came up. His brightness and efficiency, coupled with pride in himself and in those he served, made him an invaluable troubleshooter and right-hand man for former President Nixon. The strong drives for competition and achievement he developed in early life and his overwhelmingly strong pride demanded that his competence and the rightness of whatever he was associated with be recognized. Thus his country and his leaders were always right.

As the Watergate investigation began to unravel, he came to recognize the tremendous errors in which he was a participant. His view of himself and of his leaders and the government changed dramatically. Independent of any plea bargaining, he offered testimony to the crimes he had committed in planning to defame Daniel Ellsberg and consequently served a prison sentence. Following his prison term, he devoted his energies to prison reform and to a nondenominational Christian ministry among government and businessmen.

Colson's unpredictable reversal was to return to his father's emphasis upon truth at any cost. It was also to identify with a new system, replacing competition and expediency with humility and principles of love. His new view still has a strong identification with an ideal; country and leaders have been replaced with a Divine Encounter. Colson's choice was to make himself vulnerable, to acknowledge he was *not* good enough, and to express his complete dependence upon God. In this, he states, he experiences a oneness with a larger system.

Abstract of C. W. Colson's *Born Again* (Chosen Books, Lincoln, Va. 22078, 1976).

2–4 *Charles W. Colson (Drawing by Patrick Kennedy)*

how prediction may be influenced by choice; how social and environmental factors influence our life patterns as well as our choices within that pattern.

Norms   Members of society have expectations of what their members should do in certain situations. These are the *norms* of that society. For instance, one social norm dictates that home owners will keep their lawns neat. Most people have well-kept lawns. Some spend much more time on their lawns than others, but those that spend a lot of time and those that spend less than average time are still within the norm. Occasionally there may be a deviant citizen who lets his lawn go completely to weeds or a deviant at the other end of the spectrum who overdresses his lawn.

AGE NORMS.   Perception of norms is influenced by both the age and sex of the individual. For example, young people identify middle age and old age as occurring earlier than do older people. Women are viewed as middle-aged earlier than men.[23]

There is a general consensus[24] as to what behavior is appropriate for persons at different age levels. Although the specific age varies slightly from social class to social class, or by geographic region, there is a general understanding of the age at which an individual is expected by one's community to have accomplished a particular developmental task. There is a time for study, play, and entering the world of work; there is a time for marriage, for one's children to leave home, and to become grandparents.

Even within the same educational and social group there can be considerable range in the pacing of family development. For example, I am well acquainted with twin sisters who graduated from college shortly before World War II. One married during her first year of teaching; the other's fiancé was overseas and they did not marry until after the war was over. The children of the first couple now have children in elementary and junior high school; the children of the second couple have recently graduated from college. One twin has long been busy with the role of grandmother; the other is excited about becoming a mother-in-law.

My own perception of myself and my age is formulated by how the events

[23] J. Drevenstedt, "Perceptions of Young Adulthood, Middle Age, and Old Age," *Journal of Gerontology* 31 (January 1976), 1:53–57.

[24] B. L. Neugarten, J. W. Moore, and J. C. Lowe, "Age Norms, Age Constraints and Adult Socialization," *American Journal of Sociology* 70 (May 1965), 6.

in my life correspond to the expectations of events for people of a certain age period. If the age period designated by my achievements is similar to the period of my calendar age, I will think of myself as progressing on time. If my achievements are more similar to a group whose calendar age is earlier or later than mine, I will think of myself as an early or late maturer.

The guidelines of norms help us clarify our identity. They also create limitations, frustrations, and anxieties at times. The mixed reactions of older persons to the legislating of an age norm in the form of mandatory retirement illustrate the benefits and disadvantages of age norms.

Roles   Norms are associated with roles. *Roles* are the behaviors expected of individuals who occupy a given position: father, mother, son, daughter, teacher, employee. Roles exist as shared expectations. The individual knows what others expect of him, and others know what to expect him to do.

Norms and roles are part of our social inheritance; we are born or grow into them. They are, however, never completely fixed nor completely static. Each individual performs his role a little differently from the next person, although similarly enough to be within the norm. The impact of other events in the society causes some continuing modification in the expectations for each role. It is necessary that there be enough similarity in role expectation and performance for individuals to find meaning and security in life. However, the norms cannot be so narrow or so slow to change that they do not allow for individual differences, for creativity, and for group progress. In the next chapter, as we look at family roles, we will see an illustration of the processes and stresses involved as society proceeds to make changes in role definitions.

Values and Attitudes   Norms grow out of the value system of a group. The norm is the behavior that members of a group reward. Norms are more specific than values; they indicate how people may go about realizing their values. Values represent the standard or quality of life that a people consider desirable.

Attitudes are the thought and feeling processes by which an individual applies his value system to a specific situation. Attitudes also serve to modify the value system through time. They are influenced by the effectiveness of the reward system and thus reflect any changes in the way others are responding to the individual's role performance.

2–5 *Specific dress helps to clarify role identities, as illustrated by this dental assistant, who is recognized by her dress and activities although she is outside the office, and by the airplane pilot driving a car. (a, Manhattan Mercury photo; b, Kathleen Ward, photographer)*

Values and attitudes are continued from generation to generation and establish the substance of differences among social classes. Later in the book we will consider studies of middle and older adults in Kansas City and in the

2–6 *We experience our social inheritance in family gatherings.*

San Francisco Bay area that reflect social-class differences in regard to work and community involvement at different points in the life-span.[25]

ACHIEVEMENT ORIENTATION.   Three areas of attitudinal set may influence an individual's approach to achievement: *activism* (the belief that a person can manipulate the physical and social environment to his own advantage) versus *passivity; individualism* (the belief that a person does not need to subordinate his own needs to the family group) versus *collectivism; and future orientation* (the belief that a person should forego short-term rewards in the interest of long-term gains) versus *present orientation.*[26]

Higher socioeconomic groups are more often identified with individualistic, activistic, and future-oriented values. The orientations of lower socioeconomic groups are more frequently characterized as passive, collective, and present-oriented. We will discover in Chapter 3 in the discussion of work in adult life that lower-middle- and lower-social-class persons are employed in jobs rather than having careers. For them work is a means of security more than an opportunity for self-expression. Development of

[25] Neugarten, Moore, and Lowe, "Age Norms, Age Constraints and Adult Socialization"; see also M. F. Lowenthal, M. T. Thurnher, and D. Chiriboga, *Four Stages of Life* (San Francisco: Jossey-Bass, 1975), Chapter 1.

[26] See discussion of attitudes and achievement orientation in *Developmental Psychology Today,* (New York: CRM/Random House, 1975), pp. 366–370; B. C. Rosen, "The Achievement Syndrome: A Psycho-Cultural Dimension of Social Stratification," *American Sociological Review* 21 (1956), pp. 203–211; R. Coleman and B. Neugarten, *Social Status in the City* (San Francisco: Jossey-Bass, 1971).

vocational aspirations and social class is circular. Attitudes of the subculture establish an individual's approach to life and the type of work valued; they also influence what opportunities the individual will perceive to be accessible.

Differing results from studies assessing changes of men and women in preretirement and retirement years will be more clearly understood if we keep in mind the factors that influence the value orientations of different subcultures.

STEREOTYPES OF OLD AGE.   Stereotypes are preconceived ideas about particular people or groups. They often have no rational basis, but sometimes they may contain partial truths; and perceptions true for a part of a group may be generalized to the whole group.

Impressions held by the general public concerning old people provide an illustration of stereotypes that are a part of our social inheritance. They influence our relationship with old people; they also shape the way we deal with our own experience of aging.

A 1974 Harris Poll involving interviews with 4,254 persons 18 years of age and older asked a cross section of the American public about their own experiences, about their perceptions of themselves, and about their perceptions and expectations of "most people over 65." The following paragraph summarizes the American stereotype of old age:

> When judged on a list of attributes usually associated with productive, active and effective individuals, "most people over 65" received very high ratings from the public on only two counts: 74% of the public felt that most people over 65 are "very warm and friendly," and 64% considered them "very wise from experience." Seen as nice old folks who have benefited from the trials and tribulations of life, most people over 65 are not viewed, however, as very active, efficient or alert people: less than half (41%) considered them "very physically active," while only 35% said they are "very good at getting things done," 29% "very active and alert," 21% "very open-minded and adaptable," and 5% "very sexually active."
>
> In contrast to this public image, those 65 and older gave quite a different picture of their self-concept. More than two thirds (68%) said they *personally* were "very bright and alert;" 63% said they were "very open-minded and adaptable;" 55% said they were "very good at getting things done."[27]

[27] L. Harris and associates, *The Myth and Reality of Aging in America* (Washington, D.C.: The National Council on the Aging, 1975), pp. 46–47.

Two interesting facts should be observed in the responses to this question about the nature of stereotypes. Although we have just observed that the older respondent described *himself* to be quite different from the public image, the over-65 group's answer concerning "most people over 65" was almost identical with the public. On the other hand, most persons under 65 gave a self-image similar to the self-image of the older person.

How Adults Make Choices

During our discussion of the physical endowment of individuals and the environment into which they were born, we have referred to a process of interaction through which the individual becomes what he and others value. Two processes, termed learning and motivation, are the means by which this development occurs.

The Basis of Choice

Self-preservation is a principle in life. Any condition that threatens life brings discomfort. Individuals, young or old, strive to avoid situations that bring discomfort. More positively, we strive to obtain situations that bring comfort and growth; we strive for expression and recognition of our individuality and worth.

Moment by moment throughout life we are making choices of behavior. We are more conscious of some of the choices than others, yet all are under our control; for example, we choose to move our legs and walk down the street. We are less aware of making the choice about leg movement than we are about making the choice of where we are going. However, if we have had a broken leg and are just learning to use crutches, then we are very much aware of the choice and learning process involved in moving our legs.

Learning and Feedback

We learn by a process of feedback. Feedback is the report we get of what follows after a particular movement, activity, attitude, or decision. If the effect is what we desire, that behavior becomes associated in our memory with the condition that preceded it (the stimulus). When a similar condition reoccurs, we will repeat the behavior.

Learning is the modification of behavior through experience. Adaptation to a new routine or a new environment is the effect of learning. How we adapt will be influenced by our physiological and psychological condition as well as by the characteristics of the new environment.

Learning is the integral mechanism by which parts of the world outside become internalized within the brain and neural system. This is the process of forming "self," which we will discuss in Chapter 5. We continue to select, imitate, and identify with different aspects of our environment. These selections are made on the basis of extending those aspects of our being we consider essential and highly desirable at each new stage of life, whether we are just entering adult life, are well established in middle life, or are approaching old age.

We often learn skills and develop attitudes to satisfy needs of a present situation, and later these become goals in their own right. For example, a junior executive may learn about electronics to handle an account for his firm. This interest may flower into expertise, a new identity with the field of electronics, and perhaps a new career direction. Electronics has become a part of his identity along with management.

Motivation and Values

Motivation is the part of the choice-making mechanism that helps us decide from among a number of possible alternatives. In Chapter 5 we will consider the priority of motives that determine our choice of behavior. Behavior may be complex, such as making a career decision, or simple, such as moving our legs in walking. In either event it results from conscious or unconscious choice based on feedback from previous experiences.

All choices are related. Each individual is a total, or whole, unity. All our activities are directed toward the preservation and further development of the person we want to be. Because we operate at so many levels—the cells and tension of our body, the feeling and contact with the world about us, the ideas and attitudes toward others and ourselves, the memories of the past and the hopes of the future—some parts of our activity may appear to be in conflict with other aspects of our behavior. However, this is because we are not clearly able to put it all together. Operationally, we are making the responses on the basis of choices that will most enhance the person and causes with which we are identified.

Added to the complexity of our own person is the complexity of society—the variation within the norms and values, the multiple groups and roles that we identify with. Our choice of behavior involves the meaning of life's direction and the estimate of our place in relation to various segments of society. We are continually working to maintain that balance (homeostasis) within our total life sphere that sustains our present status and moves us toward what we want to become.[28]

[28] See the discussion of "Functional Autonomy of Motives," in G. W. Allport, *The Person in Psychology* (Boston: Beacon Press, 1968), pp. 167–168.

2–7 *Adults act out values that are passed from generation to generation. (Kansas State University Student Publications photo)*

2–8 *Social inheritance is passed on by policies and activities of community agencies. Here school-crossing guards are briefed for their duties.* (Manhattan Mercury *photo*)

The Transmission of Culture

Learning begins in our earliest days and continues until our last. We are thus continually taking in and reacting to the flow of social energies around us. The persons and things of our environment and the meanings they have for us are our culture.[29] Through learning we internalize our culture, as we help shape it through our responses to it. Culture can be described as those customs, beliefs, ways of behaving, and values that are passed from generation to generation as the best and most acceptable solution to problems of living. The closer the relationships between persons, generally the greater is the similarity of their attitudes. Family members are the first and continue throughout life to be among the most significant persons in the socializing process by which the culture is transmitted from generation to generation. Other socializing agencies that embody and pass on the social inheritance of a people include the church, educational institutions, peer group, government, industrial institutions, and the mass media.

---

[29] For helpful illustrations of the cultural environment, see Chapter 6 in H. V. Perkins, *Human Development* (Belmont, Calif.: Wadsworth, 1975).

Summary

Let us review briefly some of the socialization processes of an adult in the last quarter of the twentieth century. As we examine the world of adults, or the life development of one adult, we need to consider such factors as age, sex, ethnicity, occupation, and educational level. These, in turn, are influenced by the organizations and institutions of which we are a part, such as our family, religion, government, and employment.

We began life with certain predisposing conditions and our adult status reflects the interaction of that initial inheritance with the environmental influences surrounding us. That interaction is known as socialization. It is the process by which a group (family, community, nation, or race) attempts to shape the child, and later the adult, in its own image. Such shaping is confounded to some extent by the unique and vital qualities of the individual, which enables each to retain a basic element of independence no matter how powerful the environment. Thus we shape our environment as it shapes us. The efficiency and predictability of socialization is limited by the fact that the environment itself is always changing. For example, the values of a people—their picture of the ideal person, the ideal society, and the means to achieve these—are different in a period and land with vast untapped resources than in a society with overpopulation and limited energy and food.

The social group to which I belong will influence my opportunity to progress through certain roles. Because most of the members of that group will be having similar opportunities, we can expect a general pattern in aging to be characteristic of that group. Group characteristics such as high social class or working class, rural or urban, black or white have different timetables and different achievements that mark the changes in age. The period of history is also an influence; adulthood and old age were reached earlier a quarter of a century ago.

Aging is determined by the sequence of events in the life of an individual. The meaning of them will be set by the expectations that society places on those events.

We also need to keep in mind the complementary aspects of change and continuity present in every life. How time is spent is considerably different for a 20-, a 40-, and a 70-year-old. We continue to change through time, but there is also a similarity in what an individual will do at 20 and at 70. If we spend a lot of time outdoors working with our hands at 20, the chances are we will do so at 70; if we studied hard at 20, that studiousness may be expressed as a college instructor at 40 or as a reader at 70 who spends much time in a library.

There are different types of age. Some events of life are determined by the calendar, such as the ability to vote and perhaps retirement. Some events, such as menopause, may be approximately predicted according to biological age. In addition to calendar age and biological age is social age, which is reflected in movement through the social positions and roles in family, employment, and community. The extent to which others view me, and I see myself as young, middle-aged, or elderly will be influenced by my family position, be it single, engaged, married, parent, or grandparent. It may be determined by my employment as a student, apprentice, journeyman, foreman, or by my activities within the community as uninvolved or as an organization member.

Whether the processes are closely planned, as in a "brave new world," or are haphazard and without policy, socialization reflects the people's assumptions about the nature of humanness. Socialization establishes some standards of behavior. The standards are expressed in norms for behavior and in roles through which the individual relates to himself and others. Socialization ascribes an order and meaning to the expected events that mark our progress through the stages of adult life.

Suggested Activities and Further Reading

1. Ask a panel formed of persons who were of different ages when a particular event occurred—the Depression of the 1930s, World War II, Vietnam—to discuss the meaning of that event in their lives.

2. Locate articles in newspapers and magazines that report adults involved in activities especially characteristic of roles of their age level.

3. Give illustrations of stereotypes of age, sex, race, or religion appearing in television programs.

4. Inspect newspaper accounts for evidences of ageism, for example, stereotypes that imply all old people are ineffective.

5. Examine the evidences of socialization in the novel *Barry Lyndon* by William Makepeace Thackery. You may be able to see the Warner Bros. film extravaganza of this novel made in 1975.

6. Read the following books and compare the effects of social processes in the lives of poor families of different cultures:

    Oscar Lewis, *The Children of Sanchez* (New York: Random House, 1961);
    Elliot Liebow, *Tally's Corner* (Boston: Little, Brown, 1967);

Robert Coles, *Uprooted Children* (New York: Harper & Row, 1970);
James Agee and Walker Evans, *Let Us Now Praise Famous Men* (New York: Ballantine Books, 1941).

7. Identify the different sources of socialization depicted in the characters from the North and South in Stephen Vincent Benet's book-length poem, *John Brown's Body*.

8. For background in theory of socialization and aging read the following material:

V. Bengtson, *The Social Psychology of Aging* (New York: Bobbs-Merrill, 1973).

M. W. Riley, M. Johnson, and A. Foner, *Aging and Society: A Sociology of Age Stratification,* vol. 3 (New York: Russell Sage Foundation, 1972). This book presents a theoretical model; you will also find volume 1 useful as an extensive review of research on the social aspects of aging.

G. L. Albrecht and H. G. Gift, "Adult Socialization: Ambiguity and Adult Life Crises," in *Life-Span Developmental Psychology: Normative Life Crises,* eds. N. Datan and L. N. Ginsberg (New York: Academic Press, 1975).

chapter 3

Adult Development Through Family and Work Relationships

We **are created** through our interaction with other people. Throughout life we constantly reach out to be part of another person, group, or organization. Equally strong and simultaneous is our continuing desire for independence, autonomy, and privacy. In Chapter 5 we will consider the subjective aspects of relating to our intrapersonal environment. In this chapter we will consider two areas of socialization that are central in helping us to become who we are. Role achievements in family and in employment are crucial in adult development. Therefore, it is important in our study for us to conceptualize something of the larger context of family life and the world of work in order to understand the significance of roles and role transitions at different life stages.

Family as a Socializing Agent

The first significant and continuing social group in our life is our family. Although the form of family life-style may at times be questioned, the phenomenon of family is found among all people. Universally it has the same basic tasks: to provide care and socialization for the young and a network of interpersonal support and personal identity for adults. The paragraphs in Example 3–1 suggest the kinds of issues and questions that have arisen in recent years concerning forms of family life in America.

There are a variety of ways in which information about families is considered by scholars in the field. Some consider the family as a social institution and view ways in which the family interacts with governmental,

3–1 *Parenthood is a central task, beginning early and continuing at different levels of responsibility throughout the life-span.* (Manhattan Mercury photos)

Example 3–1.

Issues
Concerning
Family Life in
America

Probably never before in history have people in any one society held such widely differing opinions about the family as in America today. Some believe that the nuclear family—mama, papa, and the children—is a "biological phenomenon" . . . as rooted in organic and physiological structures as insect societies. At the opposite extreme are those who believe that a taste for family life is something that any sophisticated person naturally outgrows, like a taste for ice cream and sticky sweets. In the middle are those who believe that mother and child are the basic human couple, with the male only a fleeting and almost dispensable presence; and those who see man and woman as central and children as only an afterthought . . .

Philosophers have often remarked on how we stop noticing things that are always before our eyes, but perceive strangeness only in deviations from the familiar.

Thus we often ask:

Why did couple X get divorced, rather than why does couple Y stay together?

Why are women protesting, rather than why have they accepted an inferior status for so long?

Why is he or she a homosexual, rather than how did that "normal" person come to identify with one sex and want erotic relations with the other?

Why do people live in communes, rather than why do they live in isolated houses in the suburbs?

Why was that child beaten or driven schizophrenic, rather than what goes on behind the closed doors of the "average" family?

Why do they rebel, rather than why do they "behave themselves" in schools and jobs that oppress and bore them?

What harm comes to children from mothers who work, rather than how are children harmed by long hours in the total power of their mothers, out of sight of any other eyes?

Adapted from A. Skolnick and J. H. Skolnick, *Family in Transition* (Boston: Little, Brown, 1971), pp. vii, viii.

educational, industrial, and religious institutions. Others look more at the dynamics within the family unit and consider such things as communication patterns, the flow of power (Example 3–2), and the means of family solidarity. Some look at the family from the perspective of its organization as well as its tasks at different stages in its cycle and in the life of the individual

Example 3–2.
Life with Father

> Clarence Day has presented the mythical, authoritarian family head in his satire *Life with Father*. In the eyes of the family the world revolves around Father. Young Clarence stands in amazement when anyone intimates that Father's whims should be ignored. Father, of course, assumes the world will respond to his wishes, and in the recollection of Clarence there is little that Father cannot do. When Father said he was going to purchase a new family plot in the cemetery, one near the corner where he could get out, even Mother confided to Clarence that she would not be surprised if he could do it.
>
> Abstract from C. Day, Jr., *Life with Father* (New York: Knopf, 1935).

members. The third approach relates especially to the developmental progress of individuals through the course of a life-span study.[1]

Circumstances (the death of a spouse, the loss of employment) may intervene to change the course of life in an individual family. Historical events (war and the reduction in numbers of available men) or value changes (new roles for women) may contribute to variations in expected patterns of family living. This chapter can refer only briefly to some of these. Our intent is to introduce into our thinking an appreciation for the way in which the arena of family affords important opportunities for adults to develop skills, form identities, and find avenues of self-expression throughout the course of their lives.

We will consider some of the characteristics of family life, some of the expected patterns in the family life-cycle, and some of the different ways in which individuals are dealing with tasks of family living.

A family is composed of interacting personalities. The number of persons and closeness of involvement varies with definitions of family. Nearly all adults acknowledge some family involvement. It may be as parents or grandparents, aunts and uncles, brothers and sisters, or as sons and daughters.

Just as an individual grows and develops new competencies and goals through life, so also the family has a sequence of development. "The successful development of the family is contingent upon the satisfactory accomplishments of biological requirements, cultural imperatives, personal aspirations, and values if the family is to continue to develop as a unit."[2]

[1] R. H. Rodgers, *Family Interaction and Transaction* (Englewood Cliffs, N.J.: Prentice-Hall, 1973).

[2] F. I. Nye and F. M. Bernardo, *Emerging Conceptual Frameworks in Family Analysis* (New York: Macmillan, 1967), p. 203.

Some of the developmental tasks of the family unit[3] include establishing a suitable living arrangement, physically and sociophysiologically; finding satisfactory ways of getting and spending money; arranging for mutually acceptable divisions of labors in support of home and family; working on a growing experience in intellectual, emotional, and sexual communication; building skills and ways of working with relatives and community groups. Central among the skills required for the majority of adults in family life are skills in parenting, the art and science of bearing and rearing children.

Family Centeredness in America

One of the striking findings to come from the Kansas City study of middle adult and old age twenty years ago[4] and to come again, with even more clear-cut emphasis, from the study in the San Francisco Bay area[5] is the family-centeredness of the American way of life. Family-centeredness provides the primary orientation for individuals all along the life-span.

As we look at each of the life stages, we can note a family theme. Young adults project their planning and career preparation in terms of anticipated family roles. In the hustling middle-adult years providing food, shelter, and status for their families is a key focus of identity for most men. Sex stereotyping has often directed women's commitment to the care and nurture of all family members.[6] Regardless of the way in which the allocating of sex-role responsibilities may change in the future, parenting will still remain a primary career for most adults of young and middle years. As the nest begins to empty, the reevaluation of personal responsibilities and relationships still has a family focus—even when there is a change of marital partners. Although retirement is characterized with new role relationships, accompanied by a more dominant role for the wife, it is still the family that affords the identification center for most older adults. In retirement the exchange of services—sometimes expressed in a new movement toward mothering of the husband by the wife—provides the form of psychosocial satisfaction. The preeminence of grandparent and great-grandparent roles has emerged in

---

[3] E. M. Duvall, *Family Development* (Philadelphia: Lippincott, 1967).

[4] B. L. Neugarten and associates, *Personality in Middle and Late Life* (New York: Atherton Press, 1964).

[5] M. F. Lowenthal, M. T. Thurnher, and D. Chiriboga, *Four Stages of Life* (San Francisco: Jossey-Bass, 1975); H. S. Maas and J. A. Kuypers, *From Thirty to Seventy* (San Francisco: Jossey-Bass, 1974).

[6] It is probable that sex roles will be less arbitrary and discrete dichotomies as we approach the twenty-first century.

a much larger scope with increasing length of the average life. Four out of ten older Americans have great-grandchildren.[7]

Different Family Life-styles

The family is the first and most formative and enduring of socializing agencies. The inseparable interaction between nature and nurture or inheritance and environment is clearly present as the child formulates personality patterns, self-concept, life-style, values system, and ethnic, socioeconomic, and career identities in the early years of family life. The family provides the supportive milieu in which meaning and expectancies are fixed in the child's mind with different incoming stimuli. Members of the family and the relationships among the individuals are the security assuring the child of continued care and resources for his existence. Thus the family is experienced literally and, equally important, symbolically as providing the substance of life and continuity.

Whereas the word *family* connotes a general understanding of intimate

3–2 *Four out of ten older Americans have great-grandchildren. This four-generation picture includes the writer's wife with her father, daughter, and granddaughter.*

[7] P. Townsend, "The Emergence of the Four-Generation Family in Industrial Society," in *Middle Age and Aging*, ed. B. L. Neugarten (Chicago: University of Chicago Press, 1968). The chances of a 10-year-old child having all four grandparents living have risen from 1 in 90 in 1920 to 1 in 14 in 1970. Metropolitan Life Statistical Bulletin 53 (1972), pp. 8–10.

Example 3–3.
Types of
Family
Relationships

NUCLEAR FAMILY

Husband, wife, and offspring living in a common household; natural or adopted children. Traditional: husband the breadwinner, wife the home manager and child rearer. Evolving: wife also employed; husband sharing in home management and child rearing.

DYADIC NUCLEAR FAMILY

Childless husband and wife, one or both gainfully employed.

SINGLE-PARENT FAMILY

One parent, usually with preschool and/or school-age children; condition the consequence of death, divorce, abandonment, separation (with financial aid rarely coming from second parent), nonmarriage.

THREE-GENERATION FAMILY

Three generations in a single household, in the home of either the aged parent or the grown child; parent, grown child, and grandchildren; aged couple, their grown child, and his offspring; married couple with their children and the aged parent.

MIDDLE-AGED OR OLD-AGE COUPLE

Husband and wife; children, if any, are launched into school, career, marriage; husband only may be employed; both may be employed; neither may work (retirement stage).

INSTITUTIONAL FAMILY

Children absent from natural or adoptive parents, care being provided by orphanages, residential schools, or correctional institutions.

FOSTER FAMILY

One or more children with parents assigned by court or agency action.

KIN NETWORK

Nuclear household or unmarried members living in close geographical proximity and operating within a reciprocal system of exchange of goods and services.

Emerging experimental structures which affect children include:

COMMUNE FAMILY, MONOGAMOUS

Household or more than one monogamous couple with children sharing common facilities, resources, and experiences; socialization of children is a group activity.

COMMUNE FAMILY, GROUP MARRIAGE

Household of adults and offspring known as one family where all adults are married to each other and all are parents to the children.

UNMARRIED-PARENT AND CHILD FAMILY

Either man or woman (more often woman) and one or more children; children may be born to or adopted by the parent; marriage is not desired or possible.

UNMARRIED-COUPLE AND CHILD FAMILY

A couple who choose to live together without marriage, for varying periods of time with a child whom they have borne or adopted.

HOMOSEXUAL COUPLE AND CHILD FAMILY

A male or female couple with a child who is formally or informally adopted.

From J. W. Williams and M. Stith, *Middle Childhood: Behavior and Development* (New York: Macmillan Publishing Company, 1974), pp. 80–82. Copyright © 1974. Reprinted by permission.

reciprocal helping and committed relationships continuing through time, there are many forms in which these occur. The description in Example 3–3, adapted by Williams and Stith from the White House Conference papers, provides a helpful outline of some of the different constellations of family relationships.

Modified Extended Family Network

As the individual grows older and enters into adult life, he or she functions as a member of an intricate network of kinships, affection, and mutual aid. As our society became more mobile, the impression began to form that the extended family network was "losing out." The network of supportive relationships that characterize the extended framework of family association was thought to be in trouble as our society became more urban. The term *nuclear family* came into prominence to describe the association of mother, father, and one or two children, without continuing ties with other relatives. It replaced the picture of the family including uncles, aunts, and grandparents. The nuclear family was often contrasted with the extended family concept of some other cultures with precise patterns of lineage and responsibilities. It was anticipated that the isolated nuclear family would become the typical family situation of the mid-twentieth century. When contemplating this change, much concern was expressed as to whether there would be available sources of psychological support and material aid in times of stress or developmental transition (such as launching new families and careers). However, family-life research has continued to point out that the predicted disintegration of the extended family through industrial developments, urbanization, and mobility has not happened.

Family theorists Sussman and Burchinal[8] suggest that rather than describing the isolated nuclear family as typical of our culture, it would be better to use the concept of a "modified extended family" structure. This will reflect relationship networks and patterns of mutual aid prevailing in most families. The major activities linking the network are mutual aid and social activities among kin-related families. Cross-cultural research in Japan, England, Denmark, and the United States has found active involvement among the generations in all industrial societies.[9]

EXCHANGE OF SERVICES.   Sussman and Burchinal[10] point out that contrary to some impressions family life is active in the cities as well as in rural communities. The following four observations describe the importance of family life as reported in urban research: (1) the difficulty of establishing close relationships in the city make family contacts highly important; (2) family get-togethers are the principal leisure-time activity of the urban working class, outranking visits to friends and coworkers; (3) relatives often provide services such as the following for one another: shopping, child care, advice giving and counseling, care of the aged, hospitality for travelers, support during crises or gala occasions such as marriages, births, and deaths; (4) financial help is common between generations as youth become established in independent families, grandchildren appear, career preparation necessitates it, and illness or age present needs.

[8] M. S. Sussman and L. Burchinal, "Kin Family Network: Unheralded Structure in Current Conceptualizations of Family Functioning," *Marriage and Family Living* 24 (August 1962), 3.

[9] E. Shanas and associates, *Old People in Three Industrial Societies* (New York: Atherton Press, 1968); E. Palmore, "The Status and Integration of the Aged in Japanese Society," *Journal of Gerontology* 30 (March 1975), 2:199–208.

[10] Sussman and Burchinal, "Kin Family Network."

The national Harris Poll reported a high degree of family involvement among persons of all age levels. Eighty-one per cent of persons aged 65 and over have living children. More than half said they had seen their children within the last day or so and another one fourth had seen them within the last week.

Family interaction among the generations continues to be more than simply "family visiting." Both the older and younger generations report that older persons perform valuable services for the younger (see Tables 3–1 and 3–2). The service and monetary help was described as follows:

> In economic terms, the contribution that older people make to younger members of their family is substantial. In part, this contribution takes the form of gifts and money offered by older parents and grandparents to their offspring. In addition, however, the services performed by older people for their children and grandchildren represent substantial monetary savings for the young. As nurses for the ill, as babysitters for small children, as shoppers and errand runners, as home repairers and housekeepers, even as surrogate parents, the public 65 and over offer assistance to their children and grandchildren that would cost them dearly otherwise. Without the free services of older family

Table 3–1. Ways in Which Public 18 to 64 Say They Receive Help From Parents or Grandparents Over 65 (by Age) (Base: Have parents or grandparents over 65)

	Total Public %	Public 18–24 %	Public 25–39 %	Public 40–45 %	Public 55–64 %
Give you gifts	85	94	85	80	73
Give general advice on how to deal with some of life's problems	58	62	61	57	34
Help out when someone is ill	57	74	57	49	28
Take care of small children	42	53	46	35	16
Give advice on running a home	42	50	41	40	25
Give advice on bringing up children	40	45	40	39	23
Help out with money	35	52	34	24	20
Give advice on job or business matters	31	44	33	19	17
Shop or run errands	30	42	31	22	17
Fix things around your house or keep house for you	22	31	20	18	9
Take grandchildren, nieces, or nephews into their home to live with them	21	25	23	15	10

SOURCE: *The Myth and Reality of Aging in America,* © 1975, a study prepared for The National Council on the Aging, Inc. (NCOA), Washington, D.C., by Louis Harris and Associates, Inc., p. 81.

Table 3–2. Ways in Which Public 65 and Over Help Their Children or Grandchildren
(Base: 82% of public 65 and over who have children or grandchildren)

	Total Public 65 and Over %	Public 65–69 %	Public 70–79 %	Public 80 and Over %
Give gifts	90	93	89	86
Help out when someone is ill	68	78	65	57
Take care of grandchildren	54	65	53	34
Help out with money	45	50	44	38
Give general advice on how to deal with some of life's problems	39	45	37	32
Shop or run errands	34	46	29	23
Fix things around their house or keep house for them	26	31	25	20
Give advice on bringing up children	23	25	22	20
Give advice on running a home	21	24	21	17
Give advice on jobs or business matters	20	24	17	19
Take grandchildren, nieces, or nephews into your home to live with you	16	20	16	11

SOURCE: *The Myth and Reality of Aging in America,* © 1975, a study prepared for The National Council on the Aging, Inc. (NCOA), Washington, D.C., by Louis Harris and Associates, Inc., p. 75.

members, the young would either have to resort to hiring outside help to perform these same tasks or, more likely, sacrifice some of their own income by taking time off from jobs to perform these same tasks themselves. There is a critical, even indispensable role that older people play in the lives of their children or grandchildren which is largely taken for granted today.[11]

There are some areas where perceptions of the generations differ. Older persons think they give more child care, care to the ill, and more monetary help than the young experience receiving. On the other hand, the younger generations feel they are on the receiving end of far more advice giving than the older generations recognize.

By and large the helping relationships described prevailed across all socioeconomic levels. There was some tendency for more affluent older persons to provide more gifts, money, and job or business advice. The less affluent differed from the general population by giving more advice on

[11] L. Harris and associates, *The Myth and Reality of Aging in America* (Washington, D.C.: The National Council on the Aging, 1975), pp. 78–79.

bringing up children. Older blacks also differed significantly as a group from older whites in taking children into their homes to live.[12]

As the characteristics of family life change, along with changes in the age distribution of our population, family life will continue to offer many important areas of study. Note an excerpt from an editorial in *The Gerontologist* (Example 3–4).

Example 3–4.
The Family in
Aging Research

> . . . The family in aging research has focused on quantitative measures. The time has now come to define and learn what these mean. Qualitative interactional research is now a requisite. How do we measure the ebb and flow of interaction between the old parent and the adult child, perhaps also old? Who benefits according to what value and under what conditions? And who has more taken away under this value than that person is able to give?
>
> As we look at the family in aging, it is apparent greater qualitative knowledge is needed on the forms of interdependence by the generations. New terms are needed to define more adequately the evolving family structure in aging ranging from five generations to no relatives, from loose emotional ties with relatives to none at all or even one of hostility, and from being head of a household to residing alone.
>
> We have only begun our knowledge search on the family in aging.
>
> From J. Kaplan, "The Family in Aging," *The Gerontologist* 15 (October 1975), 5:385.

Social and
Economic
Influences in
Minority
Families

We must continue to keep in mind that each family is formed of its own heritage of previous family experiences; parents reconstruct, in a measure, the family life-style in which they were reared. Social and economic influences also do much to form different family life-styles in different cultural groups. The following excerpts of interviews with an upper-middle-class family and a migrant family illustrate the range of differences.

An upper-middle-class husband and wife from Crestwood Heights describe their activities as follows:

> WIFE: I'm on the go all the time now. Busiest woman in the community. I'm in everything—home and school, National Council of Women, Community Chest—oh, you couldn't list them all. For a long time I represented the NCW

---

[12] Ibid., p. 76.

at school-board meetings. For years I went to every school-board meeting. It is awfully important to have an active community spirit. So many people today aren't interested in anything. Do you know there are more sleeping pills sold today than you can imagine—and dope too! . . . Sometimes I have three or four, even five, meetings a day, all overlapping. Skip out of one to get to another.

HUSBAND: So we have dinner about six fifteen or six thirty. Mrs. K and I are off to meetings or occasionally we stay at home. We prefer to stay home.[13]

Observations of a migrant worker mother are described by the interviewer in the following notes:

Many times she has carried her infant to the field, done picking, stopped to go to the edge of the field, fed the child, left the child to itself or the care of its grandmother or older sister, and returned to the tomatoes or beans or cucumbers. Many times, too, she has reminded me that picking crops can be boring and repetitive and laborious, and so made very much more tolerable by the presence of good, clean, cool water to drink, a good meal at lunchtime, and, best of all, a child to feed lying nearby. She knows that the chances are that good water and food will not be available, but an infant—yes, the presence of an infant is much more likely: "To tell the truth, I do better in the field when I know my baby is waiting there for me, and soon I'll be able to go see her and do what I can for her. It gives you something to look ahead to."

She plans then. She plans her days around the crops and around the care of her children; she and her mother do that. Sometimes they both pick the crops, and nearby the children play, and indeed upon occasion the oldest child, nine years old, helps out not only with the younger children but with the beans or tomatoes also. Sometimes the mother works on her knees, up and down the planted rows, and her mother stays with the children, on the edge of the farm or back in the cabin. Sometimes, too, there is not work to be had, and "we stays still and lets the children do their running about."[14]

Ours is a pluralistic society with significantly different patterns for adult development in Spanish-American, black, Chinese, old-world European, and Indian families. Some of the special strengths of the Jewish family have been reflected in popular literature, such as Irving Howe's description of the Jewish mother.

It was from a place in the kitchen that the (immigrant) Jewish housewife became the looming figure who would inspire, haunt, and devastate generations

[13] J. R. Seeley, R. A. Sim, and E. W. Loosley, *Crestwood Heights* (New York: Wiley, 1956), p. 172.
[14] R. Coles, *Uprooted Children* (New York, Harper & Row, 1970), pp. 7–8.

of sons. She realized intuitively that insofar as the outer world tyrannized and wore down her men, reducing them to postures of docility, she alone could create an oasis of order.

It was she who would cling to received values and resist the pressures of dispersion: she who would sustain the morale of all around her, mediating quarrels, soothing hurts, drawing a circle of safety in which her children could breathe, and sometimes, as time went on, crushing her loved ones under the weight of her affection.[15]

Alfred Kazin so recalls his mother:

My mother worked in the kitchen all day long, we ate in it almost all meals except the Passover seder . . . The kitchen gave a special character to our lives; my mother's character. All my memories of that kitchen are dominated by the nearness of my mother sitting all day long at her sewing machine, by the clacking of the treadle against the linoleum floor, by the patient twist of her right shoulder as she automatically pushed at the wheel with one hand or lifted her foot to free the needle . . . The kitchen was her life. Year by year, as I began to take in her fantastic capacity for labor and her anxious zeal, I realized it was ourselves she kept stitching together.[16]

BLACK FAMILIES. There have been many differing views concerning the roles of adults in the black family. Some of them have pictured a dominant role for the woman in the black family with a weak or often absent male. Others have pictured a strong solidarity within the black family. The fact that there are few blacks in nursing homes suggests something of the nature of the extended-family concept in the black community.

Robert B. Hill, research director for the National Urban League, points out that much research based on comparisons of percentages between white and black families has given an erroneous picture of pathology in black families. He points to statistics for the majority of black families that reflect great family strength. He describes the strength of most black families as coming from strong kinship bonds, a strong work orientation, adaptability of family roles, strong achievement motivation, and strong religious orientation.[17]

Many black families take relatives into their households. These relatives are more likely to be children than older relatives. Older women tend to take

[15] I. Howe, *World of Our Fathers: The Journey of the East European Jews to America and the Life They Found and Made* (New York: Harcourt Brace Jovanovich, 1976).

[16] A. Kazin, quoted in Howe, *World of Our Fathers.*

[17] R. B. Hill, *The Strengths of Black Families* (New York: Emerson Hall, 1972). For historical context of this strength, see A. Haley, *Roots* (New York: Doubleday, 1976).

in children and younger persons rather than being taken in themselves. Blacks are less likely than whites to put children up for formal adoption. The high rate of absorption of "homeless" children by black families affords emotional and economic support to thousands of children and maintains kinship and community bonds (see Tables 3–3 and 3–4).

Hill challenges the stereotypes of the shiftless black husband, indicating that in 90 per cent of all black families the husbands work and two thirds of the wives also work. In poor black families 70 per cent of the husbands and only 44 per cent of their wives work. The ability of the wife to obtain work is often a factor distinguishing whether the black family will be able to avoid poverty. Whereas desire for work appears strong for both male and female

Table 3–3. Per cent of Related Members Under 18 in Families with No Children of Own Under 18 by Race, Age of Head, and Type of Family, March 1970

Type of Family and Age of Head	*Per cent with Members Under 18*	
	Black	*White*
Husband–wife families		
All families	13	3
Head under 35	2	3
Head 35–44	7	2
Head 45–64	16	3
Head 65 and over	14	3
Families with female heads		
All families	41	7
Head under 35	24★	17★
Head 35–44	42★	10
Head 45–64	40	13
Head 65 and over	48	10

From R. B. Hill, *The Strengths of Black Families* (New York: Emerson Hall, 1972), p. 41.

★ Base under 75,000.

SOURCE: Prepared by National Urban League Research Department from data in U.S. Department of Commerce, Bureau of the Census, Current Population Reports, Population Characteristics, *Household and Family Characteristics, March 1970,* Series P-20, No. 218, March 23, 1971, Tables 3 and 4.

Table 3–4. Imputed Effect of Out-of-Wedlock Births on Family Formation by Color, 1968–1969 (Numbers in thousands)

Disposition of Children	Black[1]		White	
	Number	Per cent	Number	Per cent
Out-of-wedlock births (1968)	184	100	155	100
Formally adopted (1969)	12	7	97	62
Foster care or institutionalized[2]	1	[3]	7	5
Retained in new family[4]	5	3	40	26
Informally adopted or retained in existing families[5]	165	90	11	7

From R. B. Hill, *The Strengths of Black Families* (New York: Emerson Hall, 1972), p. 43.

[1] The racial statistics on illegitimate births, adoption, and foster care apply to nonwhites and not only to blacks.

[2] These numbers were obtained by multiplying the increase (8,000) in the number of children in foster care or institutions between 1968 and 1969 by the proportion (12 per cent) of nonwhite children estimated by the Children's Bureau to be in homes for dependent or neglected children.

[3] Less than 0.5 per cent.

[4] These numbers represent the increase in families with a single woman as the head between 1968 and 1969. For the purposes of this presentation, it is assumed that each of these new families resulted from the birth of an out-of-wedlock child in 1968.

[5] By "informal adoption," we include both (1) the retention of out-of-wedlock children by mothers in already existing families and (2) the absorption of out-of-wedlock children by such relatives as grandmothers and aunts or by nonrelatives.

SOURCE: Prepared by the National Urban League Research Department from data in U.S. National Center for Social Statistics, *Adoptions in 1969: Supplement to Child Welfare Statistics—1969;* U.S. National Center for Health Statistics, *Vital Statistics of the U.S.: 1968, Volume I—Natality;* U.S. Children's Bureau, *America's Children and Youth in Institutions, 1950–1960–1964;* U.S. Census Bureau, *Current Population Reports, Population Characteristics,* "Selected Characteristics of Persons and Families: March 1970," Series P-20, No. 204, July 13, 1970.

blacks, lack of available employment and low salaries keeps many in poverty. Where work is available, blacks persevere. One study showed 80 per cent of black workers had held their current job for more than three years.[18]

A common assumption growing out of research reported in the 1960s has been that black families are usually dominated by the wife. The report of the National Urban League challenges that picture, suggesting that some of the early data were misinterpreted and that more recent data support the picture

[18] J. A. Kahl and J. M. Goering, "Stable Workers, Black and White," *Social Problems* (Winter 1971), pp. 306–318.

of an equalitarian pattern in which both spouses share decision-making and expected household tasks.[19] The report questions both the "matriarchial tradition" and the other popular assumption that husbands of wives receiving Aid for Dependent Children desert their families so that the family can obtain welfare assistance. Three fifths of the black women who head families work. Hill stresses that there is great variability in both the one-parent and two-parent black families. This variability is also a reflection of the adaptability of family roles. Rather than pathology, Hill suggests that the adaptability of family roles, combined with support from the extended family network, results in a strength manifested by the lower suicide rates of blacks than whites.[20]

To the extent that college attendance is an index of achievement orientation, the increasing numbers of blacks attending college reflect a family climate fostering a high-achievement orientation. More than three fourths of the black students indicate their college attendance is influenced by their parents. It is interesting to note that three fourths of the black students come from homes in which the family head had no college education.[21]

The Negro church has been a central influence in the survival of black people through the days of slavery and through their growing strength during the civil rights movement as well. The church provides a center for education, social services, and for communication regarding social issues. Even more, it maintains a world-and-life view in which family unity is part of a larger unity within the black community. Times of travail have nurtured faith among black people, and the suffering of Christ has been experienced as companionship in the dark moments of their history because His victory afforded them hope that they would overcome. The vitality of the spiritual core strengthening the black family has often come from faith formed early in life rather than through later reasoned deliberations.

Parenting and economic responsibilities for adults in black families parallel those for adults in white families. The kinship ties and family aspect of many black communities extend and create some new parenting-type roles for black adults. Economic conditions create special pressures in many instances similar to pressures experienced by poor whites.

[19] Hill, *The Strengths of Black Families,* pp. 18–20.
[20] Ibid., p. 26.
[21] Ibid., p. 30.

Other Special Families There are some adults whose arrangements concerning family life are different from the traditional family situation. Some of these include single adults, homosexual adults, and adults living in communal groups. Later in the chapter we will consider other special family types evolving from special situations in conventional family life, such as families of divorced and widowed persons.

SINGLE ADULTS. Out of every hundred people in America, three or four never marry. The trend toward remaining single seems to be increasing. From examining census data it is not clear whether this increase reflects a tendency for some young adults to postpone marriage until middle life or whether the increasing number of single young adults represents persons who will remain single throughout life.

In the past, most persons who married did so by age 40. There have been some differences in the general pattern of men and women who did not marry. Men who did not marry tended to be less educated, in lower occupations, and with lower income than those who did. Women who did not marry tended to come from above-average educational levels with higher incomes.

There are many reasons why individuals remain single. Some choose this life-style, some lack opportunity to marry, some choose life commitments such as participation in religious orders involving celibacy, some are physically or emotionally ill in institutions, some are homosexual and may not actually live as a single person, some may have financial needs or types of employment that preclude marriage.

There appears to be an increasing subculture of singles. Housing and various merchandizing groups are identifying this as a market area. Human service programs are developing recreational, educational, and other resources tailored to this population. It is probable that there exists within the broad identity of singles a number of subgroups who have little interaction with one another. These include the young nonmarrieds who will eventually marry, the older nonmarrieds who choose this as a permanent way of life, and the homosexuals who may or may not have dyadic commitments. The divorced and the widowed are also sometimes included as part of the singles subculture when programs are being considered. Each of these groups has special interests and needs, and each labors under the handicap of having no clearly defined social pattern in our society.

ADULTS IN COMMUNAL LIVING.   An alternative form of family life, with some similarities to the extended family, is communal living. This may take the form found in religious orders; it may reflect a temporary or permanent commitment. Various experimental forms of communal living have been part of the complex of family types through the years. Example 3–5, written

Example 3–5.
Living
Together

Community living sounded interesting. My assignment was to visit the Austin Community Fellowship in Chicago that included seven Wheaton alumni. I was to find out how this particular situation was working and how they hoped to improve on the common single-family unit.

After three visits with the 19-adult-member community in their three households, including several meals, much talking and even some working, I might describe their life together (as if looking through a camera) as a panorama of activity. I could focus in on the three toddlers in one household playing in the front room, or zoom in on one of the guys sauteing vegetables for supper, or catch the whole community family singing, accompanied by a ukelele, in a crowded living room. But these snapshots couldn't possibly tell a story that is now three years old and, besides, the pictures wouldn't look too different from those in most family albums. So I'll tell my story of what I experienced that was different about their family life. My story began with many questions and several criticisms but ended in sharing a simple communion service with them and also sharing many of their goals and dreams.

The large, uncurtained windows of the first old frame house that I visited captured my first criticism, a lack of privacy. Although each community member did give up some personal privacy, I began to see the community effectively solving the more important problems of continuing service ministries for which there are little financial rewards, the pull of materialism, and the over-consumption and over-work of the single family. Their common purse probably initially brings a negative reaction. But as I watched them face these issues, I concluded they have solutions to share that we can adapt and apply even apart from household structures.

Before I could see some of the advantages of community living I had to recognize my over-emphasis on privacy. Most people hoard privacy. I claim it as a right when my roommates invite their friends over so frequently that I must be careful how I look when I walk out of my bedroom. But after visiting the community, I noticed how often I savor the times when I can have our apartment, normally shared with three others, to myself. And I had to label that selfishness.

The members of the community not only realized privacy was too important to most people, but they concluded it created one of today's biggest problems, loneliness. As Steve Adelsman talked of modern suburbia's insulated loneliness, epitomized by separate family dwellings with fences around them, I remember the theme of loneliness and alienation that pervaded books like *The Invisible Man* and *The Stranger* that I read for a modern literature course. In giving up the desire to withdraw from sharing their lives, the community members also gave up a nagging loneliness labeled by sociologists as mankind's most urgent problem.

FREE TO MINISTER

Over a tunafish sandwich lunch on that first visit, Steve Adelsman demonstrated the first advantage of living together that impressed me. After an ice cream dessert, he lingered at the dining room table for several hours to answer my questions. As it was a weekday, I wondered if I should stop questioning to let him get back to work. Eventually, I learned that the community and its everyday management was his full-time job.

Steve numbers among the 40% of the adults who do not receive paychecks but minister where their abilities are most needed. Pooling paychecks of the wage earners to pay monthly bills and a $40 monthly personal allowance frees many of the members to choose an area of service without worrying about month-end bills. Glen Kehrein ('73) serves on the staff of Chicago's Circle Church as a neighborhood outreach coordinator for the Austin area. Marti Spina Adelsman's ('69) ministry centers around household management. Dan Van Ness ('71) handles criminal cases at a legal clinic connected with the La-Salle Street church.

The community dreams of involving even more of its members and their gifts in a non-profit wholistic clinic that could minister to the physical, spiritual, legal, and psychological needs of their neighborhood. Glen is working on that dream as he develops the programs of a neighborhood center located in an old house several blocks from the households. It now offers a practical learning center where kids can practice various skills such as photography and woodwork. Dan serves as the neighborhood center's part-time lawyer and Emily Schrock Bray's ('70) husband Paul offers psychological counseling four days a week.

FIGHTING MATERIALISM

The shared corporate life provides the structure to effectively resist our society's "things mania." By just surrounding themselves with more people than convenient or attractive things, people become more important. Someone commented that living with each other has become their first ministry.

I ate a grilled cheese sandwich while Dan explained the community's position on insurance that illustrates one way they resist the pull of materialism. Instead of finding security in the total listed in a bank book or insurance policy, the community finds it in each other and their mutual commitments. Dan said that most of them do not hold life insurance policies because they disagree with the popular mentality of doing all you can to prepare for the unseen calamity in the feared future.

They still have nice things like crystal and Yves St. Laurent cologne, but their common purse and careful budgeting help to curb "wanting-spending." Apart from allowances, large purchases like curtains or even a winter coat become a community decision. Dan commented that this makes you think twice before asking for a red coat because you're tired of the green one.

CUTTING CORNERS

Community living doesn't only slow down the shopping spree, it often enables the buyers to get more for their money. Most supermarkets stock economy size everything because it's cheaper. The community goes one step further in buying eight dozen eggs at a time at a wholesale price from the Water Street Market in Chicago. Along with their black and white neighbors they buy in bulk through a food co-op and save money. To get the most out of clothes the community uses the large family trick of hand-me-downs. The mothers have found this a particular advantage, first in maternity clothes and later with children's clothes that seem to shrink as the toddlers grow.

Besides money, the community households cut corners when it comes to washing dishes and cleaning bathrooms. Household chores, or "ministries," as they are labeled on a schedule tacked to the bulletin board, don't fall on one person but are spread out among all the adults. The note above the kitchen sink unpleasantly reminds the dish washer that "evening dish washing includes: . . ." and list eight specifics. But the KP schedule on the refrigerator rotates names so one person doesn't do that job two nights in a row.

They extend this principle to child care too, and call it "shared motherhood." For example, one mother lines up the three toddlers of the household in their high chairs and feeds them while another mother prepares the evening meal. On Fridays Steve Adelsman takes over feeding and changing diapers in his household to give mothers a chance to clean, read, or visit.

WOULD I LIVE IN COMMUNITY?

Probably not, at least not in a household set-up. But my story with community hasn't ended. I said good-by to the Austin Fellowship after watching them celebrate their life together in the communion of The Lord's Supper. As I watched that oneness expressed in symbol and gesture of hugging and sharing, I knew that I wanted "community" even at my apartment in Wheaton, Illinois.

From L. Havener, "Living Together," *Wheaton Alumni* (Wheaton, Ill.: June 1976).

by a journalism student in a liberal arts college whose assignment was to visit a community group in which some of the school's alumni were living, reflects something of the life-style and the motivation that may be found in experimental living arrangements.[22]

HOMOSEXUAL ADULTS.   The number of homosexual adults is unknown. The changing and indeterminate status of the homosexual relationship in the eyes of the law and society at large adds immeasurably to the difficulty of establishing continuing relationships. Adjustment difficulties experienced by heterosexual couples and families, sanctioned by society and supported by readily recognized roles, are considerably more difficult for homosexual couples. Legal groups[23] are working to clarify the rights of homosexuals in family life. Churches and other community groups are developing programs with them in mind.

The Family Life Cycle

Numerous disciplines including sociology, anthropology, and the health professions direct some aspect of their research to an understanding of family life. Home economics is the interdisciplinary applied science that makes the family the center of its professional focus.

FAMILY DEVELOPMENTAL APPROACH.   At the beginning of this chapter we alluded to a developmental perspective with which family life can be viewed. Roy Rodgers has described it in the following paragraphs:

> The developmental approach begins with the basic idea that families are long-lived groups with a history which must be taken into account if the dynamics of their behavior are to be explained adequately. Elements of the time perspective may be applied to a number of different aspects of family behavior. Let us look at two elements of the time perspective and their relationships to family behavior.
> The first element of the time perspective is historical time. One of the major contributions of the institutional approach has been its ability to show how the family institution has changed over the history of humanity. There is no ques-

---

[22] See also the report of participant observation in a number of communal groups: D. and N. Jackson, *Living Together in a World Falling Apart* (Carol Stream, Ill.: Creation House, 1974). N. Stinnett and J. Walters, *Relationships in Marriage and Family* (New York: Macmillan, 1977) offers a meaningful consideration of nontraditional life-styles and families of tomorrow.

[23] E. C. Boggan et al., *The Rights of Gay People: An American Civil Liberties Union Handbbook* (New York: Dutton, 1975).

3–3a. *The Austin Community Fellowship. (Robert Mead, photographer)* **b.** *Steve and Marti Spina Adelsman and their son, Aaron, live in the newest household of the community. Marti keeps busy with Aaron and Steve works for the fellowship on a full-time basis. (Robert Mead, photographer)* **c.** *Jan Drennan works for the Illinois Department of Children and Family Services. (Robert Mead, photographer)* **d.** *Emily Schrock Bray is doing her residency in family practice at McNeil Hospital in Berwyn, Ill. Her husband, Paul, now works nearly full time at a community clinic as a counselor. (Robert Mead, photographer)* **e.** *Steve and Carol Showers Montgomery keep busy running after Benjamin. They just moved into the community. Steve works as a data-processing manager for an appraisal company in Chicago. (Robert Mead, photographer)* **f.** *Glen Kehrein is on the staff of the Circle Church in Chicago and serves as a community outreach coordinator in the Austin area. His wife, Dicki, keeps trying to teach their daughter Tara how to walk. (Robert Mead, photographer)* **g.** *Dan Van Ness works as an attorney for the Cabrini-Green legal aid clinic in Chicago. His wife, Brenda, is considering further education. (Robert Mead, photographer)*

d.

e.

f.

g.

tion, then, that the historical time in which a given set of families is situated has effects on behavior. It is impossible to ignore the impact of the depression of the 1930s or World War Two on American family life . . .

Another dimension of historical time is the fact that the normative expectations for family behavior are not the same for all periods of the family's history. This truth is not simply a function of chronological time but is more accurately a function of social process time. By social process time I mean the periods comprised in the life space of a group or individual with a given process. For example, when we say, "He is getting an education," we are not referring to a chronological period. Rather, we are talking about a processual period. The institutional norms defining the behavior of young marrieds differs from those for couples with infants, from those with teen-aged children, from those who no longer have children at home, and so on. This time element is directly related to the idea of family life-cycle stages, which is closely identified with the developmental approach.[24]

STAGES IN THE CYCLE.   One of the most well-known and frequently adapted outlines for describing the sequence of stages in family life was formulated by a committee that Hill and Evelyn Duvall co-chaired in preparation for the National Conference on Family Life in 1948.[25]

Stage 1—Establishment (newly married, childless)
Stage 2—New parents (infant–3 years)
Stage 3—Preschool family (child 3–6 years and possibly younger siblings)
Stage 4—School-age family (oldest child 6–12 years, possibly younger siblings)
Stage 5—Family with adolescent (oldest child 13–19, possibly younger siblings)
Stage 6—Family with young adult (oldest 20, until first child leaves home)
Stage 7—Family as launching center (from departure of first to last child)
Stage 8—Post-parental family, the middle years (after children have left home until father retires)

In later chapters we will look at some of the roles and tasks of adults in these different stages as we discuss the adult development period in which these stages are most likely to appear. One of the assumptions of the family life-cycle concept is that parenting is a central career in adult family life.

---

[24] Rodgers, *Family Interaction and Transaction*, pp. 12–13.
[25] Duvall, *Family Development*, p. viii.

Parenting Parenting is one of the most popular and most challenging of adult careers (see an analysis of the role of parenthood in Example 3–6). Parenting is not only the most populated career, it is also one of the most responsible. The well-being of the nation is dependent on the training and nurture given its future citizens by their parents. Unfortunately, for all its importance, parenting is the career for which people receive the least preparation. Teachers, counselors, and nurses (to name a few of the professions whose skills and responsibilities overlap those of parents) have extensive programs of preparation for their careers. A concern has been growing in recent years to provide some preservice training by including parenting courses in high school. Parenting is a career whose nature changes considerably as the individual moves through the family life cycle. It is a different task and requires considerably different skills and understandings to parent infants and preschool

3–4 *Each level of development brings different kinds of parenting activities.* (Manhattan Mercury *photo*)

Example 3–6.
Role Analysis
of Modern
Parenthood

1. The role of parent in modern America is not well defined. It is often ambiguous and hard to pin down.
2. The role is not adequately delimited. Parents are expected to succeed where even the professionals fail.
3. Modern parents are not well prepared for their role as fathers and mothers.
4. There is a romantic complex about parenthood.
5. Modern parents are in the unenviable position of having complete responsibility for their offspring but only partial authority over them.
6. The standards of role performance imposed on modern parents are too high. This arises from the fact that modern fathers and mothers are judged largely by professional practitioners such as psychiatrists and social workers rather than by their peers—other parents who are "amateurs" and not professionals.
7. Parents are the victims of inadequate behavioral science . . . They have been told repeatedly (and erroneously) that nothing determines what the child will be like but the influence of the parents.
8. Parents do not choose their children, unless they are adoptive parents. Thus they have the responsibility for children whether they find them congenial or not.
9. There is no traditional model for modern parents to follow in rearing their children. The old model has been riddled by critical studies, yet no new model that is adequate has developed. Instead we have had a series of fads and fashions in child rearing based on the research of the moment.
10. Contrary to what some may think, parenthood as a role does not enjoy the priority one would expect in modern America. The needs of the economic system in particular come first, as can be seen in the frequency with which large firms transfer young managers and their families around the country.
11. Other new roles have been assumed by modern parents since World War I that are not always completely compatible with the role of parent. The clearest and most striking example of this would be the occupational roles assumed by millions of American mothers.
12. The parental role is one of the few important roles in contemporary America that one cannot honorably withdraw from.
13. And last but not least, it is not enough for modern parents to produce children in their own image: the children have to be reared to be not only different from their fathers and mothers but also *better*.

Adapted from E. E. LeMasters, *Parents in Modern America* (Homewood, Ill.; Dorsey Press, 1970), pp. 51–54.

children as compared to parenting older children and adolescents. Parenting continues through the middle adult years but becomes a different experience; it requires new communication skills, self-confidence, and understanding to parent married children.

Adult Developmental Tasks in Families

In the growth of an individual there are points of change in which the person moves from being regarded as a child to being regarded as an adolescent and then as an adult. Although there may be a sliding scale rather than fixed points, certain events continue to serve as transition periods. Marriage marks the beginning of a period; the birth of the first child marks the beginning of another period; departure of children from the home marks another, as does the birth of the first grandchild. At each point the individual begins to assume new responsibilities, to view himself differently, and to be viewed differently by others with new expectations of him or her. Example 3–7 shows changes in perception as reflected in excerpts from a letter to a new mother from her older sister, the mother of a 6-month-old daughter.

Social change as well as biological processes influence these stages. In recent years there has been an increase in the pace. Because marriage and children come earlier and health rates are improving, the period when parents will be alone as middle-aged and maturing couples may average twenty years. Their time together after the children leave home may be nearly the same length as the period of rearing the children. During this time the middle-aged and older adults' position in the community will change to senior status and later to retired status. Perhaps some will enter second careers.

Families of different social classes, although following similar patterns, have different ages of entry into different age-status categories.[26] For example, the higher the social class, generally the older the age of marriage. In past generations, age of marriage was influenced by economic factors; therefore, marriage usually followed on the heels of school or college graduation. Changes in recent years show many wives working to "put the husband through." A pattern reflecting an even more contemporary theme is husbands and wives working to "put us both through."

New family relationships are developing because often both young parents work outside the home and assume together home and child-care

---

[26] B. L. Neugarten and J. W. Moore, "The Changing Age-Status System," in *Middle Age and Aging,* ed. B. L. Neugarten, (Chicago: University of Chicago Press, 1968), pp. 5–21.

Example 3–7.

> Dear Sue,
>
> I've been thinking of the three of you constantly since about 3:30 when Jane told me the big news! I'm so very happy for you all! It's really killing me that I can't be there right now to share in all your joy. I feel close to you still, though, since you're constantly in my thoughts and I know you think of me and the birth of Amanda. They bring so much love with them!
>
> I'm thinking back on my first night in the hospital. I was tired of course, but so thrilled—I could hardly believe it had really happened and that that precious beautiful baby was really here, and really ours. Truly a miracle!! I know you're going through the same thing. Hope the physical discomfort is not so bad that it detracts from the thrill. Hopefully by the time you read this, the situation will be much improved already. At any rate, it's well worth it! Just about any mother will tell you that and I certainly will. Somehow things are suddenly in a new light. You do things for the baby. Your body functioned to give birth to your baby and is beautiful for that reason, whether it has wrinkles and fat or whatever. It's not that you're any less important as a person, it's just that you feel as if you want and need to put your own personal wants second behind the baby's. Not a sacrifice, a privilege really—a beautiful charge you've been given. Of course that can be overdone and if you never leave the baby or do things you really want to do, then you'll end up resenting him and both of you will suffer. You've got lots ahead of you—some hard, but mostly rewarding. That's what makes it so exciting.
>
> You hear about the night feedings being so terrible, but somehow when you see that precious little helpless baby of *yours* wanting only to be held and fed, you somehow don't mind. I could go on and on with this but you'll find it all out for yourself now! Just think of the whole new world now we can share—motherhood!
>
> We love you!
Sally

responsibilities. Younger grandparents also contribute to the changing family patterns. Communication patterns between generations and role relationships of in-laws, grandparents, and great-grandparents are important areas for future research.

CHANGES IN RELATIONSHIPS.   Family life is different at different stages in the family life cycle because of different tasks and because individual members are at different stages in their accumulation of experiences and maturity. Furthermore, the cohort concept reminds us that persons at different stages of the family life cycle represent different periods of our nation's history. Whereas we can make observations about characteristic attitudes and activities of those in different phases of the family life cycle, we need to keep in mind that the next generation occupying that stage may respond somewhat differently because their cohort is from another historical era.

Parents now in their thirties grew up in the 1950s and 1960s. Their world of rapidly changing technology, relaxing social standards, and a generally affluent economy helped them to form certain values and life-styles. These differ from the values and modes of perceiving formulated by their parents, who grew up in the 1930s. When the children of today become parents of the twenty-first century, what will be their values and life-style?

TRANSITION STAGES.   During different stages of the family life cycle, spouses come to value one another in different ways. Newlyweds look at one another in a much more personal and emotionally interactive way than do middle-aged couples.[27] In research interviews, young couples described their mates in terms of their spouse's special personality attributes. They talked a great deal about the things the couple did together and their mutual interests. Middle-aged couples described one another more in terms of their work roles. Husbands described wives as good housekeepers or mothers; wives talked of husbands as breadwinners. Older couples nearing retirement once again focused on the personality of their spouse, discussed their sharing experiences, and projected plans toward continuing interdependence and personal involvement with one another.

Lowenthall suggests that at those points where the role expectations are clear the couples tend to view one another within the role characteristics. At transition stages (for example, the beginning of marriage, the beginning of retirement) roles are less clear and there is a greater emphasis upon the personal characteristics of one's spouse.[28] It is also possible that the preoccupation with careers encourages middle-aged persons to think of one another in terms of career roles.

Recent data from interviews with working-class families suggest that the typical pattern is for the husband to be viewed as the "head of the house," or "boss."[29] Although the pattern is for men to begin with authority, there is a

---

[27] Lowenthal et al., *Four Stages of Life,* p. 25.

[28] Ibid., p. 26.

[29] Ibid., p. 28. Whether the active voices advocating equal authority and changing family life-styles are influencing only limited sectors of society or whether their effect will be felt at a later time is still to be determined.

definite change that takes place in subsequent family stages. In middle age and particularly in the retirement years, women increasingly assume leadership functions within the marriage.

THE ADVENT OF CHILDREN.   In the early phase of the family life cycle, couples are preoccupied with relationships with one another and with anticipation of parental roles. As the child-bearing and child-rearing stages appear, focus shifts to tasks at hand. Nurture of children within the home, establishing the family within the community, and provision for economic needs absorb the couple's energies during those years.

Women are recognized as carrying a major responsibility for family relationships during this period. Men tend to feel some guilt for not being more involved with the family, but they reconcile these feelings by pointing to their responsibilities in the world of work that provides the means to sustain the family. Women tend to resent somewhat the lack of time with the husband and the unending responsibilities with the home and the children.

THE DEPARTURE OF CHILDREN.   As children move through adolescence, parents begin to anticipate the empty-nest phase with mingled feelings. Both men and women anticipate that the children's departure may facilitate improved marital relationships, resulting from more opportunity to do things as couples. Both also recognize that the children's departure forces a review of present roles and reconsideration of their significance as individuals. Marital dissatisfaction is greatest among middle-aged women.[30]

Departure of children may create special strains for the marriage as wives begin to look to the outside world for avenues of self-expression. Husbands, noting their wives' restlessness, may look with new perspective upon their own career situation. With the anticipated relief from heavy financial family concerns, they see the opportunity to consider new purposes for their lives. Along with new awareness of relationships outside the family, the empty-nest period introduces a strengthening of family identities as the couple prepare for the roles of becoming in-laws and then grandparents.

THE CONCERN FOR OWN PARENTS.   The confluence of family relationships is perhaps the most complex for the couple as their children are beginning to leave home and form families. Simultaneously, the couple's own parents are

---

[30] M. T. Thurnher, "Family Confluence, Conflict and Affect," in *Four Stages of Life,* eds. M. F. Lowenthal et al., Chapter 2.

beginning to involve the couple more in their lives. Having reached retirement, the couple's parents may have more time to visit, or they may be experiencing health or other needs and require assistance from the couple. The prominence of the four-generation family is relatively new. It adds a further dimension to the picture of the modified extended family.

As the couple moves into retirement years, their relationship moves somewhat more toward one of newlyweds with interest in one another and in shared activities.

Marital Satisfaction Through Time
There have been numerous studies[31] attempting to discover what happens to the rosy glow with which the newlyweds ride off on their honeymoon. Follow-up studies at different intervals after marriage show some loss in intimacy and some drop in satisfaction, with the researchers suggesting that some of the apparent disenchantment may be simply a correction for the exaggerated idealism of courtship and marriage.[32]

The presence of children brings some dissatisfaction at the resulting lack of time parents have for each other. Children usually appear to contribute to the general state-of-life satisfaction, although conflict with marital satisfaction.[33] Couples often experience increasing dissatisfaction as children move into adolescence.

One of the most difficult periods of the marriage relationship occurs around 15 years after marriage. It is then that couples, still carrying heavy responsibilities with their families, begin to see the time when those responsibilities will lighten. They start to analyze their marital relationship and the meaning of their life.

Marital satisfaction improves when children leave home and the couple once again has time (a need) to devote more of their attention to one another. Today, couples of this age have a developmental task that was not typical before 1950. This is the task of learning to build a couple's relationship at age 40. In earlier times the husband typically died before the last child left home.

---

[31] C. S. Chilman, "Families in Development at Mid-Stage of the Family Life Cycle," *The Family Coordinator* 17 (October 1968), pp. 297–312. This article summarizes much of the research and theory related to family life in middle years.

[32] P. C. Pineo, "Disenchantment in the Later Years of Marriage," *Marriage and Family Living* 23 (1961), pp. 3–11.

[33] M. P. Hayes and N. Stinnett, "Life Satisfaction of Middle-Aged Husbands and Wives," *Journal of Home Economics* 63 (1971), pp. 669–674.

Now both partners typically live fifteen to twenty years after all the children have left home.

Public awareness in the last quarter of this century has prepared the way for a new level of regard for the responsiveness of women and men in sexual experiences. Masters and Johnson's research and education program, dealing with human sexual response, has led them to say that "our society is not only developing an infinitely greater comfort factor with the subject of sexual functioning, but we, as individuals, are growing from informed adolescence into more viable sexual adulthood."[34]

There is also some movement toward a recognition of the vitality of sexual experiences in the later stages of adult life.[35] Masters and Johnson point out that the sex drives and abilities of men and women continue to be strong throughout adult life and well into the 70- and 80-year-old groups.[36] We will refer to this in more detail in our chapter on old age. Since the early Kinsey studies,[37] there has been an increase in the reported satisfaction of women in their sexual experiences. As a matter of fact, women who find sex in marriage unsatisfactory are in a minority, according to a study conducted by Dr. Robert Bell, Robert Levin, and their wives for *Redbook* Magazine.[38] They reported that among the 100,000 women in their study, seven out of ten evaluated the sexual aspect of marriage as "good" or "very good," and two out of ten described it as "fair." This reported satisfaction continued whether the women had been married one year or more than ten, whether they had intercourse one to five times a month or more then twenty times. Women described themselves as active partners in lovemaking, which may in some way account for the increasing satisfaction they experienced. A relationship that was noted with surprise by the investigators was that the greater the woman's religious convictions, the more likely she was highly satisfied with the sexual aspects of her marriage. She tended to communicate more with her husband, engage in lovemaking more frequently, and express greater satisfaction. Levin indicates that the pattern becomes more pronounced among older women and prevails across Protestant, Catholic, and

[34] W. H. Masters and V. E. Johnson, *The Pleasure Bond* (Boston: Little, Brown, 1975), p. 9.

[35] R. N. Butler and M. I. Lewis, *Sex After Sixty* (New York: Harper & Row, 1976).

[36] W. H. Masters and V. E. Johnson, *Human Sexual Response* (Boston: Little, Brown, 1966).

[37] A. C. Kinsey and associates, *Sexual Behavior in the Human Female* (Philadelphia: Saunders, 1953).

[38] R. J. Levin and A. Levin, "Sexual Pleasure: The Surprising Preferences of 100,000 Women," *Redbook* Magazine (September 1975), pp. 51–58.

Jewish faiths. The nonreligious women tend to report greater dissatisfaction with, and less participation in, all aspects of their sex life.[39]

Oral-genital sex was practiced by about half the women in the Kinsey report published 25 years ago. In the Redbook report, nine out of ten women had experienced it, and 85 per cent engaged in it occasionally or often. Women under 20 were less likely to engage in oral-genital sex. The investigators offer two possible explanations for the age differences. The younger women were not yet comfortable enough with their own bodies or with men to experiment beyond intercourse; there was enough excitement in their early explorations of lovemaking itself so that it remained for time to develop further approaches to sex experiences.

Sex Roles in Family Life

Perhaps this is the place for us to consider the tremendous social change that has been taking place in our country since the early sixties—the concern regarding sex roles in American life. These considerations have significance for both of the socializing agencies with which we are concerned in this chapter, the family and the world of work.

In effect, a new awareness and a strong affirmation have been inserted into our public policy, emphasizing that occupational, civil, and personal rights and opportunities shall not be restricted on the basis of sexual characteristics. This has resulted in efforts of study and adjustment on two levels of activity.

In the first place, it involves a reevaluation of role characteristics and responsibilities. We have had to review the various assumptions we have made about the nature of different jobs. It has also involved a reevaluation of the means of obtaining personal identity. In what ways is personal identity separate from our sexual characteristics? This has led us to the second area of study and adjustment. How do the socializing processes—in our families, schools, churches, media, and other areas—unjustly or unwisely build into our perceptions certain attitudes about the fundamental characteristics and potentialities of persons of different sexes?

Research and writing prompted by the women's movement have increased public awareness of the important influence that the family's socializing processes have in developing an individual's identity with certain sex-role behaviors. Parents model their children's respective sex roles. By continuing subtle communications, parents establish their values and their sex-identity conflicts in the feelings of their children. Example 3–8 illustrates

[39] Ibid.

Example 3–8.
Socialization of
Boys and Girls

> The Male Machine *quotes the summary of a psychological study of children's attitudes:*
>
> Boys have to be able to fight in case a bully comes along; they have to be athletic; they have to be able to run fast; they must be able to play rough games; they need to know how to play many games—curbball, baseball, basketball, football; they need to be smart; they need to be able to take care of themselves; they should know what girls don't know—how to climb, how to make a fire, how to carry things; they should have more ability than girls; they need to know how to stay out of trouble; they need to know arithmetic and spelling more than girls do.
>
> From M. F. Fasteau, *The Male Machine* (New York: McGraw-Hill, 1974).

attitudes expressed by young children concerning the marked differences they have been taught that distinguish boys from girls. Various studies of education strongly charge that our schools limit the development of the intellectual and moral potential of girls.[40]

Example 3–9 and Example 3–10 illustrate some of the effects of sexual discrimination in career opportunities. Legislation and social pressure can be

Example 3–9.

> *Time* magazine in 1974 reported that only 7 per cent of the nation's doctors, 3 per cent of the lawyers, and 4 per cent of the architects are women. In government that year there was 1 governor, 16 women representatives, and no women senators. In industry men outnumbered women 600 to 1 in top management positions.
>
> *Time* (July 15, 1974), p. 33.

expected to continue to make significant changes in these conditions in the years ahead. For example, the French government created a top-level cabinet position, secretary of state for *la condition féminine,* to care for the "integration of women into contemporary French society."[41]

---

[40] V. L. Erickson, "Deliberate Psychological Education for Women: From Iphigenia to Antigone," *Counselor Education and Supervision* 14 (June 1975), pp. 297–309.

[41] *Time* (July 29, 1974), p. 61.

Example 3–10.
Women and
Biogerontology

. . . Many issues in the biology and physiology of adult development and aging have sex-dependent factors which have been interpreted largely on the basis of traditional, even archaic assumptions about male and female biology. In 1967 a gynecologist (male) wrote, "An important feature of sex desire in the man is the urge to dominate the woman and subjugate her to his will; in the woman acquiescence to the masterful takes a high place." As late as 1971, a gynecological text (male author) describes woman, "traits that compose the core of the female personality are feminine, narcissism, masochism and passivity." Two women, both sociologists, in 1973 finally did explore the quality of incorrect, obsolete information in the texts that socialize student physicians into that aspect of medicine uniquely involved with women of all ages.

The number of women in biology and medicine is quite low. Moreover, there has been a marked decrease over the last ten years in the rate of growth of women in science, especially noticeable at the level of full professorship and policy making. It is no surprise, then, that relatively few women natural scientists have had impact on the growth of theory and practice in gerontology. Nevertheless, it is noteworthy that in the Gerontological Society, and in other professional organizations concerned with gerontological study and practice, such women are encouraged and recognized. It is in the traditional halls of the male dominated universities that women in biomedicine find discrimination and condescension. . . .

Gerontology would profit from the intellectual and affective input of knowledgeable, creative women scientists. More women in biomedicine at large and gerontology would serve as sorely needed role models to younger female students, would raise new questions and old questions (poorly answered) with a new perspective, and would enhance the capacity of men and women to understand themselves and each other.

From R. B. Weg, "Women and Biogerontology," *The Gerontologist* 15 (December 1975), 6:483.

In family life, achieving clarity concerning flexibility of sex roles and equal opportunity for personal development is a complex task, which it will continue to be for some years to come. Of course, it has significant interaction with the involvement of men and women in the world of work as well. There is an increasing emphasis upon the statement that women's liberation involves also men's liberation.

Certain differences between men and women that have influence on family life have to do with differences in longevity. Women must plan on living longer than men. Men at 50 can expect to live about 23 years more and women nearly 29 years more.[42] This difference has continued to increase in recent years as medical technology has alleviated some of the dangers of maternal mortality and certain forms of cancer to which women are most vulnerable, whereas automobile accidents and certain stress-related deaths, such as heart attacks, have been increasing for men. In the section on widowhood we will discuss some of the effects of differences in life expectancy as these relate to future marital roles.

Because women live longer, older women will be more likely than men to live alone. They will also be more likely than men to experience poverty. Nearly half of the single, divorced, and widowed women live below the poverty level as compared with about a third of the men.[43]

Other Family Groups

There are other groups of adults whose life experience significantly alters their style of family life and, consequently, their role in adult society. These include divorced, widowed, reconstituted, and single-parent families.

Divorced Persons

The characteristics of divorced persons are as varied as those of married persons. The percentage of divorces is higher among certain groups (for example, couples who married in their teens, persons with lower income and education, blacks, couples without children, persons with divorced parents).[44]

The relative number of divorced persons, in comparison to married, is increasing steadily. This may reflect a greater acceptance of divorce itself, or a greater comfort of the divorced to remain so rather than remarry as social pressure in past years often encouraged. Census data indicate that a somewhat larger number of persons are listed as separated than are as divorced. Many persons in low-income groups do not go through the legal procedures of divorce.

Divorce involves a loss of many social signs and connections upon which the individual's identity was built. The divorced person goes through a period of rebuilding and redefining. The highest rate of suicide occurs among divorced persons. Although more women attempt suicide, more men actually kill themselves. Divorce may contribute to a loss of identity, to

---

[42] *Social Indicators.* (Washington D.C. U.S. Government Printing Office, 1973).

[43] N. E. Cutler and R. A. Harootyan, "Demography of the Aged," in *Aging,* eds. D. S. Woodruff and J. E. Birren (New York: Van Nostrand, 1975).

[44] Duvall, *Family Development,* p. 64.

feelings of aloneness, powerlessness, and despair, to the need to cry out for help.[45]

The individual's circle of friends changes. Some relationships (those at work or in other areas not central to family life) may continue.

There are many obstacles encountered by the individual going through the process of divorce and redefinition as a single person. Legal problems relating to property and financial arrangements as well as conflicting emotional attitudes involving self and former spouse are part of the developmental tasks that are as difficult as those of adjusting to marriage.

Divorce involves self-evaluation. Sometimes questions of self-confidence, anxiety, and guilt are aggravated by difficulties in communicating the meaning of the present life situation to children or to other relatives and close friends. A mother writes in Example 3–11 of her experiences in divorce following thirteen years of marriage.

Example 3–11.
After Thirteen
Years

> With the passage of my marriage, I also lost a part of me. . . We had gloried in college together, shared the agony and the hopes of building dreams for the future, the birth of children. No matter how logical the decision to divorce, how can one forget the intimacy of viewing "our child." So there is grief, perhaps even more difficult grief than that of the widow, for it is confused with the later hurt and anger—the confusion of change that sets in after the fact of divorce compounds the issue. Personalities adjust to new lives and it becomes difficult to realize that the person angrily combatting for reduced child support on the witness stand in court is the father of your children and your former "beloved husband." Pride prevents the display of grief that the widow may freely display. Friends' reaction are bewildered. What responses are to be made? In all, the loneliness increases with the inability to share the depth of emotions encountered.

There is a period in which the individual again goes through many of the learning experiences of adolescence, for example, developing dating strategies. Middle-aged persons forming such new associations may feel awkward and juvenile. Most divorced persons begin dating within the first year after their separation. Many needs intermingle that prompt the divorced person to reach out (for example, desire for security, assurance of worth, need for social contact, and sexual desire).[46]

[45] *Behavior Today* 7 (June 7, 1976), 23:4.

[46] R. S. Weiss, *Marital Separation* (New York: Basic Books, 1975).

Many divorced persons find it difficult to meet potential dates. An increasing number of groups are being formed by churches, travel associations, and educational and recreation programs to help divorced persons faced with loneliness. Although more and more divorced persons remain single longer, most eventually remarry.

Dating is more complicated for persons with children because it involves baby-sitters and children's questions. Divorced persons also have to work out the place and meaning of sex in their new relationship. Social values have often changed since they were single, and they themselves have changed. Sex relations often have an important role for divorced persons exploring their ability to trust themselves with other people.

Widowhood   It is rare that both spouses die simultaneously. Therefore, widowhood will be experienced at some time by a large part of the adult population. With the increasing length of life, widowhood can be expected to last for a longer time. The tendency for women to live longer than men makes it unlikely that there will be much increase in the rate of remarriage among widows.

Let us consider the words of a young widow describing this aspect of adult development. Lynn Caine has written of her experiences as a woman in her thirties, mother of two children, whose husband was struck with cancer and died after several months of illness.

> After my husband died, I felt like one of those spiraled shells washed up on the beach. Poke a straw through the twisting tunnel, around and around, and there is nothing there. No flesh. No life. Whatever lived there is dried up and gone.[47]

She tells how it seemed to her that with the loss of her husband she also lost her personal identity. This sense of loss was in part because of our society's treatment of marriage and male/female identities. It is also a part of the steps of bereavement.

Her account of "crazy" economic ventures and desperate efforts at restructuring her life-style underscores the importance of the waiting period during the first months of widowhood and the value of counseling from someone who understands the process of adjustment in widowhood.

Ms. Caine experienced discrimination as a woman and as a widow. Acts of discrimination included the greater difficulty, compared with men, to obtain disability insurance, the paranoid exclusion from gatherings of former friends who were married couples, and increased tendencies among men

[47] L. Caine, *Widow* (New York: Bantam Books, 1974).

friends toward sexual exploitation. She also observed the greater opportunities for males than for females to remarry after the death of their spouse.

Widowhood is a most difficult stage of growth, but many move through it to a greater strength. Caine wrote in the closing of her book:

> Widow is a harsh and hurtful word. It comes from the Sanskrit and it means "empty." I have been empty too long. I do not want to be pigeon-holed as a widow. I am a woman whose husband has died, yes. But not a second-class citizen, not a lonely goose. I am a mother and a working woman and a laughing woman and a concerned woman and vital woman. I am a person. I resent what the term widow has come to mean. I am alive. I am part of the world . . .
>
> But what of love? The warmth, the tenderness, the passion I had for Martin? Am I rejecting that too?
>
> Ah, that is the very definition of bereavement. The love object is lost . . . Grief is as much a lament for the end of love as of anything else.
>
> Acceptance finally comes. And with it comes peace . . . I owe the person I am today to Martin's death . . . Today I am someone else. I am stronger, more independent. I have more understanding, more sympathy.

Nearly five out of six widowed persons are female. The majority of widowed persons are over 65. Between one and two out of ten widowed persons live in institutions. The majority of others maintain their own home and live alone. When widowed persons live with relatives, it is more likely to be with a daughter than with a son.[48]

Bereavement, along with age, adds to the complications of the adjustment experience that otherwise has many similarities to the adjustment processes of a divorced person. Research reports that some widows declare they have never gotten over their grief.[49]

MALES.   There are problems in adjusting to widowhood that are relatively unique for men. Among these is the probability that the loss of a wife will produce a marked change in the home-living pattern for the surviving husband. Generally, the man is not well experienced in maintaining many of the household responsibilities. Preparation of meals can often produce problems

---

[48] H. Carter and P. C. Glick, *Marriage and Divorce: A Social and Economic Study* (Cambridge, Mass.: Harvard University Press, 1970).

[49] H. Z. Lopata, *Widowhood in an American City* (Cambridge, Mass.: Schenkman, 1973). Stinnett and Walters, *Relationships in Marriage and Family*, pp. 318–349, provides an excellent discussion of widowhood along with other aspects of family relationships in later years.

for the newly widowed husband. Cleaning and numerous types of general domestic care are not familiar to many men.

If there are children in the home, the widowed husband will be faced with parenting situations probably not previously confronted. The task of clothing, feeding, and supervising social activities of children may present overwhelming challenges to the man still grieving over his personal loss of his companion. In our society much of the wife's traditional role involves caring for her husband. With that support gone, the husband finds it difficult to carry on the roles that are normally his, not to mention taking on the additional responsibilities that were previously his wife's.

Widowhood, like divorce, is a critical situation that involves both social and personal disorganization. Old statuses and roles are lost and new relationships must be substituted in order to effect a satisfactory adjustment to a changed situation. The maintenance of a set of personally satisfying self-conceptions depends on the availability of alternative patterns of roles and relationships. The elderly widowed person is likely to face a vaguely defined situation lacking clear-cut cultural guidelines. Unclear and often contradictory expectations become the social context of the new status confronting the aged widowed survivor.

Transition to widowhood is made difficult not only by the lack of clearly defined cultural expectations but also by the absence of supportive relationships. The loss of a significant role partner tends to strain and dissolve other relationships of the individual, for example, kin networks, neighbor relations, friendships, and memberships in formal organizations. Aged widows and widowers often find themselves in isolated situations.

Bernardo suggests that the precariousness of widowhood appears to be experienced more by the aged male than by the female.[50] Numerous social factors aid the adjustment of widows but impede the satisfactory transition for widowers. We have referred to the domestic roles with which the female is quite familiar and which she continues to perform; these become a problem to the widower. The female is also more likely to be involved in a kin network because the maintenance of relations with kin has relied more heavily on female than male activity. The elderly widow is more likely than the widower to maintain membership in formal organizations and to continue to participate in these and in other community relationships.

The relatively greater isolation of the aged widower is related to, and

---

[50] F. M. Bernardo, "Survivorship and Social Isolation: The Case of the Aging Widower," *The Family Coordinator* 18 (1970), pp. 11–25.

probably aggravated by, his retirement. He is removed from a chief source of self-identity—his occupational role and his relationships with his friends and coworkers.[51]

The adverse manner in which some individuals respond to widowhood, for example, mental illness, suicide, high death rate, and unhappiness, is found to be more prevalent among the elderly males. The occurrence of these responses, particularly suicide among the elderly widowed persons, has been explained primarily in terms of their greater isolation. The elderly widowed, especially males, are more likely than their married counterparts to commit suicide, not just because they have lost a significant role partner, but also because they are isolated in many other ways from kin, friends, neighbors, and formal organizations.

FEMALES.   For the widow, new roles must be filled, old roles must be reassessed, and social relations must be redefined by her and by the people with whom she interacts. Most relations undergo a change; some to be terminated, others to be adjusted. Helena Lopata has probably done the most extensive research in the area of widowhood. As she points out, widowhood clearly means the loss, reorganization, and acquisition of social roles. In ceasing to be a wife, a woman can no longer function as her husband's nurse, confidant, sex partner, or housekeeper; on the other hand, she may have to assume unfamiliar roles like financial manager, handyman, or worker. Other social relations may also be disrupted. Intimacy with in-laws does not seem to survive the husband's death. In Lopata's study, only a quarter of Chicago widows saw their husband's relatives with any frequency.[52]

The widow may find that she is a "fifth wheel" in couple-oriented interaction. She may also find that she can no longer maintain old social contacts because her entertainment budget is limited, or she does not drive and public transportation is not readily accessible.

New activity patterns, friends, and gratifications may eventually replace old ones. Half of Lopata's widows had so adjusted to their new life-style as to see compensations in widowhood, such as independence or reduction of workload.

Financial problems may be a major concern for younger and older

[51] Z. S. Blau, "Structural Constraints on Friendships in Old Age," *American Sociological Review* 21 (1961), pp. 429–439.

[52] Lopata, *Widowhood,* p. 52.

widows. Young widows have problems of child support. Widows over 65 and unable to work may have little Social Security or other income. In a survey of young, widowed mothers it was found that they were more than twice as likely to be in the labor force than mothers with living husbands.[53] Employment opportunities (including potential jobs on the labor market), previous education, socioeconomic background, and previous work status influence a widowed woman's choice of work.[54] A nationwide survey of young, widowed mothers and their dependent children who were receiving survivor benefits under Social Security programs showed that the median income of these families was only slightly above poverty level.[55]

The young widow, whose loss is typically sudden and unanticipated, is more likely to be shaken by the death of a spouse than is the older woman who has had more time to ready herself psychologically and economically.[56]

A study comparing problems of younger and older widows found loneliness to be the problem most frequently cited by both groups.[57] A frequently mentioned form of loneliness was that of missing "having someone around with whom to share a joke, a bit of news, or discuss a problem." A second problem mentioned in both groups was that of home maintenance and car repair. This was more of a problem for the older widows.

Other problems often mentioned by the younger widows, but not considered problems by the older group, included child rearing, decision-making, absence of sex life, and managing family business. Problems for widows in the 60 years and over group, which were not cited by the under 60 group, were learning basic finances, lack of transportation, and fear of crime such as robberies and muggings. The older widow reported a decrease in activities and in the amount of work since the death of her husband; the younger widow saw an increase in activities and in the amount of work she had to do.

[53] E. Palmore, G. L. Stanley, and R. H. Cormier, "Widows with Children Under Social Security," U.S. Department of HEW (Washington, D.C.: Government Printing Office, 1966).

[54] L. W. Hoffman, *The Employed Mother in America* (Chicago: Rand McNally, 1963).

[55] Palmore et al., "Widows with Children."

[56] D. K. Heyman and D. T. Gianturco, "Long-term Adaptation by the Elderly to Bereavement," *Journal of Gerontology* 28 (1973), 3:359–362; I. Gerber et al., "Anticipatory Grief and Aged Widows and Widowers," *Journal of Gerontology* 30 (March 1975), 2:225–229; present the negative effects of physical strain of anticipatory grief.

[57] M. V. Wyly and I. M. Hulicka, "Problems and Compensations of Widowhood: A Comparison of Age Groups," paper presented to annual meeting of the American Psychological Association, 1975, p. 6. (Department of Psychology, State University College at Buffalo, New York).

REMARRIAGE.   Remarriage probabilities are very high for persons widowed before age 35. Less than one fourth of men widowed after age 65 remarry. Less than 50 percent of women widowed after age 55 remarry.[58] There is little social support and many obstacles for the remarriage of older persons. Although there is an increeasing awareness of the potential, there is as yet no upsurge in new marriages for older people.[59]

There are several reasons why men are more likely than women to marry after 65. Due to sex differences in mortality and widowhood, there are more single women than men in the population over 65. Older men, however, are not restricted by social norms to marrying older women. Twenty percent of grooms over 65 attract brides under 45, whereas only 3 per cent of older brides wed men under 45.[60] When looking at these statistics, it is interesting to note that women are seen as "old" sooner than men.[61]

The fewer children, the greater the chance for remarriage by middle-aged men and women. It has been found that if a man with children at home remarries, he is more apt to do so when the children are under the age of 6 and much less apt to as the children approach adolescence. For both widowed men and women, there are more remarriages in the fifties than in the forties.[62]

ALTERNATIVE LIVING ARRANGEMENTS.   Despite the benefits married living may have, there are obvious demographic constraints on the numbers of older people who can pair off in traditional unions. Unlike widowed men, widowed women appear to have a far greater tendency to band together with other widowed women rather than with divorced or single women.[63]

Alternatives to conventional marriage may offer solutions to the unmet intimacy needs of some older widowed people, just as foster grandparent programs can furnish affectionate integenerational contacts. Nonmarital

[58] W. P. Cleveland and D. T. Gianturco, "Remarriage Probability After Widowhood: A Retrospective Method," *Journal of Gerontology* 31 (January 1975), 1:99–103.

[59] J. Treas and A. Van Hilst, "Marriage and Remarriage Rates Among Older Americans," *The Gerontologist* 16 (April 1976), 2:132–136.

[60] National Center for Health Statistics, 1969, Table 1–18.

[61] B. L. Neugarten, J. W. Moore, and J. C. Lowe, "Age Norms, Age Constraints, and Adult Socialization," *American Journal of Sociology* 70 (May 1965), 6.

[62] L. J. Bischof, *Adult Psychology* (New York: Harper & Row, 1969), pp. 84–85.

[63] Ibid.

cohabitation, polygamy, group marriage, communes, and homosexual companionships are some suggestions being offered.[64,65]

Reconstituted Families

Families in which both parents have had previous marriages (terminated by death or divorce) present special circumstances in the challenges of adult development. The extended family has been enlarged to include relatives of both previous and present marriages. Parenting responsibilities include assisting children to relate to step-siblings—sometimes representing a wide age span. Divorced parents may need to adapt schedules and psychological circumstances to visitation arrangements.

The well-known writer Catherine Marshall tells of her own experience of entering a new marriage after ten years of widowhood. With her son in college and her writing going well, she had entered into a period of tranquillity when she fell in love and married a man with three children in public school. Adjusting with his two sons was largely getting used to the hurly-burly of boys in the house after some years of quiet. The larger task was developing a relationship with her husband's daughter.

> Soon after Len and I were married and were living in Westchester County, New York, my new daughter Linda was entering the sixth grade. It became apparent that my stepmother role was not going to be easy. There was the usual playing of one parent against the other and the tussels over clothes and curfews most mothers have with their daughters . . .
>
> When fun times were planned especially for Linda, such as a party or a shopping trip, immediately afterwards she would turn into her worst self. This odd sequence happened so often that we knew a warped force was at work. It was as if she was saying, "Please, I can't stand any special demonstration of love." . . .
>
> Such behavior was especially discomfiting to a stepmother. The relationship to which I had looked forward was not what I had hoped. I felt like a rejected parent. Then I caught myself resenting this child and her attitudes.

It was not until after Linda's graduation from college and a family crisis concerning another member of the family that a reconciliation came.

> "I thought I wanted a loving relationship with you when you married Dad," Linda told me. "But resentment crowded in. The reason was that at a gut level

[64] F. Conklin, "Should Retired Women Live Together?" *NRTA Journal* 25 (1974), pp. 19–20.

[65] R. S. Covan, "Speculations on Innovations to Conventional Marriage in Old Age," *The Gerontologist* 13 (1973), 4:409–411.

I thought you were taking Dad away from me. I would no longer be Number One in his life."

During this long evening of honesty and confession among the three of us, many barriers came crashing down. For Linda it was the release of years of hostility and guilt. For us, it was a facing up to mistakes and fears and lack of understanding.[66]

Single-parent Families

There is a relatively small, but possibly increasing, number of adults—mostly female—who choose to rear a child without entering into a continuing relationship with an adult partner. Some of the challenges, handicaps, and satisfactions experienced by divorced or widowed persons will also be experienced by single parents.

In most instances the parent bears a child out of wedlock; however, the possibility for single persons to adopt children is increasing. For some there may be social pressures and family conflicts associated with the mother having borne a child out of wedlock. When the mother is in her teens, there may be problems of continued education and arrangements for child care. The young person may have a special difficulty with the transition from youth to adult-role status.

Summary of Family as a Socializing Agent

We have discussed a variety of ways in which the family commitments provide roles and productive responsibilities and in which relationships in varying degrees of intimacy afford support, nurture, and meaning for adults throughout life. Whereas the most frequent type of relationship is one termed the nuclear family, consisting of two parents and a few children relatively close in age, this does not mean a lack of connection with more extended parts of the kinship network. Frequent contact, often in the form of exchange of services, links young couples with their parents and grandparents. Because families maintain autonomous units by generation while still nurturing intergenerational relationships, the American family structure is often termed a modified extended family type as contrasted with an isolated nuclear family type.

There are also complex families in which previously divorced parents have formed new families still maintaining varying degrees of relatedness with

---

[66] C. Marshall, *Something More* (New York: McGraw-Hill, 1974), pp. 45, 46, 50.

family networks from the earlier marriage. There are also single-parent families and communal families.

Family life provides the milieu in which adults achieve such developmental tasks as the capacity for intimacy, the capacity to model sex-role behavior, and the capacity to serve other parenting responsibilities. Changing social patterns are providing an opportunity for more variation in family responsibilities. Day-care programs allow more freedom from continuous supervision of children. Sharing household tasks and joint husband–wife responsibilities for family financial support make sex roles less arbitrary than in earlier generations.

It is difficult to understand the development of individual adults without understanding their family interactions. Because the family is a complex system of interacting personalities, opportunity for adult development depends greatly on how the family functions. Each member is socializing, shaping, and providing other family members with encouragement for different behaviors. As with any system, the family is different than the sum of the individual members. Educational, economic, or service resources aimed at facilitating successful adult development and aging will have to take the family and its needs into account for effective program planning.

Our understanding of adult behavior involves not only the interaction within the family, but also an awareness of the developmental stages through which the family moves, called the family cycle. Families are different in the periods of newlyweds, young parents, empty nest, widowhood. Each stage in the cycle creates different responsibilities. How the individual perceives and responds to those responsibilities is influenced by the pattern of interaction that has prevailed in the family up to that point.

The increasing length of life, coupled with smaller families, has resulted in an extension of the family cycle with the postparental period taking on substantial length and significance. The characteristics of the different periods of the family cycle are influenced by social and economic status of the adult and by the particular periods of history in which the family is living. Ethnic and socioeconomic status of the family also influence adult roles.

Whereas parenting is a definitive career occupying a primary place in the developmental processes of the majority of adults, there are a significant number of adults who never marry or who do not choose to have children. Family relationships for these persons take on different patterns. However, nearly all adults have identifying relationships with their family.

Personal identity and psychological and environmental support for adults is obtained primarily within the context of family life. Employment is the second most universal resource in the maintenance of adult development through the life-span, with religious and other community associations offering resources whose significance varies with the individual and the situation. We turn next to a consideration of the place of work as a developmental influence throughout the life-span.

The World of Work

As salesman Willie Loman reviews the events of his life and the reasons for choices he made in *Death of a Salesman*,[67] we recognize how close the intermingling of our illusions and ambitions is for our family life and for our work. The milieu of the family forms the pathway along which the adult progresses in a series of roles, each contributing to the continuing expression of his personal identity. To understand adult personality throughout the sequential stages of life, we must consider the world of work and the adult's vocation.

Nearly a hundred years ago, in 1888, Edward Bellamy presented a utopian picture of Boston in the year 2000 in the novel *Looking Backward*. Work was planned so that all jobs would be attractive by arranging varying work periods and equal amounts of "pay" (government credit card). Everyone received a broad general education until age 21 and then was guided with appropriate training into suitable employment. When people retired at 45, they were prepared intellectually and emotionally for continued study and recreation and the furtherance of their life vocation. A creative relation between work and other aspects of life is a continuing challenge in adult development.

The meaning of the word *vocation* includes the concept of a calling. It suggests a sense of destiny and purpose, a reason to be. This is a larger concept than job, or occupation, or even career. It is a helpful reminder of the central place that work has in the process of being human and being creative adults. It suggests that each life is designed to contribute to something beyond itself.

We sometimes limit the concept, with unfortunate consequences. Some illustrations of this are the mother and homemaker who marks "unemployed" on a questionnaire, or the 70-year-old retired railroad conductor

---

[67] A. Miller, *Death of a Salesman* (New York: Viking Press, 1949).

a.

3–5 *Men and women find satisfaction in all kinds of jobs.* (a, b, c, Manhattan Mercury *photos; d,* Kansas State University Student Publications *photo)*

b.

c.

d.

who maintains a hothouse, cultivating prize roses, yet similarly checks "not working."

It is easy to think of work in a utilitarian fashion as supplying the means to pay for food and shelter or as being the vehicle of social status. It is interesting to observe how frequently our introductions of one another include our occupation as part of our identification.

Work serves many functions, but in all of them there is an element that relates in some way to self-worth, identity, and purpose. Whether the work is through a carefully planned career or through a series of disconnected and sporadic jobs, whether its pay is monetary or in other more intangible coin, work is crucial to the adult's development and continuity of personhood. Some aspects of work may be expressed in *leisure*. We will discuss these and some of the social affect associated with that term later in the book. In this chapter we will consider some of the characteristics of the world of paid employment and how these influence the development of individuals throughout their adult life.

The writer Studs Terkel spent three years talking to people in a wide variety of occupations—washroom attendants, entertainers, mail carriers, and lawyers—to see what they did in their jobs and how they felt about their work. He put these together in a book of word sketches capturing the attitudes and experiences of working people. In the Introduction he said the book is about his search, but even more it is about every man's search expressed in the job.

> It is about a search for daily meaning as well as daily bread, for recognition as well as cash, for astonishment rather than torpor; in short, for a sort of life rather than a Monday through Friday sort of dying. Perhaps immortality, too, is part of the quest. To be remembered was the wish, spoken and unspoken, of the heroes and heroines of this book.[68]

Opportunities for employment, the nature of the work place, and the meaning of job changes as society changes. We have already observed that changes in family roles influence the participation of male and female workers. There are also changes in the work place.

Four-day workweeks are being promoted as means for saving energy and for improving productivity and morale. The majority of workers in such experimental programs report improved family life, recreation, and job satisfaction and employers report productivity gains.

[68] S. Terkel, *Working* (New York: Avon Books, 1974), p. xiii.

"Flextime" is an experimental approach whereby the worker has more control over the hours he works.[69] He is hired for a definite number of hours but may put them in (within a certain time range) at his own discretion. For example, he may choose to come in early or late, or work in split periods. This helps the traffic and also gives the worker more responsibility and sense of trust.

Most adults are employed for about 40 years of their 70-year life-span. They begin preparing for this even in the nursery and toddler years when parents provide them with toys representative of future occupations. Levels of aspiration are formed early; they reflect family influences and other role models. The satisfaction we experience as adults and the approach we will take at times of transition in middle and later life reflects our perception of the world of work. It reflects our understanding of the reward system and the way other aspects of living are related to the world of work. For this reason, a brief background review of such issues as occupational stereotypes, interests, and career ladders may help us as we later examine the developmental tasks of adult life and retirement.

[69] J. M. Rosow, *The Worker and the Job* (Englewood Cliffs, N.J.: Prentice-Hall, 1974), pp. ix–x.

3–6 *The building stones of career goals are often formed out of early childhood role playing and our identification with childhood heroes. (Kansas State University Student Publications photo)*

Occupational Stereotypes

From early childhood play as firemen, nurses, doctors, and cowboys, we fantasize about occupations. Acting out, in practice or imagination, the work of our parents or other significant individuals was one way to know those persons. Then, when the time came to think of careers, we had already formulated a repertoire of stereotypes, picturing personal qualities of individuals in the different occupations.

Study of occupational stereotypes was an active research topic in the early 1950s. The stereotypes reflect the values our culture ascribes to different activities. Research reported, for example, that medicine and law were viewed as careers encompassing many of the rewards and virtues of society: money, status, intelligence, responsibility, and confidence.

For my master's thesis, I asked college students to rank twenty industries on a scale of prestige. It made little difference whether the student was asked to rank laborers or executives in the industry, medicine still ranked number one and manufacturing still ranked number twenty.[70]

Stereotypes grow out of day-by-day social exchanges with members of one's community. Special coloring is taken on by accounts, either heard about or witnessed, of the heroic significance of certain persons and certain occupations. Some of these touch base with values being formed or with skills we have experienced. Thus in addition to general stereotyping, there is also the fantasy world into which we project our ambitions for the "good life." Family influences help to bolster both the stereotypes and fantasy. Indeed, it is often the efforts to accommodate the family values that stimulate our fantasy. Some families create the expectation, explicit or implicit, that the child will follow the footsteps of parents or others in the family line. Other families stimulate the imperative that the children shall carry forward to new heights the family's striving for upward mobility. Parents reared in Depression years wanted their children to secure themselves in different occupations so they would not be vulnerable to the hard times the parents experienced. Keniston describes how children having absorbed the values of their parents implemented them in a fashion some parents did not recognize (or in ways that conflicted with the behaviors of their parents) even though they expressed the values their parents taught.[71]

---

[70] A. H. Brayfield and C. E. Kennedy, "Social Status of Industries," *Journal of Applied Psychology* 38 (1954), 4.

[71] K. Keniston, *Young Radicals: Notes on Committed Youth* (New York: Harcourt Brace Jovanovich, 1968).

Occupational Interests

Studies of different professional groups reflect the development of a central focus or basic interest beginning fairly early in life for individuals entering some professions. For example, McClelland[72] identified eight characteristics found to be reoccurring in the lives of "creative physical scientists." They are generally male and masculine in interests, from Protestant background (though not themselves religious), shy in interpersonal contacts, obsessed with their work, distressed by complex emotions and seek to avoid them, fond of music but dislike poetry, and they have a strong desire to analyze the structure of things. Roe,[73] on the other hand, found artists having little in common with one another except an intense satisfaction with the experience of painting. What characteristics do you associate with different occupational groups?

Tests such as the Strong Vocational Interest Test[74] have keys for different occupations. The keys have been created on the basis of a significant proportion of an occupational group having responded in the same fashion to a group of attitude statements. The fact that vocational-interest tests can be produced underscores the fact that early socialization and/or inborn traits have created a large area of commonality among the workers. It is also probable that some of the commonality has resulted from the worker's identity with and participation in the occupation.

Occupational Rewards and Influences

Occupations influence the persons involved in them. This is done by the codes and rules to which they subscribe. For example, large sectors of life were willed away by schoolteachers of another era when they signed contracts agreeing not to marry during the school term. Some self-concepts or dispositions might be considered occupational hazards of certain professions, for example, "attitudes of omniscience" that emerge for some physicians who are confronted daily by endless numbers of patients awaiting diagnosis.

Occupational positions influence those who hold them by providing a pattern of privileges, opportunities, requirements, and restrictions. The result is to extend personal experience in some directions and limit it in others. The lawyer constantly deals with people who are abused, angry, and contentious.

[72] D. C. McClelland, *Roots of Consciousness* (Princeton, N.J.: Van Nostrand, 1964).

[73] A. Roe, *The Making of a Scientist* (New York: Dodd, Mead, 1953).

[74] E. K. Strong, Jr., "Permanence of Interest Scores Over 22 Years," *Journal of Applied Psychology* 35 (1951), pp. 89–91.

The businessman is most regularly exposed to human nature in its aspects of competition for material gain. The doctor lives in a world of sickness. The woman who chooses homemaking as her vocation is selectively exposed to childlike behavior and to adults who are tired after a day's work.[75]

There are two types of significance associated with work: one is the intrinsic satisfaction in the activity itself; the other is the satisfaction of being able to perform a job and earn money to contribute to my and my family's maintenance. For millions of workers it is their job that primarily affords them the secondary satisfaction—being employed and earning a living.

Many workers are employed in an unnumbered series of jobs; others may work for years at jobs they only endure. The words of a telephone receptionist express some of their feelings.

> The machine dictates. This crummy little machine with buttons on it—you've got to be there to answer it . . . Your job doesn't mean anything. Because *you're* just a machine. A monkey could do what you do . . . You try to fill up your time with trying to think about other things: what you're going to do on the weekend or about your family.[76]

Some workers need to try out several different types of situations before they find one they can tolerate. Studs Terkel interviewed a truck driver who had formerly worked as a bookkeeper.

> I've been outside for seven years and I feel more free. I don't take the job home with me. When I worked in the office, my wife would say, "What was the matter with you last night? You laid there and your fingers were drumming the mattress." The bookkeeping and everything else, it was starting to play on my nerves. Yeah. I prefer laboring to bookkeeping.[77]

Whether the job is viewed as providing opportunity for self-experssion or for food for the table, whether the individual works as a member of a team or on a solitary task, the rewards and significance of his work must be taken into account to understand the context of development in an adult life.

---

[75] R. W. White, *The Enterprise of Living* (New York: Holt, Rinehart and Winston, 1972), p. 437; J. Mortimer, "Occupational Values Socialization in Business and Professional Families," *Sociology of Work and Occupations* 2 (February 1975), 1:29; R. Simpson, "Review Symposium on Work in America," *Sociology of Work and Occupations* 2 (May 1975), 2:182–187.

[76] S. Terkel, *Working*, pp. 58–59.

[77] Ibid., p. 150.

The Career Ladder

The individual himself also influences the occupation he enters. There is in each occupation considerable room for individuality and there is within each individual considerable room for common attitudes and values, along with aspects of his personality that are uniquely his own.

Becker and Strauss have described the career lines and channels within various organizations. They describe not only upward and downward but also lateral movements. In understanding adult development we must keep in mind the interrelationship of the individual with the "life" of the industry or organization with which he works. The age of the company, whether it is a new company with many openings or an older one where promotions come slowly, influences the pace of career movement. In every career there are periods of greater opportunity than at other times. The relationships of careers of various workers are interdependent. To understand the development of an individual requires an awareness of the other persons who have had an influence at various periods in his career. For example, how near to retirement the person above him was would have influenced his opportunities for advancement.

An understanding of the career development of an individual requires an awareness of the economic history that intersected his life. Was it a period of expanding job opportunities? Becker and Strauss observed, "The crises and turning points of life are not entirely institutionalized, but their occurrence and the terms which define and help to solve them are illuminated when seen in the context of career lines."[78]

The irony of historical influences was frequently experienced in the early days of World War II. In the peace-time army, advancement to master sergeant usually took 15 to 20 years. With the outbreak of war, many new companies were formed and promotions came rapidly to fill the ranks. I can still recall the look of scorn and pain with which a sergeant of 20 years of service looked at the armful of chevrons I wore as an eager 20-year-old master sergeant.

Career success may also have negative side effects. Success may involve long hours away from the family. It may require neglect of home or community involvement. It may involve uprooting the family with frequent moves. As the escalator of success lifts the husband higher, friendships for his children may be pulled apart and personal identity for his wife fragmented, as is the case of a corporate wife in Example 3–12.

---

[78] H. S. Becker and A. L. Strauss, "Careers, Personality and Adult Socialization," *Journal of American Sociology* 62 (1956), 3.

Example 3–12.
The Case of the
Corporate Wife

Psychiatrist Robert Seidenberg cites the case of a successful woman, successful in having a good early childhood in a secure family setting, successful with leadership and roles in high school, successful in nurses' training and in working as a nurse while her husband was finishing law school. As her husband succeeded in a law firm, she also succeeded socially, having—at the family's encouragement—left nursing and devoted her interest to her own family, to Junior League, and other community enterprises. She was successful socially and a success as a wife.

Her husband moved because of professional opportunity for advancement and she moved also. In the new community she went into a continuing condition of depression. She took to alcoholism and was not able to profit from therapy. She eventually separated from her family. In the years that followed she was never able to really take an active part in community involvement after her move to the new community.

The psychiatrist's interpretation is that because she had achieved a well-defined identity associated with her success in the first town, she was not able to pick up life again in the new town. She had suffered a loss of identity in the move; her identity had been associated with her accomplishments in the first town. To move into the social activities of the new community would mean moving in either on her husband's reputation or starting at the bottom. In either event it would be without personal identity or personal credentials. His thesis is that had she not been so successful earlier, she would probably have moved with less trauma. "The human spirit," he says, "is apparently such that it does not take easily to diminution or anonymity once it has known better things. Even safety and security do not suffice where matters of personal worthiness and identity are the issues. Charles Reich (in *The Greening of America*) reflects on what is perhaps the inordinate importance placed on credentials in our society: 'In a world where men are recognized only by their credentials, to lose credentials is to cease being a human being. Agreeing with this statement in general, some, however, would substitute the word 'persons' for 'men.'"

Adapted from R. Seidenberg, *Corporate Wives—Corporate Casualties?* (New York: Anchor Books, 1975).

Job Satisfaction

Job satisfaction is dependent not only upon the work an individual does, but also upon the extent to which the accompanying life-style enables him to play the kind of role he wants. The status in the community to which an individual aspires as well as his aspirations for career advancements influence an individual's reactions to the employment position he holds. Whereas we have suggested that some job satisfactions may be influenced by the opportunities his career opens for community status, Wilensky[79] has pointed also to another dimension relating work and community involvement.

Wilensky has found that an individual's participation as an active member of his community is greatly influenced by the nature of his employment situation. The more his employment position can be described as orderly, the more active will be his involvement in the community. By orderly we mean that his job has a predictable future and line of promotion. Persons employed in jobs with frequent, unexpected periods of unemployment or in situations where they are frequently moved from job to job will develop little identity with their work and also will feel fewer ties to or responsibility for their community.

> Excluding churches, there appears to be a general curve of participation in formal associations (clubs, etc.) which closely parallels a job satisfaction curve—a sharp drop in the early 20s, especially among young, hard-pressed married couples, a climb to a peak in the middle years, a slight dropoff and then a final sag in the 60s—and these cycles seem to be interdependent, although good longitudinal data are as usual lacking.[80]

The relationship of work to community involvement and personal identity is an area certain to receive attention as debates over mandatory retirement loom on the horizon. Claims will be made for the *centrality* of the work experience and statements will present work as *peripheral* to the personal life of the individual. To reconcile the contradictory statements, one will need to examine the life course of persons with different personality patterns; type of work is also a factor to be considered. Maddox expresses the two aspects of work in the following statement:

> In addition to his source of income, a man's job means a point of personal and social anchorage with considerable significance, both for the emergence and maintenance of a satisfactory self-identity and for the experience of adequate social intercourse with his family and peers . . . [There is also] evidence indicating that among selected industrial workers work is not the central life interest and the work place is not the locus of the most rewarding social experiences for the worker . . . Specifically, Dubin found that only one in ten industrial workers in his survey sample perceived their important primary

---

[79] H. L. Wilensky, "Orderly Careers and Social Participation: The Impact of Work History on Social Integration in the Middle Mass," *American Sociological Review* 26 (August 1961), 4.

[80] Ibid.

social relationship to be located in the work place; instead, the job was endured as a necessary condition to secure satisfaction elsewhere.[81]

More recent research among young people entering the labor force indicates that unskilled workers as well as white-collar workers increasingly will demand their jobs provide more intrinsic satisfaction. This is forecast as an area of potential national concern.[82]

Vocational Development: Life-span Perspective

Many years ago, Freud suggested that the major task of achieving adult maturity is to reconcile the competing demands of work and love.[83] Future research will have to consider the effects of two social movements that relate self-actualization at different life stages to personal values and social opportunities. These are the women's movement pressing for equal opportunities, and the older persons' challenging the retirement law's arbitrary termination of work. Each will require a rationale that will place work within the context of life-stage development.[84]

PERSONAL AND CAREER IDENTITIES.   The constructive tension of relating personal and career identities as we move toward greater meaning in the course of our lifetime search has been beautifully recounted by anthropologist Margaret Mead concerning her close friend, Ruth Benedict (see Example 3–13 for a profile drawn from her biography). Homemaking and careers outside the home are issues that may be confronted by women at any stage of life.

In 1974 a study found that college women who aspire to a career outside the home are less likely to describe themselves as having career-women characteristics. Women who aspire to careers *within* the home are inclined to describe as similar the characteristics of homemakers and thier own. Although those with homemaking aspirations had a more congruent view of themselves and their roles than had the career-oriented, their self-esteem scores

---

[81] G. L. Maddox, "Retirement as a Social Event in the United States," in *Middle Age and Aging,* ed. B. L. Neugarten, pp. 359–360.

[82] Rosow, *The Worker and the Job,* p. 42.

[83] E. J. Shoben, "Work, Love and Maturity," *Personnel and Guidance Journal* (February 1956), pp. 326–332.

[84] Students particularly interested in theories of vocational development may wish to consider the life-span perspective presented in D. B. Hershenson, "Life-Stage Vocational Development System," *Journal of Counseling Psychology* 15 (January 1968), 1:23–30.

Example 3–13.
The Several
Worlds of Ruth
Benedict

Ruth Benedict was a woman living in a time of transition. She was to some extent before her time professionally and in her experiences as a woman. It was her attempts to reconcile her conflicts with her identity as a woman that moved her into the academic sphere in which she was to play such a pivotal role in the evolution of the young science of anthropology.

Although strongly imbued with the conviction that women were created for motherhood, she resented the price this exacted in limiting women's creativity. Even more, she, through her own personal expereince, grieved for the anguish women suffered waiting to be "chosen"; or having been chosen, waiting for fate to bless her with motherhood.

Mrs. Benedict was an extremely shy and brilliant person. Both of these conditions contributed to her separateness and her periods of loneliness. Upon graduation from college she saw little ahead of her for a creative life. Marriage possibilities seemed remote. The kinds of work available for women in the early 1900s were teaching and social services, both of which she considered worthy but unchallenging. During her three years as a teacher in a girls' school, her pain was at times desperate beyond measure as she suffered loneliness while watching the educational process instill vacuity into the lives of young women.

Marriage brought a brief interlude of joy and hope. Hope was soon dimmed, however, as the possibility for children did not materialize. Her husband immersed himself increasingly in his chemical research. Because she was so efficient, the maintenance of housekeeping occupied but a slight portion of her day. Her intellect, spiritual and artistic sensitivity combined to keep her from finding contentment in hobbies or social causes. Her own pain forced her to seek meaning in life.

It was in this condition at age 35 that she encountered an anthropology lecture and began to see this discipline as a challenge to the many dimensions of creativity within her. She went on to achieve a place of prominence following her doctorate. The rich blending of her capacities as an artist, poet and scholar enabled her to introduce a new perspective into the study of human experience. Much of the impetus in contemporary cultural anthropology derives from her book, *Patterns of Culture,* and the ensuing research she directed during the next few years.

Although the several dimensions of her talent contributed to the richness of her personality which in turn changed the direction of anthropology, she continued to keep the several areas of her life separate. Her poetry interests were shared with a small group, for the most part unknown to her colleagues in anthropology. Likewise her family life was separate. Even her closest friend, Margaret Mead, met her mother and sister only once and her husband rarely. Mrs. Benedict published her poems under the pseudonym of Anne Singleton.

Her writing as a professional anthropologist used her married name, which, she once observed, also seemed to her to be a pseudonym.

The unusual talent of this person was enhanced by the fact that she was a woman born in the late 1800s. The several factors—her brilliance, the period of history into which she was born and the physical problems preventing her from having children—combined to direct her into a career of significant contribution. A concomitant condition—we cannot know whether to call it a price—was a private life of great loneliness.

Abstract from M. Mead, *An Anthropologist at Work* (Boston: Houghton Mifflin, 1959).

were medium to low. Richardson's observations were that the results reflect "the ambivalence experienced by women who pursue a traditional course of development (homemaking) in a society which devalues this feminine role."[85] Concerning the career-oriented women, Richardson wrote, "The lack of relationship between self-career congruence and career orientation suggests that the development of an integrated personality which incorporates career-role aspirations consistant with self-and-role concepts is incomplete in the senior year of college . . . One can speculate that the developmental process for women who are deviating in some way from the traditional female role is a more difficult and prolonged one affected by a variety of internal and external factors."[86]

Clarification of personal and career identities does not appear to have become easier for women during the course of the last twenty years. As a beginning counselor twenty years ago, I consistently encountered two different groups of college women, who expressed career goals either in terms of career outside the home or career within the home. These differences in career orientation were accompanied by differences in personal preferences on a number of styles of interaction, such as autonomy, nurturance, and achievement.[87]

[85] M. S. Richardson, "Self Concepts and Role Concepts in the Career Orientation of College Women," *Journal of Counseling Psychology* 22 (1975), pp. 122–126; see also M. S. Richardson and J. L. Alpert, "Role Perceptions of Educated Adult Women: An Exploratory Study," *Educational Gerontology* 1 (April–June 1976), 2:171–185.

[86] Richardson, "Self Concepts and Role Concepts in the Career Orientation of College Women," p. 126.

[87] D. P. Hoyt and C. E. Kennedy, "Interest and Personality Correlates of Career-Motivated and Homemaking-Motivated College Women," *Journal of Counseling Psychology* 5 (1958), 1:44–49.

Research with women has helped to initiate greater awareness of a sequential approach to careers in and outside the home. Taylor[88] found that a group of college graduates in their mid-thirties, most of whom were principally occupied with rearing families, were expressing a great deal of satisfaction with their situation. They had been employed before beginning their families and looked forward with confidence to returning to outside careers at a later time. This variety in their lives seemed to afford them somewhat greater satisfaction with their lot than was expressed by their husbands, whose careers had had less variety.

CAREER PLANNING. The increasing number of retired persons beginning new careers highlights the phenomenon of second careers as an area for study. This need is also promoting the development of counseling resources for middle-and older-aged persons, along with a rapidly expanding demand for educational programs geared to the needs of persons planning new careers.

Career planning is a continuing process throughout life rather than a once-and-for-all decision made in high school or college. Involving at different times different skills and competencies, job changes and promotion opportunities, modification of self-concept and satisfactions, family and community roles, each new stage of life requires some reintegration and review of career plans. Chickering, having made the case for the educator and vocational counselor to build his program on a well-informed understanding of adult developmental stages, summarizes his case with the following paragraph:

> We can thus better recognize that the 35-year-old who comes for clearly specified professional knowledge or competence needed for a promotion or a new opportunity will define a program and approach it very differently from the 45-year-old who wonders whether all those long hours, family sacrifices, short-changed human relationships, and atrophied interests were really worth it. Both of these students will be different from the 25-year-old eagerly exploring the potentials of a first career choice. The 30-year-old housewife whose husband thinks she should become more sophisticated, develop broader interests, get out more, and define her own career will be very different from the 25-year-old just settling into the challenges and satisfactions of new babies

---

[88] J. Taylor, "The Relationship of Life Satisfaction and the Determinants Associated with the Fourth Decade of Life," Ph.D. dissertation, Kansas State University, 1975.

and a new home, and from the 50-year-old who is building a more rich and easy existence with a devoted husband.[89]

Women Workers   There has been in recent years an increasing influx of women into the work force. They now number about 40 per cent of all employed persons with significant implications for our future.[90] Women enter the world of work for a variety of reasons. Some work because they are the sole providers for their families, others to augment their husband's income either "to make ends meet" or "for extras," and about three out of ten,[91] place personal fulfillment as the main reason for working.

Women continue to face discrimination in employment, although the pressures they and their supporters are putting on employers are having positive effects. Correction of inequities will not come overnight. Women are still congregated in relatively few occupations and at low occupational levels. A fourth of all employed women are in the traditionally female jobs of secretary, retail sales clerk, bookkeeper, elementary-school teacher, or household worker.[92] Many women continue to receive less pay than men for comparable jobs.

Until recently, young women have lacked role models for high-level positions and in new careers areas. This is changing rapidly through the success experienced by some women and the effective publicity given to these stories.[93] Books to guide women in availing themselves of their rights[94] and legislation are helping to open avenues for further opportunities for women.

As society moves toward new types of working conditions, the entrance of women into the work force will confound the job satisfactions of many men. Yankelovich[95] points out that to many men who are working in jobs that offer little intrinsic satisfaction, the presence of a working wife may

[89] A. W. Chickering, "The Developmental and Educational Needs of Adults," paper presented to annual meeting of the American Personnel and Guidance Association, April 1975, New Orleans, p. 16.

[90] S. J. Brody, "Policy Issues of Women in Transition," *The Gerontologist* 16 (April 1976), 2:181–183.

[91] Rosow, *The Worker and the Job,* p. 44.

[92] Ibid., p. 63.

[93] For example, the book *What's a Nice Girl Like You Doing in a Place Like This?* by J. Teitz (New York: Coward-McCann & Geoghegan, 1972), describes the experiences of eleven women near their early thirties in varied professions with salaries ranging up to $25,000 and averaging around $12,000.

[94] C. Bird, *Everything a Woman Needs to Know to Get Paid What She's Worth* (New York: David McKay, 1973).

[95] D. Yankelovich, "The Meaning of Work," in *The Worker and the Job,* ed. J. M. Rosow, p. 45.

3–7 *Women pursue increasingly varied jobs. Pictured here are a college dean and a road construction worker. (Kansas State University Student Publications photos)*

create a personal crisis. The man's motivation for keeping at the job was "to provide for the wife and kids." If this need is removed, his job may become intolerable.

Adults need opportunities to sort through periodically the conflicting meanings experienced with varying roles and abilities. Different types of life-planning workshops, career exploration meetings, and strength groups are making these opportunities available. The letter in Example 3–14, from the leader of such a group reporting a follow-up gathering, reflects some of the growth experiences in career and life-planning activities. Women in that group ranged in age from 22 to 58 years. The workship had had eight 2-hour meetings.

Employment continues for some persons past the retirement marker. Nearly a third of the persons over 65 are working outside the home, full or part time. Research points up a substantially high unemployment rate of

3–8 *Some women find guidance and encouragement from one another in life-planning workshops and evening study groups as they consider entering the world of work. (Photo, University for Man, Manhattan, Kansas)*

people in their late fifties and early sixties, suggesting the possible need for occupational retraining opportunities of this age group.

Many retired persons still want to work. More than three out of ten retired persons express this desire. Those with lower incomes are more likely to want to continue working. Half of the black retired persons and 46 per cent of the persons with incomes below $3,000 indicated they were forced to retire.

Two out of ten persons of all working ages feel frustrated at the lack of opportunity to use or to develop specific skills. Persons approaching retirement and young school graduates feel that no one will give them a chance to use some of their skills. A study of attitudes toward work and retirement was summarized as follows:

> Government and the private sector have until now aimed their job-training efforts where the demand is greatest: among young people in their 20s and 30s. What this study reveals, however, is a substantial demand for similar programs by people in their 40s, 50s, and 60s.

Example 3–14.

> Dear Jean, Cindy, and Pam:
>
>   Many of us from our first workshop got together for dinner, wine, and mutual support last evening at the Hilltop Tea Room. We thought of you and wished you were there. Mary Allen had been experiencing some very rewarding professional recognition in having had some of her work accepted at the New Beginnings Art Show on campus. She had a very successful exhibit of her wall hangings in the Monroe Public Library and a piece had been accepted for a showing of contemporary Midwest artists. Sue Hampton was exploring the feasibility of going on in architecture. Gayla was happily at home for now; she was exploring tole painting and tentatively planning to volunteer her services as a teacher's aide next year to test her level of teaching interest. Sally Heinz was happily combining job and family and finishing her B.A. this June; planned a summer respite (and maybe longer) before going on with graduate study or work. Sheila King was at peace with her conviction that counseling was her interest and that when she was ready that would be the field she would pursue. Terry Hill was jubilant; she had just this week passed her M.A. orals in English. Jill had received a grant which enabled her to complete her undergraduate pre-med work; she had already given her notice to her employer.
>   We wined and dined and talked from 7:15 to 11:15. We felt the mutual sharing of triumphs and debacles had been supportive. We found we still like the company. And we agreed we would keep touch in person or by mail.
>   Therefore this letter!
>
>   Sincerely,

  Many of these older people may be expressing an interest in career variety and simply feel that it is time for a change or for advancement. Others, however, may be recognizing that mandatory retirement is not too far off and that they had better prepare themselves for it by learning an occupation that they can continue until they are ready to stop working.[96]

  The experience of the adult in retirement will be influenced by several factors: how central work has been in his personal identity, expected benefits

---

[96] L. Harris and associates, *The Myth and Reality of Aging in America,* p. 94.

in retirement, and his ability to project meaningful activities into the retirement years.[97],[98]

Summary of Social Influences of the World of Work

An expression of job satisfaction is an expression of satisfaction with oneself and, in a measure, with one's place in life. The women's movement has helped dramatize the intimate relationship that exists between opportunity for personal expression through employment and one's sense of self-worth. The freedom of choice in employment has been recognized as a crucial factor in the concerns of workers in general, and especially of those upon whom special constraints have been placed, such as minorities, women, and the elderly.

There is a close interaction between the worker's satisfaction, his effectiveness on the job, and his satisfactions in family life. Disharmony at work puts strains on the family. Embarrassment caused by type of employment extends to embarrassment with one's life-style and social position. Through the amount of income and/or social contacts it affords, employment significantly influences the family's place in the community. Special demands of the job—such as night shift, travel, frequent transfers—shape the form of family interaction. Lack of employment places economic pressures on the adult and his family and contributes to feelings of inadequacy and low worth on his part.

Choice of occupation is to some extent a misnomer in that family, school, and the community have narrowed greatly the range of occupations available to the young person. The role models available to the young set the stage against which they may measure their satisfaction in adult life. There may be a series of models as the individual is drawn first into an occupational field and then develops more specialized identification through success and experience in the field.

The economic and social status of the family creates occupational role expectations for the young person. Opportunity for preparation and entry into

---

[97] W. J. Goudy, E. A. Powers, and P. Keith, "Work and Retirement: A Test of Attitudinal Relationships," *Journal of Gerontology* 30 (March 1975), 2:193–198.

[98] F. D. Glamser and G. F. DeJong, "The Efficacy of Preretirement Preparation Programs for Industrial Workers," *Journal of Gerontology* 30 (September 1975), 5:595–600.

an occupational area are greatly influenced by the family. The social status, values, and relationships within the family either offer encouragement and resources or conflicts and barriers to the individual's pursuit of an occupation. Many occupational opportunities are never recognized or considered by a young person because his family, his peers in the community, and his classification by the school have caused him to form certain types of perceptions about himself and the world.

The occupational role expectations expressed by others and internalized by the individual continue to guide the adult throughout his working career. There are marks of success, such as the type of firm by which he is employed and the rate of advancement, that influence the motivation and self-esteem of the adult. Even as there are role changes for the adult in family life, there are also role changes during his work career, paralleling to some extent chronological age. There is an expected time to be an apprentice and later a foreman; a man of 40 is rarely a junior executive. Competence and esteem experienced on the job carry over to be related in a reciprocal fashion with the feedback the adult gets from other roles in family and community life. Workers whose work history is steady and predictable will be the persons who are also active and responsible in community groups.

As the adult continues his career, the occupation provides the outlet for and continued cultivation of personality traits and values that were influential in his choice of occupation. The attitudes and values he develops through his adult years are increasingly similar to those of other persons in his occupation. However, there is always a degree to which the individual shapes or socializes his job as he is being socialized by it.

Suggested Activities and Further Reading

1. What family roles have you occupied in the course of your life? How have these contributed to your development through adult life stages?

2. What observations can you make concerning changes and stability of the family in the future?

3. Have you had experiences with any of the special family groups discussed in this chapter? If so, what special strengths and what special needs did you observe that have implications for adult development?

4. For futuristic ideas about the family read the following books:

   H. A. Otto, ed., *The Family in Search of a Future* (New York: Appleton-Century-Crofts, 1970);

J. S. and J. R. Delora, *Intimate Life Styles: Marriage and Its Alternatives* (Pacific Palisades, Calif.: Goodyear, 1975);

A. Toffler, *Future Shock* (New York: Bantam Books, 1970), Chapter 11.

5. For a more extensive consideration of the effect of the family in the transmission of values see V. L. Bengtson, "Generation and Family Effects in Value Socialization," *American Sociological Review* 40 (June 1975), pp. 358–371.

6. An area needing further research is that dealing with ethnic influences in adult development and family life. A beginning is being made in the study of the black aged and black families. In addition to Hill's *The Strengths of Black Families,* see also:

J. J. Jackson, "Plights of Older Black Women in the United States," *Black Aging* 1 (December 1975–February 1976), pp. 12–16;

I. F. Ehrlich, "Toward a Social Profile on the Aged Black Population," *The International Journal of Aging and Human Development* 4 (Summer 1973), 3:271–276;

J. J. Jackson, "Comparative Life Styles and Family and Friend Relationships Among Older Black Women," *The Family Coordinator* 21 (October 1972), 4:477–486.

7. Review some of the popular books on parent education, such as Thomas Gordon's *Parent Effectiveness Training* (New York: Peter H. Wyden, 1970) and Brenda Maddox's *The Half-Parent: Living with Other People's Children* (New York: M. Evans, 1975). How do they deal with adult development stages?

8. Discuss how work experiences contributed to your feelings of adult status. Are there situations in Studs Terkel's *Working* that seem familiar?

9. What are the occupations with which you associate high status? What are the factors underlying the status system you have in mind—money, power, intelligence?

10. To follow through a theory attempting to explain the processes by which occupational choices are made, skills acquired, and fields of work selected, see J. D. Krumboltz et al., "A Social Learning Theory of Career Selection," *The Counseling Psychologist* 6 (1976), 1:71–81.

chapter 4

Physiological Processes

Health care is a large item in the budgets of the adults in our society and in our national budget. Often this money is spent for remedial rather than for developmental and preventive services. The objective of this chapter is to relate the physiological aspects of human development to other developmental dimensions in order to see the wholeness and patterns that characterize adulthood. We will consider the importance of balance in the functioning of different systems of the body and see a continuity in the flow of energy within and surrounding us.

Energy

Let us think of an example. We know diet influences our supply of energy, thus our alertness, our responsiveness to others, as well as our appearance. These in turn influence the responses of others to us, which influence our feelings about ourselves. Our self-concept can have a significant effect upon our moods that feed back into the endocrine functioning and the body chemistry. This brings us back full circle to the body's processing of the food (see Example 4–1 for an illustration of the interaction of diet with psychological and physiological functioning).

Each of us requires a continuous supply and effective processing of the energy that maintains our body and influences the quality of our personality. Nutritional requirements vary from individual to individual. They vary according to the kind of activities in which we are engaged and according to our age. Most of us in middle life use around 2000 calories a

4–1 *Society's awareness of the importance of exercise is reflected in this "benefit" jog. Teen-agers to college president and adults of all ages participated in a cross-country exercise to raise money for a special cause.* (Manhattan Mercury *photo*)

Example 4–1.
A Matter of
Diet

A neuropsychiatrist described the case of a young student who had been doing poorly in school because of fatigue and inability to concentrate. He began to develop further emotional problems growing out of feelings of worthlessness prompted by his work and social situation. Shortly before his emotional problems began, he had experienced a major disappointment when failure to pass an eye examination caused him to be turned down for a position he wanted badly.

The student was diagnosed as having a condition of hypoglycemia and put on a special diet. Within a month his energy returned, his vision improved, and other physical symptoms such as itching, excessive thirst, and urination problems were alleviated.

Abstract from S. Walker III, "Blood Sugar and Emotional Storms: Sugar Doctors Push Hypoglycemia," *Psychology Today* 9 (July 1975), 2:69–74.

115

day, but most of us take in from our food considerably more than 2000 calories.

Units of Measure Calories are the units of measure telling us the amount of energy that is being taken in or is being "burned up" in the metabolism, which changes food to usable energy for the body. One calorie is the amount of heat energy it takes to raise the temperature of 2.2 pounds of water one degree centigrade. We can think of calories in terms of the amount of calories present in the food we eat. For example, one gram of the different nutrients yields a different number of calories.

One gram of fat yields 9 calories.
One gram of protein yields 4 calories.
One gram of carbohydrates yields 4 calories.[1]

Fats It is obvious that fats are highly concentrated calories, and adult diets are susceptible to a preponderance of fats: gravies, dressings, spreads. Alcohol also contains a high concentration of calories: one gram yields 7 calories. An 8-ounce glass of beer has more than 100 calories; one cocktail averages better than 200 calories. Carbonated beverages carry nearly the same concentration; a coke has between 70 and 100 calories. Except when sugar and cream are used, coffee and tea are virtually without calories.

Fats are deceptive. A minimal amount is essential for body functioning. They are often hidden in various meat and dairy products and are taken into the body without our being aware of them. Excess fat is not only a problem for persons concerned with appearance, it also interferes with the work of the heart and the blood circulation, and the functioning of other parts of the body.

Proteins Proteins are important for growth and repair of tissues; they also form the enzymes in the body that activate a wide variety of chemical functions associated with digestion and various circulatory and endocrine functioning. Most of our protein comes from meat, fish, milk products, and eggs.

[1] W. J. Darby, "Nutrition," in *Family Medical Guide,* ed. D. G. Cooley (Des Moines: Meredith, 1974), p. 493.

Carbohydrates   Carbohydrates furnish most of the free energy in the body. They allow the energy potential of protein to remain in the form used for specialized functions. Thus, carbohydrates are the "swing" group. An undersupply of them causes the body to draw upon its fat reserves; an oversupply causes the abundance to be stored as fat.

Vitamins   Vitamins are chemical compounds that, with trace amounts of certain minerals, are required for good nutrition. They do not contain energy as does a calorie; rather, they are catalysts to activate actions within the body. Although minute in amount needed, their presence is indispensable. When any of the vitamins is absent, the body does not function efficiently. Vitamins and their significance in many aspects of biological and mental health are receiving much study. Our increasing appreciation for the rhythms of the body suggests possibilities for more ways of approaching the use of vitamins than previously thought possible.

    The intimate relationship between nutrition and biological and mental health should encourage adults to continue to observe balanced diets and amounts of calories needed as their life-style changes.

Excess Calories   Fat tends to accumulate in our bodies after we reach 25 years of age. This is because the rate of the metabolism needed to maintain body functioning slows down. We are generally less active; physically we have achieved most of our growth. Therefore, less energy is needed for growth and maintenance. However, we continue to eat as much or more than we did when younger. This means that the extra calories not burned up to operate the body are converted and stored as fat.

    People in middle life can plan in two ways to regulate their weight. They can either reduce their diet to the calorie intake needed to maintain a certain weight, or they can exercise each day to burn up the excess calories. Probably a combination of the two is best. Exercise without setting a limit on calorie intake may result in an increased appetite, which brings in more calories than the exercise uses. For example, it takes a 30-minute walk at a brisk pace to use up the calories of one doughnut. Exercise has the added benefit of strengthening and keeping organs and muscles of the body in good tone.

Malnutrition   Malnutrition results from the lack or from the overconsumption of certain foods, which may contribute to heart trouble and/or obesity. Fad diets often

a. b.

4–2 *Adults find many ways to keep physically fit. (a, Photo University for Man, Manhattan, Kansas; b and c, Manhattan Mercury photos)*

c.

result in an oversupply of some nutrients and a severe lack of others; whereas crash diets may reduce weight while consuming vitally needed stores of other nutritional reserves. Poverty may cause families or aged persons to be unable to obtain a balanced diet. And lack of nutritional information or awareness may keep people in poor health.

Metabolism:
A Process of
Conversion

The cells of the body use energy for three major activities: maintenance of the body, growth, and physical activity. About half of the average person's calorie intake each day is spent on the energy the body requires for circulation, respiration, secretion, and the maintenance of the metabolism of cells during sleep. Perkins[2] points out that it takes energy just to stay alive.

Metabolism is the chemical process through which the body frees energy present in food to be used for the three major body activities. Energy is obtained from the oxidation of sugar. Complex food molecules are broken down during digestion into glucose molecules and then transported in the blood stream to the innumerable cells of the body. In the cells each glucose molecule is refined to produce 2 molecules of lactic acid; these then move into the Krebs citric-acid cycle that further breaks them down to 36 molecules with energy in a form available to the cell for carrying on life processes.

The adult person's system, operated by this energy, has several closely synchronized units. The characteristics and functioning of the units are modified slightly and use energies in different ways as we move through the years of adulthood. Let us look briefly at each of the units. We will note how each is related to the other and how the units influence and are influenced by our awareness of self.

Systems of the Body

Growing
New Cells

The cell is the key member in the physiological organism forming the body, or house, of our "being." In some ways a miniature of the human body, each cell takes in nutrients and oxygen and disposes of wastes.

The size and shape of the cell varies with its specific task, such as the blood cell, skin cell, brain cell. Many cells reproduce through duplication and division. The age and health of the adult will influence the efficiency with which broken bones and ruptured skin heal through formation of new cells. Nerve

[2] H. V. Perkins, *Human Development* (Belmont, Calif.: Wadsworth, 1975), p. 91.

cells do not reproduce; however, in case of damage or decay, certain functions may be taken over by remaining cells.

The Older We Grow, The Shorter We Get

The skeletal system contains the bones providing the support and form of the body, and the bone marrow manufactures the red blood cells. The 200 bones are held together by ligaments and cartilage that allow for movement, and each joint is encased by a capsule filled with fluid. As we become older, our physique changes. We usually become slightly shorter. Disturbances or upsets in the body chemistry through stress or the malfunctioning of certain glands may contribute to conditions causing pains in the joints, such as arthritis.

Muscles and Systems of Exercise

The striated, or voluntary, muscles hold the skeleton together by a system of planned tensions. They are long fibrous bundles attached to the bones and have the ability to contract and relax. Pairs of voluntary muscles act in oppositional contraction. This ability to change provides the mechanics for body movement. The involuntary, or smooth, muscles work parts of the body not associated with the skeleton, such as the stomach, intestines, and the arteries. The heart is constructed like a voluntary muscle but its function is involuntary. (See chapter 6 for discussion of biofeedback's influence on involuntary activity.)

THE FILTERS AT WORK.   Two important filtering systems are controlled by our kidneys and lungs. Exercise is a key factor to keeping up the elasticity of the cardiac muscle that provides healthy heart contractions and therefore better exchange of air in the lungs. The blood carries nutrients and oxygen to all parts of the body and transports waste material back to the lungs and kidneys.

The kidneys are crucial in filtering poisons from the body. As our food is broken down to chemical form through the digestive processes of the stomach, intestines, liver, and pancreas, there are some materials remaining that are poisonous. Ammonia is one such substance that the kidneys filter as they help to regulate the balance of chemicals circulating in the blood stream. Because the "workload" of the kidneys is influenced by the amount of poisonous material needed to be taken from the blood, illness and particularly drugs may wear down a kidney, making it less able to perform well its surveillance function. Decreased effectiveness of the kidneys may appear with advancing age or with alcoholism.

AGING AND APPEARANCE.   There is some loss of elasticity in muscles beginning in mid-life. Individuals differ greatly because of inheritance and amount
of exercise. An individual's speed and coordination are not as likely to
change with age as with disease, injury, or disuse.[3]

Changes in our physical appearance as we age are the result of the loss of
elastic fibers of the skin and by the thickening in the connective tissue fibers
that lie between the cells of the body.[4] Changes in collagen, a gelatinous sub-

[3] D. B. Bromley, *The Psychology of Human Ageing* (Baltimore: Penguin Books, 1974), Chapters 5 and 6.
[4] Ibid., p. 82.

4–3 *A 60-year-old city official gives an impromptu demonstration that he is as agile as ever. (Kansas State University Student Publications photo)*

stance found in connective tissue, bone, and cartilage, account for much of this effect. As cells reproduce, the "wear and tear" effects of collected wastes or cell damage may be alleviated at the time of division, with the new cells tending to possess the undamaged form of their original endowment. Through time, however, slight mutations result in a modified version of the original cell, and some cells slow down the frequency of reproduction. In tissues with slow reproduction or with no reproduction, there will in time result a collection of damaged cells and a loss in total number of cells. These cells then function less effectively and their ineffectiveness is compounded by the ineffectiveness of other cells.[5]

Glands and Nerves

We cannot overstate how finely tuned the interaction of the body's systems is. Keys to the timing involve two messenger services of the body, the endocrine system and the nervous system.

The term *endocrine* means "inward secreting." Many organs manufacture chemical substances, known as hormones, and deposit them directly into the blood stream. The chemical composition of certain hormones causes them to affect various organs. For example, the presence of hydrochloric acid, protein, and fat-digestion products in the small intestine causes the tissue of the intestinal walls to secrete a hormone that acts upon the pancreas and gall bladder. In response these organs secrete the bile and pancreatic juices needed to break down the food during the digestive process.

More well-known than the endocrine system as a vehicle for communication is the network of billions of nerve cells forming the nervous system. The central nervous system is composed of the large mass of nerve cells forming the brain and the spinal cord. The peripheral nervous system, including the motor and sensory branches, extends the communication network to all parts of the body.

MOTOR BRANCH.   There are two subsystems in the motor branch: the autonomic and the voluntary systems. The autonomic nervous system serves all

---

[5] Birren comments: "What seems likely is that in the cells there are characteristic sites on the chromosomes that are susceptible to damage with time. It is most unlikely that there is a simple gene or group of genes that does nothing except limit the length of life. Cells that do not or cannot divide seem to show aging more than do cells that divide." J. E. Birren, *The Psychology of Aging* (Englewood Cliffs, N.J.: Prentice-Hall, 1964), pp. 76–77.

of the visceral organs where the action is largely involuntary. When we discuss in Chapter 6 the processes of biofeedback, we will recognize that the distinction between voluntary and involuntary is less clear than previously thought. However, functioning of the autonomic system differs from the voluntary system in several ways. The action and reaction of organs in the autonomic system are relatively slow compared to the voluntary system controlling the skeletal muscles. Organs regulated by the autonomic system, such as heart and lungs, require continuous regulation. The circuitry of the autonomic system differs from the voluntary system's circuitry by including antagonistic impulses. For example, one set of nerves coming from the brain to the heart increases contractions of the cardiac muscle; another decreases the contractions.

The voluntary system controls the skeletal muscles in quite another way. It is an "all or nothing" system. Screening out antagonistic impulses in the voluntary system occurs at an earlier point in neural functioning. Only when the neural impulse is sufficiently strong to stimulate a muscle contraction does a message go out on the voluntary network.

SENSORY BRANCH.   The sensory system engages the world about us through our senses of sight, sound, taste, smell, and touch. Persons in the mid-forties and fifties begin to have difficulty seeing details at close distances. Limitation in ability to see things well at close range sometimes begins during youth. "After the age of about ten, the best viewing distance lengthens gradually until, by the age of 50, many people need to wear glasses with lenses to correct this 'long-sightedness.' The lens of the eye 'ages' even from infancy, and becomes more opaque and less elastic in adult life."[6]

Most people do not begin to suffer hearing loss before age 50. Trouble appears first with high-pitched sounds, whereas lower tones are more easily heard. Bromley points out that loss of hearing for speech sounds may include other factors, such as attention or lack of familiarity with the context of the thought being communicated.[7]

Capacities to taste and smell do not change much until the late fifties, with moderate decline thereafter. There is some suggestion that people in their sixties and beyond have higher thresholds for pain or other touch sensations—that is, they do not feel pain as readily. Laboratory data for this conjecture are confounded by the older person's tendency to wish to be sure

[6] Bromley, *The Psychology of Human Ageing.* p. 102.
[7] Ibid., p. 103.

before offering a response. This tendency toward "slowness" confounded with "deliberateness" will be discussed when considering slowness of reactions with aging.

There are many psychological and physiological factors involved in the phenomenon of pain. Treatments and research on intractable pain indicate this is an area about which we will be receiving new information in the years ahead.[8] Acupuncture has also added another dimension in the study of pain.

Biological Rhythms   As discussed earlier in this chapter, hormones serve as connective and balancing agents for chemical transmission. They are important for adjustments that must be made in the body. For example, the blood-sugar level is regulated by the combined action of a number of hormones. Important is that this control system operates in such a way that an increase in the blood-sugar level stimulates the mechanism that prevents the level from going too high. Conversely, when the level starts to fall, this decrease triggers the particular chain of events which cause an increase.

Plants, animals, and man have a 24-hour cycle as the major rhythm. Our body temperature, blood pressure, blood-sugar level, and a multitude of other factors in the body rise and fall in predictable fashion during the circadian (Latin, meaning about 24 hours) cycle. Our strength and moods vary with the biological time of day. There is much research suggesting that stimuli have different effects on people or animals depending on the time of day. For example,[9] a loud noise had little effect on a rodent at one period of the day; it drove him into convulsions and death at another period. More pregnant women go into labor at night or in the early morning hours than in the afternoon. Physicians also report that during the late hours they receive the most calls from patients with coronaries.

People are usually aware that there are certain periods of the day when they are most alert or most dull. Jet travel has highlighted the difficulty of adjusting individual biological clocks to society's clocks on two different sides of the world. A factory worker, nurse, or police officer being shifted from day to night duty experiences a biological adjustment that may require a week or more to recover from.

---

[8] R. Melzack, *The Puzzle of Pain* (New York: Basic Books, 1973).

[9] The illustrations in this section on biological rhythms are taken from Gay Luce's *Body Time* (New York: Random House, 1971). They are only a small sample of the multitude of the provocative situations and research reports contained therein.

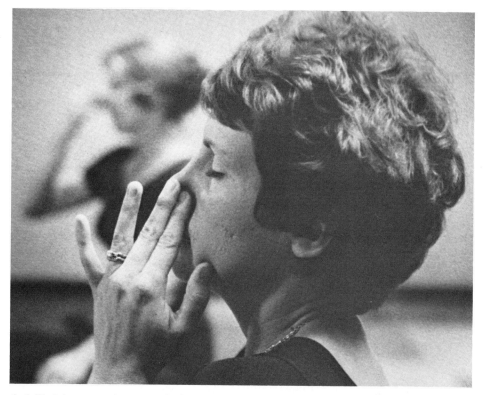

4–4 *Training groups in yoga and other meditative and health exercises prepare individuals to sharpen their awareness of body rhythms.* (Manhattan Mercury *photo*)

In the meantime the systems may be out of phase. One researcher commented on the effect as follows: "A glandular tissue may be in the phase of hormone production while another organ, being in another phase, cannot make use of the hormone; or an enzyme may be very active in a particular tissue at a time when its substrate is not available."[10]

The fine tuning of the systems can work against the individual if something upsets it. Unexpected pressures from the environment—either physical or psychological—can send reverberations through the whole body. We refer to these reverberations as stress.

[10] Quoted by G. Luce in "Biological Rhythms," in *The Nature of Human Consciousness,* ed. R. E. Ornstein (San Francisco: Freeman, 1973), p. 436.

Stress

Stress is frequently described as the number one health problem in our country.[11] Heart-attack victims and those who suffer from ulcers, migraines, and arthritis are usually under great stress. But stress itself is not a disease; it is the response of the body to any demand made upon it. The demand—whether an argument with a friend or the threat of losing one's job—requires some mobilizing of resources in the body. There may be a tendency, however, for overkill—that is, the body gears up more than is necessary. The pituitary and adrenal glands produce the hormones ACTH, cortisone, and cortisol, which protect us from attacks on the body and counteract inflammatory substances. The feedback mechanism of the body also calls forth antiinflammatory hormones to offset the proinflammatory hormones activated by threat.

General Adaptation Syndrome

The heavy load of combative agents in the system (combating the intruder and combating each other) often initiates a chain reaction when the effect of the general reaction to stress upsets systems throughout the body. If there are vulnerabilities—a predisposition toward heart trouble, for example—stress may provide sufficient "protective" disturbance in the system to bring the latent condition into full bloom.

Any strong emotion can effect overproducing of epinephrine and glucocorticoids that induce a state of emergency in the body, which stimulates the release of free fatty acids from the body's fuel deposits. Though anxiety and tension do not require the physical fight-or-flight preparation made by the body, they continue to cause the blood stream to be flooded with lipids, which, if continued over long periods of time, affect the heart and lead to hardening of the arteries.[12]

Adult Diseases: Diseases of Adaptation

Prolonged disturbances within the endocrine system can lead to damaged organs of the body. Also, the disturbance of the endocrine balance may result in reduced immunity and greater susceptibility to disease.

HEART ATTACKS.   The heart is one of the most frequent victims of the adaptation diseases. The effect of stress is always a mingling of factors: our in-

[11] H. Selye, *Stress of Life* (New York: McGraw-Hill, 1956).

[12] W. McQuade and A. Aikman, *Stress* (New York: Bantam Books, 1974).

herited "machinery" and predisposition, our diet and life-style, and the surrounding climate of circumstances.[13] In the chapter on middle adult life we will discuss the type of persons who are prime candidates for heart attacks. These individuals are continually in the midst of battle for achievement, have a higher quotient of lipids in their blood, faster coagulation, and a generally greater excretion of stress hormones.[14]

ULCERS.   The stomach and intestines are influenced by factors of stress. The mucous lining that protects the stomach is constantly being influenced—even its color changes—by the effects of our emotions. When we are angered or frightened, the lining becomes inflamed and red, and the stomach produces excess acid that can eventually eat a hole in its lining, creating an ulcer.

Sometimes, instead of affecting the heart or stomach, stress may find a target in the bowels. Ulcerative colitis is an extremely painful and often dangerous condition that seems directly associated with stress.[15]

DIABETES.   Although also influenced by heredity and overweight, problems of diabetes are frequently associated with stress. Sugar is the body's main source of energy and comes chiefly from the carbohydrates in our diet. After being digested from our food, sugar is stored in the liver until needed, then released into the blood stream as glucose. Our body can only avail itself of the energy when the glucose actually enters the individual cells of the body. Insulin, a hormone from the pancreas, is required to enable the glucose to enter the cells. If insulin is not present, the glucose simply accumulates unused in the blood. To dispose of the excess glucose, the body draws water, salt, and potassium from the tissues and eliminates the glucose in the urine. Meanwhile, the body demands glucose, and without its availability begins to burn fat stored in the cells. The burning of fat releases other chemicals into the blood that further upset the balance.[16]

HYPOGLYCEMIA.   A relatively new term, hypoglycemia is becoming familiar through the media. Its symptoms are chronic fatigue accompanied by irrita-

---

[13] The point should be kept in mind that all stress is not destructive. Stress is involved in all our adapting, creating, and coping with life. H. Selye discusses the matter of balance and the creative uses of our life energies in *Stress Without Distress* (Philadelphia: Lippincott, 1974).

[14] L. Levi, *Stress* (New York: Liveright, 1967), p. 62.

[15] McQuade and Aikman, *Stress,* pp. 55–57.

[16] Ibid., pp. 58–60.

bility, anxiety, and emotional distress. Hypoglycemia is the condition of excessively low blood sugar. It is described not as a disease but as a fault in the body chemistry and can often be corrected by a high-protein diet with limited intake of carbohydrates and refined sugars. Counseling may be needed at times.[17] Example 4–2 provides an instance where psychotherapy, nutrition, and endocrinology are finding a common, though often controversial, focus.

Example 4–2.
Counseling and
Hypoglycemia

A 26-year-old woman admitted herself to a hospital because of her urge toward suicide. She had been in counseling for more than a year without making progress. A physical examination revealed periodic numbness in different parts of her body. She was always thirsty, craved sweets, and had skin problems. Glucose-tolerance and other tests led to a diagnosis of hypoglycemia. She was placed on a special diet and her physical symptoms cleared up. She was then able to re-enter psychotherapy and within six months her emotional concerns were relieved.

Abstract from S. Walker III, "Blood Sugar and Emotional Storms: Sugar Doctors Push Hypoglycemia," *Psychology Today* 9 (July 1975), 2:69–74.

There is a danger of oversimplification that results in "fads" of popular diseases. The point is that we are complex organisms and to look only at emotional concerns, or at diet, or only at endocrine or neurological functioning would be to see only part of the picture.

Summary

The human body is an engineering marvel—the interworking of the systems of the organism is beautifully balanced. Complementarity is seen throughout the systems: some muscles tense while their opposites relax; some hormones speed the system up as others slow it down. Balance is the key word in body functioning. Illness or other trouble comes when this balance is upset, when one of the systems gets out of phase with the others. This can happen when

[17] G. Watson, *Nutrition and Your Mind: The Psychochemical Response* (New York: Harper & Row, 1972), Chapter 2.

excessive stimulation sets off an extensive adjustment process throughout the systems. The adjustment process attempts to restore the normal balance in the various organs of the body. Sometimes this attempt and failure to adapt can reverberate in great disturbances as each new adjustment triggers another. The resulting condition is known as stress or body "wear and tear". Each system has a tolerance or an adjustment range. When a subsystem has, either as a result of heredity or of conditioning and prior experience, built up an action potential near its limit of tolerance, a minor reverberation through the system may set off an unexpected action of that subsystem. The latent condition illustrates the principle of a "necessary but not sufficient cause".

By considering the functioning of our body as a whole, rather than treating or exercising one part without regard to its interdependent relationship, we will be more likely to maintain good health. As we listen to our body, we will be better able to sense its rhythm, and by flowing with it, we will realize a greater measure of our potential.

Our body's functioning is not only an outcome of the balancing among its organs, it is also an expression of our interchange with the world around us. The climate of heat or cold, the nutrients in our food, the schedules of our day, the acts of gratitude or revenge, the images in our mind, and the hope or despair in our spirit—these are part of the network of reciprocal influences participating in the harmony of our body's functioning.

Suggested Activities and Further Reading

1. Write a brief paper of your reactions to the author's approach to physiological processes in the book *Nutrition Against Disease* by Roger J. Williams (New York: Bantam, 1973).
2. List the different types of special diets and exercise routines among people of your acquaintance.
3. Interview persons whose work schedule changes periodically from day to night shift to discover what physical and/or psychosocial effects they experience with the change.
4. Interview a random sample of persons from different age groups—young, middle, and late adult—to find how many have a physical limitation in some system of the body: sensory (sight, hearing), endocrine, circulatory (heart, blood vessels, spleen), skeletal, or muscular (arthritis, etc.). You may be surprised at the high percentage of adults of all ages with a physical limitation. Note also the number who have learned to accommodate so they are not incapacitated by the limitation.

5. The following books provide further background reading at different levels:

American Medical Association, *The Wonderful Human Machine* (535 N. Dearborn Street, Chicago, Ill. 60610).
A brief, informed, and well-illustrated overview of the systems of the body.

C. H. Best and N. B. Taylor, *The Physiological Basis of Medical Practice (Baltimore: The Williams & Wilkins Co., 1966).*
An extensive technical discussion of each of the systems of the body.

The Boston Women's Health Collective, *Our Bodies, Ourselves* (New York: Simon & Schuster, 1975). A popular book written by women who desired to share their information with others.

H. T. Lief et al., *The Psychological Bases of Medical Practice* (New York: Harper & Row, 1963).
Written in 1963, this is still one of the best collections of articles dealing with the interrelationships between the person and the disease.

R. B. Weg, "Changing Physiology of Aging: Normal and Pathological," in *Aging,* eds. D. S. Woodruff and J. E. Birren (New York: Van Nostrand, 1975).

D. B. Bromley, *The Psychology of Human Ageing* (Baltimore: Penguin Books, 1974), Chapter 3.

J. D. Palm, *Diet Away Your Stress, Tension and Anxiety* (Garden City, N.Y.: Doubleday, 1976).

chapter 5

Self-Processes

"**S**elf," "ego," or "I" is the developmental process that brings together the social and physiological dimensions we have been discussing in earlier chapters. In some respects the self is the most expressive aspect of adult development, and it has been implicit in our discussions of social roles and values. We have referred to it when we talked of the psychological influences in our physical health.

It is the changes in the self—in the awareness of who we are and how we are to act—that experientially mark our movement through periods of adult life. Stated in its briefest form, we define self to be the phenomenon of being aware of our experience. It is the "knowing" aspect of me. It is the awareness of the present moment and it is the holding in storage of the awarenesses of past moments. It is the putting together and making sense of my awarenesses—the creation of my identity—so that I project this identity into the future. I anticipate how it will be, or should be, and I make decisions on the basis of maintaining my identity or my self.

An Overview of Self

As I sit at my desk writing this chapter, my hand carries forward the pen, a part of my brain formulates ideas, another part handles the details of words and spelling. I have a general awareness, or feeling, of the picture or information that I want to communicate.

While occupied with the task of writing, I also have other awarenesses at different levels of clarity and intensity. At times I am aware of physi-

131

5–1 *Self-processes are the putting together of our awarenesses.* (Manhattan Mercury *photo*)

cal tension in my back or legs and I shift my position. Occasionally I hear sounds of television in another room.

In addition to the biological machine processing these data, there is an awareness—a conviction is perhaps a better term—of existence and continuity. There is an "I" receiving the input. *Self* is a term for that receiving entity.

Obviously much that makes up the I, or self, or the receiving and computing entity, is the creation of what is processed. I am that which I experience; however, I shape and select what I experience.

Beginning with our first breath, and probably a number of months before that, a patterning was begun in our brain in the awareness of our senses. In their intricate network of connections, each awareness influences the other. Each new experience, each sound, each decision slightly changes the pattern of connections. The general direction of change is toward making stronger or clearer the already existing patterns. Thus a fundamental law is the maintenance of self—homeostasis, the regulating principle.

Imbedded in the principle of maintaining self is the process of growth. Life cannot stagnate. We are always incorporating, reevaluating, and restructuring our awarenesses and our goals. As we seek to maintain our position with our employer, for example, we are making choices and looking ahead to the opportunities that will establish more securely our skills and our identity in the firm.

The principle of striving for balance prevails through all levels of our body and personality. Without a fair degree of balance there would be such disorganization as to immobilize and perhaps disintegrate the system. Said another way, balance is a key to integration. However, our body and our personality are open systems—that it, they are continually growing and taking in new materials and experiences; thus as we grow, the balance is upset slightly. The body and mind then work to accommodate this new condition and restore a state of temporary equilibrium in our energy systems.

Our total self is a rich mingling of our identities and commitments in many groups. In each life situation we function in terms of our own ideal for that group and in terms of relating that investment of our self to our investment in other situations. I have a concept of my ideal self as father, teacher, man, husband, citizen, and colleague, as leader in one group and follower in another.

When we talk about my responding as an adult to the role expectations of my social group, we assume the presence and functioning of my self. Because the self is the connecting link between my inner and outer world, it is difficult to describe its operation in simple terms. There is, of course, much that we do not know about the phenomenon self. But because it is the self that registers changes resulting from growth and it is the self that makes the decisions that lead to growth-producing action, we need to set forth as clear a picture as we can of its functioning. Therefore, it will be helpful if we go back a bit and begin to build our description of self-processes "from the ground up." Because self is experiencing of awareness, let us see how the fundamental faculties for awareness develop. Let us look at the "machinery" of our brain and how it is in time interrelated with the less tangible world of ideas and meanings.

Machinery for Thinking   The brain of the average adult weighs about three pounds and can easily be held in two hands. It is formed of more than 100 billion cells, of which 90 per cent provide the centers where the 10 billion neurons do the main work of the brain. Complexity and organization make the brain succeed.[1]

[1] R. W. Gerard, "What Is Memory?" *Scientific American* (September 1953).

5–2 *Self-actualization is experienced in the creative way we relate our daily behavior to fulfilling our innate, positive potential. (Kansas State University Student Publications photo)*

Each single neuron may be connected to 60,000 others in the labyrinth of dendrites and axons. Each cell contributes to behavior by firing or failing to fire. The *pattern* of these discharges accounts for memory, which retains past awarenesses. Organized or patterned through time, they form a foundation of self.

Self stores and interprets our past experiences through a biological process called cell assemblies (see Example 5–1). Each event in our life modifies the makeup and connections of our brain cells with other parts of the body. We are able to review the events through processes of memory and consciousness. By the time we reach adulthood, we have stored in an awareness system called consciousness an endless array of past experiences. We can "relive" any of them by simply calling to awareness a past scene or feeling.

RETICULAR FORMATION.   Stimulation of the "thinking area" (cortex) of the brain has no effect unless the brain is awake. A piece of nerve fiber two or

Example 5–1.
Cell Assemblies

In thought processes an elementary idea consists of activity in a complex closed loop of brain cells called a "cell assembly." This network of neuroactivity is developed as a result of repeated stimulation during childhood. One or more of these simultaneously active cell assemblies can excite another in a series called a "phase sequence." The firing of a cell assembly comes about as a result of summation of the necessary amount of neural energy. Because there needs to be a summation or build-up of electrical charges before an impulse will move from one group of cells to another, we can exercise "selectivity" and directiveness in our individual train of thought.

A moderate degree of emotion is important in organizing and integrating our thought processes. However, there are disorganizing effects with excessively high emotion. Excessive threat may induce disintegration of the brain organization so that our volitional processes are paralyzed and the individual is unable to "will" behavior.

Abstract from D. O. Hebb, *The Organization of Behavior* (New York: Wiley, 1949).

three inches long has the important task of serving as the alarm system for wakening the brain to incoming stimuli. This alarm system is called the reticular activating system (RAS). The RAS alerts the cortex and in turn receives impulses from the aroused cortex to which it responds in a continual feedback-confirmation arrangement. Thus it directs the traffic of messages in the nervous system, monitors the myriads of stimuli that affect our senses, and tempers and refines our muscular activity and bodily movements.[2]

BIOFEEDBACK: UNITING MIND AND BODY.   For years we were taught that activities under the influence of the autonomic nervous system—heart rate and brain waves, for example—could not be voluntarily (consciously) controlled by us. The "body" did it on its own and "I" was separated from my body.

The 1960s will be remembered for many things; one will be the reuniting of mind and body. The process termed *biofeedback*[3] came into popularity in practice and research. Through this procedure I can observe a record of physiologic activities, such as heart rate or brain waves, as they are going on at this moment in my body. I am also simultaneously aware of other feelings or thoughts I am having. As I observe the effect of changes in my feelings or

[2] J. D. French, "The Reticular Formation," *Scientific American* (May 1957).

[3] B. Brown, *New Mind, New Body-Biofeedback: New Directions for the Mind* (New York: Harper & Row, 1974).

thoughts while they accompany changes in my heart record, I can learn to adjust the various states of my body and mind to bring about the heart rate I desire or the degree of body temperature or the amount of tension in my muscles. We will discuss biofeedback further in Chapter 6.

Balance Is the Key

As mentioned earlier, the basic or underlying component in all my parts and systems is energy. Everything about me can be broken down to a level of energy.[4] Essentially I *am* energy. There are different levels and forms of energy involved in the functioning of my body and person. As they interact, they create different degrees of tension in the state of balance among the systems. This principle of homeostasis works to maintain a *loose* equality of tensions.

The balance needs to be seen in overall terms because at times certain activities may seem to be deliberately attempting to upset the balance. There is an intricate network of communication among the different systems of our being. This includes communication between the organic systems and the systems of values, roles, and perceptions. Frequently our behaviors are serving functions in systems quite remote (and unrecognized) from the more obvious system in which they are involved.

The intrinsic patterning of activity within each minute cell contributes throughout life to a consistency of rhythm and pattern underlying our total functioning. The molecular material in the cell, known as DNA, is an extensive storehouse of information.[5]

As previously indicated, any frequently repeated stimulation in the cells of the brain will lead to the development of a cell assembly, which then functions as a group having contact with other cell assemblies (see Example 5–1). As events stimulate a series of cell assemblies to activate each other, this phase sequence constitutes the "thought process." It is by sustained activation of groups of cell assemblies that an individual focuses attention.

---

[4] The Book of Hebrews refers to the fundamental form of the universe as expressed in the Creator's Word of Power. New American Standard Bible, Hebrews 1:3.

[5] DNA embodies in its structure a highly condensed molecular 'code' bearing all the information needed to design a living organism . . . The goal of biologists is to discover just how DNA instructs the cell to perform the thousands of chemical reactions needed to produce proteins in countless varieties, and ultimately specifies the construction of the whole organism. It seems probable that DNA even carries within it the recipe for all sorts of inborn patterns—all the complex things that insects, birds, and animals, including men, instinctively know how to do without being taught." *Fortune, Great American Scientists* (Englewood, N.J.: Prentice-Hall, 1961), pp. 92–93.

There are two main factors that insure consistency in the brain's activity at different times. One is the intrinsic organization[6] in the cells of the brain; the other is the steadily increasing influence of the individual's environment that adds new cell assemblies.

NEUTRAL PATTERNS.   There is a neural pattern operating at birth, and each new movement through a behavior involves a pattern of neural responses that become simultaneously more fixed (lower thresholds) and more extended (more interweaving). Each new experience I have interweaves some new associations in the circuitry. This learning seems to go on continuously without any consideration of "reward."

There is another kind of continuous learning. As an adult, my absorption of new experiences is not random or haphazard. Through the years my association with different experiences has given them certain pleasant or unpleasant values. Those events and situations that strengthen the concept I have of myself are pleasant—more specifically, the most pleasant and most valued experiences are those that cause the concept of me to be viewed as more nearly my ideal.

Self-Concept   My concept of an ideal self has been formed through the years by direct and indirect teaching. It is formed essentially of the compilation of attitudes and behaviors of persons who have been close to me. Because people close to me were of different ages and backgrounds and held different values, my own *ideal* system is unique. No one else is striving to become exactly the person I am striving to become. This is part of the conflict in each person's life. I want to be like those persons I value. I fear rejection and oblivion if I am different. And yet, I find that to be completely like one individual conflicts with those parts of me that have been formed out of experiences with other people important to me.

Fundamentally the imperative for growth is greater than the fear of being different. Therefore, most of us are able to place our highest values on developing toward an *ideal* self which—while maintaining the central core—is always changing slightly with new experiences.

[6] D. O. Hebb, *The Organization of Behavior* (New York: John Wiley, 1949), pp. 121–122. "The intrinsic organization of cortical activity is so called because it is opposed to the organization imposed on the cortex by sensory events . . . At birth the intrinsic organization is completely dominant; in psychological development its dominance decreases, but it continues to recur periodically, generally in a diurnal rhythm."

*From
Concepts to
Consciousness*

From the cell to the self there is a patterning of behavior. As the organism moves through time, some extensive networks become firmly established, and because of their prominence, they direct behavior. These reigning hierarchies (regnant processes)[7] come to serve as the center for the organization of personality. They are "self-consciousness" and provide the sense of identity that I know to be me. With self-consciousness comes personhood. At this point, we bring together the biological and the mental. Each of these areas has at different periods of scientific thought been relegated to a "nonexistent" status. It is encouraging to see both once again respected and united. In Example 5–2 note the comments of Roger W. Sperry, professor of psychobiology at California Institute of Technology, upon receiving the Passon Foundation award.

*From Persons
to Groups*

Our description having moved up in complexity to the level of social organisms, we look to the concepts of symbolic interaction theory to describe these relationships. We interact with others through the use of shared symbols. We come to share common symbols through projecting ourselves into the position of other people and "feeling" the activities and perceptions they experience. George H. Mead illustrated this by showing that we "play" baseball by putting ourselves in the place of each player who is involved when the ball is hit. Thus we learn the meanings of gestures and rules—the shared symbols.

Gestures become significant symbols when they implicitly arouse in us the same response they explicitly arouse in the person to whom they are addressed. When I throw the ball to first base, I feel the process that the first baseman will perform in catching the ball.[8]

In time, the reigning neural patterns, which are my sense of identity, come to be highly valued. "Valued," in operational terms, means that my homeostatic balance is disturbed when the environment introduces new or conflicting stimuli at a rate that the reigning pattern cannot assimilate.

---

[7] For a discussion of regnant processes, as used in this text, see Chapter 2 in H. A. Murray, *Explorations in Personality: A Clinical and Experimental Study of Fifty Men of College Age* (New York: Science Editions, 1938, 2nd printing, 1965).

[8] G. H. Mead commented, in *Mind, Self and Society* (Chicago: University of Chicago Press, 1934) that there are certain common responses each individual has toward certain common things. Insofar as those responses are awakened in the individual when he is affecting other persons, he arouses his own self. The structure, then, on which the self is built is this response common to all because one has to be a member of a community to be a self.

Example 5–2.
Consciousness:
Mind and Brain

One of the important things to come out from brain research in recent years is a greatly changed idea of the *conscious* mind and its relation to brain mechanism . . . Instead of dispensing with consciousness (as we have in the past) as just an "inner aspect" of the brain process or as some passive "epiphenomenon" or other impotent by-product, as has been the custom, our present interpretation would make the conscious mind an integral part of the brain process itself and an essential constituent of the action.

As a dynamic emergent property of cerebral excitation, subjective experience acquires causal potency and becomes a causal determinant in brain function. Although inseparably tied to the material brain process, it is something distinct and special in its own right, "different from and more than" its component physiochemical elements. This is seen in the power of the whole over its parts, in this case the power of high order cerebral processes over their constituent neurochemical components . . . Not only does the brain's physiology determine the mental effects, as has been generally agreed, but now, in addition the emergent mental processes are conceived to control the component neurophysiology through their higher organizational properties. Terms such as "mental imagery" and auditory images are no longer taboo.

The scheme provides a conceptual explanatory model for the interaction of mind with matter in terms that do not violate the principles of scientific exploration or those of modern neuroscience. After more than 50 years of strict behaviorist avoidance of such terms as mental imagery . . . in the past five years these terms have come into wide usage . . . Old metaphysical dualisms and the seemingly irreconcilable paradoxes that formerly prevailed between the realities of inner experience on the one hand and those of experimental brain science on the other have become reconciled today in a single comprehensive and unifying view of mind, brain and man in nature. Within the brain we pass conceptually in a single continuum from the brain's subnuclear particles on up (through atoms and molecules to cells and nerve-circuit systems without consciousness) to cerebral processes with consciousness.

Adapted from R. W. Sperry, "Left-Brain, Right-Brain," *Saturday Review* 2 (August 9, 1975), 20:30–33.

Our tendency to see food in ambiguous pictures when we are hungry illustrates the influence of a reigning pattern attempting to maintain its balance. It causes us to perceive stimuli in accord with our prevailing value systems and present need. We avoid seeing perceptions that threaten our usual patterns of operation.

In these last few paragraphs we have passed over aspects of self-processes

5–3 *Gestures become significant symbols when the response they evoke in the receiver is the same as that experienced by the sender. (Kansas State University Student Publications photo)*

about which much research and theory has been generated. We need to identify a few of these factors for background as we will encounter different activities associated with them in different developmental periods.

Learning Research and writing about self or psychological processes follows along certain topics that help us describe our behavior choices. These topics include learning, motivation, developmental tasks, defenses, identification, and self-actualization.

We were discussing learning when we mentioned the storing of experiences and the association of each new experience with past experiences. As we recognize the subsequent reaction from others or within ourselves to the presence of a given behavior or attitude, we build up connections and a tendency to repeat or avoid similar situations in the future (see Example 5–3).

Motivation What happens if I am confronted by a situation in which there are a number of behaviors possible? As I visualize the consequences of each behavior, I find

Example 5–3.
Learning

> Sign learning is the acquisition of "positive" (rewarding) and "negative" (punishing) feedback associated with stimuli that have accompanied an action or an experience. If a particular activity has resulted in satisfaction to me, then all the incidental stimuli, both internal and external, which have been associated with this rewarding act will be tied in with brain associations of a positive nature.
>
> In the future any of those cell assemblies when activated will also activate tangetially related positive assemblies with which they have now become associated. Thus they will have the capacity to guide me to repeat that activity. For punishing activity the same process of establishing connection, this time associating cell assemblies with unpleasant effect, creates the tendency for me to avoid those activities in the future. My behavior, at any given time, is my "self's" best effort to find the line of action with the greatest likelihood of being satisfying.
>
> Abstract from O. H. Mowrer, *Kentucky Symposium: Learning Theory and Clinical Research* (New York: Wiley, 1954).

each has some positive and some negative consequences. The sorting of these alternatives is guided by some criteria that we assume to be built into the Western way of responding. Either they are intuitive or were learned early in life. A. H. Maslow refers to these as "needs." The assumption is that self-preservation is the underlying motivation of all behavior, and a series of other motives have been identified in a hierarchy of importance for the preservation of the individual (see Example 5–4). Until the basic survival fac-

Example 5–4.
Maslow's
Hierarchy of
Needs

> 1. Physiological needs
> 2. Safety needs
> 3. Love and belonging needs
> 4. Self-esteem needs
> 5. Need for self-actualization
> 6. Desire to know and understand
>
> From A. H. Maslow, *Motivation and Personality* (New York: Harper & Row, 1970).

tors (food, shelter, safety) are satisfied at least at a minimal level, I cannot entertain other kinds of behavior choices. Once the basic physical needs are met, I can work to secure satisfactions in other areas, each somewhat less vital than survival. As I move up the need hierarchy, the expression of my individuality becomes more interlaced with other needs so that self-preservation becomes increasingly associated with behavior choices that contribute to the development of my personal identity.

Growth of Self

Patterns of Growth

As behavior becomes more complex so that preservation of identity influences the majority of our behavior choices, another principle of growth helps to direct our activity. This is the principle of developmental stages and readiness for growth. As I move through the adult years, two types of input will form the pattern of attitudes, values, and feelings constituting self. One input will be information from my social interaction and observation of the behaviors expected of persons of certain ages and in certain situations. The other input comes from awareness of physiological and deeper emotional changes within me.

DEVELOPMENTAL TASKS.   The input leads to a series of interrelated, interdependent learnings called developmental tasks, which are types of learning and development that all individuals within a given society encounter as they progress through life. I need to accomplish the tasks of an earlier stage before I can handle effectively the learning of the next stage—that is, I must be comfortable with the skills and attitudes of young adulthood before I can take up the tasks of middle adult years. I may move into middle years in some areas of life and still be working on the tasks of achieving intimacy characteristics of young adulthood. An outline for the young adult period such as Havighurst's, presented in Example 5–5, is helpful for thinking about my unique experience and development associated with each maturity level. We will consider it and suggested developmental tasks for other adult stages in later chapters.

DEVELOPMENTAL STAGES.   Another related approach to looking at development is Erikson's developmental stages described in Example 5–6. Each stage has special ego qualities that emerge from critical periods of development, and each is a further step in the maturity of the interrelated attitudes, feelings, and intuitions of ego or self. Erikson's stages refer to basic orientations associated with skills and social interaction, whereas Havighurst's tasks refer more to specific competences.

Erikson's stages represent challenges, each rising as a special opportunity

Example 5–5.
Havighurst's
Developmental
Tasks of Early
Adulthood

1. Selecting a mate
2. Learning to live with a marriage partner
3. Starting a family
4. Rearing children
5. Managing a home
6. Getting started in an occupation
7. Taking on civic responsibilities
8. Finding a congenial social group

From R. J. Havighurst, *Human Development and Education* (New York: Longmans, Green, 1957).

for growth at a particular period in development. Each stage prepares the adult for growth toward the next stage. Erikson has described the stage as a time when the individual has a general preoccupation with developing a characteristic attitude and way or relating, as developing a "sense of." For example, the young adult is usually completing the task of developing an organization of the self (an ego state) that has a sense of identity versus role confusion and is beginning to work on skills and attitudes to gain a sense of intimacy versus isolation. Although a particular issue is a central focus at a designated stage, that issue is also one of the dimensions of personality at all periods of life. Thus Erikson's eight stages may also be seen as presenting a picture of eight dimensions in the self, with each having its greatest growth in a designated stage of life.

DEFENSE MECHANISMS.   Although all my experiences have input with my self, some are in conflict. They threaten the preservation of my ideal; they

Example 5–6.
Eight Stages
of Self-
Development

1. Infancy—TRUST versus MISTRUST
2. Early Childhood—AUTONOMY versus SHAME AND DOUBT
3. Play age—INITIATIVE versus GUILT
4. School age—INDUSTRY versus INFERIORITY
5. Adolescence—IDENTITY versus ROLE CONFUSION
6. Young adult—INTIMACY versus ISOLATION
7. Middle adult—GENERATIVITY versus STAGNATION
8. Maturity—INTEGRITY versus DISGUST AND DESPAIR

From E. H. Erikson, *Childhood and Society* (New York: Norton, 1950), Chapter 7.

predict unpleasant future experiences. It is possible for the awareness mechanisms of the self to choose not to bring these to consciousness. The self may also through this selective process organize distorted pictures of the world and my interaction with it. This is termed defenses; the distortion is attempting to "defend" my present self. All growth causes some threat to the self because it involves a change.

As I move through adult life, I take up new roles, develop new skills, establish new relationships, and experience new conditions in my body and in the deeper psychological regions of my being. The composite at any one time is my perceived identity. The more uncertain I am about my relationship with others and the more of my contradictory experiences I keep repressed in my unconscious, the more I need to maintain a fixed and definite identity. We all fluctuate, being more rigid and defensive at certain times than others. When the social pattern for my particular stage is unclear or when my relationships with close friends is strained, then my external support system is weak and I am more likely to be arbitrary and absolute and perfectionistic in the organization of my self.

As I come to have confidence in my ability to survive in new and changing circumstances, I will become more open in the organization of the feelings, ideas, and commitments that are my self. I will be better able to tolerate contradictions and be in touch with the deeper regions of my being. I will be freer to risk my self in making choices that are more clearly expressions of the unique organizations of experience and abilities that is "me." As I am thus freer to risk failure, I become freer to succeed and to move more toward behaviors that are fuller expressions of self. I will be able to respond to an inner urge for competence.[9]

We tend to reduce our anxieties by highlighting the positive aspects and ignoring the negative in situations that we cannot change. For example, elderly persons were found to be much more critical of their housing situation when they had opportunities to move to better accommodations.[10]

Self-Actualization   In the formation of self, and throughout life in the maintenance and growth of self, it is crucial that the individual have the sustaining relationship of knowing that he is being deeply understood and accepted by at least a few

---

[9] R. W. White, "Motivation Reconsidered: The Concept of Competence," *Psychological Review* 66 (1959), pp. 297–333.

[10] F. M. Carp, "Ego-Defense or Cognitive Consistency Effects on Environmental Evaluations," *Journal of Gerontology* 30 (November 1975), 11:707–711.

other people. Carl Rogers summarizes this well with the following statement.

> A finely tuned understanding by another individual gives the recipient his personhood, his identity. Laing has said that "the sense of identity requires the existence of one other person by whom one is known." Buber has also spoken of the need to have our existence confirmed by another. Empathy gives the needed confirmation that one does exist as a separate, valued person with an identity.[11]

The existence of a certain amount of experience that the individual cannot accommodate in the reigning patterning, or self-concept, results in tensions that I attempt to resolve by various defense mechanisms. Such unassimilated experiences also account for the guilt anxieties I experience.

TENSION AND GROWTH.   In the secure, psychologically adequate person, the various aspects of the personality work together harmoniously. Such a person may be under considerable physical stress. For example, he may be hungry, in danger, or in pain, but as long as the various parts of the personality are functioning in an organized, unitary way, the individual will experience no great psychological stress. If, however, the circumstances are such

5–4 *Understanding from another gives the recipient his personhood.* (Manhattan Mercury *photo*)

---

[11] C. R. Rogers, "Empathic: An Unappreciated Way of Being," *The Counseling Psychologist* 5 (1975), 2:7.

that the parts are thrown into conflict so that the unified functioning is threatened, then the individual will experience normal anxiety.[12] It is normal because the individual can identify the origin of his distress. The individual in such cases makes decisions and undertakes action that will bring the "parted selves" back into harmonious operation. Normal anxiety is necessary for the development of the individual.

TOO MUCH TENSION.   Anxiety is an experience of tension that results from perceived threats to one's security. The infant develops (through an empathic relationship with his mother) a sense of security and also a sense of anxiety that is experienced by the mother. This early anxiety is the beginning of the defense system of the adult. The infant learns to identify anxiety with certain phenomena and adopts ways of behaving that will help him to avoid or prepare for these threatening phenomena. This repertoire of responses (or defense system) stands between the person and his environment. Early emotional associations of accompanying responses formed around significant individuals tend to be personified and to determine our responses to new individuals in remotely similar situations. Thus an adult man may respond to employers or other status figures in the same way he responded to his father.[13]

When conflict is so severe that resulting anxiety cannot be handled by ordinary modes of responses, the process of dissociation takes over. One part of the conflict situation is repressed—its demands are denied consciousness. The immediate relief coming from this denial puts together a positive value with a neurotic procedure. This sometimes leads to a continuing condition of neurotic anxiety, depending on the strength of the individual's personal identity and the strength of the material repressed. Mowrer says that the experience excluded from consciousness retains much of its energy.

> As the combined force of the dissociated elements begins to approximate that of the remaining parts of the personality, there is growing danger of counterattack by the banished elements . . . Depression, inferiority feelings, obsessive doubting, loss of sexual responsiveness, psychosomatic disturbances, and related experiences are the ways in which the dissociated forces attack,

---

[12] O. H. Mowrer, *Psychotherapy: Theory and Research* (New York: Ronald Press, 1953). See Chapter 3 for Mowrer's outline of steps in normal development.

[13] There are some individuals whose socialization has caused them to want to avoid introspection that would help them recognize these motivations. A classic study describing this is T. W. Adorno, E. Frenkel-Brunswik, D. J. Levinson, and R. N. Sanford, *The Authoritarian Personality* (New York: Harper & Row, 1950); see also E. Hoffer, *The True Believer* (New York: Mentor Books, 1951).

punish, harry, and try to contact and communicate with the conscious self, and when these forces attack with special fury, the individual experiences *neurotic anxiety,* i.e., anxiety which, because it occurs out of context, without warning or explanation, is perceived as meaningless, mysterious, and malevolent.[14]

Empathy For the adult to take the risks that result in growth, there must be present in his life some elements that assure him that he (his self or person) is known and valued regardless of his success or failure. Love and a particular aspect of it, empathy (see Example 5–7), are necessary in the lives of most persons

Example 5–7.

Empathy Means:
1. Entering into the private perceptual world of the other person.
2. Being sensitive moment by moment to the changing felt-meanings which flow in the other person.
3. Temporarily living in the other person's life, not making judgments, sensing meanings of which he/she may be scarcely aware but not trying to uncover feelings of which the person is totally unaware, since this would be too threatening.
4. Communicating my sensing of his/her world as I look with fresh eyes at elements of which the other person is fearful.
5. Frequently checking with the other person the accuracy of my sensing and being guided by his/her responses.
6. Being a confident companion of the other person in his inner world.
7. Pointing to the possible meanings in the flow of his experiencings, I help the other person focus on this useful type of referent, to experience the meaning more fully, and to move forward in experiencing.

From C. R. Rogers, "Empathic: An Unappreciated Way of Being," *The Counseling Psychologist* 5 (1975), 2:2–10.

who successfully accomplish the risk-taking steps of creative growth throughout the adult years.

Whereas many factors may contribute to the social isolation of men living on skid row, significant among them is the fact that most of the men have no contact with family, employment, or friends.[15]

[14] Mowrer, *Psychotherapy: Theory and Research,* p. 77.

[15] J. F. Rooney, "Friendship and Disaffiliation Among the Skid Row Population," *Journal of Gerontology* 31 (January 1976), 1:82–88.

a.

b.

5–5 *To know that another knows us helps us to keep in touch with our own self; to feel alone and unknown causes us to lose our bearings.* (a, Kansas State University Student Publications *photo; b,* Manhattan Mercury *photo*)

Each of us needs to know that someone else understands what we are experiencing. This we encounter through empathy. To know that another person knows us helps us to keep in touch with our own self; to feel alone and unknown causes us to lose our bearings, to distort and misread our awarenesses. "At all times there is going on in the human organism a flow of experiencings to which the individual can turn again and again as a referent in order to discover the meaning of experience."[16] Gendlin suggests that this ongoing psychophysiological flow is the authenticating and most intimate phenomenon of human existence. Self-awareness and self-concept derive from this flow.

How the Self Changes

Change is generally associated with growth, with further expression of potential, with developing new skills or relationships. Where change is toward constriction, it will be seen somewhat in the same light. In each instance the individual changes toward behavior and attitudes that will enable him to satisfy the tension within. When an individual is overwhelmed with fears and self-doubt, relief comes through retreating. For example, one may hesitate to apply for a transfer to a job that is a promotion. When an individual feels valued and accepts himself, the imperative is to reach out, to extend oneself.

Clarity in one's identity and establishing congruence between values and life-style are factors influencing positive change. For example, it has been found that older persons who reminisce frequently have higher scores on measures of ego integrity.[17] The lack of clarity in role criteria or lack of a feeling of being valued may contribute to vacillation and lack of authenticity in choice making.

A quotation from a study of young adults illustrates the importance for each of us to have occasions periodically to review the meaning of our past experiences in light of new challenges and opportunities.

> In all young men and women the advent of adulthood releases immense new energies and potentials, which in most are centrally involved in establishing new intimacies with the opposite sex. This new learning is seldom smooth; but

---

[16] E. T. Gendlin, *Experiencing and the Creation of Meaning* (New York: Free Press of Glencoe, 1962), p. 195.

[17] W. Boylin, S. K. Gordon, and M. F. Nehrke, "Reminiscing and Ego Integrity in Institutionalized Elderly Males," *The Gerontologist* 16 (April 1976), 2:118–124.

when it is severely blocked by unresolved needs and frustrations from the past, it takes but a slight catalyst—and often no catalyst at all—to transform these energies into rage, scorn, and aggression, often symbolically directed against those who have stood in the way of full adulthood.[18]

We often find the opportunity for such review through helping relationships with a spouse, friend, relative, or professional counselor. Such helping relationships are an important and normal part of self-growth. Sometimes earlier life experiences have created significant obstacles to self-growth that require opportunities for relearning.

Counseling is Relearning

Theorists of psychotherapy point out that some people come out of childhood with an impairment of mental life and an inhibition of power to act in critical life areas. In their early years, neurotic persons have been frightened out of their capacity to think, love, and work at a high level.

Because new habits can be learned only under new conditions, a new

[18] K. Keniston, *The Uncommitted: Alienated Youth in American Society* (New York: Harcourt Brace Jovanovich, 1965), p. 53.

5–6 *A young mother seeks help from an older relative in sorting through events in her life. (Kathleen Ward, photographer)*

learning situation must be created. This is the goal of psychotherapy.[19] In therapy the individual fearfully recites his thoughts and intentions and awaits the thunderclap of disapproval he has learned to expect. When it does not come in the course of repeated trials, his fear is extinguished, and once frightening sentences lose their power to create alarm. As fear is reduced, new thoughts can occur, especially those that formerly have been opposed by anxiety. The individual begins to learn new habits by verbally trying them out; but effective learning or effective therapy requires that these new habits be experienced in relation to people. The first occasion for this is the recognition that therapy is a social encounter.

RECOGNIZING OUR IMAGES.   Karen Horney[20] indicated that instead of developing a basic confidence in self and others, the neurotic develops in childhood a basic anxiety—a feeling of being isolated and helpless in a world potentially hostile. In order to keep this basic anxiety at a minimum, there is a change in his spontaneous moves toward others. He tries to solve his conflict by making one of these moves consistently predominant and becomes compulsively compliant, aggressive, or aloof. In time the neurotic begins to fulfill some of his needs by daydreaming that he is a particular kind of person. The "idealized self," often quite different from the real self, in time becomes the ruling figure in the person's life. He acts, or attempts to act, as though he really were his "idealized self," and he is hurt and angry when others do not treat him in that fashion. He also comes to hate his real self. The consistent conflict between the real and the ideal self results in excessive compulsions and "shoulds" that the individual develops to rule his life.

IDEAL AND REAL BECOME CLOSER.   Studies of group and individual counseling[21] suggest that growth in individuals may reflect an increased consistency between the way an individual sees himself and the way he would like to be. Among clients where counseling has been termed successful, the individuals were freer to talk about themselves and freer to accept, respond to, and plan for their immediate activities in contrast to talking about the past or a vague future. Clients judged successful by the therapist also showed increasing use of the relationship with the counselor as a person. When the

[19] J. Dollard and N. E. Miller, *Personality and Psychotherapy* (New York: McGraw-Hill, 1950).

[20] K. Horney, *Our Inner Conflicts: A Constructive Theory of Neurosis* (New York: Norton, 1945).

[21] L. J. Braaton, "The Movement from Non-Self to Self in Psychotherapy," *Journal of Counseling Psychology* 8 (1961), 1.

client feels free enough to view the relationship to the therapist as a source of new experience, change seems to be forthcoming.

As we move through the developmental stages of adult life, we will experience transition periods involving crucial life reviews (see Example 5–8). In

Example 5–8.
New Beliefs
About Oneself

Childhood delivers most people into adulthood with a view of adults that few could ever live up to. A child's idealized image of an adult can become the adult's painful measure of himself. Without an active, thoughtful confrontation of this image, the impressions of childhood will prevail. An adult who doesn't undertake this thinking and confrontation lives out his or her life controlled by the impossible attempt to satisfy the magical expectations of a child's world.

The process of change means coming to new beliefs about oneself and the world. Habitually unorganized beliefs are more felt than thought, yet these beliefs must be thought about before they can be modified by experiences.

While children mark the passing years by their changing bodies, adults change their minds . . . Increasing age also brings changes in biological functioning, changes in the ages of one's parents and children, and changes in the cultural expectations about what a person should be doing . . .

I believe that it is through the constant examination and reformulation of beliefs embedded in feelings that people substitute their own conception of adulthood for their childhood legacy.

From R. Gould, "Adult Life Stages: Growth Toward Self-Tolerance," *Psychology Today* 8 (February 1975), 1:78.

these reviews we examine our own feelings and perceptions in light of the feedback and views of life shared with us by others[22] in helping relationships. Thus we relate our life choices to the identity that continues to build consistently through time.

How the Self Is Maintained and Expressed

There is a gyroscopic momentum[23] that keeps the self returning to its own unique course. In early life the sequences of movement are mostly unrelated.

[22] P. Tournier, *The Meaning of Persons* (New York: Harper & Row, 1957).
[23] Murray, *Explorations of Personality*.

Trends are not persistent and discoordination is the rule. Opposing drives and attitudes succeed each other without apparent friction. With age comes conflict, and after conflict, resolution; there is synthesis and creative integration; action patterns are coordinated; enduring purposes arise and values are made to harmonize. It is in defense or support of these various attitudes, self-concepts, and values that much of human behavior occurs. Prescott Lecky proposed that self-consistency is the integrating process for the mentally healthy person.[24]

Self-Consistency

Throughout life we strive to maintain the self that was begun early in life and that continues to be the central guiding force in all our choices. Each new experience modified only slightly the person we know ourselves to be. We continue to grow in each stage of life to be a more complex and mature version of our younger self.

An illustration of self-consistency may be seen in a study that attempted to learn how well developed the self-concept is at the time students seek entry to medical school.[25] The investigators wanted to know what happens to this concept when the individual encounters obstacles to its implementation. Is there a general identification with the field of medicine so that the individual continues to seek means of self-expression in that area? Over 300 students who had been rejected in their application to medical school at the University of Minnesota were sent a questionnaire follow-up after a period of four years. It was found that nearly two thirds of the rejected students were in medical or related occupations.

The drive for self-expression is not partitioned according to years. In Example 5–9, Santiago, Hemingway's hero in *The Old Man and the Sea,* captures spiritual victory from circumstances of disaster and material defeat.

Self-Concept Through the Life-span

There is generally a progression in the positive nature of the self-concept through the life-span. The late-adolescent/young-adult individual generally describes himself as insecure and discontented; the older young adult expresses confidence, energy, and spontaneous activity; the middle adult, while maintaining this confidence, reflects a more controlled and orderly sense of

[24] P. Lecky, *Self Consistency* (New York: Island Press, 1945).

[25] R. R. Stephenson, "Occupational Choice as a Crystalized Self Concept," *Journal of Counseling Psychology* 8 (1961), 3.

Example 5–9.
The Old Man
and the Sea

> Santiago, the old experienced fisherman, had gone for eighty-four days without catching a single fish. Still buoyed by the pride of his calling, though now destitute, he ventured on the eighty-fifth day too far out into the Gulf; but he caught the largest marlin ever seen in those waters. And then the battle began. After several days, using all his wiles and physically exhausted he gained the victory over the marlin. When he lashed him to the side of the skiff, the marlin extended beyond the length of his boat. Triumphant but physically worn out, the old man started the long journey to the mainland and discovered that the distance had put him at the mercy of the sharks. They stripped the marlin carcass clean. His fortune gone before it was gained, he slept round the clock in his shack dreaming of future conquests, while the townspeople marveled at the size of the fish Santiago had won and lost.
>
> Abstract from E. Hemingway, *The Old Man and the Sea* (New York: Scribner, 1952).

power. The mature person of later middle life expresses the most satisfaction with self. The older adult expresses confidence but less competitiveness; he generally is more oriented toward interpersonal relationships.[26]

DREAMS AND LIFE PLANNING.   We form dreams[27] early in life—projections of our future selves. These dreams often are unrecognized in our conscious planning, but we continue to be restless and unsatisfied until we begin to move toward their fulfillment. We can illustrate this in terms of vocational development. Often we project our personal identity in terms of careers or in terms of the style of life that will come as the result of benefits from our work. Vocational choice is not a single event in some one moment of life, rather, vocational development is part of the ongoing processes of self-development.[28] The self utilizes the opportunities and resources of the environment to express the potential the individual feels within. We continue to express creativity and imagination as we see the present moment with the eyes of future goals. The soliloquy of Lorene in the novel *From Here to Eternity* illustrates this point.

> Lorene was a girl of single ambition—to marry a man with social prestige. To do this she found she must herself have wealth, prestige, and position. In

[26] M. F. Lowenthal, M. T. Thurnher, and D. Chiriboga *Four Stages of Life* (San Francisco: Jossey-Bass, 1975).

[27] C. Jung, *The Undiscovered Self* (New York: Mentor Books, 1959).

[28] D. E. Super, *Psychology of Careers* (New York: Harper & Row, 1957).

her reasoning, it all came back to money. To gain the money necessary for her plan she became a prostitute serving the military forces in Hawaii. She once told a customer, "After I go home with a stocking full of bills, after I build the new home for my mother and myself, after I join the Country Club and take up golf . . . then the proper man with the proper position will find me as a proper wife who can keep a proper home and raise the proper children." Two years later a woman meeting Lorene en route to the States and observing her excellent poise, modest carriage, and exquisite dress, commented to a friend that the girl had the face of a Madonna.[29]

As we proceed through adulthood and into old age, the developmental stages continue: the physiological, the social, and the psychological. Our bodies continue to change, bringing differing degrees of effectiveness and society ascribes different statuses and expectations to us. These influence how we perceive ourselves and how we integrate the match between our effectiveness and the expectations society has created for us in our different roles. It is this ongoing awareness—the evaluative, willing, and integrative activity—that we have considered self-processes.

In the following chapter we will consider ways in which the self responds to other, wider dimensions than the perceptual framework created by a particular culture. We will consider the transpersonal processes in adult development.

Summary[30]

Self is anchored in the biological mechanisms of thinking and perceiving; it is shaped by the social content received from its environment. It provides the continuing awareness, the entity with which others interact. It assumes responsibility, experiences hope, and projects future, even as it is built upon the accumulation of past awareness.

Self is an emergent process. From infancy until death we are differentiating among stimuli, forming meaning patterns, and modifying these patterns as a result of new experiences.

Self is unique. Each of us has a different endowment with which we begin. We therefore experience a slightly different world from anyone else, and the

---

[29] J. Jones, *From Here to Eternity* (New York: Signet Books, 1953).

[30] Various ideas for this chapter and its summary were suggested by the chapters on self in H. V. Perkins, *Human Development* (Belmont, Calif: Wadsworth, 1975), pp. 231–297.

meanings we deduce from our experiences are different from anyone else's. We value and we fear this uniqueness.

Self is organization. The pattern of meanings derived from experience provides the basis for continuity and change. The self directs action toward maintaining the pattern of its identity, the composite formed of past experiences. Situations challenging the pattern create tension, and behavior that reduces the challenges reduces tension.

Self-process is dynamic. Whereas maintaining organization, the self adjusts to new aspects in growth and experience so that these become congruent with the self.

There are different levels of consciousness within the self. Much of the activity involves conscious awareness (such as self-concept). Operating below conscious level are also patterns of meaning that influence behavior and provide an existential basis for persons.

Self is an inferred process. Subjectively, I am aware of meanings and patterns of thought and behavior that I experience in relation to the life about me. This awareness is not visible and can only be measured by inference, using external instruments created of hypotheses about the character of self.

More than the sum of its parts, self touches dimensions of experiences beyond self and person and points to the transpersonal and spiritual aspects of life.

Suggested Activities and Further Reading

1. Think about the different concepts you have of yourself. Are you aware of variations between the self that your family, your friends, and your instructor recognize you to be?

2. Find illustrations from fiction or real life of individuals in stages 5, 6, 7, and 8 of Erikson's stages of self-development.

3. What makes you feel free? What types of conditions cause you to be tense? Describe a situation where you have "frozen" on an examination or have become immobilized or less effective as a result of threat.

4. Which one is lonelier, the student or the retired person? A study at the University of Nebraska found that students are lonelier. See J. C. Woodward and M. J. Visser, "Loneliness: When and Whom Does It Touch?" *Quarterly Serving Farm, Ranch and Home* (Lincoln: University of Nebraska, Fall 1972).

   Have a panel discuss the topic of aloneness. Consider whether anyone can really know what another person is experiencing. What aspects of our society faciliate community and what fosters separateness? What factors influence loneliness in different groups—young adults, young marrieds, divorced, widowed, retired?

5. Prepare a reaction paper after reading one of the following books:

E. Fromm, *The Art of Loving* (New York: Harper & Row, 1956);

S. Jourard, *The Transparent Self* (New York: Van Nostrand, 1964);

C. Moustakas, *Loneliness* (Englewood Cliffs, N.J.: Prentice-Hall, 1961);

J. Powell, *"Why Am I Afraid to Tell You Who I Am?"* (Niles, Ohio: Argus Communications, 1969).

6. Discuss Keniston's view of the self-processes of commitment and alienation as he describes development of young adulthood in two different periods of history in *The Uncommitted* and *Young Radicals*.

7. Compare the views of self-development reflected by the following writers:

Simone de Beauvoir, *Coming of Age* and *All Said and Done;*

Paul Tournier, *The Meaning of Persons* and *Learning to Grow Old;*

Albert Camus, *The Plague;*

Martin Buber, *I and Thou;*

F. M. Dostoevski, *Letters from the Underground.*

8. Relate the ideas of "transactional analysis," "behavior modification," and "encounter groups" to your understanding of self-processes.

chapter 6

Transpersonal Processes

As adults move through the stages of young, middle, and older life, their development is influenced by changes occurring within them and by changes in the social world about them. The resources adults use to assist them in achieving new orientations and new capacities for coping reflect the expectations of their society. There is a social construction of reality that the student of adult development must take into account if he is to understand the developmental experiences of adults of a given historical period.

Social Reality for the 1980s
Aging must be examined in the context of the events in the lives of individuals and the meaning these events give to the lives of the people studied. Traditional meanings for some events may be changed if the context in which the events are experienced changes significantly. Time has a different meaning for older and younger persons, for persons in time of stress (Example 6–1) and in time of tranquillity. Competence and autonomy mean different things according to the amount of control an individual perceives to be available. Biofeedback has expanded the possible range of the adult's control of his physiological processes. The fallout from new theories of physics and the resurgence of mediation and mystical activity have extended the boundaries of time and space for today's adults. Studies of death and programs of death education have challenged taboos on that subject, with science adding a further dimension to the legends of the man in the street. Example 6–2 gives excerpts from an in-interview with a leading investigator that appeared in a popular magazine.

6-1 *Today's adults are caught between two alternative views of life: rationalistic and romantic. (Kansas State University Student Publications photo)*

Life review is an important aspect of adult development, especially in later years. Today adults of all ages are participating through various groups and resources in studies of consciousness. They are reliving earlier experiences and projecting their futures with new meaning through various modes of transcendence. Although we cannot discuss in detail the different aspects of the varied changes, it is important to remind ourselves of some of the kinds of social changes surrounding the adults we are studying.

As we consider what it is like to be an adult in the last quarter of the twentieth century, one of our observations must be that there is a great shaking of our philosophical foundations. Older adults grew up with the philosophy of rationalism and scientistic idealism of the 1920s. Middle adults had the beginning of American existentialism in the 1940s during their formative years. Younger adults went through school in the 1960s learning that "God is dead." Today they find themselves confronted with a new world view that some are adopting and about which many are puzzling. An editor of *Psychology Today* described today's adults as caught between two alternative visions: rationalistic and romantic (Example 6–3).

To be an adult in the last quarter of the twentieth century means that many of us will have to find ways of communicating with our children or grandchildren who report finding significant meaning in mystical experi-

Example 6–1.
Sudden Danger
Alters
Consciousness

Human beings facing sudden life-threatening danger experience remarkable alterations of consciousness. If death appears to be imminent, certain subjective phenomena are almost universal. Outer events take place in extremely slow motion, but internal processes are speeded up.

The old saying, "My whole life flashed before me," seems to be a literal description of the typical near-death experience.

Russell Noyes and Roy Kletti of the University of Iowa College of Medicine studied 114 such cases, including falls, near-drownings, automobile accidents, cardiac arrests, battlefield explosions and allergic shock.

The experiences in the Iowa study were characterized by a curious sense of detachment. A feeling of unreality was coupled, paradoxically, with heightened vision or hearing. More than half said they felt no emotion at all, not even fear.

Subjective phenomena included revival of memories (47 per cent), enhanced understanding (43 per cent), colors or visions (41 per cent), sense of harmony or unity (39 per cent). Out-of-body-experiences, voices, music, vivid mental images and a sense of being controlled by an external force were commonly reported.

The time-distortion aspect was described by a 21-year-old college senior who swerved to miss an oncoming car, lost control and saw a bridge abutment looming ahead. She experienced a calm, dreamlike state "at peace with everything. Then I saw an endless stream of past experiences—there must have been hundreds—go through my mind . . . They were all pleasant. During all of this, time stood still."

Typically, the flashing memories are chronological, beginning with early childhood, and include some events that the individual does not consciously remember but accepts as probably true.

Noyes and Kletti emphasized that the depersonalization felt by these individuals differs in important respects from that described in pathology. "It seems to have represented a normal reaction to suddenly presented, life-threatening danger," they said.

From *Brain/Mind Bulletin* 1 (May 3, 1976), 12:3; see also R. Noyes and R. Kletti, *Psychiatry* 39 (February 1976), 1:19–27.

ences. It means taking into account that what we once thought to be beyond our control—such as heart rate, temperature, brain waves—can be directed at will through scientific, and increasingly popular techniques of biofeedback and other forms of voluntary control of involuntary processes.

Example 6–2.
Dr. Kubler-Ross
Shares Reports
from Beyond
Death

Q. Do you think there is life after death?
A. I have always felt something significant happens a minute or so after "clinical" death. Most of my patients got fantastically peaceful expressions, even those who had struggled terribly with death.

Q. What would you describe as your first positive evidence?
A. About seven years ago, a patient who had been declared dead despite heroic last-minute resuscitation efforts spontaneously came alive 3½ hours later. She shared with me how she felt she had floated out of her physical body and watched herself being worked on. She described in minute detail the resuscitation team—who was there, who wanted to give up, who wanted to continue, who told a joke to relieve the tension. This gave me my first clue.
   Since then I have investigated scores of clear-cut cases from all over the world, both religious and nonreligious people. One had been "dead" 12½ hours. All had the same basic experience.

Q. How did these people describe the experience of dying?
A. They virtually shed their physical bodies, as a butterfly comes out of a cocoon. They describe a feeling of peace, no pain, no anxiety. And they were perfect—completely whole. A young man whose leg was cut off in an automobile accident floated above the crash scene and observed the rescue effort. They were so content that they resented, sometimes bitterly, the attempts to bring them back to life because they were returning to a dreadful existence—cancerous bodies, amputated limbs. Not one of them was afraid to die again.

From E. Kubler-Ross, "When Face to Face with Death," *Reader's Digest* 109 (August 1976), 652:81–84.

Growth
Groups

Adults of all ages are being exposed to new ways of relating to their inner beings, their environment, the present, and to their past as part of the present (Examples 6–4 and 6–5). Growth groups encourage creativity through guided imagery or offer increased opportunities to grow through mystical journeys into their past for the healing of memories (Example 6–6).

Some adults see their imaginations as participants in groups teaching assertive training. Others obtain relief from severe migraine headaches by using their imaginations to visualize scenes of tranquillity, warmth, or

Example 6–3.
An Alternative
World View

We are caught between two alternative visions, two competing world views . . . Both of the alternative visions have defenders and advocates within the psychological and healing professions. A number of psychologists have followed the new star and are proclaiming the emergence of a "fourth force in psychology." (The first three: psychoanalysis, behaviorism, humanistic psychology.) They call the fourth force transpersonal psychology and they now have a journal and an association with regular meetings. Therefore legitimacy.

As a self-conscious movement, transpersonal psychology began with the heretical wonderings of Abraham Maslow. Abe began to talk about *metaneeds,* B. values, and peak experiences, and when he turned around he found to his surprise that a whole tribe had followed him out of the desert of Freudian reductionism and push-pull-click-click behaviorism into the lush wilderness of humanism. Humanistic psychology was born, and with it a new ideal of self-actualization.

But Maslow soon found that the self that was actualized could still be isolated in an alien world. Man longs to transcend his aloneness and belong to the cosmos. Even when he has fulfilled every secular need, the hunger for transcendence is not satiated. So it was a short step from actualization to transcendence, from peak experiences to God. Abe didn't say out loud that psychology was once again flirting with theology. But, like William James and Carl Jung before him, he was struck by the idea that normality and the one-dimensional consciousness of secular society were adequate ideals only for those unimaginative persons who sought a minimal adjustment to the savage glory of the human condition. By 1969 Maslow had joined Anthony Sutich to create an association and journal of transpersonal psychology.

From S. Keen, "The Cosmic Versus the Rational," *Psychology Today* 8 (July 1974), 2:56.

coolness in biofeedback sessions. They are learning to regulate the temperature in their hands and their muscle tension.

Some persons report experiences in which they have left their bodies.[1] And an anthropologist[2] produced a series of best-selling books describing how he was trained by a Mexican sorcerer to enter other realms of being (Example 6–7).

[1] R. Monroe, *Journeys Out of the Body* (Garden City, N.Y.: Doubleday, 1971).

[2] C. Castaneda, *The Teachings of Don Juan: A Yaqui Way of Knowledge* (New York: Ballantine Books, 1969); *A Separate Reality* (New York: Simon and Schuster, 1971); *Journey to Ixtlan* (New York: Simon Schuster, 1972); *Tales of Power* (New York: Simon and Schuster, 1974).

Realms of Consciousness

To understand the experiences of adults in today's world inevitably involves a consideration of various realms of consciousness. In addition to the alteration of states of consciousness through sleep, dreams, and waking, there are the alterations from alcohol, drugs (prescription and nonprescription), hypnotism, religious activities, and various physiological and psychic processes.

We will introduce here briefly some of the states of consciousness that occupy important segments of the life of many adults. Each will bear further study depending upon the reader's interest and area of professional service.

When we consider consciousness, we are thinking not only of the problem-solving processes of our experience, we are considering also our awareness of ourselves as we participate in the action. Thus there is a "self"-conscious aspect to our experience. There are times, also, when we are aware of aspects that seem to involve ways of knowing that do not rely on words or conventional thought processes. Sometimes we refer to these awarenesses as intuitive.

Sometimes we experience a special relatedness with the elements around

6–2 *Growth groups encourage creativity through guided imagery or offer increased opportunities to grow through mystical journeys into the past for the healing of memories.* (Manhattan Mercury *photo*)

Example 6–4.
Conference
Program on
Exploration
into the Forces
of Life

LIFE MAPS

An overview and introduction of the conference will explore the developmental tasks of the various stages of life.

TRANSFORMATION AND HUMAN CONSCIOUSNESS

An exploration into the role of transformation and consciousness will compare drug and non-drug techniques for inducing unusual states of being and discuss the relevance of such states for group stability, creativity, and psychological well-being. The focus will be on the character and function of trance and possession states induced by non-drug techniques, and those states which occur as a result of using psychedelic substances.

THE EXPERIENCE OF BIRTH

As a new life is forming in the womb a new relationship is evolving for the parents. If we avail ourselves to the particular sensitivity, so much a part of this stage of the life-cycle, we can use it to transcend outmoded ways of relating.

TRANSFORMATION, INITIATION, AND VISIONARY STATES

An exploration into the nature of human consciousness in which the relationship between initiation rites such as puberty, marriage, aging, death, initiation into secret or sacred societies and healing rituals; mystical experiences; and the phenomenology of psychedelic states will be examined.

TRANSFORMATION AND THE EXPERIENCE OF DEATH

Among the areas to be covered will be the phenomenology of dying, subjective experiences of clinical death, and the therapeutic potential of mystical experiences.

Excerpt from a conference program at a Midwest university.

us; or we respond to a conviction, an imperative, or relatedness deep within us. These are experiences referred to as transcending—going beyond—our self-consciousness.

It is interesting to note that in Sanskrit there are twenty terms used to differentiate consciousness, whereas our culture distinguishes only conscious versus unconscious.[3]

---

[3] K. Ring, "A Transpersonal View of Consciousness: A Mapping of Farther Reaches of Inner Space," *The Journal of Transpersonal Psychology* 6 (1974), 2:125.

Example 6–5.
Senior
Actualization
and Growth
Explorations
(SAGE)

SAGE is a project which works in a creative and holistic manner with men and women 65 years and older for self-improvement and growth. By viewing aging as the creative interplay of the forces of life rather than as a deterioration process, we have discovered that older people can grow, change, and develop as much as younger people. In almost every case, there has been considerable improvement in the overall health and well-being of the participants as well as a renewed interest in life and self-responsibility. Since its inception the SAGE Project has extended its resources into private homes, local churches, community centers, growth centers, hospitals, nursing homes, senior residences, and universities.

An introductory workshop is provided for professionals, paraprofessionals, and those interested in working with older adults to revitalize their lives. During this four-day training the nature and evolution of the SAGE Project is explained, explored, and discussed. There are demonstrations of the methods and techniques utilized in an integrated manner as means toward improved health, and greater appreciation of self in the older adult. Techniques such as deep breathing, relaxation training, EMG biofeedback, hatha-yoga, bodymind awareness exercises, massage, shared discussion groups, individual counseling, meditation, taichi, art, and music therapy are demonstrated. Specific attention is paid to applications of SAGE processes to institutional, therapeutic, and community settings. Video-tapes and experiential exercises are employed in this process.

Excerpt from an announcement of a program on the West Coast.

NO EGO BOUNDARIES.   According to the theory of transcendence, the essence of an individual is not limited by one's own ego boundaries. When functioning in the extraterrestrial region, my consciousness can apparently go anywhere in the universe. This sounds fantastic only because we are accustomed to thinking of ourselves as bodies having the property of consciousness. If, instead, we think of ourselves as essentially consciousness and not bodies, and if we can entertain the belief that our consciousness can operate independently of our bodies, then the notion of our consciousness traveling to distant spaces of the universe may be seen as a theoretical possibility.

Researchers and other writers have begun to develop maps of the various regions of consciousness. Ring, Grof, and Lilly formulated a map with eight

Example 6–6.
The Gift of
Inner Healing

"Faith-imagination creates an objective experience. It does not approximate or simulate one," writes Ruth Carter Stapleton in describing her approach to inner healing. The following account from her book is an illustration of the kinds of experiences influencing the development of some adults today:

(Jeff was reared by an overcontrolling, aggressive mother. In mid-life he was still unable to relate effectively to a woman.) After the healing begins, Jeff must deal with each successive anger-hurt reaction as quickly as possible. He should get quiet and use faith-imagination to visualize his mother in some earlier overcontrolling situation. Love may be visualized without feeling it. Creative imagination makes all things possible in a forgiving state of mind; healing love is applied. He can then see his mother coming to be reconciled, each asking forgiveness of the other, then embracing. In this way, a habit-formed positive image replaces the negative.

A friend told me how she applied this method. She was standing in line at the ticket counter at a large municipal airport. A man walked up and placed his bags right beside her. Then, ignoring the line, he pushed in front of her and asked the agent for a ticket. She said to the ticket agent, "Excuse me, I was next."

The agent snapped, "Lady, wait your turn."

She felt a surge of tremendous anger. Realizing this was the reaction of her inner child, she moved out of line, sat down in a waiting area, and asked the Spirit of God to help her. Her mother's unfortunate tendency to treat her unfairly had been heard in the agent's unwitting mistreatment. With faith-imagination she "saw" her mother and prayed for her. The moment she did, peace poured in. She then prayed for the agent and for the inconsiderate man. As she returned to the line, she was thrilled with the victory. Her mother was more beautiful; she herself was more beautiful, and the whole world was a little better place because she took those few minutes to bless instead of curse.

From R. C. Stapleton, *The Gift of Inner Healing* (Waco, Texas: Word Books, 1976), chapter 3.

regions.[4] The teachings of transcendental meditation[5] discuss seven levels of consciousness. In the New Testament the apostle Paul speaks of the realm of the third heaven.[6]

[4] Ibid., p. 126.

[5] A. Campbell, *Seven States of Consciousness* (New York: Harper & Row, 1974).

[6] New American Standard Bible, II Corinthians 12:12.

Example 6–7.
An
Anthropologist
Comments on
the Teachings
of Don Juan

Anthropology has taught us that the world is differently defined in different places. It is not only that people have different customs; it is not only that people believe in different gods and expect different postmortem fates. It is, rather, that the worlds of different people have different shapes. The very *metaphysical presuppositions* differ: *space* does not conform to Euclidean geometry, time does not form a continuous unidirectional flow, causation does not conform to Aristotelian logic, man is not differentiated from non-man or *life* from death, as in our world. We know something of the shape of these other worlds from the logic of native languages and from myths and ceremonies, as recorded by anthropologists. Don Juan has shown us glimpses of the world of a Yaqui sorcerer, and because we see it under the influence of hallucinogenic substances, we apprehend it with a reality that is utterly different from those other sources. This is the special virtue of this work.

Castaneda rightly asserts that this world, for all its differences of perception, has its own inner logic. He has tried to explain it from inside, as it were—from within his own rich and intensely personal experiences while under Don Juan's tutelage—rather than to examine it in terms of *our* logic. That he cannot entirely succeed in this is a limitation that our culture and our own language place on perception, rather than his personal limitation; yet in his efforts he bridges for us the world of Yaqui sorcerer with our own, the world of nonordinary reality with the world of ordinary reality.

The central importance of entering into worlds other than our own—and hence of anthropology itself—lies in the fact that the experience leads us to understand *that our own world is also a cultural construct.* By experiencing other worlds, then, we see our own for what it is and are thereby enabled also to see fleetingly what the real world, the one between our own cultural construct and those other worlds, must in fact be like.

From W. Goldschmidt, Foreword to *The Teachings of Don Juan: A Yaqui Way of Knowledge,* by C. Castaneda (New York: Ballantine Books, 1969).

Altered
States of
Consciousness

Charles Tart makes the distinction between states of consciousness and altered states of consciousness by likening them to computer programing. The computer has many subroutines. It depends on the program as to how the different subroutines will process the data. Study of one program will not tell us much about how another program will process the data, although many of the same subroutines may be used. "The new program with its input-output interactions must be studied in and of itself. An altered state of consciousness (ASC) is analogous to changing temporarily the program of a

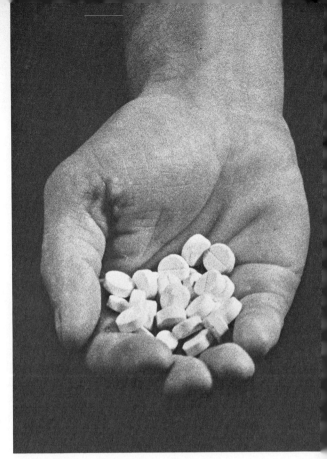

6–3 *Some seek chemical escape from routine through altered states of consciousness induced by drugs or alcohol. (Kansas State University Student Publications photo)*

computer."[7] The ASC is defined by the nature of the pattern experienced, not by the technique used to induce the pattern.

ALCOHOL AND DRUGS.   Nearly half a century ago the science fiction *Brave New World*[8] described the "soma" that would provide a chemical means for man to escape from his normal "humdrum" state. Man has continuously sought this through various forms of intoxication. Some have benefited from their trips to altered states by means of alcohol or drugs; others have been harmed. Society at different periods has been alarmed and punitive about use of alcohol and drugs. At other times their use has been encouraged. One researcher observed that "Studies of alcohol have been biased—biased by the prohibition-nurtured conviction that alcohol is a drug with bad effects; biased by the inability of psychologists to produce joy in the labora-

[7] C. T. Tart, "States of Consciousness and State-Specific Sciences," *Science* 176 (June 16, 1972), pp. 1203–1210; see also C. T. Tart, "The Basic Nature of Altered States of Consciousness: A Systems Approach," *Journal of Transpersonal Psychology* 8 (1976), 1:45–64, for a theory of the basic nature of ASC.

[8] A. Huxley, *Brave New World* (New York: Bantam Books, 1932).

tory; biased by the American belief that action is real and important, fantasy unreal and unimportant."[9]

Whatever problems society may have in discovering why some people profit and some are destroyed by it, the use of alcohol as a means to ASC is an important part of the experience of many adults at some point in their developmental experience.

Marijuana, too, is a resource available to many. Amphetamine and a variety of prescriptions and over-the-counter drugs figure actively in the day-by-day experiences of people across the land (Example 6–8).

> The span of effects man can attain with drugs extends from such minor alterations as relief from tension to major psychological changes that include escape from lethargy, from boredom and depression, through varying degrees of release from sexual and aggressive inhibitions and, ultimately, to altered states of consciousness. They may even transport a person to an entirely different emotional or psychological state. The potential for transport is graphically portrayed in recent psychedelic literature. Prior to the introduction of LSD, however, there were descriptions of the effects of alcohol and marijuana that were almost as varied and gripping. It is this capacity to transport a person from one conscious state, reality, or self, to another that appears to be common to all these drugs. Man has always appeared to have this requirement.[10]

Whatever age we may be studying in adult development, alcohol and drugs must be recognized as an influential factor in the individual's environment. For some, intoxication offers a means of running away; for others, a means of extending and reaching out beyond new horizons.

We can think of vast numbers of adults adding pills on top of pills to control their daily lives; or we can read of the estimated $25 billion cost of alcohol misuse each year.[11] We can also remember that many have found that intoxication stimulates the mystical capacities of human nature.[12] Perhaps here, as with so many aspects of human development, the significance of an experience is determined by the way the individual is coping with life as a whole.

---

[9] D. C. McClelland, "The Power of Positive Drinking," *Psychology Today* 4 (January 1971), 8:40.

[10] M. M. Katz, "What This Country Needs Is a Safe Five-cent Intoxicant," *Psychology Today* 4 (February 1971), 9:30.

[11] *Second Special Report to the U.S. Congress on Alcohol and Health from the Secretary of Health, Education and Welfare* (Washington, D.C.: U.S. Government Printing Office, 1975).

[12] Katz, "What This Country Needs Is a Safe Five-cent Intoxicant," p. 39.

Example 6–8.
Amphetamine,
Alias Speed

Chemists first synthesized amphetamine in 1887, but no one evaluated it systematically until 1927, when experimenters reported that laboratory animals dosed with the drug became hyperactive and lost all interest in eating or sleeping. Five years later a pharmaceutical house introduced the drug into clinical medicine under the name Benzedrine.

Scientists isolated two different forms of the drug. One of them rotated polarized light to the right—clockwise; the other rotated it to the left. Gordon Alles found that the right-handed dextro-form was a much more potent central stimulant than the left-handed, levo-form. Soon dextroamphetamine (Dexedrine) was with us.

Dexedrine and Benzedrine, both marketed by Smith Kline & French Laboratories, were the primary commercial amphetamines until 1945, when Burroughs Wellcome & Co. joined the market with methamphetamine (Methedrine), now notorious under the name speed . . .

Drug users I interviewed said that Methedrine is the favored amphetamine because it produces more euphoria than the others. (Heavy users are often referred to as speed-freaks; as the habit increases they are vulnerable to amphetamine psychosis). Most speed-freaks, aware of this effect, expect sooner or later to experience severe paranoid psychosis . . .

Some terms refer descriptively to the uses and effects of amphetamine: crank, pep pills, uppers, lid-poppers, wakeups, eye-openers, truck drivers, copilots, coast-to-coasts. Other terms identify specific pills by their chemistry or appearance: bennies, dexies, meth, whites, black beauties, purple hearts, greenies, footballs.

But it is the ultimate frequent effect of amphetamine that has inspired the simplest and most telling catchphrase of all: SPEED KILLS.

From S. H. Snyder, "Amphetamine—A Sketch," *Psychology Today* 5 (January 1972) 8:45.

PSYCHIC PROCESSES. An increasing number of adults acknowledges experiencing phenomena that lie beyond our present understanding of normal sensory perceptions. More than half the adults in America believe they have had telepathic experiences.[13] As the boundaries of "normality" expand, individuals are freer to recognize and report what are called psychic experiences. And increasingly research energies are being directed to this study, an area in which the Soviet Union has until recently held the leadership. Today, in re-

[13] P. Chance, "Telepathy Could Be Real," *Psychology Today* 9 (February 1976), p. 40.

search centers of more than a dozen universities, physicists, chemists, neuro-biologists, psychologists, psychiatrists, and physicians are engaged in this study.

One writer has described the work of a center for study of consciousness as follows:

> We have worked with hundreds of research subjects, representing a wide sampling of the population . . . We have seen the remarkable speeding up of normal mental processes, the control and enhancement of all senses, the modulation of pain and pleasure. We have learned much about religious and "peak" experiences, about the nature and facilitation of creativity, about the programming and practical uses of dreams. We have investigated some of the phenomena associated with parapsychology. We have been able to impart, through biofeedback training, physiological control of internal and involuntary states. We have learned the body can be re-educated . . .
>
> Training to restore an integral sense of body-mind comes first . . . Breaking through the surface crust of what we ordinarily called consciousness—the "cultural trance"—is all important to success. The best place to start is outside the range of this "normal" consciousness. [14]

BIOFEEDBACK.   We have already referred to training becoming increasingly available that allows individuals to develop voluntary control over physiological processes once thought to be involuntary (see Example 6–9). However, biofeedback has led individuals to experiences that seem to verge on other levels. The theory is that mind is an energy structure and all matter is energy related to the mind. Our thoughts are of the same substance as the energy forming the cells of the body. But because we have not learned to listen to our own unconscious, we are not usually aware of the oneness between our thoughts and our body. Because our minds are of the same energy as material objects around us, those who have learned to listen to their unconscious can control external objects.

Biofeedback was used early in student counseling with students searching for new understanding of self and of their future or for new effectiveness in study and human relations. [15] Persons suffering from various states of tension

---

[14] J. Houston, "Putting the First Man on Earth," *Saturday Review* 2 (February 22, 1975), 11:29. For further definitions of parapsychology see C. Ponti, *Supersenses* (New York: Quadrangle, New York Times Book, 1974).

[15] D. Danskin and E. D. Walters, "Biofeedback and Voluntary Self-regulation: Counseling and Education," *Personnel and Guidance Journal* 51 (1973), 9:633–638.

Example 6–9.
Biofeedback

Biofeedback provides visual or audible feedback, such as a flashing light or a buzzer. With these signs the individual soon learns to control what is happening in areas once thought to be unconscious. Regulating flow of blood to different parts of the body, the rate of heart beat, the pattern of brain waves are all illustrations of bodily functions individuals are now learning to control by means of biofeedback.

A further training aid often used with biofeedback is autogenic training. Autogenic training is explicit and effectively toned with suggestive imagery to facilitate a desired mood or state in some part of the body. Coupled with biofeedback reports which inform the person of progress being made, the individuals rapidly learn to bring about desired conditions in the body. The migraine headache was one of the first medical complaints to look to biofeedback training for treatment. Patients were taught to cause their hands to become warmer. This "voluntary" action relaxed the autonomic nervous system and brought relief from the migraine pain.

From J. D. Sargent, E. D. Walters, and E. E. Green, "Psychosomatic Self-regulation of Migraine Headaches," *Seminars in Psychiatry* 5 (November 1973), pp. 415–428.

6–4 *The technology in biofeedback labs assists individuals to recognize and control behavior once thought to be involuntary. (Photo by Danskin and Lowenstein, Applied Biofeedback Lab, Kansas State University)*

and from migraine headaches were among those profiting from early services of biofeedback.[16]

Elmer Green and colleagues at the Menninger Foundation are among the leaders in research[17] and application of skills in voluntary control of involuntary processes. Included among persons with unusual abilities whom they studied in their laboratories is Swami Rama from India. When the Swami was wired to machines so that observers could read his physiological processes, he showed his ability to stop his heart for a brief period of time. He was able to direct by his mental concentration the movement of a needle located five feet from him. Another visitor was Jack Schwarz, a man reared in Holland who for many years has practiced psychotherapy in Selma, Oregon. Schwarz demonstrated how through "communication with his subconscious" he was able to perform feats such as carrying hot coals or inserting a long needle through his biceps without pain or bleeding.

MEDITATION

> Meditation, only a decade ago, was something that we vaguely knew was done by yogis in India, a few hippies, and some far-out church groups in America. Now it is being practiced more and more by students, housewives, business and professional men and women, and a wide variety of other people. Meditation has at last become respectable. Recently the National Institute of Mental Health gave Harvard a grant to study one form of this activity—Transcendental Meditation.[18]

The research psychologist, Lawrence LeShan, who wrote that paragraph is well known for the book whose title illustrates how diverse the directions are from which comes an appreciation of man's expanding consciousness, *The Medium, the Mystic and the Physicist.* LeShan points out that meditation is an arduous, disciplined program of exercise through which one strengthens the integration of mind and personality. It enables many to become "more at ease with themselves, with others and the universe we live in."[19]

The integration of medical research and transpersonal practices is illus-

---

[16] J. D. Sargent, E. E. Green, and E. D. Walters, "Preliminary Report on the Use of Autogenic Feedback Training in the Treatment of Migraine and Tension Headaches," *Psychosomatic Medicine* 35 (1973), pp. 129–135.

[17] E. Green and A. Green, "The Ins and Outs of Mind-Body Energy," *Science Year, the World Book Science Annual* (Chicago: Field Enterprises, 1973).

[18] L. LeShan, "The Case for Meditation," *Saturday Review* 2 (February 22, 1975), 11:26–27.

[19] Ibid., p. 27.

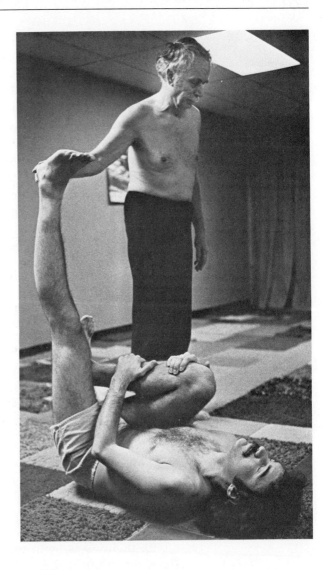

6–5 *Meditation is practiced more and more by businessmen, housewives, and a variety of persons from all walks of life.* (Manhattan Mercury *photo*)

trated by early research conducted on the physiological concomitants of meditation. Research on Zen monks in Japan revealed a slowing of metabolism during meditation, as evidenced by the fact that they reduced their consumption of oxygen by about 20 per cent as well as their output of carbon dioxide. In the intervening years, numerous studies of physiological correlates of meditation have been conducted. In a recent review of the literature, Wallace and Benson report that data from studies of transcendental meditation, Zen, and other meditative experiences have generally common findings. Meditation is accompanied by a "wakeful hypometabolic state: reductions in oxygen consumption, carbon dioxide elimination and the rate and volume of respiration; a slight increase in acidity of the arterial blood; a marked decrease in blood-lactate level; a slowing of the heartbeat; a considerable increase in skin resistance; and an electroencephalogram pattern of intensification of slow alpha waves with occasional theta-wave activity."[20]

The greater relaxation, evidenced by increased skin resistance and lowered blood-lactate level, was accompanied by a wakefulness contrasting with sleep patterns. There was some similarity in the general pattern to that of the "fight-or-flight" alarm pattern described many years ago by Walter B. Cannon. However, this pattern is the counterpart of the fight-or-flight reaction.

Transpersonal Processes in Education

Young and middle-aged adults with school-age children may be confronted with "far-out" reports from the schoolroom. A part of their developmental task may be to learn how to relate their children's efforts in creative activities to their own intuitive experiences, some of which they may have thus far deliberately or subconsciously screened from awareness.

Educators are studying ways in which imagination, dreams, fantasy, concentration, biofeedback, and meditation may be included in student experiences. They point out that the development of the several realms of human consciousness are important educational areas for children and adults, along with cognitive processes and areas of academic content. Those in teacher training are examining ways in which transpersonal abilities in students may contribute to other areas of schoolwork.[21] Some possibilities are that meditation may improve grades, help social relationships, and lower drug abuse. The ability to relax, focus on internal processes, and block out conflicting external signals temporarily are thought to contribute creativity in sciences as well as arts. Studies of creativity among mathematicians reveal how Einstein, Faraday, and others used visual and even kinesthetic sensation of muscle motions in their scientific discovery periods.

Some high school English teachers let students use their dreams as an introduction to poetry. One writer suggests that children naturally seek to

---

[20] R. R. Wallace and H. Benson, "The Physiology of Meditation," *Scientific American* 226 (February 1972), pp. 85–90.

[21] T. B. Roberts, *Four Psychologies Applied to Education* (New York: Schenkman, 1975), pp. 395–550.

experience altered states of consciousness through whirling, through squeezing one another's chests or throats to near-unconsciousness, and through smelling volatile solvents. He suggests that later on youth find they must resort to alcohol and drugs to experience the altered states of consciousness they desire, although their preference is to learn other more constructive approaches to entering altered states.[22]

Transpersonal Processes in Health

Adult classes in dance, martial arts (such as karate), massage, and body corrective systems (such as Rolfing and the Alexander technique) are involving many people of all ages in programs defined either as health or spiritual activities. They are seen as ways of opening the individual to greater oneness with body and more consciousness of the flow of psychic and physical energies.

Thousands of adults are involved in some fashion with biofeedback training and other approaches to the voluntary control of involuntary processes. Mental and physical health practices are utilizing it in some aspects of treatment. A national conference with keynote addresses by the president of the American Medical Association, the president of a psychiatric foundation, and a leading endocrinologist offered clinical sessions to "provide an explanatory introduction to new techniques which present breakthrough evidence of mind/body and vital energy field interaction and their application to the theory and practice of medicine."[23] Specific areas dealt with included biofeedback, acupuncture, altered states of consciousness, psychic diagnosis, bioenergetics, mind/body interaction.

Describing an ASC experience he associated with improvement in his leukemia condition, columnist Stewart Alsop commented, "Perhaps my decision not to stop at Baltimore [a reference to his ASC experience] had nothing to do with my astonishing recovery. But there are mysteries, above all the mysteries of the relationship of mind and body, that will never be explained, not by the most brilliant doctors, the wisest scientists or philosophers."[24]

[22] Ibid., pp. 417–420.

[23] From the seminar program, "First National Congress on Integrative Health," The Academy of Parapsychology and Medicine, Los Altos, Calif. Keynote addresses were presented by endocrinologist Hans Selye, American Medical Association president M. C. Todd, and president of the Menninger Foundation Roy Menninger.

[24] S. Alsop, *Newsweek* 83 (March 11, 1974), p. 92. See also G. A. Maloney *The Breath of the Mystic* (Denville, N.J.: Dimension Books, 1974) for a consideration of uncreated energies within man relating him to the universe.

Transpersonal Processes in Religion

The excerpt in Example 6–10 from a program of a large Midwest church is illustrative of the new lines of church activity to which adults in the 1980s must make adjustment. A new vitality for the mystical aspects of the Judeo-Christian tradition also has emerged. The possibility of achieving oneness with God is an active pursuit of many newly formed "charismatic" groups within most of the established Catholic and Protestant churches. The presence of God, as Divine Spirit, active within the personality of the individual is literally affirmed rather than as a figure of speech.[25]

Example 6–10.
New Wineskins

> The current spiritual hunger is quickening as more and more people desire growth in the inner life and an experience with the transcendent dimension of life. For substantial numbers, the answers are coming through such channels as the charismatic movement, conservative Christianity, Transcedental Meditation and other forms of Eastern religions, and the new emergence of transpersonal psychology. Mainline and liberal churches seem to be offering little in the way of dynamic alternatives to the above mentioned movements. Old wineskins are still in use and they are inadequate for the new wine of spiritual hunger. There is a new and extraordinary research project, based at First Community Church, Columbus, Ohio, which is developing new wineskins.
>
> Spiritually significant insights have been gleaned from such fields as biofeedback, dream research, transpersonal psychology, meditative techniques, telepathy research and experimental hypnosis. These are being synthesized into a Christian concept of prayer—a technique called "Meditative Prayer"—to be used within mainline churches. The workshop "New Wineskins II: Dreams" focuses upon the understanding of dreams and how they may be used to enhance creativity to keep us in tune with our everyday world and its problems and how they can act as revelation of God's purpose in our lives.
>
> From brochure "New Wineskins II: Dreams," First Community Church, Columbus, Ohio (April 1976).

Programs of physical healing and other manifestations of divine energy are a part of many of the group experiences. In some instances conventional medical practice and Christian healing centers are being jointly established.[26]

[25] R. D. Wead, *Catholic Charismatics* (Carol Stream, Ill.: Creation House, 1973); D. J. Bennett and R. Bennett, *The Holy Spirit and You* (Plainfield, N.J.: Logos Press, 1971); C. Marshall, *Something More* (New York: McGraw-Hill, 1974).

[26] The Christian Medical Foundation (6021 West Buffalo Avenue, Tampa, Fla. 33614; coordinator W. S. Reed, M.D.) sponsors an annual conference concerning the Holy Spirit in the practice of Medicine.

A Blending of New and Old

We noted near the beginning of this chapter that adults of the 1980s will continue to face a resurgence of a transpersonal world-and-life view as well as a strongly established rationalistic and materialistic view. The dichotomy is a part of the paradox of the nature of man. Each new generation adapts its discoveries and its traumas, modulating somewhat the agreed-upon "grounds of reality."

The Nature of Reality

In previous chapters we discovered that our socialization process equips us with common ways of viewing. We share with others common expectations that certain actions or words mean predictable consequences. We also share with them, either implicitly or explicitly, common views about what is possible and impossible. Our culture has created for us our experience of reality and truth. There was a time when a trip to the moon was not thought to be within the realm of possibility. Similarly the idea that we could see and talk with persons thousands of miles away once would have been described as lunatic thinking.

> Any community of people holds in common certain assumptions about reality. Our language itself is a set of common assumptions, shared for the convenience of easy discourse . . . Each scientific community of physicists, mathematicians, psychologists, or others share an additional set of implicit assumptions, called the *paradigm* by Thomas Kuhn. The paradigm is the shared conceptions of what is possible, the boundaries of acceptable inquiry . . .[27]

Within recent years, activities in several areas have been gradually preparing the way for new boundaries to our world of possibility. LeShan has dramatized this issue by presenting a list of sixty statements from the writings of mystics and physicists. He challenges the reader to identify whether the author of each statement were writing as a mystic or as a physicist.[28]

The flood of data from drug experiences, the changing view among scientists concerning time and causality, the new technology available for biochemical and electrophysical research and the forthcoming information from

[27] R. E. Ornstein, *The Psychology of Consciousness* (San Francisco: Freeman, 1972), p. 3.

[28] L. LeShan, "Physicists and Mystics: Similarities in World View," in *The Medium, the Mystic and the Physicist* (New York: Viking Press, 1974).

brain and biochemical studies, the extensive involvement of numerous persons in various religious experiences—such as transcendental meditation, Eastern thought, and charismatic Christianity—and finally, parapsychological research involving conventional research tools together have brought influences and pressures requiring each adult to adapt to somewhat new perceptual categories.[29] The extent of adaptation may be greater for persons in some parts of the country than in others; it may be more difficult for persons of some age levels or cultural background than for others.

Duality in Man

A focus on the transpersonal is not new. In the famous Gifford Lectures of 1901–1902, philosopher-psychologist William James presented the results of his extensive survey of reported religious experiences, including the experiences of mysticism, conversion, and saintliness.[30] Nearly fifty years later, for the same prestigious philosophical symposium, Reinhold Niebuhr[31] addressed himself to the duality in man. Man is basically self-centered, Niebuhr suggested, but he has the capacity to rise above himself, to stand outside himself and with his conscience evaluate his behavior.

The nature of man combining biological instincts and drives with the spiritual capacities of faith and love causes a state of constant tension. Some attempt to deal with this tension or anxiety by denying one of the two aspects of man's being—either his limitations as a biological creature or his freedom as a spiritual being. Denial of man's limitations results in various forms of destructive or self-limiting pride, such as pride of power in group superiority, pride of knowledge resulting in conflicting ideologies, pride of virtue and moral self-rightousness, pride of spirit as in religious fanaticism. He may also attempt to eliminate anxiety by denying his freedom and emphasizing his creatureliness. Such deceptions compound man's insecurities and reduce his ability to deal with reality.

Man's capacity for self-transcendence enables him to see in every human act the possibilities he did not fulfill. Niebuhr said it is only in the recognition that God is self-giving love that man can accept the continual judgment

---

[29] A. Weil, *The Natural Mind* (Boston: Houghton Mifflin, 1972); W. Heisenberg, *Physics and Beyond* (New York: Harper Torchbook, 1971); B. Brown, *New Mind, New Body-Biofeedback: New Directions for the Mind* (New York: Harper & Row, 1974); J. Lilly, *Center of the Cyclone* (New York: Julian Press, 1972); G. Krishna, *The Awakening of Kundalini* (New York: Dutton, 1975); D. J. Bennett, *Nine O'Clock in the Morning* (Plainfield, N.J.: Logos International, 1970).

[30] W. James, *Varieties of Religious Experience* (New York: Mentor Books, 1952).

[31] R. Niebuhr, *The Nature and Destiny of Man* (New York: Scribner, 1943).

of his behavior through self-transcendence. Man's duality in nature means that his historical condition will not change—every greater possibility for good brings with it a proportionally greater possibility for evil. Therefore, politically speaking, "man's capacity for justice makes democracy possible; man's inclination to injustice makes a democracy necessary."[32]

Platonic Heritage   Niebuhr in the mid-twentieth century was reintroducing views of earlier generations. As literature from the ancient Orient has provided the insight of meditation and acupuncture coupled with modern medicine, therapy, and education, so also the writings of the Greek philosopher Plato have a strangely contemporary ring, blending the new thought of physics with the traditions of conventional science. Plato saw the world in perpetual change, though having an essential unity in all things. He said that man knows the world through sense experiences and through spiritual realities. The spiritual realities give permanence; they are unchanging elements in the chaotic world of change. He referred to spiritual realities as the realm of *Ideas.* Spiritual realities, he said, do not come to man through sense experience or reason but are reached through direct contact and participation in the realm of the eternal.

Plato thought man had three basic ways of knowing: through sense experience, through reason, and through inspiration. It is through inspiration or madness that man is given access to the realm of the nonphysical that include prophecy, healing, artistic inspiration, and love.

Morton Kelsey[33] notes that the Greek words *prophecy* and *madness* are related. Madness as Plato used it is not the illness concept we have associated with it. It referred to experiences that possessed the mind and the mind could not be changed. Sense experiences were viewed as irrational and akin to madness, too. In prophecy man is possessed by the gods and often given glimpses of the future or of the meaning of the present. Kelsey notes that it never occurred to Plato to doubt that man can be possessed by the divine and so have touch with the nonspace-time world in a prophetic way. He believed man could encounter the world of spirit and learn from the encounter.

In discussing the way Platonic thought had served as a theoretical framework for communicating the Christian tradition, Kelsey notes that half of

---

[32] Ibid.

[33] M. Kelsey, *Encounter with God* (Minneapolis: Bethany Fellowship, 1972), pp. 51–59.

the writing in the New Testament is devoted to describing some aspect of the spirit/man relationship in the present world.[34]

Back from the Moon

The blend of East and West, new and old involved in transpersonal study was expressed by astronaut Edgar D. Mitchell, a leading student of human consciousness and president of the Institute of Noetic Sciences. He wrote:

> When I went to the moon, I was as pragmatic a scientist engineer as any of my colleagues. I'd spent more than a quarter of a century learning the rational-objective-experimental approach to dealing with the universe. But my experience during Apollo 14 had another aspect: It showed me certain limitations of science and technology. It began with the breathtaking experience of seeing planet earth floating in the immensity of space . . . I underwent a religious-like peak experience, in which the presence of divinity became almost palpable, and I knew that life in the universe was not just an accident based on random processes. The realization was subjective, but it was knowledge every bit as real and compelling as the objective data the navigational program or the communications system was based on . . . Human beings . . . have a dimension that transcends the entity of the person and takes them into the category of the transperson . . . We need to study the nature of consciousness in all its manifestations . . . The rational-objective-experimental mode of Western science based on materialism is insufficient by itself . . . The intuitive-subjective-experimental mode characteristic of religion and of Eastern traditions has much to contribute.[35]

The subject matter and the wide range of persons contributing to the discipline of transpersonal processes was well illustrated in the following description of a research center studying human consciousness:

> This exploration of the farther reaches of human consciousness typifies a new kind of mind research already well begun. Scientists, psychologists, and technicians of every stripe are gathering together with priests, shamans, mystics, artists, madmen, healers, and yogis, in conferences, academic seminars, laboratories, and ashrams, in a curious blending and interchange of ancient gnosis with contemporary know-how. The result is a strange yeasting of East and West, science and ritual, the distant past and the emergent future.[36]

[34] Ibid., p. 58.

[35] E. D. Mitchell, "Outer Space to Inner Space: An Astronaut's Odyssey," *Saturday Review* 2 (February 22, 1975), pp. 20–21.

[36] Houston, "Putting the First Man on Earth," p. 29; see also A. J. Sutich, "The Emergence of the Transpersonal Orientation: A Personal Account," *Journal of Transpersonal Psychology* 8 (1976), pp. 5–19.

Summary

In the seventeenth century the physicists set the boundaries of the "possible" in such a way that the Western world learned to operate with laws of cause and effect, time and motion. This separated Western thought from much of Eastern thought and caused human experience and ancient writings to be translated into mechanistic and predictable ways. What did not fit this framework was said to be supernatural or superstition. This was the dominant perceptual framework of the world into which today's adults were born. A second more intuitive and cosmic awareness was in the background.

Many profound changes have been taking place during the years we have been growing in and through adulthood. Those in old age witnessed the advent of the airplane, telephone, and radio; those in middle age, television, heart transplants, and artificial insemination; the young adults grew up with men in space and the moon landings. Each event strained credulity slightly further.

As the revolution of the 1960s pushed toward abolition of traditions, laws, and roles, a flood of data was brought forth by experiences with drugs, psychic phenomena, and religious mysticism that could only be accommodated with new definitions of reality. Implications from the new physics (propounded in the 1930s) were gradually being inserted into the consciousness of the Western community. While some were writing "God is dead," others were writing "Cause, effect, and time are dead." When violence was recognized in the midst of peace movements and Watergate in the midst of government, those now moving into young adulthood were in the period of life to build their own philosophy. Those of us now in middle and later life found our philosophic underpinnings fiercely shaken. We will for the rest of our lives be involved with attempting to find correspondence between what our lenses take in and what those wearing the lenses of the new age perceive.

Suggested Activities and Further Reading

1. The cover story of *Newsweek,* "Getting Your Head Together," (by K. L. Woodward, J. Huck, D. Gram, and L. Howard, September 6, 1976), describes several of the multitude of approaches and groups of all ages in what the writers term "the consciousness revolution." It is, they state, "a diffuse but culturally pervasive movement that may well turn out to be this century's version of colonial America's Great awakening."

2. The effects of marijuana on various body functions and on perceptual and spiritual processes are reported in *Psychology Today* (May 1971) in articles by S. H. Synder of the Johns Hopkins University School of Medicine and Charles T. Tart of the University of California.

3. Some of the terrors and some of the delights of intoxication appear in fiction and biography. In the novel *Lost Weekend,* by C. Jackson, Don Birnam's terror, anticipating the agony of being without alcohol, expresses graphically the effect of the changing balance of the body's chemistry for the alcoholic. Biographies by Elizabeth Burns, *The Late Liz* (Old Tappan, N.J.: Revell, 1957), and by Johnny Cash, *The Man in Black* (Grand Rapids: Zondervon, 1975), offer insights into the experiences of adults who at some period in their lives found themselves involved with alcoholism or drugs. A national study of young adults provides useful background information that distinguishes the small percentage of drug abusers from among the drug users: D. Yankelovich, "Drug Users Versus Drug Abusers," *Psychology Today* 9 (October 1975).

4. Whereas much poetry evokes the transpersonal dimension in life—for example, Blake, Milton, the Brownings—some poetry and music have seemingly more direct references to the effect of drugs, such as Coleridge's "Kubla Khan" and the Beatles' "*Lucy in the Sky with Diamonds.*" Find examples from poetry or other literature—for example, De Quincy, Huxley—relating to the positive and negative influences of drugs on creativity.

5. Study the works of some contemporary poets, such as Robert Lowell or Dylan Thomas, for their expression of man's experiences in transcendence. Consider their perception of transcendence at different stages of life. Robert Lowell's book *Selected Poems* (New York: Farrar, Straus & Giroux, 1976) reflects the intertwining of poetry and the events of his life in a poetic biographical profile of adult development over the past thirty years.

6. Interview members of a church congregation to see what changes in their view of reality may have come from the popularity of such books as W. P. Blatty's *The Exorcist,* the evangelist Billy Graham's *Angels: God's Secret Agents,* and Charlie Shedd's *Getting Through to the Wonderful You,* a biblical guide to meditation.

7. The variety of books and articles on transpersonal processes spans the gamut from popular to technical.

> *Brain/Mind Bulletin* (Interface Press, P.O. Box 42211, Los Angeles, Calif. 90042).
> A monthly newsletter that provides abstracts of contemporary research and writing relating to consciousness and to biological research.
> Adam Smith, *Powers of the Mind* (New York: Random House, 1975).
> Profiles in popular form research ideas and personalities along with reports of consciousness groups and other contemporary mystic and psychic activities.

S. Ostrander and L. Schroeder, *Psychic Discoveries Behind the Iron Curtain* (Englewood Cliffs, N.J.: Prentice-Hall, 1970).
Reports on early psychic research in Russia.

B. Brown, *New Body, New Mind* (New York: Harper & Row, 1974).
Provides a useful background to the science of biofeedback.

O. C. Simonton and S. S. Simonton, "Belief Systems and Management of the Emotional Aspects of Malignancy," *The Journal of Transpersonal Psychology* 7 (1975), 1:29–47.
Describes the application of transpersonal techniques to the treatment of cancer.

O. Roberts, *The Call* (New York: Avon Books, 1971).
The autobiography of the president of Oral Roberts University describes the process of faith healing.

W. P. Wilson, "Mental Health Benefits of Religious Salvation," *Diseases of the Nervous System* 33 (June 1972), pp. 382–386.
Professor of psychiatry at Duke University reports research on spiritual aspects of psychosocial behavior.

Alan Watts, "Psychotherapy and Eastern Religion," *Journal of Transpersonal Psychology* 6 (1974), 1:18–31.
A lecture on the metaphysical bases of psychiatry to staff of a psychiatric hospital by the famed exponent of Zen Buddhism.

D. Blazer and E. Palmore, "Religion and Aging in a Longitudinal Panel," *The Gerontologist* 16 (February 1976, Part 1) 1:82–85.

Part TWO

STAGES OF ADULT DEVELOPMENT

chapter 7

The Study of Adult Development: An Overview

The Beginning of a Discipline

It is indeed a mind-boggling undertaking to bring together the many-faceted aspects of one life and from the collected data formulate a picture reflecting the sequence and order of human development. To accomplish this formulation with sufficient numbers of lives in order to see some pattern in life-span development has required a long-term dedication and vision for researchers. Because of the complexity of the task and some tendency to think that adults are simply large-sized children, there have not been many scholars in this field until recent years.

Early Leaders One of the pioneers in the study of development through the life course[1] was Dr. Charlotte Buhler. She contributed much to the vision and investigative procedures used in the early programs at the University of Chicago and at Berkeley. Her method was developed during her years of clinical work in Vienna, Austria. She and her close colleague, Else Frenkel-Brunswik, collected hundreds of biographies from people of varied

---

[1] Papers presented at the West Virginia conferences on life-span psychology in 1969, 1971, and 1972 provide a history and review of the evolution of theory and method in life-span developmental psychology: L. R. Goulet and P. B. Baltes, eds., *Life-Span Developmental Psychology: Research and Theory* (New York: Academic Press, 1970); J. R. Nesselroade and H. Y. Reese, eds., *Life-Span Developmental Psychology: Methodological Issues* (New York: Academic Press, 1973). P. B. Baltes and K. W. Schaie, eds., *Life-Span Developmental Psychology: Personality and Socialization* (New York: Academic Press, 1973).

187

7–1 *The new interest in the study of human development during adult years and aging is reflected in the departments and centers of gerontology being established on many campuses. One of the newer and more extensive is the Andrus Gerontology Center pictured here. (Photo courtesy of the Ethel Percy Andrus Gerontology Center, University of Southern California)*

nationalities, occupations and social classes. The life stories were then individually analyzed and compared with one another.[2]

There were three kinds of information included in the Buhler studies: (1) external events of life (what a person does, his job, his friends, etc.); (2) internal events (what the individual feels and thinks about his life); (3) accomplishments and products from the life.[3] The three areas describe the general organization of material used by students in most longitudinal studies as they gather information from groups of people.

In her early comparisons of biographies, Buhler related the social and the psychological data to the biological. She and subsequent researchers recognized a biological age dimension in human development. We are becoming aware, however, that the relationship between biological change and chronological age is not as close in adult years as in infancy and childhood. The significance of a given event may be described better in some instances in terms of some dimension in the life-span rather than in terms of biological or

[2] E. Frenkel-Brunswik describes the Buhler method as well as some of their findings in "Adjustments and Reorientation in the Course of the Life Span," in *Middle Age and Aging,* ed. B. L. Neugarten (Chicago: University of Chicago Press, 1968), pp. 77–84.

[3] Ibid., p. 78.

chronological age. For example, a major longitudinal study of adults in the San Francisco Bay area was begun with groups of people selected because they were at transitional points in careers rather than because they were certain ages.[4]

It is interesting that the formulation of the human-development theory has until recently been associated with the study of child development. This probably represents some of the financial practicalities of research funding. The Child Study Program of the Commission on Teacher Education of the American Council on Education (ACE) provided much of the support for the work of Erik Erikson and Robert Havighurst, who formulated outlines useful in the study of human development through the life-span.[5]

[4] M. F. Lowenthal and associates, *Four Stages of Life* (San Francisco: Jossey-Bass, 1975). The life stages being anticipated were (1) first job, college, or marriage, (2) parenthood, (3) postparental "empty nest," (4) retirement.

[5] R. J. Havighurst, "History of Developmental Psychology: Socialization and Personality Development Through the Life-Span," in *Life-Span Developmental Psychology: Personality and Socialization,* eds. B. P. Baltes and K. W. Schaie (New York: Academic Press, 1973), pp. 3–24.

7–2 From early childhood through college graduation these twins proceeded at a similar pace. In later years a war delayed the marriage of one, thus also the stages of parent and grandparent.

Formulations of Developmental Stages   In Chapter 5 we referred to Erikson's book *Childhood and Society,* which outlined eight developmental stages, each with a prevailing identifying task: achieving basic trust, autonomy, initiative, industry, identity, intimacy, generativity, and integrity. This book,[6] published in 1950, brought depth psychology together with current social, psychological, and philosophical thought within the applied context of establishing teacher-training programs and educational philosophy. It found a wide response. The ACE program provided the setting for an emerging group with a developmental life-span orientation. One of the members of the group was Robert Havighurst. He adapted Erikson's ideas about ego development to problems of planning in the public school, and from this formulated his theory of developmental tasks in education. He conceptualized education as helping individuals deal with the new tasks characterizing each stage of growth. The new tasks were responses to biological development at different periods of life and to changes society expected in the individual's performance at different life periods.[7]

An orientation to adult life stages usually brings a synthesis of Havighurst's developmental tasks, along with a listing of Buhler's and Erikson's stages. Studies of moral development by Kohlberg[8] and others have begun to add to the literature on adult development. Jane Loevinger's work[9] on methodology offers promise for adapting to adult study concepts from Piaget and developmental theorists whose past work has been utilized in the child-development areas.

The Meaning of Development

Direction of Change   As students of human development extended their range beyond childhood, the term *development* became increasingly confusing. The intent of the study of adult development is to describe the changes that take place at different periods of life. Because child development and biological development usually imply movement toward a more complex, efficient, and generally "higher" order, some would assume that this should be the meaning for

[6] E. H. Erikson, *Childhood and Society* (New York: Norton, 1950).

[7] R. W. Havighurst, *Human Development and Education* (New York: David McKay, 1954).

[8] L. Kohlberg and R. Kramer, "Continuities and Discontinuities in Childhood and Adult Moral Development," *Human Development* 12 (1969), pp. 93–120.

[9] J. Loevinger and R. Wessler, *Measuring Ego Development* (San Francisco: Jossey-Bass, 1970).

adult development. There are, however, many changes during adult life. It is difficult to know with the present information just to what extent a change represents more or less efficiency, complexity, and goal attainment. We do know that in advanced stages of aging there are changes that reflect decreasing efficiency.

It is better to think of development as referring to any change in an individual, rather than as referring to change in a predetermined direction. The study of adult development is the study of the characteristics of individual behavior, and of biological, social, and psychological pressures, expectations, and goals experienced by individuals and groups of different age levels.[10] The study looks at the sequence of events in the course of adult life and the meaning society gives to these events. It recognizes the unique core of individuality that provides continuity in behavior changes in the developing personality. The events of adult life occur in a context. The context of life is the environment as it is perceived and "not perceived" by the individual and the inherent intuitive and biological constitution of the person. The study of adult development seeks to learn more about the patterns of life events as a background for appreciating the uniqueness of the individual life.

Age Differences and Cohort Differences

In our study of adult development, we will be interested in observing differences in attitudes and behaviors of people in their twenties through their seventies and eighties. This will help us more effectively to understand, plan for, and relate to persons of different ages. However, in order to understand what may have caused the differences, we will need to remind ourselves continually of the tendency to confuse differences resulting from aging itself with differences resulting because people were born at different points in his-

---

[10] B. L. Neugarten, "Personality Change in Late Life: A Developmental Perspective," in *Psychology of Adult Development and Aging,* eds. C. Eisdorfer and M. P. Lawton (Washington D.C.: American Psychological Association, 1973), pp. 312–313. "The term developmental refers here not only to those processes that are biologically programed and inherent in the organism, but also to those in which the organism is irreversibly changed or transformed by interaction with the environment. As the result of one's life history with its accumulating record of adaptations to both biological and social events, there is a continually changing basis *within the individual* for perceiving and responding to new events . . . For the present, the student of adult personality will find it strategic to accept age relatedness alone as the criterion, that is, to call developmental those processes that can be demonstrated to vary in an orderly way with age regardless of the direction of change . . . The psychologist is eventually concerned not with the passage of time itself, but with the biological, social and psychological events that give substance and meaning to time. In exploring an uncharted field, however, it is a justifiable first step to use age as a preliminary index and to determine which, if any, personality phenomena are more associated with age than with other gross variables such as sex, health, ethnicity, level of education or social class."

tory (cohort differences). Persons born at different periods of history live through different social and cultural events. These different socializing conditions have created differences in the personalities of people not expected to occur to another group experiencing that same age span but in a different historical period.

In the following chapters we will look in detail at information associated with four periods of adult life: young adult, middle adult, maturity, and old age. Before we examine the specific stages, it will be helpful to provide some background through a brief overview of generalizations arising from several extensive research projects.

University of Chicago Studies

Sociocultural Influences on Development

The Committee on Human Development at the University of Chicago has given significant leadership to the study of sociocultural influences on development. One emphasis of their research has been to identify and describe the prevailing issues that occupy the energies and attention of persons at different periods in the adult life. Included among such issues are

1. how time is perceived by people of different ages;
2. how we visualize ourselves as stronger or weaker at certain life periods;
3. the meaning that work and family have in our lives at different periods;
4. how we conceptualize death;
5. how we formulate values, life style, and use of time.[11]

AGE-STATUS SYSTEM.   One of the findings from the University of Chicago research that contributed to a framework for viewing adult development is the age-status system. Their research emphasizes that most people have definite ideas about what are the appropriate ages for life events such as leaving school, taking a job, marriage, and parenthood. How we feel about where we are with this schedule has important implications. In our framework for looking at the regularity or orderly patterning of changes underlying the total life-cycle, we need to include age status as well as biological status. In

---

[11] B. L. Neugarten, "Adult Personality: Toward a Psychology of the Life Cycle," in *Middle Age and Aging,* ed. B. L. Neugarten (Chicago: University of Chicago Press, 1968), p. 139.

the following quotation, Neugarten suggests implications for developing a theoretical framework to view adult life.

> These studies have relevance for a theory of the psychology of the life-cycle in two ways: First in indicating that the age structure of a society, the internalization of age-norms, and age-group identifications are important dimensions of the social and cultural *context* in which the course of the individual life line must be viewed;
>
> Second, because these concepts point to at least one additional way of structuring the passage of time in the life-span of the individual, *providing a time clock* that can be superimposed over the biological clock, together they help us to comprehend the life-cycle. The major punctuation marks in the adult life line tend (those, that is, which are orderly and sequential) to be more often social than biological—or, if biologically based, they are often biological events that occur to significant others rather than to oneself, like grandparenthood or widowhood.
>
> If psychologists are to discover order in the events of adulthood, and if they are to discover order in the personality changes that occur in all individuals as they age, we should look to the social as well as to the biological clock, and certainly to social definitions of age and age-appropriate behavior.[12]

TIME SINCE BIRTH AND TIME LEFT TO LIVE.   Neugarten has set forth a time-related construct for describing the internal frame of reference for an individual. She suggests that somewhere in the early or mid-forties an individual passes through a time line. He stops thinking in terms of how many years he has been living and starts thinking of how many years he has left. The importance of the change in perspective is expressed in the following comment:

> Neugarten, more than any other theorist, elaborates the role of age and timing in adult development. The shift from "time since birth" to "time left to live" sets boundaries for other major changes: from sense of self-determination to sense of the inevitability of the life cycle, from mastery of the outer world, through re-examination, to withdrawal and pre-occupation with inner self and sponsoring others, from achievement to self-satisfaction. She found that when normal events were "on time"—children leaving home, menopause, death of a spouse—they were not seen as crises and generally were not traumatic or damaging. Departure and death of loved ones causes grief and sadness as does the prospect of one's own leaving, but when it occurs at times and in ways consist-

[12] Ibid., p. 146.

ent with normal expected life cycle, most persons manage without major upset.[13]

Kansas City Studies of Adult Life

During the 1950s and 1960s a group of investigators on the Committee on Human Development at the University of Chicago carried forward a series of investigations on changes in personality associated with the second half of life. Field work for many of these studies was done in the Kansas City area.[14] There have been two series of investigations. The first set were cross-sectional studies dealing with 700 men and women. The participants ranged in age from 40 to 70 and represented all levels of social status. The second series consisted of in-depth interviews with a smaller group, about 300 men and women aged 50 to 90 years. The persons were interviewed at regular intervals during a six-year period.

An important theory on social-psychological aspects of aging in adult life grew from those studies: the *disengagement theory*. This theory has gone through considerable modification as researchers in the Kansas City studies continued to analyze their data and profited from the findings of other research and writing prompted by the theory.

The principal finding from the study is that there is considerable difference between (1) an individual's day-by-day, active, effective, energetic problem solving and (2) his internal, subconscious organization of feelings and perceptions. The researchers found that there was not a noticeable decrease in competence of performance in adult work and social roles, nor a lessening in involvement in social interaction until the mid-sixties or early seventies. People carry forward business as usual in a rather effective fashion.

They did discover, however, through analysis of inferences in in-depth interviews and projective tests that there was a definite increase in inward orientation and a decrease in emotional attachment to outer-world events beginning in the late forties and fifties. This change was described as increased "interiority." We will discuss these changes in further detail in our chapters on middle adult and maturity.

[13] A. W. Chickering, "The Developmental and Educational Needs of Adults," paper presented to annual meeting of the American Personnel and Guidance Association, April 1975, New Orleans, p. 8.

[14] B. L. Neugarten and associates, *Personality in Middle and Late Life,* (New York: Atherton Press, 1964). The book presents much of the material from the Kansas City studies. Neugarten puts these studies in perspective with ongoing research in developmental psychology in her chapter, "Personality Change in Late Life: A Developmental Perspective," in *The Psychology of Adult Development and Aging,* eds. C. Eisdorfer and M. P. Lawton (Washington, D. C.: American Psychological Association, 1973), pp. 311–334.

DISENGAGEMENT THEORY.   The disengagement theory stimulated much controversy because it seemed to be a departure from the view of aging that had been held by most people through the years. The prevailing view at the time was what the researchers termed *activity theory*. It held that except for changes in biology and health, older people have essentially the same psychological and social needs as middle-aged people. When confronted with the fact that in old age people are less active, less socially interested, and less involved, the popular response has been that this is because society has squeezed the older person out. Society was said to have isolated and ignored the older person. The failure to include them in the ongoing affairs of society was said to be against the desires and well-being of older persons. The popular view was that the healthy way to grow old was to stay active and to carry forward as much as possible the life-style of earlier years.

The disengagement theory set forth by Cumming and Henry in the book *Growing Old* picked up the other side of the picture.[15] They said that the withdrawal process was a mutual action. The older person desired to withdraw and so did society. The older person withdrew because his emotional interests and energies were shifting from an external to an internal orientation. This was based on some of the findings in the "interiority" data where intrapsychic changes were seen to precede changes in the external coping behaviors of individuals.

Growing Old presented the further postulate (which had many implications for community planning as well as for family and social guilt feelings) that in old age it is the disengaged—not the socially active—person who will have the greatest sense of well-being and life satisfaction.

The breadth of generalizations presented in the first version of the disengagement theory did not hold up as the Chicago group continued their analysis of their data. Rather, they found that the level of activity associated with life satisfaction was influenced by personality and the characteristics of previous life-style. In the time the previous postulate was reversed[16] to say that high life satisfaction is more often present in persons who are socially active and involved than in persons who are inactive and uninvolved. However, there is much diversity among older persons. Whereas the researchers later found that there was a positive relationship between *engagement* and life satisfaction, they also found that this relationship was not consistent. As a

[15] E. Cumming and W. E. Henry, *Growing Old* (New York: Basic Books, 1961).
[16] B. L. Neugarten, "Personality Change in Late Life," p. 328.

matter of fact, they found four life-satisfaction patterns: high activity and high satisfaction, low and low, high and low, and low and high.

Their case data reflected interesting patterns of interaction of previous life-style, personality, old-age activity, and life satisfaction. Some persons preparing for old age begin to relinquish responsibilities and involvements with a sense of satisfaction; some become unhappy at the prospect of dropping out of their leadership role; others have had a life-style of little social involvement and, as they move into old age, there is not a major change in either their pattern of activity or their level of involvement.

Personality organization is the key factor in predicting who will age successfully. Adaptation is the key concept. Patterns of aging reflect longstanding life-styles; consistencies rather than inconsistencies in coping patterns predominate as the individual moves from middle age through old age. Patterns of aging are predictable from knowing the individuals in middle life.[17]

The Kansas City studies observed trends between the sexes that were later expressed with greater clarity in the San Francisco Bay area studies. As men become older, they become more receptive to affiliative, nurturant, and sensual emotions than young men. As women become older, they become more receptive to impulses toward self-expression and more aggressive and managerial in interpersonal relationships. Men move toward more theoretical, abstract, and introspective style with age; women move toward a more direct, applied, and expressive style with age.[18] With increased age, members of both sexes move toward an increasing preoccupation with their own personal lives and needs.

Transitional Longitudinal Study— University of California

Four Transitional Groups Majorie Fiske Lowenthal, chairperson, and others in the Human Development Program at the University of California at Berkeley have taken as their focus the events and experiences associated with persons as they proceed through one of the several major *transition periods* of adult life. They chose to look at two "positive" transition periods, termed positive because the transition is viewed as "voluntary" and as moving the individual toward more ex-

---

[17] Ibid., pp. 328–329.
[18] Ibid., p. 320.

panded and socially valued life status. The two stages (1) leaving high school and moving toward job, college, and marriage; (2) leaving the stage of newlyweds and moving toward parenthood.

They also chose two transitional stages sometimes described as "negative" because they are thought to be "involuntary" and as moving individuals toward reduced expression and less valued social status. The two stages were (1) the postparental, or "empty-nest," stage, moving the individual toward career changes within the home and forecasting the nearing of change of status in community and job activities; (2) retirement stage, moving the individual into a new social role "outside the world of work."

The study[19] is continuing with periodic interviews with 216 men and women who live in the central part of San Francisco. They are mostly middle and lower middle class. The plan for selection of the participants was built around one senior high school in the city. The geographic boundaries of that school formed the district from which all four transitional groups were drawn.

The youngest group was selected from the graduating class: 25 males and 27 females. The senior class records were used to identify the empty-nest group, finding among the seniors those who were the youngest in their family and letting their parents serve as the group from which 27 middle-aged men and 27 middle-aged women were selected. The newlywed group consisted of 25 men and 25 women who had been married less than 12 months when selected and had not yet started a family. They were friends of either the seniors or their parents, or some were residents of the district and had applied for marriage licenses within the 12 months preceding the selection of participants. The group from which the retired sample was selected were friends of the high school and middle-aged groups or were persons whose names were on the to-be-retired rolls of local organizations.

Understanding Stress

We will have occasion to discuss various aspects of the characteristics and life histories of persons in these groups in the following chapters. At this point we must be content to observe the theoretical context while seeking a further understanding of the influences of stress in adult development. It is the investigators' assumption that all changes, whether "positive" (entering a new

[19] M. F. Lowenthal, M. T. Thurnher, and D. Chiriboga, *Four Stages of Life* (San Francisco: Jossey-Bass, 1975).

job) or "negative" (loss of a job), are potentially stressful. They describe their rationale as follows:

> The anticipation of an impending transition often serves as a stimulus to examine, and possibly to reorient, goals and aspirations, and to reassess personal resources and impediments in the light of the probability of their attainment. In searching out commonalities and differences in such coping processes among persons about to undergo four very different types of transition, we hope also to contribute to the understanding of the more gradual adaptive processes evoked by less dramatic changes that most people sense in themselves, their immediate milieu, and the broader society as they grow up, mature or do not mature, and grow old.[20]

Sex Differences in Aging

As mentioned earlier, there was considerable similarity between the San Francisco and the Kansas City studies in the findings of different aging patterns for men and women. In early and middle life, men are heavily involved in mastery of the environment, in managing and producing. As they mature and move into retirement, there is a mellowing and a laying aside the "hassles" in favor of fellowship and family life. In early life, although oriented toward family, women may become involved in dealing with the world of work. However, the group of young women in this study did not have their hearts in competitive striving of careers outside the home. In mid-life, home and family predominate; there is a general tendency to see the husband as boss and needs of the family coming first. As the children leave home and the husband begins to "mellow," women also change. They begin to present many of the attitudes and behaviors of men in early middle life. They are more self-assertive and more interested in starting new careers, and they are interested in developing new roles and relationships in their community.

Family Centeredness

The most striking and singularly pervasive finding from the study is the high degree of family centeredness that was found across all four life stages.

Young men and women leaving high school think of work as how it will enable them to establish and support a family. Newlyweds are already projecting toward parental roles. The empty-nest and retirement years establish

---

[20] Ibid., pp. x–xi.

a renewed dependence of the husband and wife on the mutuality of their relationship to meet needs of nurturance and succorance.[21]

The investigators suggested that the people in this study perhaps reflect some homogenizing of social class values. They seem to represent "that increasingly mixed (blue- and white-collar) segment which may in part be beginning to assimilate values of professional and artistic elites but remain primarily job-and-family oriented."[22] There appears to be little influence from the national focus on changing orientations toward family and sex roles. In this study conducted in the early 1970s, "the presented and projected life-styles of these young people of both sexes were family-centered and male dominant. As though reflecting on their parents' prospects, their hopes for themselves at postparental and retirement stages amounted to little more than financial security, a modicum of comfort, and freedom from occupational and parental responsibilities."[23]

We will refer frequently to this study as we discuss changes in women's life at postparental and retirement years. Concerns growing out of it regarding the lack of planning for adult and late-life stages will also be discussed in our section on old age and in a consideration of life satisfactions in each of the adult stages.

Intergenerational Studies in Development and Aging—Berkeley

Forty-Year Follow-up   In the 1930s the Institute of Human Development at Berkeley was actively studying the development of young children. Their approach involved periodic tests and interviews with the young children and their parents. Data from the interviews with the parents (then about 30 years old) form the first part of the study reported by Maas and Kuypers, *From Thirty to Seventy*.[24] The second part consists of interviews and tests with 142 of the parents who are now in their seventies.

The object of the study was to look at how the young-adult and old-age phases of the adult life course are related. They were interested in looking at

---

[21] M. T. Thurnher, "Family Confluence, Conflict and Affect," in *Four Stages of Life,* ed. M. F. Lowenthal et al., pp. 24–27.

[22] Lowenthal et al., *Four Stages of Life,* p. 242.

[23] Ibid., p. 244.

[24] H. S. Maas and J. A. Kuypers, *From Thirty to Seventy* (San Francisco: Jossey-Bass, 1974).

the diversity of life-style and personality in old age and about how different life-styles in early adult years relate to living and psychological orientations in later life. The people participating in this study were above average in financial and health status. Most were born around 1900. The men served in World War I and were young adults in the 1920s. They suffered the 1930s Depression and rolled with the tides of our nation's economy to ride the wave of prosperity in the late 1940s through the 1950s. Almost 80 per cent of the men had had occupations as small-business owners, executives of large organizations, or were professionals; more than half of them were college graduates in comparison to the approximately 5 per cent of the national population over 70 who have college educations.[25]

Life-styles Through the Years

One of the observations from this review of the 40-year span of adult life has to do with differences between the sexes. It was found that there is greater similarity among men in their early life-styles (their thirties) with their later life-styles than is true for women.[26] That is, the kind of life lived by younger women is usually quite different from the kind of life lived by older women. A woman's adult life course includes several discontinuities. Women experience role and other changes in occupational, marital, and parenting areas, and cumulative effects of these changes are likely to have considerable influence on how they live their daily lives.

Personality Patterns Through the Years

Women not only differ from men by having greater differences in life-styles between young and older periods of life, they also differ from men in having greater similarity of personality patterns in early and late life.[27] Continuities in personality, with early signs flowering into anticipated personality patterns in old age, were more evident for women than men. They were most evident in women whose old-age personality is characterized by anxiety and ineffective functioning. There was also the suggestion that psychological weaknesses that may emerge in old age have more visible signs in young adulthood than do the incipient strengths. However, the data did not suggest

[25] U.S. Department of Commerce, Bureau of Census, *Statistical Abstracts of the U.S. 1974*, p. 117.

[26] Mass and Kuypers, *From Thirty to Seventy*, p. 203.

[27] Ibid., pp. 203–204.

that there were fixed and immutable problems in young adult personalities that lead unalterably to pathology in old age.[28]

Strong at Seventy   Maas and Kuypers feel that one of the striking findings is the optimistic picture presented by interviews with 142 people ranging in age from 60 to 82 years. They state: "Popular beliefs that aging ushers in a massive decline in psychological functioning or a narrowing down of ways of living find no support in our evidence."[29] There is, indeed, rich diversity in the lives reported. It is interesting to note that the investigators found considerable variation of personality patterns within each of the life-styles. As a matter of fact, they also found that the hypothesis of certain combinations of personality patterns being required for long-term marriages was not supported in their data. Couples who had been living together for forty years did not necessarily share patternable pairings of personality types or life-style. They report, "Just about every kind of mother, as classified by her life-style, was married to just about every kind of father, as categorized by his life-style . . . nor was there any evidence that long-lasting marriages occur only when wives of personality type A live with husbands of personality type B."[30]

Duke Longitudinal Studies

Since 1955, Duke Medical Center has been conducting longitudinal studies on normal aging. The persons being studied are middle-aged and aged community residents who were willing and able to come to the center for one or two days of examinations. Some of the persons come in every two years; others are brought in annually, according to different phases of the research.

The studies are focused on common or typical aspects of aging rather than on abnormalities. The investigators come from various disciplines and they include medical, psychiatric, psychological, and social examinations for each participant. Erdman Palmore, coordinator of the Longitudinal Studies of Aging, made the following observation concerning the value of interdisciplinary and longitudinal methods of research.

[28] Ibid., p. 199.
[29] Ibid., p. 200.
[30] Ibid., p. 209.

Since aging is by definition a process of change over time, it would seem that the best way to study aging is longitudinally, by repeated observations over time. This is not meant to deny the value of cross-sectional studies, nor to deny the technical and methodological problems connected with longitudinal study, but it is meant to reassert the unique advantages of longitudinal studies such as the following: each panel member can be used as his own control, consistent trends can be distinguished from temporary fluctuations, errors due to retrospective distortion are minimized, early warning signs of disease or death can be studied, cohort differences can be distinguished from age changes, and the effects of one kind of change on another kind of change at a later time period can be studied.

The interdisciplinary nature of the study is useful because aging affects many interrelated types of behavior and functioning. When specialists from different disciplines work together, the mutual stimulations, correction, and combination of perspectives can result in more accurate, thorough, and comprehensive understanding of the aging process.[31]

Findings from the studies have contributed especially to information on concomitants of physiological conditions of old age. Although noting some decline with age in immunities, skin conditions, vision, hearing, health ratings, and sexual activity, they also noted considerable variation and with some individuals they noted improvement rather than decline. They found little decline in social and psychological effectiveness that could be attributed to age.[32] References to the Duke data appear frequently in other chapters of this book.

Ethel Percy Andrus Gerontology Center

One of the newer institutions giving leadership in education and research in aging is the Andrus Gerontology Center, University of Southern California. Its research staff[33] is especially distinguished by its interdisciplinary representatives of anthropology, architecture, biochemistry, biochemical engineering, neurobiology, physiology, experimental and social psychology, social work, and urban planning.

---

[31] E. Palmore, ed. *Normal Aging II* (Durham: Duke University Press, 1974), pp. 3–4.

[32] Ibid., pp. 289–290.

[33] D. S. Woodruff and J. E. Birren, eds., *Aging: Scientific Perspectives and Social Issues* (New York: Van Nostrand, 1975). This text, prepared by members of the Ethel Percy Andrus Gerontology Center staff, provides an orientation to the work of the center as well as course material for students of aging.

Graduate students are involved in urban studies, relating issues of adult development to architecture and regional planning and to the problems of social work. Public administrators are also studying the issues of management and the needs of the aging. And a number of ongoing studies are in progress in the biological and social sciences.

In the Environmental Studies laboratory at the center, a group of researchers are looking at the degree of integration of aged persons with persons of similar and other ages. They are interested in how different kinds of living arrangements influence social relationships. They are examining how housing design for the elderly influences their physical and mental health.

The "generation gap" is the focus of another research group.[34] Several hundred three-generation families are being studied to examine the degree of family cohesion through time. The investigators are finding similarity, not difference, to be a dominant pattern when comparing parents and offspring, thus raising questions about the validity of the popular stereotype of a generation gap.

A project under the direction of Vern Bengtson is gathering data from middle-aged and elderly people in three ethnic groups—black, Mexican-American, and white—to understand how different groups adapt to aging. They are investigating particularly the individual's relationship to families, to the political process, and to the delivery of social services.

A related project is surveying societal policy makers—politicians, professionals, and business and union representatives—to determine how they are likely to respond to the complex social issues associated with developing policy and services for effective aging. A third aspect of this project involves study in Italy, Tanzania, Yugoslavia, and Israel to determine how people in these different cultures are responding to the problems of aging.

Other Resources for Study of Adult Lives

The ongoing studies of adult life described here briefly are to alert the student to available resources for a more in-depth look at some aspects of adult development. Extensive data and commentary from each of these studies are presented in available books.

[34] V. L. Bengtson, "Generation and Family Effects in Value Socialization," *American Sociological Review* 40 (June 1975), pp. 358–371.

HARRIS POLL—AGING IN AMERICA.   Another current and extensive collection of data that we will refer to frequently in the following chapters is *The Myth and Reality of Aging in America*.[35] This book reports the results from a Harris Poll conducted in the summer of 1974. Interviews were conducted with 4,254 persons, serving as a "representative cross-section of the American public 18 years of age and over, selected by random probability sampling techniques."[36]

The interviews were designed to obtain information in eight areas having to do with aging. The thrust of the study was toward a better understanding of the attitudes and experiences of people 65 years of age and older and of how the younger public views people in that age group. However, the data also provide information on characteristics of adults at all age levels. The interviews asked respondents to indicate experiences as well as to speculate on the experiences of people 65 and over. Thus, the data tables provide opportunity to compare self-reports of people at young and middle adult ages with those of people 65 and over.[37]

As you will remember from our discussion of this study in Chapter 2, there is the clear generalization that most people have a very different perception of what old age is like than does the individual who is over 65. Most older people feel their condition is better economically and socially than the general public believes it to be. Interestingly enough, most older people share the public image of what most people over 65 are like. Each simply thinks his situation is different from the "typical" person over 65 years of age.

STUDIES OF YOUNG ADULTS.   Also extremely helpful in terms of information on adult development and as a method of study of lives are the books of Robert W. White, *Lives in Progress* and *Study of Lives*.[38] White presents case studies from personality research carried out in the 1940s and 1950s in the Harvard Psychological Clinic under the direction or in the tradition of

---

[35] L. Harris and associates, *The Myth and Reality of Aging in America* (Washington, D.C.: The National Council on the Aging, 1975).

[36] Ibid., p. v.

[37] Ibid., pp. 53–55.

[38] R. W. White, *Lives in Progress: A Study of the Natural Growth of Personality* (New York: Holt, Rinehart and Winston, 1966). R. W. White, ed., *Study of Lives* (New York: Atherton Press, 1963).

Henry Murry.[39] These studies begin with persons during their college years with follow-up studies at later periods of life.

The research activity and writing on student development by Nevitt Sanford gave impetus to a short burst of activity across the nation in the 1960s directed toward the study of development in young adult years. The Vassar studies, which he directed in the 1950s, served as a model for longitudinal studies on several campuses. In the 1960s, Sanford's mammoth book *The American College*[40] highlighted the existing information on development of the young adult with recommendations for research activity needed for this phase of adult life. We will refer to other resources in the study of college student development in the chapter on the young adult years, including the work of Kenneth Keniston,[41] another associate of Henry Murry at the Harvard Psychological Clinic.

HUMAN AGING STUDY—BESTHESDA, MARYLAND.   Another well-known study of aging is the *Human Aging*[42] longitudinal study conducted by 22 investigators at the National Institute of Mental Health in Bethesda, Maryland, between 1956 and 1967. James E. Birren, later head of the Andrus Center, directed the study, which consisted of two groups of older men and a control group of young men in their twenties. The older men were as close to complete physical, mental, and social well-being as possible. Group 1 were men with extraordinarily good health without any or only slight evidence of trivial disease; group 2 were men who were the conventional picture of healthy older men with only slight evidence of disease with possibly serious implications, but so slight as to be undetectable in any but the most sophisticated examination. They ranged in age from 65 to 91 with a median age of 71. About one third had been laborers, the rest had been professionals and businessmen. They were matched with a comparison group of healthy young men with a mean age of 21. The men were tested in 1956 and again five and eleven years later. The findings emphasize that if individuals retain their health, there is remarkably little difference between the young and the old.

---

[39] H. A. Murray, *Explorations in Personality: A Clinical and Experimental Study of Fifty Men of College Age* (New York: Science Editions, 1938, 2nd printing 1965).

[40] N. Sanford, *The American College* (New York: Wiley, 1962).

[41] K. Keniston, *Young Radicals: Notes on Committed Youth* (New York: Harcourt Brace Jovanovich, 1968).

[42] J. E. Birren and associates, eds., *Human Aging I* and *Human Aging II* (Washington, D.C.: National Institute of Mental Health, 1971). DHEW Pub No. ADM-74-122, ADM-74-123.

OTHER RESEARCH.   In 1974 the National Institute of Aging was established as a separate institute in the National Institutes of Health. The first director was Robert Butler, a member of the Human Aging study team. Some of the emphases of the institute are suggested in an early comment by the director.[43]

It is presumptive to single out a few research centers from among an increasing number of centers and academic departments staffed with well-prepared scholars who are giving able leadership to the field. The intent of this section has not been to present a review of the literature or an evaluation of existing programs; rather, it has been to provide an introduction to the kinds of issues and approaches that characterize the study of adult development and aging. It has also been to give you an introduction to some of the people and studies influential in my thinking and to whom we will be making frequent references in the pages to come.

Most major universities have one or more staff members involved in research on some aspect of adult development. Several have centers that have made significant contributions to the development of this field of study. There are also nearly 30 professional organizations pertaining to aging; each state has an agency associated with the U.S. Administration on Aging; and the National Council on Aging has listed 284 national organizations with programs in the field. One third of the articles appearing in *The Gerontologist* from 1961 to 1975 came from 20 leading institutional sources; two thirds came from individuals on other campuses and agencies representing a broad base of research involvement.[44]

This is a rapidly growing area of study. There are two bibliographies to which you may refer to obtain a more adequate perspective of the people involved in research on adult development and aging. The National Council on the Aging publishes a quarterly bibliography, *Current Literature on Aging,* and the *Journal of Gerontology* contains a quarterly "Index to Current Periodical Literature."

And again—as a reminder—let me mention the variety of "reports" of observations and interpretative "research" on stages of adult development that have been done by novelists and poets. Example 7–1 contains notes of the poet James Agee considering a scene he was preparing for a musical version of *Candide.*

[43] R. N. Butler, "Guest Editorial; Early Directions for the National Institute on Aging," *The Gerontologist* 16 (August 1976), 4:293–294.

[44] J. D. Rasch, "Institutional Origins of Articles in *The Gerontologist* 1961–1975," *The Gerontologist* 16 (June 1976), 3:276–279.

Example 7–1.
Life Events

I will write of Eldorado, the Earthly Paradise, and this scene should be entirely in verse, entirely sung, and most of it, probably danced. I think of centering it around three events in court, in which "the people" bring before their mild, saintlike king, not pleas, but three events or statements of intention, for his hearing, and his blessing: the celebration of a birth; the intent for divorce and re-marriage; and the intent to die. The first is self-evident, as among people who need fear no evil, and only sorrow which is to be accepted in gratitude and reverence. The second: the husband, in the presence of the community and of his wife and her lover, declares that he yields her to her lover. Candide: "But don't you *love* her?" Husband: "How, otherwise, could I yield her up and wish her so well?" Candide (after trying to describe the agonies of jealousy): "Don't you *desire* her?" Husband: "How could a true man, or woman, desire one whose desire is for another?" The third: A very fine old man, surrounded by four generations of his magnificent family, appears before the king. The old man is a farmer: "I have loved God; and the poets; and my wives; and their children; and theirs; and I have loved the soil, and have dealt with it reverently. Now, I declare my wish to die." He briefly describes two main things: that he has, of late, after being ever more grateful for life, decade after decade, begun in every way to tire: to long for the unknown, whatever it may be; and to tire in his faculties. He can foresee an ever saddening decline, which he does not wish to inflict either on those who love him, or upon himself. And so: The king nods, and signals; a draught is brought; he sings an extempore farewell to his loved ones and to the world and to life, drinks, and dies quickly and without pain, surrounded by his family.

From J. Agee, *Letters of James Agee to Father Flye* (New York: George Braziller, 1962), pp. 217–218.

Summary

Research in adult development and formulations of patterns of growth may come from several approaches. There are the impressions, folklore, and intuitive wisdom reflected in fiction[45] and poetry. There are biographies and oral histories, clinical studies with thematic outlines and personality theories formed from in-depth observations of psychotherapy. There are longitu-

---

[45] N. J. Hendrickson, D. Perkins, S. White, and T. Buck, "Parent-Daughter Relationships in Fiction," *The Family Coordinator* 24 (July 1975), 3:257–262. The article points to some safeguards when using fiction in teaching human development.

dinal and cross-sectional studies that take up particular questions and compare individuals of different ages or different periods of history in regard to life satisfaction, emotional problems, physical activities, cognitive functions, and family or work experiences. Each approach provides a dimension of information necessary in the building of a framework for understanding and predicting adult development. The types of information differ in levels of abstraction, in specificity, and in qualities of control. Our task will be to recognize the values of different sources. Our need for certain kinds of information to answer questions in the formulation of our framework may in turn direct us toward conducting certain types of investigations for ourselves.

Suggested Activities and Further Reading

1. Prepare a brief biographical introduction responding to the question, "Where am I in relation to developmental stages of adult years?" Do you think of yourself as a young adult, middle adult, in maturity, or in old age? Is it possible that none of these designations fit you exactly? Why?

2. What particularly important experiences have you had with persons in other stages of adulthood?

3. In association with each of the remaining chapters of this book, we suggest that you prepare a *time line* describing events going on in the world during the periods through which each age group has been living. Thus, at the end of the book you will be able to compare the time lines of young adults with the time lines of middle adults, adults of maturity, and adults of old age. In preparation for creating the time lines, prepare a time line to show significant events surrounding you as you passed through childhood and as you have grown through adult years.

   On your time line, list at one end the national events that were happening at the time you were born and in the years before you entered school. What did you sing? What movies or television programs were popular? In the high school section of your time line, list the events and national successes or crises that you remember were important along with personalities and programs from the media or the arts, sports, and science world. Continue your time line to your present period, marking off those times that seem to represent a time of transition in your life, times when you moved into new status and new roles. Include on your time line the national and community events of those periods that stand out in your memory.

4. Discuss the possible applications of the life-course approach to research and to study of adult development as it is presented by R. C. Atchley, "The Life Course,

Age Grading, and Age-Linked Demands for Decision Making," in *Life Span Developmental Psychology: Normative Life Crises,* eds. N. Datan and L. N. Ginsberg (New York: Academic Press, 1975).

5. Have a panel consider the different uses of *life review* in program development. Have a task force develop guidelines for the use of a *life history approach* to the study of adult development. The following references will help you begin your consideration.

> B. G. Myerhoff and V. Tufte, "Life History as Integration," *The Gerontologist* 7 (December 1975), 6:541–543.
>
> R. N. Butler, "The Life Review," *Psychiatry* 26 (1963), pp. 65–76.
>
> M. I. Lewis and R. N. Butler, "Life Review Therapy," *Geriatrics* 29 (1974), pp. 165–173.
>
> G. W. Allport, *The Uses of Personal Documents in Psychological Science* (New York: Social Science Research Council, Bulletin 49, 1942).
>
> J. Dollard, *Criteria for the Life History* (New York: Peter Smith, 1949).
>
> L. L. Langness, *The Life History in Anthropological Science* (New York: Holt, Rinehart and Winston, 1965).
>
> H. A. Murray, *Explorations in Personality* (New York: Science Editions, 1965), Chapter 4.

6. Make a list of individuals, agencies, and groups in your region who are engaged in research on adult development.

7. Prepare a list—with brief identifying sentences—of the different approaches to, and tools used in, research in adult development. The series on *Life-Span Developmental Psychology,* in footnote 1 of this chapter, will provide a place to begin.

chapter 8

Young Adult Years

Getting Our Bearings

As we consider a developmental period, we will look first at information that describes the characteristics of people in that age range. We will look also at the developmental significance of this period. We will try to understand how different approaches to some of the situations people are experiencing in this time period may influence future directions in their development. Looking from the other direction and clarifying a general picture of this age, we may better understand the meaning a particular situation has for the young adult and why he may respond as he does—that is, why he may respond differently than a middle adult or an adolescent.

For purposes of our discussion we will arbitrarily use 18 as the beginning age of the young adult. We will consider the next five years as being the introductory period. During this time, 18 to 23, the young person is seeking, and preparing for a life career (perhaps trying out in apprenticeships and summer employment). This is the period of searching for and finding his identity in many aspects—values, roles, self-concept.

The next ten years, from 24 to 34, are the entry years. They are the beginning of a career commitment, the beginning of marriage, and usually the beginning of parenthood.

The age range we are suggesting is an arbitrary framework. In thinking developmentally, we need to remember that it is the sequence of stages that provides the framework as much or more than the chronological age or (especially in adult life) biological changes. It is important to remember that there is a powerful social awareness surrounding an individual that

8–1 *During the young adult years, individuals are taking the beginning steps on paths to careers and independent lives. (Photo University for Man, Manhattan, Kansas)*

becomes internalized as an age-status.[1] We are aware of developmental tasks and accomplishments appropriate—socially expected—of persons at different ages. The specific ages vary somewhat with different social classes. The calendar moves a little faster for the low social class: people go to work earlier, marry earlier, and so on. Upper social classes are slower than the middle class in career entry.

Let us look first at some general descriptive information to remind ourselves of the characteristics of the young adult. We are fortunate that this age group, especially the beginning phase, was much in the public's attention during the past decade and a fair body of literature was developed. Research money seems to follow rather than precede areas of national tension. Child development study grew out of public awareness of child neglect. Study of late adult life has begun after that population has already started to tip the scales of social concerns and population balance. The study of youth and

---

[1] B. L. Neugarten and J. W. Moore, "The Changing Age-Status System," in *Middle Age and Aging,* ed. B. L. Neugarten (Chicago: University of Chicago Press, 1968), pp. 5–21. B. L. Neugarten, J. W. Moore, and J. C. Lowe, "Age Norms, Age Constraints, and Adult Socialization," *American Journal of Sociology* 70 (May 1965), 6.

young adult years began after the crisis of "campus rebellion" was well aflame and long after the years of the "apathetic generation."[2]

Impact of the Past Decade

During the past decade our nation has gone through great agony, with much vacillation, in attempting to evaluate how best to help the young person prepare for and become established in the world of work.[3] The tradition of the immigrant finding a new future through education, of establishing public schools, of compulsory education until age 14,[4] of the land-grant institutions and the junior college—all these express the thought that formal and eventually higher education were the way for *all* people to prepare for life. As the 1960s began, we were approaching the position that not a high school diploma but a college degree should be the norm.

As the 1970s dawned, that position was being seriously questioned.[5] It was found that students were "being processed" through college—often against their will—with little effectual change or preparation for life. Industry was saying college graduates did not have the skills needed. They were also saying that technology was changing so fast that the skills must be learned on the job. Students were saying, "We do not know what we want or what potential abilities we have. We are not sure what the meaning of life and our society is."

During the period of expanding employment, young people were going directly to work out of high school. Career education became a national policy with an effort to begin early in life to help the child recognize future avenues of work and creativity. It is difficult to anticipate what the next years will bring as we approach the 1980s. Tightened economy has redirected the flow of young people toward the campus as education provides the "holding" function of keeping the young out of the labor market.

---

[2] This term was sometimes used for the alienated young people of the 1950s. For a discussion of this period, see K. Keniston, *The Uncommitted: Alienated Youth in American Society* (New York: Harcourt Brace Jovanovich, 1965).

[3] At times the concern has been phrased more broadly: "How best to help the young person to prepare for effective citizenship or self-realization."

[4] Some of the flavor and the problems of these aspirations are reflected in W. L. Warner, R. J. Havighurst, and M. B. Loeb, *Who Shall Be Educated?* (New York: Harper & Row, 1944).

[5] F. Newman, *Report on Higher Education* (Washington, D.C.: HEW, U.S. Government Printing Office, 1971); see also F. Newman, "A Preview of the Second Newman Report," *Change* (May 1972), pp. 28–37.

We need to look at two groups of young people to form an overall picture of activities and characteristics of the young adult during the first five years of this stage.[6] The two groups are (1) those who go directly into apprenticeships and vocational schools, the military, or beginning occupations; (2) those who enter some aspect of higher education.

National Profiles of Young Adults

Under the sponsorship of several philanthropic organizations, Daniel Yankelovich[7] has been studying changing patterns of attitudes of young people (16 to 25 years) since 1967. In 1974 he reported vast changes between the profiles of the 1960s and 1970s. The most striking finding was the speed with which the attitudes and values of a rather extreme forerunner, or counterculture, group of the 1960s had been selectively, but extensively, adopted by the majority of young noncollege and college people.

Example 8–1 presents a comparison of outlook and activities in the '60s and '70s. Yankelovich suggests two factors as largely responsible for these changes of outlook and behavior. The first, of course, was the Vietnam war. The second is the diffusion of new values moving through college and noncollege young adults and influencing society at large. They group the new values into three areas: (1) moral values, (2) social values, and (3) selffulfillment.[8]

New Moral Values   Within the area of new moral values the changes have come in four aspects. There is a change in sexual morality toward more liberal sex mores. There are changes in the way individuals regard established institutions such as

---

[6] This period has been referred to as the "leaving family" period (LF) by D. Levinson et al. in "Periods in the Adult Development of Men: Ages 18–45," *The Counseling Psychologist* 6 (1976), 1:21–25, and D. Levinson et al., "The Psychosocial Development of Men in Early Adulthood and the Mid-Life Transition," in *Life History Research in Psychopathology*, vol. 3, eds. D. F. Ricks, A. Thomas, and M. Roff (Minneapolis: University of Minnesota Press, 1974). G. Sheehy terms it the "pulling-up roots" period in *Passages: Predictable Crises of Adult Life* (New York: Dutton, 1976). R. Gould observed differences between the 16 to 18 group (escape parental dominance), 18 to 22 group (substitute friends for family), and 22 to 28 group (active in becoming competent in the real world), in "The Phases of Adult Life: A Study in Developmental Psychology," *American Journal of Psychiatry* 129 (November 1972), 5:521–531.

[7] D. Yankelovich, *The New Morality: A Profile of American Youth in the 70's* (New York: McGraw-Hill, 1974).

[8] Ibid., pp. 5–7.

Example 8–1.

LATE 1960s

The campus rebellion is in full flower.

New life styles and radical politics appear together: granny glasses, crunchy granola, commune-living, pot smoking, and long hair seem inseparable from radical politics, sit-ins, student strikes, protest marches, draft card burnings.

A central theme on campus: the search for self-fulfillemnt *in place of* a conventional career.

Growing criticism of America as a "sick society."

The Women's Movement has virtually no impact on youth values and attitudes.

Violence on campus is condoned and romanticized; there are many acts of violence.

The value of education is severely questioned.

A widening "generation gap" appears in values, morals, and outlook, dividing young people (especially college youth) from their parents.

A sharp split in social and moral values is found within the youth generation, between college students and the noncollage majority. The gap *within* the generation proves to be larger and more severe than the gap *between* the generations.

A new code of sexual morality, centering on greater acceptance of casual premarital sex, abortions, homosexuality, and extramarital relations is confined to a minority of college students.

The challenge to the traditional work ethic is confined to the campus.

Harsh criticisms of major institutions, such as political parties, big business, the military, etc., are almost wholly confined to college students.

The universities and the military are major targets of criticism.

The campus is the main locus of youthful discontent; noncollege youth is quiescent.

Much youthful energy and idealism is devoted to concern with minorities.

The political center of gravity of college youth: left/liberal.

The New Left is a force on campus: there are growing numbers of radical students.

Concepts of law and order are anathema to college students.

The student mood is angry, embittered, and bewildered by public hostility.

EARLY 1970s

The campus rebellion is moribund.

An almost total divorce takes place between radical politics and new life styles.

A central theme on campus: how to find self-fulfillment *within* a conventional career.

Lessening criticism of America as a "sick society."

Wide and deep penetration of Women's Liberation precepts is underway.

Violence-free campuses; the use of violence, even to achieve worth-while objectives, is rejected.

The value of education is strongly endorsed.

The younger generation and older mainstream America move closer together in values, morals, and outlook.

The gap within the generation narrows. Noncollege youth has virtually caught up with college students in adopting the new social and moral norms.

The new sexual morality spreads both to mainstream college youth and also to mainstream working-class youth.

The work ethic appears strength-

cned on campus but is growing weaker among noncollege youth.

Criticism of some major institutions are tempered on campus but are taken up by the working class youth.

Criticism of the universities and the military decrease sharply.

Campuses are quiescent, but many signs of latent discontent and dis-satisfaction appear among working-class youth.

Concern for minorities lessens.

No clear-cut political center of grav-ity: pressures in both directions, left and right.

The New Left is a negligible factor on campus: the number of radical students declines sharply.

College students show greater acceptance of law and order requirements.

There are few signs of anger or bit-terness and little overt concern with public attitudes toward students.

From *The New Morality: A Profile of American Youth in the 70's* by Daniel Yankelovich. Copy-right © 1974 by the JDR 3rd Fund. Used with permission of McGraw-Hill Book Company.

government. There is less automatic obedience or respect for the authority of the police or the "boss" at work. There is less dependence on the guidance of organized religion for moral behavior and less patriotism for "my country, right or wrong."

New Social Values   Changes of attitudes toward work are most noticeable in the area of new so-cial values, with special complications for the noncollege person. Attitudes toward work are influenced by the changed attitudes toward self-fulfillment.

Essentially, young people are saying that the compartmentalized view of separating work and personal life is not valid. They reject the idea of working all week in order to pay for the privilege of time for family, friends, and hobbies on weekends and holidays. Young people strongly express the desire to work hard, but they reject the idea that hard work per se brings its own rewards. They are expecting work to provide adequate financial and prestige compensation, but they are saying their work must also be meaningful, challenging, and satisfying in its own right.[9]

This is where Yankelovich sees the modification of work values as fitting the future for the college student but setting up great frustration for the non-college young person. The contrasts between important job attributes valued by blue-collar workers, and their reports of job satisfaction (Table 8–1) supports Yankelovich's prediction of a frustrated future work force. He suggests these frustrations pose a challenge to society. "We are reaching one of those critical turning points in our social history where the options of the future and the opportunities to create new institutions are truly open. The die is not yet cast. The majority of young people continue to bring to their work a

Table 8–1. Most Important Job Attributes Among Blue-Collar Workers

Work interesting	66%
Pay good	65%
See results of work	60%
Chance to use mind	58%
Chance to develop skills/abilities	57%
Participating in decisions	56%
Recognition for job well done	52%
Chance to make a lot of money later on	39%
Good pension plan	39%
Job in a growing field/industry	35%
Work socially useful	35%
Not caught up in a big, impersonal organization	34%
Job not too demanding	26%
Not expected to do things not paid for	24%
Job not involving hard physical work	18%

From *The New Morality: A Profile of American Youth in the 1970's* by Daniel Yankelovich. Copyright © 1974 by the JDR 3rd Fund. Used with permission of McGraw-Hill Book Company.

[9] Ibid., pp. 28–37.

deeply rooted desire to do a good job and a hunger for work that will satisfy some of their deepest cravings—for community, for fellowship, for participation, for challenge, for self-fulfillment, for freedom, and for equality."[10]

New Values for Self-fulfillment

Today's Young Adults—working through Erikson's stages of identity development and development of intimacy[11]—are surrounded by a climate that says, "There must be something more to life than keeping one's nose to the grindstone making a living." There is a certain degree of self-centeredness, of valuing oneself, that says, "My own needs are equally important along with attending to the needs of my family, my employer, and my community." Yankelovich points up the importance of this in the following paragraph.

> As the New Values spread from a small minority of privileged college students to the mainstream of college youth, and from college youth to the noncollege majority of young workers, housewives, high school students, etc., they evoked new questions and posed new dilemmas for each of the various subgroups in the population. When people's expectations are raised and their values transformed, they seek out new patterns of fulfillment, depending on their circumstances. The well-educated and well-trained college graduate, for example, finds himself in a better potential to gratify his new desires than someone who is less well trained, less well educated and privileged, even though both persons may share similar desires.[12]

Alternatives: College or Work

"Three out of four of both college and noncollege young people call for more emphasis on self-expression and self-fulfillment as personal values."[13] Among blue-collar workers, "job security" ranked 15 points below "interesting work" as a job criterion.[14] The chance to make a lot of money ranked at the bottom of a list of possible job criteria. Although noncollege young people express nearly as strong desires as college students that their jobs offer

[10] Ibid., p. 37.

[11] E. H. Erikson, *Identity: Youth and Crisis* (New York: Norton, 1968), p. 135.

[12] *The New Morality: A Profile of American Youth in the 70's* by Daniel Yankelovich. Copyright © 1974 by the JDR 3rd Fund. Used with permission of McGraw-Hill Book Company. pp. 6–7.

[13] Ibid., p. 29.

[14] Ibid., p. 29.

a.

8–2 *Some young adults choose to go directly into the world of work; others elect college or other training experiences.* (Manhattan Mercury photos)

b.

c.

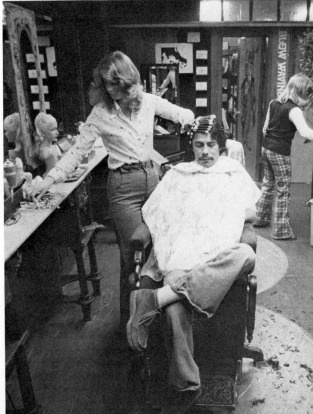

challenge and interest, the probability of this is much less for noncollege people.

Although the nature of our technological society poses serious problems, the young blue-collar worker feels that lack of education is a major barrier to getting a job of his liking. In their interviews with Yankelovich, 68 per cent said they would welcome the chance to get a six-month training or education program that would lead to a better job, even if it meant taking a 20 per cent pay cut while taking the course.[15]

The Yankelovich interviews presented five alternatives to the present limited work-versus-college choice.

Plan 1. A start-your-own-business program would feature training and interest-free loans.

Plan 2. New types of technical schools would offer certified training for skills needed in expanding industries.

Plan 3. A career-planning year would expose the individual to many different fields and job opportunities and feature new forms of career counseling.

Plan 4. New types of apprenticeship programs in industry, the arts, unions, or service organizations would offer the individual minimum wages while he learns new skills.

Plan 5. A six-year job-and-college program would involve working steadily at a job and receiving a college degree for both work and formal courses taken at a nearby college.

Asked how they would react to each of these alternatives if they were graduating from high school today, here is how the blue-collar workers responded:

Seventy-six per cent said they would give serious thought to a career-planning year.

Seventy-one per cent would give serious consideration to the six-year combined job-and-college program.

Sixty-eight per cent expressed interest in the new types of technical school.

Sixty-six per cent were interested in the new types of apprenticeship programs.

---

[15] Ibid., p. 33.

Fifty-five per cent reacted favorably to the start-your-own-business program.[16]

Interestingly, college students share the blue-collar workers' enthusiasm for the career-planning year and the six-year work-college program but are less interested in the start-your-own business program or in the new types of technical schools.

The Yankelovich report suggests that the young adult of phase 1 (years 18 to 23) has distinctive characteristics reflecting this stage of his life and this period of history. He is less fearful of economic insecurity than past generations (the specter of breadlines does not haunt him). Many are somewhat pessimistic because of their feeling that their employers cannot provide the kind of interesting and challenging work the young adults desire. They are not as awed by authority, nor as automatically obedient or loyal to their company or other organizations as their parents were. They are more aware and expressive of their own needs and rights. They are better educated than their parents, even without a college degree.

The social changes reflected in this profile of the young adult (phase 1) express attitudes that color ways in which adults of other ages will be dealing with work and personal development.

> That the majority of noncollege youth face the prospect of growing difficulties with their jobs must be regarded as a matter of serious concern to the society. These young people, after all, represent the great bulk of the new labor force. The problem they face is compounded by the multiplier effect of higher expectations with lower opportunities: their New Values inevitably clash with the built-in rigidities and limited responses of the traditional work place.[17]

College Grades and Postcollege Success

Donald P. Hoyt, director of educational research at Kansas State University, stimulated much dismay but clarified some goals and methods of education when he reported that there was little relationship between college grades and measures of postcollege success. In discussing these findings, he pointed out some discrepancies between the educational experiences in college and the application experiences in the larger community.

> [Concerning] the minimal correlations between college grades and measures

[16] Ibid., p. 35.
[17] Ibid., p. 37.

of post-college success, I'm inclined to think one reason for that is that the life situation simulates the puzzle-type approach more than the mechanistic approach we often seem to get at in our examinations, where we call for limited numbers of responses to givens. Givens are never quite so clear in business or industry. Often decisions have to be made in life from fairly ambiguous information, which calls for thought processes that are more complex or shrewd. I believe it's this discrepancy between the academic exercises we provide students typically and the challenges that face them when they leave us that accounts for the appalling lack of relationship between what we told them was "success" and what they accomplish later on.[18]

This discrepancy is perhaps illustrated, on the one hand, in the contrast between the "live" or seemingly more relevant issues in the dormitory bull sessions or the working through of social skills and values in college friendships, and on the other hand, in the more formal presentation of information in class work. In any event, it is a provocative finding that graduating seniors consistently indicate that they "learned more" outside than in the classroom.

Transition Period: Choice of Locale

Young adult phase 1 is the transition period—the time when the individual is half in and half out of the family.[19] Whether he will elect to enter the world of work while continuing to live at or near home, or whether he will elect college or the military as avenues of transition, will be influenced by community and family expectations.

If a young person's parents have attended college, the chances are that he will attend too.[20] Peers and friends also exert important influences.[21] The neighborhood and the school create a similar climate and career orientation in the young adult. A study conducted of ten rural communities illustrates

---

[18] D. P. Hoyt, in J. Sistrunk, A. Fretwell, and C. E. Kennedy, *Windows into Student Life: Growth and Change During College Years* (Manhattan, Kansas: Kansas State University, 1972), p. 234. For a more complete discussion, see D. P. Hoyt, "Rationality and the Grading Process," *Educational Record* 51 (1970), pp. 305–309.

[19] Levinson, "Periods in the Adult Development of Men," p. 21.

[20] J. W. Trent and L. L. Medsker, *Beyond High School* (San Francisco: Jossey-Bass, 1968), p. 25; a national study indicated that one third of students entering college had parents who attended college. In contrast, one tenth of high school graduates not attending college had parents who attended college.

[21] Ibid., p. 26. The study indicated 84 per cent of high school graduates who did not enter college reported having no friends who planned to attend college.

some of the differences.[22] It was observed that five communities sent a high percentage of their students to college or to post-high-school training. The five communities were then matched on various demographic variables with five other communities that had much lower percentages of young adults entering post-high-school training. The study examined the attitudes of parents, townspeople, teachers, and students on a variety of issues. The clear impression from this study is that there were two different types of community climate and that this influenced students in many ways. Parents, teachers, and leaders of communities that sent a high number of students to college had more optimistic views about the future, about possibilities for change in the community, as well as about the value of education. Differences perceived by students paralleled differences in attitudes and perceptions expressed by parents, teachers, and community leaders, suggesting that students' motivations for educational activity may reflect an internalization of community values and social climate.

More than a million students enter college each fall. However, over half of them drop out in two years, and about one third of the million completes four years of study.[23] Most students who leave college before graduation give more than one reason, but almost invariably included is a statement of dissatisfaction with college and a desire to reconsider personal goals and interests.

For many students, other learning experiences and direct vocational preparation are more interesting and helpful than college. Often a semester or year of college provides students with an opportunity to establish their independence and confidence. They are then ready to move into the world of work, not really looking for the scholarship or skill preparation required by four years of college. According to a national follow-up study in the late 1960s of high school graduates who did not attend college, most of the men entered employment in factory-type jobs and most of the women entered clerical positions.[24]

---

[22] J. Sistrunk, "Community Attitudes Affect Post High School Plans," *Student Development Series* (Manhattan, Kansas: Department of Family and Child Development, Kansas State University, 1972).

[23] Newman, *Report on Higher Education;* a higher percentage of students who enter colleges with low admission standards drop out before completing college than do students who attend colleges with rigorous admission standards. This probably reflects a variety of factors, such as purpose for attending and prior preparation both academically and within the home.

[24] Trent and Medskar, *Beyond High School.*

Transition Period: Focus of Interest

Today's students come to college from a wide cross section of the population, and they come for diverse reasons[25]: some to prepare for a career; some see the main purpose of college as a time and place to make new friends and contacts; others see college as a time of pursuing new ideas and formulating a philosophy of life; still other students use college as an opportunity to be on their own, to experiment with gaining a new independence from parents. Those attending college may be divided into four types according to their predominant motivations.[26] Similar motivations probably influence the activities of noncollege young people at work or drifting during their first years out of high school.

VOCATIONAL.   Vocationally oriented college students may fall into two categories. There are those who come to college with the main goal of acquiring a specific set of skills to qualify for a particular career. Others may see completing required courses and obtaining the degree as an end in itself. It is more difficult for such people to relate to subject matter. Their commitment is to complete the course demands and obtain a "union card" (the degree) that will admit them to jobs in the outside world.

Some young people go to work immediately after high school. They may see the beginning job as preparing them to move into more responsible positions or they may look upon the job as simply providing a paycheck. Although we have discussed the increasing desire for the job to be a means of self-expression, nearly half of the young adults think in terms of compartmentalizing work and personal life.[27]

SOCIAL.   Some students look upon college as the opportunity to widen their scope of acquaintances, develop added skills in leadership, and be able to handle social functions. For these students, extracurricular activities are an

[25] Much of the following discussion of college student life is adapted from Sistrunk et al., *Windows into Student Life,* the report of a four-year longitudinal study at a midwest university.

[26] B. W. Clark and M. Trowe, "The Organizational Context," in *College Peer Groups: Problems and Prospects for Research,* eds. T. M. Newcomb and E. K. Wilson (Chicago: Aldine, 1966), pp. 17–70; the authors describe four subcultures they believed to exist on most college campuses: the collegiate culture, the vocational culture, the academic culture, the nonconformist culture. B. Ringwald et al., "Conflict and Style in the Classroom," *Psychology Today* (February 1971); these authors describe eight clusters of classroom behaviors exhibited by college students: compliant, anxious-dependent, discouraged, independent, heroes, snipers, attention seekers, and silent students.

[27] M. F. Lowenthal, M. T. Thurnher, and D. Chiriboga, *Four Stages of Life* (San Francisco: Jossey-Bass, 1975), p. 16.

important part of college life. Campus organizations, dormitory, fraternity, or sorority programs occupy much of their time. Mate selection is also a significant factor in their goals for college.

The same motivations and interest in social contacts and peer relationships may direct the activities of young people who enter work directly out of high school. Clarification of identity and achieving new capacities for intimacy require opportunities for young adults to try themselves in new social circumstances and in different roles.

LIBERAL EDUCATION.   There are a few students who look upon college as the "pursuit of ideas." These are usually young people who come from home situations where the necessity to prepare to earn a living is not urgent. They differ from the vocationally oriented student in that they look upon college as equipping them with general understandings and ways of thinking. They focus upon ideas, development of sensitivity, and problem-solving skills.

Some students have described the main goals of a liberal education as having college prepare them for a life of continued learning. The pursuit of ideas at one time was less likely to characterize young people entering the world of work. However, as young people have begun to question the "programing" of higher education, more are choosing to pursue self-directed learning. They often will work at a job for a livelihood while pursuing their own line of artistic or philosophic inquiry.

MARKING TIME.   Many students come to college because this is "the next notch up the educational ladder." They are, in a sense, marking time. They need a period for further exploration, perhaps for separation from their family, and a chance to gain some sense of identity and direction. Sometimes they come to college because their parents expect it; sometimes because their peers are coming. Often they come because they don't really know of anything else to do. Sometimes they come for a year while they are waiting for something else to happen, such as a job or marriage. This is not an undesirable situation if the students (and their parents) can accept the experience as a time of exploration, understanding that their primary task is one of gaining a clear awareness of various possibilities.

There are perhaps as many noncollege young people in the first year or so out of high school who are "marking time" in various ways. Some are trying out different kinds of work; others are trying out different places to live or different life-styles.

Satisfactions with Early Adult Years

Nearly half of the people of all ages consider the teens and twenties to be the best years of a person's life.[28] The teens, especially, are seen as a time of limited responsibility with many opportunities for fun. The twenties are also perceived to have less responsibilities than later years, but two out of ten persons point out that this is the period in which one develops ambitions and sets goals. The anxieties experienced in making choices and risking new roles and friendships seem to fade from memory.

For some, however, the young adult years are not seen as times of great enjoyment. When the 18 to 24-year group was asked in a study[29] to nominate the "worst years of life," the teen years received more nominations than did any period except "over 70 years." The twenties, however, received few nominations for being the worst. Those who chose the teens as the worst years generally described that period as unsettled and a time when "you're not mature."

Developmental Tasks

Erikson indicates that the development of a sense of *identity* is the task of late adolescence, and the development of the capacity for *intimacy* is the task of the young adult. These tasks are closely related and the period of young adult encompasses them both. As we prepared to share with students the results of our four years of weekly interviews, we found that their experiences fit into four dimensions.[30] These refer to much the same dynamics as the two Eriksonian stages.[31]

*Gaining a
Sense of
Identity*

As the young adult makes the decision to attend college (or not to attend college) he is adding dimension to the picture he has of himself. As he selects a particular school he is projecting or clarifying that picture somewhat further. He is not only saying to himself, "I am a college-type person," he is also

---

[28] L. Harris and associates, *The Myth and Reality of Aging in America* (Washington, D.C.: The National Council on the Aging, 1975), pp. 3–6.

[29] Ibid., p. 13.

[30] The dimensions we used were (1) dependence-independence, (2) intimacy-isolation, (3) extension-restraint, (4) identity-alienation; see Sistrunk et al., *Windows into Student Life*, pp. 39–41, 57–60, 76–78, 94–96.

[31] Erikson, *Identity: Youth and Crisis*, pp. 128–137.

saying, "I am a person like the people at such and such school or college." Colleges have a public image such as "friendly," "elite," "liberal arts," "practical." Although there are several other factors (Table 8-2) entering into the choice of school, the young adult is to some extent saying, "I think I'm like this group or I want to become like the people I know to be graduates of this kind of institution." This process of projection is an important aspect of developing one's sense of identity, a central task of young adulthood.

Young adults entering directly into the labor force go through a similar process of projecting themselves into different roles and statuses. We dis-

Table 8–2. Choosing a College

Students at Kansas State University gave the following reasons for choosing their university*:

Special curriculum	57%
Desirable location	40%
Low-cost college	39%
Good faculty	36%
High scholastic standards	33%
Size	28%
National reputation	27%
Close to home	25%
Advice of parents	20%
Desirable social climate	20%
Offered a scholarship	17%
Advice of high school teachers	16%
Advice of high school counselor	15%
Friends are (will be) going	15%
Campus visit	13%
Comprehensive physical and educational facilities	12%
Desirable intellectual atmosphere	9%
Emphasis on religious and ethical values	5%
Progressive liberal outlook	4%
Has fraternities and sororities	4%
Has good athletic program	4%
Talked with the college admissions counselor	4%

From J. Sistrunk, A. Fretwell, and C. E. Kennedy, *Windows into Student Life: Growth and Change During College Years* (Kansas State University, 1972), p. 187.

* Percentages add up to more than 100% because of multiple responses.

cussed in Chapter 3 that statuses are associated with different occupations and different industries.

Choosing the school also involves the young person in choosing a course of study. Although students often fear their curriculum choice in college locks them in a job for life, we continue to make career decisions throughout life.[32] The advocates of career education emphasize that the dilemma of choosing a vocation is compounded by the fact that a student usually has not had contact with people in his intended career. Even more likely, he has never had any practical experience in his desired vocation. A greater frustration occurs when a student has finished years of specialized training, goes into the real world, and finds he dislikes his vocation. This is not unusual. Often a student completes his premedical curriculum without ever coping with a sick person. Another student may complete training for teaching in elementary school without confronting children until his last semester. Career education urges an earlier exposure to the occupational world and more interspersing of classroom and work activities.

Learning Independence

Young people entering the world of work directly may try several jobs before settling on one. Final selection may be determined as much by other situations developing in their lives as by the characteristics of the job per se.

Phase 1 of young adulthood occurs during years when the individual has the rights and responsibilities of adult life, including the right to vote, to bear arms, to marry and procreate. It is, nevertheless, a time of transition. The affirming and the relinquishing of various role behaviors associated with change from youth to young adult is not easy, nor is it accomplished overnight.[33]

In our discussion of maturity in Chapter 10 we will consider some of the experiences of the parents of the empty nest and the patterns of communication between students and parents.

Nevitt Sanford[34] has pointed out that while the young adult is a student, he is learning to deal with responsibility for himself, with standards for himself and others, and how he will relate to people of authority. College teachers may serve various roles as the student works toward new relationships

[32] See W. Ogg's discussion of students' experiences in choosing a vocation in Sistrunk et al., *Windows into Student Life,* pp. 189–190.

[33] M. Curry catches something of the tones of that struggle in her essay. "Sunday—A Day of Severence," in Sistrunk et al., *Windows into Student Life,* pp. 192–194.

[34] N. Sanford, *The American College* (New York: Wiley, 1972).

with parents and other adults and as he decides about how much he will accept responsibility for his own life and decisions. The following summary from a series of interviews with students and campus leaders suggests three kinds of relationships students have with faculty. Nonstudents away from home and in apprenticeships or beginning jobs are going through learning experiences and responding to supervisors in ways similar to the students described in the following paragraphs.

The majority of students see the professor as a *dispenser of academic information*. They are unaware or unconcerned about the professor as a functioning social being outside the classroom situation. Students often judge professors in terms of how they may affect the students' survival in college. Students evaluate faculty as "good" when they provide adequate assistance in academics. Because part of the teacher's job is to evaluate academic performance, students often assume and may even desire a remoteness in the student-faculty relationship.

A few students see beyond the professor's classroom role, viewing him as an esteemed member of the community. But few students actually choose to interact with the professor on a personal level. This is supported by our data that many of our students did not choose the professor as a confidant in personal matters, nor did they wish to meet faculty members at informal gatherings.

A few students are able to develop a *colleague relationship* with members of the faculty when joined in a common project. However, a colleague relationship between student and professor rarely happens during a student's early years in college.[35]

Developing New Capacities for Intimacy

Although college students identify out-of-class experiences as the most formative and most alumni remember with nostalgia their college friends, students report relatively few close friends during their college years.[36] Selected friendships from home still carry forward and students maintain an active communication with their families.[37] After the first year or two of college,

[35] Sistrunk et al., *Windows into Student Life*, pp. 202–235. Included are excerpts from interviews with faculty and student panels. For an account of stimulating faculty-student relationships, see E. Raushenbush, *The Student and His Studies* (Middletown, Conn.: Wesleyan University Press, 1964).

[36] G. Peters and C. E. Kennedy, "Close Friendships in the College Community," *Journal of College Student Personnel* 11 (November 1970), pp. 449–456.

[37] E. Bloom and C. E. Kennedy, "The Student and His Parents," *National Association of Women Deans and Counselors* 33 (1970), 3:98–105; C. E. Kennedy, "Patterns of Parent-Student Communication," *Journal of Home Economics* 63 (1971), 7.

they narrow their range of close friendships toward a steady dating or marriage relationship.[38]

Preparation for family life influences much of the early decision making of young adults. Some marry within a year or two after high school. Those who marry after age 20 look upon their work situation in terms of how it will relate to the family life they anticipate. Marriage adds a dimension of realism to occupational attitudes of young men that may not be present earlier.

Lowenthal found that 84 per cent of the newlywed women were working. For them, as for most of the young men, working was not something they looked forward to; it was an accepted fact of life, the means of obtaining the kind of home and social life they wished.[39]

During the newlywed period usually both husband and wife are working and activities outside of work are usually shared with the spouse. Men and women in this period tend to have many social roles and activities.[40] People in the 18 to 24-year range are the most active of any age group in social and family contacts.[41]

Extending and Integrating Values

Early in this chapter we discussed the impact of attitude changes for young adults. The young adult period is the stage when individuals may most likely move beyond the conventional values of conformity. Keniston's research, using Kohlberg's stages of moral development, suggests that the development of some young adults moves beyond the conventional stage 3 to stages 5 and 6[42]; that is, while the majority of society is at stage 3, ("conformist: oriented to interpersonal relations and approval for its own sake"), an increasing number of young adults is expressing more autonomous values and values oriented to universal human ethical principles.

[38] Nearly a fourth of the students at Kansas State University in 1971 were married. The percentage increased the longer the students were in school. One out of a hundred freshmen was married, but nearly seven out of ten graduate students had spouses. About one out of three was married by the time the students graduated from college. A decade earlier, B. L. Hembrough reported in "A Two-fold Educational Challenge: The Student Wife and the Mature Woman Student," *Journal of National Association of Women Deans and Counselors* 20 (1966), 163, that at the University of Illinois, three out of five undergraduate men were married in comparison with one out of five undergraduate women.

[39] Lowenthal et al., *Four Stages of Life,* p. 19.

[40] Ibid., pp. 13–14.

[41] Harris, *The Myth and Reality of Aging in America,* p. 169.

[42] K. Keniston, "Youth: A 'New' Stage of Life," *American Scholar* Autumn 1970), pp. 631–654; see also C. Widick, L. L. Knefelkamp, and C. A. Parker, "The Counselor as a Developmental Instructor," *Counselor Education and Supervision* 14 (June 1975), pp. 286–296.

8–3 *Gaining the capacity for intimacy is a developmental task of young adulthood. For many, marriage comes within a year or two after high school; others wish to become established in careers before they marry. (a, Kansas State University Student Publications photo; b, Manhattan Mercury photo)*

b.   **a.**

The interviews of Lowenthal, conducted with working-class young adults shortly after the Keniston interviews, found most of those young people to be *not* reflecting much impact from current issues such as the Vietnam war or the women's liberation movement.[43] The value changes reflected in the Yankelovich data may come as changes in social mores to which new groups of young people adapt rather than reflecting an autonomous value system.

Some young adults are moved more rapidly into adult positions without a lengthy period of introspection and testing. The roles and responsibilities they take in the late teens and early twenties are characteristic of older young adults to which we refer in phase 2 (Example 8–2). In some instances the searching and preparatory period of phase 1 has been bypassed in an accelerated adolescence. In other instances the preparatory period of phase 1 is exceptionally brief (Example 8–3). In some instances the supportive climate of family, army, or college assists individuals as they take on adult responsibilities early (Examples 8–4 and 8–5). Lack of role models or developmental opportunities in phase 1 may make it difficult for young adults to assume responsibilities of phase 2 (Example 8–6).

In any event, young adult years involve individuals in many acts of com-

[43] Lowenthal et al., *Four Stages of Life,* pp. 16–17.

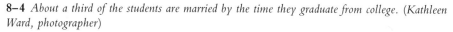

8–4 *About a third of the students are married by the time they graduate from college. (Kathleen Ward, photographer)*

Example 8–2.
Teen-age
Mother of
Three

Kerry's father died when she was 8. They lived in Cincinnati. She had three other sisters and a brother. Her mother worked in a factory and finances were a continual problem. At age 12, Kerry went to live with her older sister near a military base. In a matter of months she met John and they were married. John is a sergeant and career man in the Army. John learned to be responsible early in life as he was the only child of working parents. His father was a carpenter in a factory and his mother worked on an assembly line. They praised him when he performed the assigned tasks around the house and made good grades in school. They encouraged him to find a job with security in it because they all remembered times of factory layoffs. So when John graduated from high school, he entered the military. He is small in stature and very protective of Kerry, who is 10 years younger than he. Kerry appreciates John's help and solicitation about her personally and especially his help with work around the house and care for their children. They had a child each year during the first years of their marriage. Kerry's third child was born the day before she became 18.

Most of their leisure time is occupied with the care of the children and shopping for furniture and household gadgets. They often buy kits from the post exchange and assemble furnishings, radios, and other equipment. From time to time they have developed friendships with other couples in the military. They get together to listen to music or play cards. These are transitory friendships because one of the couples is soon transferred. Kerry gets along with the men in the other couples better than with the women. She finds that the women seem bossy to her. Men find her attractive and she indulges in harmless flirtations, knowing that John is patient and understanding and will not be too perturbed as long as her responses to the joking and interests of the other men is not extreme.

mitment. It is a time of clarifying their value system and how they see their values being expressed in relationship and career choices.

White describes the transition stage of young adulthood as the individual moving toward choosing a career and establishing a family, as a time of focusing of energies, and as a time of seasoning ideas and ideals.

Young adulthood is a time during which significant developments of a fairly complex nature take place. The making of lasting commitments has the general effect of concentrating the sphere in which one lives. Entering an occupation usually implies staying in one place, at least for the time being, and pursuing one line of activity. Marriage means bringing a diffuse liking for the

Example 8–3.
Laura and Casey

Laura's mother has always worked, helping to support the family. Laura's father, a construction worker, has had employment intermittently with bouts of alcoholism.

Laura knew that it would be important for a woman to be able to help with the family finances. So she talked with the high school counselor about careers and at first thought of secretarial work. She was encouraged by the counselor to prepare for key-punch and computer work and took a thirteen-week course after high school graduation. She eventually found employment with a large firm in the community. She has worked steadily for the three years since high school graduation.

She was married to Casey shortly after she finished the key-punch training. She had known Casey in high school, not well, but she admired him from a distance. She found him attractive and at the same time somewhat of a worry to her as he began to show interest, because she knew that he had a tendency to be in trouble with the school. He had been in trouble also a time or two on drinking and assault charges. She appreciated the fact that even in high school he had developed skills as a carpenter and worked part time with a local carpenter.

During the three years of their marriage he has worked intermittently. Mostly, he goes hunting or sits in the bar. He has a separate bank account for his money. Laura's money goes into a joint account and maintains the family budget. They own a trailer out in the country and two acres of land. Casey's money is to go for special things for the house or for trips. However, his bank account is usually empty, having been spent for beer and for Casey's hobby of citizens band radio.

Their life has been turbulent ever since they were married. Casey is very demanding and abusive. When Laura talks of leaving him, he threatens to kill her if she does. She is not sure whether she stays with him because of fear or because of attraction and love for him and the hope that sometime he will change. She now has a one-month-old baby girl, Peggy Lee. She had hoped that with the baby Casey might change, becoming more considerate and working regularly. The baby has not made any great change. Casey is proud of Peggy Lee, though. And when he and Laura have arguments, it now ends with a threat from one or the other that they are going to leave, taking the baby and not allowing the other person to see her.

other sex to a focus on one representative with whom the daily details of life are shared. Having a family means translating a benign feeling toward the young into loving one or more children for whom one has become responsible. If the quality of life is judged wholly in terms of *breadth,* these trends could

Example 8–4.
To Retire at 37

Eric was a high school athlete of considerable renown. And it was a great disappointment to his coaches when at the end of his junior year he volunteered for the army. His parents wanted him to finish high school, but when he told them he would lie about his age if they did not give him permission, they agreed to his joining the army. During his first year in the army, Eric completed the GED tests for a high school diploma. He has done well in his work as an engineering technician in the army and has received regular advancements.

In his first overseas assignment he married a German girl, Natasa. She lived with his parents in Oregon for several months before he was settled in a place where Natasa could join him. Eric's parents became very fond of her. They look upon her as a true sister for their daughter Emily. Emily is divorced and lives with her parents so that they can care for her young son. Natasa says Emily was a great help to her in becoming acquainted with American life and with her new family. She thinks it is the confidence she gained through the acceptance and "training" by her new family that has helped her to carry the responsibilities she has as the wife of one of the top noncommissioned officers in her husband's unit. At 35, Eric is beginning to make plans for retirement in two years. He thinks he may go into some form of sports equipment or recreational management work.

Example 8–5.
Married
Students

Judith was born in a large city in Tennessee. She is white and both of her parents are schoolteachers. After high school she went to a college in Ohio and graduated in education. She met Frederick, a black athlete and outstanding student, during their freshman year. They were married during the summer before their sophomore year. Fred received an ROTC commission and they went directly to his first assignment after graduation. Judith has been able to secure teaching positions in each of the three communities in which they have lived. Nearing the end of his six years of military obligation, Fred is taking evening classes in business administration in preparation for further graduate study. Judith is in the midst of a masters degree program. They both look forward to active professional lives and are uncertain as to whether they wish to have children. Both sets of parents are letting them know, through various subtle encouragements, that they would very much like to become grandparents.

Example 8–6.
High School
Dropout

> Marti was born in Birmingham, Alabama. Her father was black and her mother Indian. She was one of fourteen children, eight of whom were older than she. She grew up moving from home to home in the Birmingham area, living with her older brothers and sisters or at times with other relatives. When she was 10 she got a job in a restaurant washing dishes, and she worked part time in similar positions until she was 15 and a sophomore in high school. Then she got a job as a checker in a dry-cleaning shop and quit school. She was soon able to pass for 18 and got a second job in a bar. For the next few years she usually combined two jobs. She lived in a number of different living arrangements with girl friends, boy friends, and groups. By age 20 she was the mother of three daughters.
>
> Hal met her that year in the bar. He was in the army and on temporary duty near Birmingham. He wanted to marry her and adopt the girls. When she went to be with his parents in Dakota while he was making arrangements for living quarters near his new assignment, it was difficult for his white parents to accept a black daughter-in-law and for her to accept white parents. Hal became increasingly hostile toward his parents during that period. When Marti and the girls joined him at his base, their relationship strengthened but the estrangement from his parents increased. He soon began to be in conflict with his superiors in the army. In frustration he went AWOL for a few days. This messed up his pay and increased his frustration. He began to write bad checks. In a matter of weeks he spent time in both civilian and military confinement and was up for court martial.
>
> Hal's parents came when he was being tried and the family was reconciled. His father, who was about to retire from a service station job, decided to stay on and hold the position for Hal. Hal is now out of the army with a general discharge after ten years of service and has the service station job of his father's. He, Marti, and the girls live in a moderately new trailer house on the lot with his parents.

be construed as constriction. If it is judged on a dimension of *depth,* they appear as desirable opportunities for growth.[44]

Young Adult—Phase 2: Transition

During phase 2, the later years of the twenties and beginning thirties, the young adult who has gone to college is now beginning to launch his career.

[44] R. W. White, *The Enterprise of Living* (New York: Holt, Rinehart and Winston, 1972), p. 424.

8–5 *For some young adult women becoming a mother signals a change in place of work and focus of interest for the next few years.* (Manhattan Mercury *photo*)

The noncollege person will also have become more settled in his field of work. Most will be married by their mid-twenties. Neugarten found a general concensus among middle class middle-aged persons that 20 to 25 was the expected age to marry and 24 to 26 the expected age to be settled on a career.[45]

The young adult phase 2 will begin to take on some of the role expectations and attitudes of the middle adult period. As he becomes a parent, fits into his career, and moves a step or so on the ladder of success, the feelings of

[45] Neugarten, Moore, and Lowe, "Age Norms, Age Constraints, and Adult Socialization."

8–6 *Young adulthood may involve adjustment to intimacy with spouse and with children. (Kathleen Ward, photographer)*

expectancy and the opportunities for seeking and choosing jobs, roles, and relationships may seem to be fading.

Ambiguities present in our society concerning family are difficult factors with which the young adult must contend in achieving a satisfactory sense of intimacy. Young adulthood involves the period of adjustment to intimacy with spouse and children or (if an alternate life-style has been chosen) to a close relationship with an individual or group, as contrasted with an individual solitary existence.

For men, phase 2 of young adult years means moving more definitely into one of the career areas he has been exploring. For women, phase 2 may mean an interruption—at least for a time—of their career identities as members of the labor force. Although most women work after marriage, the birth of a child focuses their attention on their role in the home. Some may return to work shortly after the baby arrives. For some, becoming a mother signals a change of place of work and focus of interest for the next few years.

237

For example, the transition from career as a librarian to that of full-time mother is reflected in this first letter from a new mother to *her* mother.

> I was going to write much earlier, then you called, and every day this week seemed really full, so never quite got to it. Wanted to say THANKS! again, Mom, for all your help last week. Steve and I both really appreciated you coming and all the things you did to help out. Dad, thank you, too, for getting along without her for the week, making the trips here and back, etc.
>
> Lucy is pretty well on a three-hour schedule. At nights it almost seems like she has a built-in alarm clock—almost exactly three hours. Every once in a while she'll sleep longer. Like this morning, instead of waking at 7:00 it was about 8:15. She's gotten so she stays awake more in the late afternoon and evenings. Sometimes she seems like she just wants to be sociable, is very good. Other times she is fussy—you know how she can be, don't you, Mom?
>
> Really, it's been a pretty good week. I've been feeling fine. Although the days go by quite fast, I've been able to keep up with the things that need to be done, but there are lots of things I'd like to do. I'm sure it will taper off and I'll get more done later. Really though, it's enjoyable just taking care of Lucy. She's showing her personality already, with the funny expressions on her face and little things she does. I'm going to have Steve help me give her a tub bath on Saturday.

A part of the developmental tasks of the new mother is getting information about child care and establishing criteria for progress. Some of the rewards are sharing of the child with the family. Young parents have new skills to learn (Example 8–7) and new identities to appropriate.

Daniel B. Levinson has described the period of the twenties as the "getting into the adult world" (GIAW) time. From his intensive study of forty men, he describes GIAW as a "time of exploration and provisional commitment to adult roles, memberships, responsibilities and relationships . . . the overall developmental task of the GIAW period is to explore available possibilities of the adult world, to arrive at an initial definition of oneself as an adult, and to fashion an *initial life structure* that provides a viable link between the valued self and the wider adult world." [46]

The young adult phase 2 may accomplish the necessary transition through making a tentative commitment to an occupation and entering a position, reserving, at least in his thinking, the possibility that this may not be exactly what he wants. After a few years he will reevaluate to see whether he needs

---

[46] D. Levinson et al., "The Psychosocial Development of Men in Early Adulthood and the Mid-Life Transition," p. 246. G. Sheehy has termed them the "trying twenties," in *Passages,* p. 27.

Example 8–7.
Lucy's
Six-Weeks'
Checkup

> . . . Now about Lucy's six weeks' checkup. The weather was beautiful and it was nice to be out. Lucy behaved pretty well I think. The appointment was at 11:40 in the Medical Building. That sounds like plenty of time, but I really had to organize our activities to get me ready, Lucy have her bath and a bottle (so she wouldn't be hungry while we were there) and still allow enough time for parking, etc. I was glad we had gone out the day before so that I was used to getting her situated in the car seat. She went to sleep after we'd been driving a while but awakened shortly after we arrived in the waiting room.
>
> Lucy was really enjoying playing on the table in the nude as we waited for the doctor to come in. She was kicking her legs and moving her arms, inching around on the table and "talking"—gurgling, cooing sounds—she wasn't doing much of that when you were here, was she, Mom?
>
> The doctor came in and examined her thoroughly, but quickly. He said to her, "Tell your mom that you're perfect." Wow, was that good to hear! He gave me a sheet with things she can eat next, but said not to push any of it . . . This next six weeks will be a fun six weeks, he said. She will start to respond and develop a lot more. I can already notice quite a difference in the last several weeks. I know you probably will too . . .

to make a change. Somewhere around age 30 the young adult makes a rather definite commitment. He decides either that he has found the right line of endeavor and moves toward a deeper commitment, or he decides he has not made the right choice and moves to a new career and perhaps new life-style.

As the young adult tests the waters of the adult world, he is reconciling the high standards of his adolescent idealism with the practicalities of the daily tasks. The age-30 review may reveal some inconsistencies and prompt new commitments (see Example 8–8).

There are numerous illustrations from fiction and in biographical accounts highlighting this time of introspection. These accounts emphasize the intermingling of career, family, and life-mission goals. For example, in *Of Human Bondage*[47] the confining influences of a clubfoot and the early social training in the life of Philip Carey illustrate some of the different obstacles to independence a young adult must surmount. It was only after years of "bondage" and the completion of several internships that the young physician realized the importance of a family and what he really wanted from life. It was

---

[47] W. S. Maugham, *Of Human Bondage* (Garden City, N.Y.: Doubleday, 1915).

then he also discovered that because of his deformity he had never done what he wanted to do, but always what he thought he should do.

Special circumstances may come to bear at any period of life to bring forward earlier intuitions and fuse need with latent ability to bring about realization of an individual's creative potential. An example is Eleanor Roosevelt. The retiring and homebound Eleanor started on the road toward becoming one of the leading women of the world when as a young wife she "stood in" politically for her husband while he was recovering from illness.[48]

The need to look at one's own life is a vital part of the equipment of a novelist. George Webber, the journalist in *You Can't Go Home Again*,[49] writes of his early life experiences. But when he tries to return to that world of an earlier period, he finds it is no longer there. Through George we learn that each new stage of life involves some severing of ties with the past, some reaching out in new commitments.

For some young adults the searching and the growing independence of phase 1 has continued through most of the years of the twenties. As 30 approaches, there is an imperative to shift from the transient to a more settled

[48] J. P. Lask, *Eleanor and Franklin* (New York: Norton, 1971).
[49] T. Wolfe, *You Can't Go Home Again* (New York: Harper & Row, 1940).

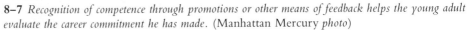

8–7 *Recognition of competence through promotions or other means of feedback helps the young adult evaluate the career commitment he has made. (Manhattan Mercury photo)*

Example 8–8.
Commitment at
Thirty

Commitment to an ideal was a familiar word in our home. Eventually the idea of commitment became a kind of standard to me, in every area of my life but one. I came to share not only my family's abhorrence of corruption in government, but also their respect and admiration for those leaders who upheld the most noble precepts of our nation. My childhood heroes included nearly as many political figures as cowboys and athletes . . .

Through reading, I acquainted myself with great leaders of the past and the present and tried to discover the secrets of their success. I discovered that the most effective leaders were those who dedicated themselves to the highest ideals and who worked unceasingly for the realization of them. From the enthusiasm of Jefferson to the dedication of Lincoln there was a contagious spirit about them, and I found myself dreaming of how best to serve my country . . .

In politics, for example, it was easy for me to see the value of commitment. In fact, I used to expound it to my classes when I was a political science teacher at Williamette University in Salem, Oregon.

"Take a stand!" . . . "Join a party, meet the candidates, ring door bells, get involved." . . . "get down off the bleachers and into the rough-and-tumble where the issues of life are decided."

In 1950, to prove my point further, I announced that I was going to file my name as a candidate for the state legislature . . . After winning the election and serving two terms in the lower house, I went on to the state senate . . . All of these honors were highly encouraging to me as an aspiring young politician. But with these outward advancements came a disturbing inner awareness of inadequacy in the area of my spiritual life . . . For months my words in the classroom had been coming back to mock me. I was urging my students to stand up and be counted. But I was a very silent and very comfortable Christian. One night in the quiet of my room the choice was suddenly made clear. I could not continue to drift along as I had been doing . . . I made the choice that night, many years ago; I saw that for thirty-one years I had lived for self, and I decided I wanted to live the rest of my life for Jesus Christ . . . Now, the decisions, the policies, the programs which I follow in my official life I try to root first of all in prayer.

M. O. Hatfield, *Conflict and Conscience* (Waco, Texas: Word Books, 1971), pp. 95–99.

existence. Levinson's study of men suggests that if a man does not begin to restructure his life toward stabilized commitments by about age 34, the chances are slight that he will in the future be able to form a satisfying life structure. He refers to the movie *Five Easy Pieces* as an illustration.

In our discussion of self-processes we discussed the sense of self-expression, the central core of identity toward which the individual continues to orient at a deeply personal level. Levinson refers to this as the individual's dreams.[50] The young adult at about age 30, and at subsequent self-evaluative transitional periods, compares his present life to the dream; see Carol Kennicott (Example 8–9). References to authenticity, of being

Example 8–9.
Carol Kennicott

> When Carol Kennicott graduated from Blodgett College in Minnesota, she was determined to transform the world. As young Dr. Will Kennicott told of Gopher Prairie, she visualized that her mission was to help the people of Gopher Prairie to find enlightenment. The years of young adult phase 1 were a painful process of accommodation in her idealistic zeal to bring cultural enlightenment to her husband's community. In the early years of their marriage she could not yet feel it to be her home.
>
> With the birth of little Hugh, Carol and the ladies of the community had somewhat more to share. But Carol worried that by keeping her son buried in the small Midwest community, away from "the world," she would be handicapping him. She left Will and Gopher Prairie, taking Hugh with her to the challenges and culture of war work in Washington, D.C. There she found the people of the city to be only an accumulation of people from thousands of other little Gopher Prairies from all over the country. Life was still Main Street.
>
> In the year that she lived in Washington, Carol began to find ways of asking the questions of life with more patience and more relevance. When Will came asking her to return, she found that her bitterness toward Gopher Prairie had burned itself out. She could feel the searching and the hope beneath the superficial routines of the town's club women. Her search for meaning could proceed with sympathy rather than vengeance. Her neighbors had missed her. After more than five years of marriage and now with little Hugh walking about, Carol began to feel at home in Gopher Prairie.
>
> Abstract from S. Lewis, *Main Street* (New York: Harcourt Brace Jovanovich, 1920).

true to oneself, of self-actualization, of accomplishing one's purpose, refer to this relating of oneself with the spiritual dynamics that come from integrating life's activities with the core of one's being.

As the young adult passes the 30-year mark and solidifies his commit-

[50] Levinson et al., "The Psychosocial Development of Men in Early Adulthood and the Mid-Life Transition."

ments, he is preparing to move into the stage of middle adult years that we will discuss in the next chapter. It is good to remind ourselves of many kinds of life satisfactions the young adult has had and of the events that have been so formative in structuring this early part of his adult life. The satisfactions of entering the world of work, becoming married, becoming a parent are the "firsts" that highlight this period. Each requires decision making and some modeling of attitudes and life-styles. Each requires some new skills in relationships, some working through of past attitudes toward authority, toward one's own potency, toward one's attitudes in relation to members of the opposite sex.

The young adult has made the transition from youth into the real world of adult careers and families. Now "over 30," he is of another generation; he knows where he is going and is much in the thick of "getting there," which we will discuss in the next chapter.

Summary

The young adult years encompass the developmental tasks of leaving home, of preparing for and entering an occupation, of developing the capacity for intimacy, and of deciding on marriage or another life-style. And in many instances young adult years are the time for becoming a parent.

In young adult phase 1, about 18 to 23 years, the individual goes through a transition process of gaining gradual independence from the family through moving into new, more autonomous living arrangements and of becoming less financially dependent. In this period he is completing the Eriksonian task of gaining identity versus role diffusion. Some sort of structured work and living—such as college, the military, or paying one's own rent—usually provides the transitional framework for leaving the family.

Friends and other groups are substituted for some of the family influences. The young adult in phase 1 begins to form relationships with adults on a peer level and thus begins to experience himself as an adult. Beginning to embrace an adult role, he must overcome the perfectionistic standards that his adolescent anxieties have caused him to hold against adult society.

As the young adult makes his place in society and finds less of his energies associated with making changes in his family relations, he moves into phase 2, which extends through the later twenties and early thirties. This is the time when the individual has made a tentative commitment in a career area and is beginning a more enduring interpersonal relationship in marriage. He has put searching behind for the time being and is occupied with learning the ropes. He is intent on demonstrating to himself and others that he can make it in these new adult responsibilities.

There is the excitement of first recognitions of competence by advancements on the job. There is the pleasant stress of marriage proposals and weddings. Parenthood presents new dimensions in relationships, new wonders in creation, new challenges—and new awareness of the enduringness of commitments.

Near the end of phase 2 the young adult experiences a period of reassessment. He makes decisions about the choices he has made. He feels sufficiently established to look around for a minute and ask, "Am I on the right track? Is this the path I want to follow?" For most, this is a reassuring review preparing them to plunge into the course they have set for themselves without further reservation. For some, the review brings contrary reflections from earlier goals and ideals. Changes in work, family, or community relationships are usually initiated before the individual moves into the full commitment of the middle adult years. The 30-year review is for some young adults an occasion for beginning the settling-in experiences others began five or six years earlier. For the more transient as well as for the other young adults, the stocktaking at the beginning of the thirties is a crucial step. Society and the individual himself will expect people in their thirties and older to perform the maintaining and the building work of the full-fledged adult.

Suggested Activities and Further Reading

1. Prepare a time line for people now in phase 1 and another for people now in phase 2 of young adult years. Phase 1 people were born in the late 1950s, phase 2 people in the late 1940s. Include on your time lines the worldwide events, the people in the news in our nation, and the kinds of music, movies, and television that were providing the environment for them as children, as youth, and as young adults.

2. Discuss John Dos Passos' novel *USA* (New York: Houghton Mifflin, 1937), concerning the approaches he has used in presenting the lives of young adults that might be helpful to you for the time lines you are preparing.

3. Have a panel of high school students and young adults discuss their present views regarding such topics as family relationships, community values, and work.

4. Have a panel of young adults who have gone directly into the world of work and young adults who are in college or other training situations discuss ideas and experiences concerned with developing a sense of identity.

5. Prepare a reaction paper to one of the following novels from this perspective: (1)

what the novel says about development of identity and (2) how it relates to your own experiences of young adult years.

> James Joyce, *A Portrait of an Artist as a Young Man* (New York: Viking Press, 1916).
>
> J. D. Salinger, *The Catcher in the Rye* (Boston: Little, Brown, 1951), *Franny and Zooey* (Boston: Little, Brown, 1961), or *Raise High the Roof Beam, Carpenters* (Boston: Little, Brown, 1959).
>
> Chaim Potok, *The Chosen* (New York: Simon and Schuster, 1967).

6. Write a paper on the place of parenthood as a developmental task. For a start in your discussion, see J. Benedek, "Parenthood as a Developmental Phase," *Journal of the American Psychoanalytic Association* 7 (1959), pp. 389–417.

7. Examine the experiences of college students today; see B. D. Lokitz and H. D. Sprandel, "The First Year: A Look at the Freshman Experience," *Journal of College Student Personnel* 19 (July 1976), 4:274–279. Talk with staff in the student personnel services on your campus about their research and programs. Find out about programs of nontraditional studies. Become acquainted with professional organizations, such as the American Personnel and Guidance Association (1607 New Hampshire Avenue, N.W., Washington D.C. 20009), concerning services for and research on young adult years. See journals such as *Personnel and Guidance Journal, Change,* and *Educational Record.*

8. In addition to references in this chapter, the books of Nevitt Sanford, R. W. White, and Kenneth Keniston, to which we have referred in Chapter 7, provide important background for a study of young adult years. In *Education and Identity* (San Francisco: Jossey-Bass, 1969), A. W. Chickering describes dimensions of development during college years. Although its data stops before 1970, K. A. Feldman and T. M. Necomb's *The Impact of College on Students,* vols. 1 and 2 (San Francisco: Jossey-Bass, 1969) helps raise questions to consider for study in its extensive summary of research on student development.

chapter 9

Middle Adult Years

For our second plateau in the arbitrary age ranges we are using to describe the sequences of adult development, we will be thinking of the span of years from 35 to 50. It seems clear that there is a period—after the individual has completed the searching and testing and established the commitments of young adult life—when he is totally immersed in those tasks and roles to which his young adult commitments aligned him. This is the late thirties and the decade of the forties. It precedes a more relaxed and supervisory era, the maturity period of the fifties and early sixties.

As we saw two phases in the young adult years, so also we can detect two phases in the middle years. The first might be called the "stop dallying and let's get on with it" phase. It is green lights and full speed ahead; then, after about ten years, there begins a slight but growing questioning. Phase 2 is those later years of the forties when the individual begins to feel he has made the first round and wonders what next—or perhaps what the battle was.

Stop Dallying and Let's Get On with It

The late thirties and early forties are extremely busy. The middle adult is strongly product oriented. The vacillation over personal identity and career choice is ended. Commitment is made and the task at hand is to produce, to get established at home, in the career, and in the community. This achievement orientation is probably most typical of the middle class; however, the hassle of the job is much a part of all social classes in their thirties and fifties.

246

9–1 *Middle adults are involved in expanding their career successes.* (Manhattan Mercury *photo*)

A Bonafide Member

Children are in elementary school. Parents juggle assignments as PTA officer, Scout Master, Sunday School teacher, Little League coach. The transportation schedule during after-school hours may include music lessions, swimming lessons, and the orthodontist.

Opportunity for one more big move—to accept promotion or obtain a more secure niche with the firm—may cause some moments of pain and readjustments. A new and larger house may need to be purchased when phase 1 moves into phase 2. Each of us has some private bench marks for success: before age 40 to be a construction supervisor or a full professor or a vice-president. These goals keep pushing us.

Leisure is talked about more than experienced. Afternoons on the golf course or in the fishing boat are often planned, only to be canceled by last-minute business or a family crisis. It will be another three or four years

9–2 *Getting children to activities and appointments is one of the many responsibilities of the middle adult parent.* (Manhattan Mercury *photo*)

and into phase 2 before the middle-aged adult will know a regular time with golf clubs or fishing tackle or bridge cards.

In phase 1 of the middle years the individual is being established in his career. He is past the internship or junior executive status, a tenured member of the firm.

Likewise, he is an "old hand" at PTA and other parenting activities if his choice of life-style has been family and parenthood. Or if the choice has been not to include marriage and children, the initial ambivalences are fairly well settled; personal identity is established as a bachelor or member of a cooperative living group or some other life-style.

248 Middle adults are viewed as the leaders and workhorses in industrial and in

civic enterprises. They are settled in the community and experienced in the workings of their institutions.

Daniel Levinson[1] suggests there is another process going on during this busy period of middle years that is a climaxing of the "making it" drive. It is different from the upcoming questioning transition experience of middle adult phase 2; in a sense, it is preparatory for it. He terms it the BOOM experience (becoming one's own man). It results from the gradual awareness that one is still being controlled, not by the original family, but by goals engendered by the institutions, reference groups, and persons one holds in high regard. We knock ourselves out to achieve recognition from them. As we near 40, we experience a shift; we restructure some dependent relationships and begin to serve as reference figures and mentors for other persons. We are becoming our own person.

It is, indeed, this awareness of being settled in, of being a part of the establishment, that will begin to cause some rethinking as phase 2 (late forties) approaches.

> Is this all there is? Have I bet on the right career? Did I choose the right husband or wife? What is the real purpose of life anyway? Have I missed something along the way? Do I want twenty more years of this same life?
>
> What about the doctor's warning of heart conditions if I don't cut back on weight and quit smoking? Did those warnings mean something more serious? What if I really have only three or four more years to live? Wow!

These are only unspoken questions operating in the back of the mind of the busy middle adult phase 1. They will demand answers three to five years later in middle adult phase 2.

Matters of Health

Under the steady pressure of his full schedule and unacknowledged discontent and questioning of his lot in life, the middle adult's body begins to act strangely. Men notice fatigue and some flabbiness of muscles; women encounter friends in the midst of menopause and wonder what this experience will mean in their lives.

---

[1] D. Levinson et al., "Periods in the Adult Development of Men: Ages 18–45," *The Counseling Psychologist* 6 (1976), 1:23.

Worries About Menopause

The climacteric is often confused with menopause. Climacteric refers to the gradual process of reduced ability to reproduce. It is more pronounced in women than in men, leading eventually to a loss of procreative power at menopause. The major event, menopause, does not occur for most women before their fiftieth birthday, although the confusion with earlier signs causes them to worry throughout much of the decade of the forties (Example 9–1).

Men also experience a climacterial imbalance. As ovaries manufacture estrogen, which has considerable influence on other systems, so the testes produce testosterone. The production of testosterone is influenced by the pituitary hormones FSH and ICSH and their amount in the bloodstream is

Example 9–1.
Anticipating Menopause

The ovaries are crucial in the rhythm of endocrine functioning in women. They are the main source of estrogen. Ovaries secrete an abundance of estrogen during the part of the monthly cycle preceding menstruation. In addition to regulating ovulation, estrogen is associated also with functioning of the thyroid and other glands that affect the central and sympathetic nervous systems and the circulatory system, including the amount of tissue fluids and salts.

As the ovaries near the twenty-year mark in their active functioning, their effectiveness begins to lessen. They may produce less estrogen in some months than others; occasionally, they may produce the follicle but without an egg for impregnation. The next month may have all the fullness of earlier cycles. The tendency of the organs to maintain balance stimulates an increase amount of the hormone FSH, by which the pituitary activates the ovaries to produce estrogen. The ovaries are not able to respond to this increase of FSH; so rather than establishing balance, the increased FSH only adds confusion to endocrine functioning, resulting in some of the discomfort and symptoms of the climacteric. Included among these symptoms are hot flashes and perspiration, emotional and nervous disturbances, fatigue, depression, and metabolic changes that may include additional weight and broadening of body contours.

These symptoms may be triggered by the estrogen-FSH changes and are disturbing to women. Unsure of what is going on, her anxiety may evoke further stress reactions. Attempts to "correct" some of the symptoms may result in medications and routines that are themselves disturbing and compounding in their effect. In time, the pituitary will stop trying to stimulate the ovary with floods of FSH and the adrenal cortex will in turn begin to secrete another steroid with many of the balancing effects of estrogen. This restoration of internal harmony usually occurs sometime after age 50 with menopause and the termination of reproduction.

regulated by testosterone. Although there is reciprocal influence between FSH/ICSH and testosterone, the reciprocal functioning is not cyclic but continual. Perhaps it is this continual rather than the cyclic functioning that facilitates a longer life function for testes than ovaries.

Although less recognized than changes in women, there does begin a lessening of testicular activity, usually in the early forties. The reduction in supply of testosterone has repercussions in the endocrine system of men similar to that described for women: fatigue, circulatory and metabolic disturbances, arthritic tendencies, emotional effects of depression and irritability. The effects are less pronounced, possibly for several reasons. The rate of reduction of estrogen is more rapid and probably occurs earlier in life than change in testosterone. The cyclic nature of the endocrine functioning in women is more visible and dramatic, thus changes tend to be more anxiety provoking. The sudden appearance of facial hair or the word that a 45-year-old neighbor unexpectedly became pregnant can worry a woman who thought she had reached the "safe" period of sex life.

Worries About Heart Attacks   Neugarten's group of middle-class, middle-aged persons designated the years 35 to 50 as the period when a man has the most responsibilities.[2] The years 30 to 45 were the years they designated when a woman accomplishes most.

In the studies of four life stages, Lowenthal found that it was during the middle adult period that men worried considerably and often expressed frustration over matters of employment.

> Work-related stresses were critical for the middle-aged men, mostly stemming from lack of occupational advancement and anxieties about retirement income. In view of the fact that the majority of these men were firmly entrenched in the probable security of civil service and related bureaucracies (indeed most of them selected such work primarily because of its security), and above all in view of the comparative remoteness of their retirement (10–15 years), it would appear that much of this preoccupation is attributable to a combination of job frustration and economic and political factors which they perceived as beyond their control . . . The mixture of strain and boredom in

---

[2] B. L. Neugarten, J. W. Moore, and J. C. Lowe, "Age Norms, Age Constraints, and Adult Socialization," *American Journal of Sociology* 70 (May 1965), 6.

the middle-aged men struck us as a threat to their mental and possibly their physical health in succeeding years.[3]

Whereas many men talked much about their stresses, there was another group Lowenthal thought might represent even greater health problems.

> Roughly a third were in the category which we call, in a stress typology reported elsewhere, the challenged. These men had had and continued to have considerable presumptive stress but did not dwell on it. In some ways they resembled the Type A reported by Friedman and Rosenman, hard-driving, comparatively ambitious men whom these authors found to be at risk of heart attack or stroke.[4]

Although many diseases have been known through the ages, heart attack is a modern phenomenon. It has been suggested that the growth in heart disease parallels the growth in the gross national product. As the pressures and the product orientation of technology advance, so does heart disease. Diet and lack of exercise have been pointed to as contributors. However, it is stress—often self-imposed—that has the most influence. Stress makes the difference of whether an inherited tendency toward high cholesterol will create problems. For example, cholesterol readings for accountants have been found to rise markedly during the pressure periods of January and late March, with a return to normal during less rushed periods.[5]

Those persons most vulnerable to heart attack are described by Friedman and Rosenman as personality "Type A." Their motors are going at full speed continually, and they are usually juggling two telephones or carrying on multiple tasks simultaneously. Personality of the Type A individual is indicative of the stress and tension under which he keeps himself. He is always impatient, always in a hurry, usually at work. Even when he relaxes, he works at it. Fingers drumming on the desk or tunelessly humming, the Type A far outranks in heart attacks the Type B people, the other category in which Rosenman and Friedman have grouped the American population. For example, in a study of 257 heart-attack victims 70 per cent were Type A individuals.[6]

---

[3] M. F. Lowenthal, "Psychosocial Variations Across the Adult Life Course: Frontiers for Research and Policy," *The Gerontologist* 15 (February 1975, Part 1), p. 9.

[4] Ibid., p. 10.

[5] W. McQuade and A. Aikman, *Stress* (New York: Bantam Books, 1974), pp. 21–25.

[6] M. Friedman and R. H. Rosenman, *Type A Behavior and Your Heart* (Greenwich, Conn.: Fawcett Crest, 1975), p. 80. McQuade and Aikman, *Stress,* p. 29.

We often think of men as more vulnerable to heart attacks. The distinguishing factors seem to be stress and personality. There are Type A women, too, and they are just as vulnerable.

Generativity Versus Stagnation

The developmental stage Erikson terms *generativity versus stagnation* characterizes the growth potential during middle adult phase 1 years. Generativity means the concern for establishing and guiding the next generation. Erikson describes it thus:

> Once we have grasped this interlocking of the human life stages, we understand that adult man is so constituted as to *need to be needed* lest he suffer the mental deformation of self-absorption, in which he becomes his own infant and pet. I have, therefore, postulated an instinctual and psychosocial stage of "generativity" beyond that of genitality. Parenthood is, for most, the first, and for many, the prime generative encounter; yet the perpetuation of mankind challenges the generative ingenuity of workers and thinkers of many kinds. And man *needs* to teach, not only for the sake of those who need to be taught, and not only for the fulfillment of his identity, but because facts are kept alive by being told, logic by being demonstrated, truth by being professed . . . As adult man needs to be needed, so—for the strength of his ego and for that of his community—he requires the challenge emanating from what he has generated and from what now must be "brought up," guarded, preserved and eventually transcended.[7]

Generativity involves developing a capacity for caring about other adults, about the continuation of society. It means a growth in personal maturity. He no longer feels himself a child to be nurtured or a young man seeking approval from his mentors. Levinson suggests that having had a mentor[8] is important in laying the affective foundation in the self for the later maturing of generativity. He points to the growing away from dependence on one's mentor as part of the BOOM experience, a necessary step allowing one to take on generative relationships with others.

---

[7] E. H. Erikson, *Insight and Responsibility* (New York: Norton, 1964), pp. 130–131.

[8] In the story of Martin Arrowsmith's struggle to find his way between private practice, public health, and medical research, we see some of the young professional's dilemmas of destiny. We also see the important role of his mentor, Professor Gottlieb, and how he provides role-model inspiration and tangible professional contacts and assistance. S. Lewis, *Arrowsmith* (New York: Harcourt Brace Jovanovich, 1925).

Erikson's description of generativity seems to speak of an active creating and procreating, a nurturing, and later a preserving aspect. It is probable that this task is an extended one. It is being realized during the active, busy, productive years of the late thirties and mid-forties. There comes an interruption and the middle adult grows through a process of reevaluation and recommitment. We will see generativity come to the fore again in the early years of maturity in the preserving and extending of social institutions.

Growing (working) through the crisis of generativity is not easy. It means shifting from a "me and mine" to a "thee and thou" orientation. It means hours of labor for an end outside oneself. New parents may find the excitement of their anticipation of a new toy changed to frustration and resentment when they discover their child makes demands for *himself* and *his* amusements and needs. When their midnight services bring little overt appreciation from the child, the foundations of generativity are being formed. At the office, when the late nights of donated work "to get a project off the ground" appear to be taken for granted or when they are elected over a specially planned recreational outing, the foundations of generativity are also being formed.

White[9] describes a young Ph.D. who had not yet achieved the sense of generativity. The young professor resigned from his teaching position in the middle of the year, stating that neither his colleagues nor his students were intellectually stimulating. He was still occupied with finding a mentor rather than serving as one.

Whereas growth in generativity versus stagnation is the prevailing task of the middle adult period, earlier accomplishments, such as intimacy, will require reworking in light of new growth and circumstances. In some instances, such as with single, divorced, or widowed persons, intimacy becomes a major developmental task.[10]

On the Go One of the characteristics of phase 1 of middle years is that the individual is so busy that there is little time to think. He has become immersed in the social system and the force of the stream rushes him along. Each year on the

---

[9] R. W. White, *The Enterprise of Living* (New York: Holt, Rinehart and Winston, 1972), p. 467.

[10] In Ashton-Warner's book the spinster, Anna Vorontosov, seems to struggle with intimacy (in relation to adults), whereas her fellow teacher, Paul Vercol, may still be occupied with identity versus role diffusion. S. Ashton-Warner, *Spinster* (New York: Simon and Schuster, 1960); see also L. Caine, *Widow* (New York: Bantam Books, 1974).

job moves the individual one step closer to a goal, only to discover that achieving this has created a new opportunity, a new goal, and a new drive to achieve is on. Getting children through elementary school means that they are now in junior high—and their younger siblings move from nursery to elementary school. The new house purchased when the family was just starting becomes too small; but buying a house the second time is more easily taken in stride.

There are other, more taxing, issues. Children become adolescents as parents near 40. It is difficult to know how to relate to one's flesh and blood who, seemingly overnight, has developed the physical stature of an adult and is challenging the various "turf" prerogatives that one had assumed were innate and unchanging "givens." There is indeed much that keeps the middle adult hopping to keep ahead of the next day's development—to keep up with his responsibilities, to fulfill in a respectable fashion the obligations of parent and community member. In a sense, his life is being lived "for the sake of" the family and the career.

And then one day, the first child graduates from high school. The husband

9–3 *Promotions often require uprooting the family and moving to a new community.* (Manhattan Mercury *photo*)

receives his "fifteen-year pin" with the company.[11] Someone takes a deep breath and says, "I think we can begin to see daylight." Phase 2 of the middle years is beginning. It doesn't happen this neatly or this clearly but is more interspersed with the steady pace. The very intermingling causes growing uneasiness.

What's Next?

The mid-forties of phase 2 has been termed by some as the transition period of "middlescence."[12] It is a period of reexamination similar to the self-examination of adolescence and of the age-30 transition. Some of the goals for both husband and wife are nearing fulfillment. Other more idealized dreams have been recognized as out of range in this lifetime. As he moves toward the security of recognized accomplishments on the job, in the home, and in the community, some questions begin to surface privately: "Is this what life is? "Is this all there is?" "What have I missed?" "What's next?"

Children are graduating from school. The more obvious requirements for parenting no longer dictate fidelity in marriage. "What ties are there?" Along with sampling of new uses for leisure may come sampling of new forms of intimacy.

Some attempt to avoid confrontation with the meaning of life by plunging into an additional career. Others may change jobs, perhaps seeking the re-membered excitement of the first days of proving themselves to be able workers.

We might almost imagine Sinclair Lewis was attempting to depict the travails of middlescence. The characters in several of his novels express a varied range of results from this period of life review.

As middle-aged real-estate broker George Babbitt[13] witnessed his friend Paul's existential searching and marital travail, he began to feel that his own wife was a habit and his way of life superficial. He turned from conservative to liberal political views, took a mistress, and was terribly unhappy. His wife's illness provided a catalyst for the reintegration of separate pieces of his life.

Sam Dodsworth,[14] approaching 50, realized that he had given all of his life

---

[11] Some who entered the military or industry directly out of high school and are on a 20-year work plan may retire before their fortieth birthday.

[12] B. Fried, *The Middle-Age Crisis* (New York: Harper & Row, 1957).

[13] S. Lewis, *Babbitt* (New York: Harcourt Brace Jovanovich, 1922).

[14] S. Lewis, *Dodsworth* (New York: Harcourt Brace Jovanovich, 1929).

9–4 *What's next? The mid-forties involve a time of reexamining life goals. (Kansas State University Student Publications photo)*

to the Revelation Automobile Company. With his son in college and daughter married, he decided to sell some of the stock and see the world. During their travels through Europe, Sam began to see his wife, Fran, and their relationship in a new way. Her self-centeredness and pretentiousness at first made him pity her and then despair of her. At the end of their travels Sam and Fran divorced and Sam returned to Europe to marry Edith Cartright, a widow he had met in Italy.

Cas Timberlane[15] was a distinguished district court judge in his forties

[15] S. Lewis, *Cas Timberlane* (New York: Random House, 1945).

when he met Jinny, a working girl in her twenties. His friends were not only surprised but downright critical and unsupportive. They said such a marriage would never work, but it did.

A Time for Rethinking

Fried[16] has described for the popular reader some of the emotions, turbulences, and behavior of the condition she calls "middlescence." She points out numerous ways in which social, psychological, and biological conditions of the years following 40 parallel those of the years following 14. She points out that the "foolish forties" and the "dangerous years" are a frequent theme in novels and plays. The person of 40 is experiencing new feelings. He is questioning old loyalties and seeking new meanings of life. This is usually done alone—there is not an event, a rite of passage, that creates the occasion for personal review. In the midst of being mother, father, shopkeeper, there are these impulses, these moods. It is the period of preparation for a new life stage.

A New Social Era

Until recently the adult went directly from the struggles of work to the status of old age at 50 plus. With the lengthened middle years, coupled with a changing technology that threatens to shorten the working period, society is faced with new social and psychological dynamics.

Developmental crises, at whatever period, serve to prepare us for the next stage. In this case the "being 40" syndrome or the "case of middlescence" prepares us for the next ten to fifteen years of maturity and the anticipation of retirement.

Middlescence is a period of growth when our bodies and minds respond to pressures from within and around us, pressures setting off changes in personality and attitudes, and forecasting changes in physiological functions. Women, with an increasing life-span, now live three decades after childbearing years are over. This has prompted a new consideration of life goals.

---

[16] Fried, *The Middle-Age Crisis.*

More Years After Child Bearing

The emergence of a psychosocial condition of middlescence may well reflect the social evolution going on in our society. Fried points to a similar historical change that contributed to the evolution of the psychosocial condition now accepted as adolescence.[17] In colonial days, people went directly from childhood into adult responsibilities. A boy became a man when physically able to hold the ax or serve a full day in the field. Girls became mothers at 14 or 15. Life ended at a little past twoscore years and there was little time to waste. As life lengthened, there was a longer period of preparation—children remained longer in the home and in schools. This created a new phenomenon in terms of relationships, business, industry, and education. The adolescent was the term given to the focal point of that phenomenon. So with further social and health changes, there is now more time available for adults and a new developmental stage.

Dissatisfaction with Social Role

One of the changes occurring in the middle years of many women is the return to work. More women will, of course, be in the labor market during the next developmental period, maturity. In 1970, 28 per cent of the young adult wives were working outside the home as compared with 48 per cent of the middle adult wives.

In Chapter 10 we will discuss in more detail some facets of the changing roles for women. However, it is of interest at this point to note that Lowenthal's interviews with working-class women, in an environment she described as highly family centered, reflected the women of middle years phase 2 to be the most unhappy of any of the four age periods. They sense their "mothering" career may soon be ending. They feel unappreciated by their husbands and children and frustrated with many aspects of their family situation. Furthermore, they are uncertain whether they will have a place of significance once the children are gone from home. Lowenthal described them as follows:

> Despite the manifest boredom with jobs and uneasiness about finances among the middle-aged men, on nearly all counts, the women confronting the post-parental period appeared to be in a considerably more critical state. They were vague and diffuse in regard to the stresses which may have accounted for their extreme malaise, which alternated with anxiety. While they said that they were in general pleased by the prospects of the youngest child leaving home, they had a much less positive stance toward the future than older women. In

[17] Ibid., p. 10.

fact, women facing the empty nest were more negative, apprehensive, and at the same time inarticulate, about their pending transition than any other group we studied. They were also far more likely to report an increase in marital problems, a state of affairs not reflected in the reports of their male counterparts, nor in those of the older women.[18]

Symptoms of Middlescence

Symptoms of middlescence are boredom, restlessness, inclination to question life. It is this impetus to reevaluate that enables middlescence to be a creative opportunity. During the latter years of young adult and the early years of middle adult, the individual has been pretty well dominated by the system. And now, with some respite, when the individual begins to examine his feelings, he exaggerates his reactions. Boredom and frustrations, previously minimal, become monumental. The result may be depression or a throwing overboard of long cherished values, or a running away, or an impetuous affair.[19]

As with 14-year-olds, no one—particularly the younger sibling—understands them. Who has more impatience with a "moony" adolescent than his 10-year-old brother or with an "irresponsible" middlescent than his 30-year-old junior executive brother?

In the turmoil of middlescence, the middle adult again seems to be working through earlier stages of ego development: the crises of identity, intimacy, and generativity. I was impressed with the relationship between the searching of middlescence and the searching of the young adult when prompted by Fried's suggestion that the play *After the Fall*[20] acts out many aspects of middlescence, I reread a review I had prepared several yares ago for the *Journal of Counseling Psychology*. In that review I pointed out the usefulness of the play as a counseling tool with college students[21] (Example 9–2).

---

[18] Lowenthal, "Psychosocial Variations Across the Adult Life Course," p. 10.

[19] Discussion of Gauguin, who abandoned his family and successful banking career at the age of 45 to go to Tahiti and paint, can invariably evoke spokesmen for both sides of the issue.

[20] A. Miller, *After the Fall* (New York: Viking Press, 1963).

[21] C. E. Kennedy, "After the Fall: One Man's Look at His Human Nature," *Journal of Counseling Psychology* 12 (Summer 1965), 2.

Example 9–2.
"After The
Fall": One
Man's Look at
His Human
Nature

Arthur Miller is no stranger to introspective dialogue or to attempts at presenting the dilemmas of modern man. Willie Loman in *Death of a Salesman* reaped the vacuous fruits of every man's inferiority-propelled dreams of success. Joe Keller in *All My Sons* suffered every father's torments of filial misunderstanding. Miller's works have dealt with family conflicts, guilt and prejudice. They have employed the method of flash-back and soliloquy. In his new play *After The Fall,* Miller employs an unusually intense form of flash-back and soliloquy: "The action," he states, "takes place in the mind, thought and memory of Quentin." It is portrayed on a bone bare and darkened stage, sculpted to represent a brain. Recalled vignettes of past experience light one portion of the stage for an instant before the cerebral circuit breaks and another thought illuminates another sector.

> This play, then, is a trial; the trial of a man by his own conscience, his own values, his own deeds. The "Listener," who to some will be a psychoanalyst, to others God, is Quentin himself turned at the edge of the abyss to look at his experience . . . (Miller, 1963, Introduction)

And what is the experience he sees?

He sees his mother soured because she was denied an opportunity to attend college. He hears the diatribe that passes for marriage between his parents. He feels the obligation to success for the sake of mother and father and older brother and he simultaneously knows the paradoxes of love and hate and an irrevocable guilt. There are his two wrecked marriages—one by divorce, the other by suicide. Dare he contemplate another such relationship? The lecherous wife of his friend and mentor lights the stage for an instant as does the recollection of a girl who blesses him. The relief he felt when his friend's suicide freed him from the obligation to defend that person before a Congressional investigation turns to questioning and guilt.

If all this sounds heavy and morbidly somber, it is perhaps because this listing has not included Quentin's soliloquial search for meaning. It has not taken into account his strengths and successes. It has not suggested the vitality of Quentin's friends—distilled into the moments of confrontation and encounter, flooding his memory and overwhelming the apperception of the reader.

Henry Hewes (1964) comments in the *Saturday Review* "Whatever drawbacks one may find in Arthur Miller's *After The Fall,* the size of its concerns are impressive." Elia Kazan (Meyer, 1964) hails it as one of the few truly great plays with which he has come in contact and confesses that he came to direct the play so awed by its magnitude that he felt a rare but serious concern for his ability to bring it off.

Notwithstanding the merits of the play as worthy art, one may still ask why bring it to the pages of a professional journal of counseling?

The answer is simply that this writer's response to reading the play was stimulating and meaningful to him. He shared vicariously some of the player's emotions and was moved to introspection and inquiry by the concepts being considered. In addition to his own personal experience with the play, the writer found himself responding to the play in terms of its meaningfulness as a forum for student discussion. The play seems to possess properties that would facilitate the communication and introspection of some college students. The hero, on the verge of re-entry into the world, is not unlike the college student on his edge of entry into the world of the post-AB. Both are concerned with commitment, with process of choice, with the search for authenticity and with tasks of dealing with responsibility and guilt.

The language of the play commends itself to college students in two respects. One of these is the introspective, counselee-counselor style. The other is the vocabulary and symbols. Critics of the play have described its language as sophomoric and adolescent. Its "obviousness" has been lamented.

> The vocabulary in which Quentin's discoveries are enunciated fans out in many directions. Much of it is religious, even Christian, but none, I am afraid, carries that freshness of tone which is the mark of authentic personal discovery. Instead we hear of familiar themes in familiar words: innocence and guilt, finding and losing identity, loneliness and community, hope and despair, belief and unbelief, saving others and being saved, crucifixion and resurrection. Watching the play, one does not doubt that Arthur Miller is, in Dr. Earl Loomis' phrase, a "self in pilgrimage." . . . . what bothers one is that the pilgrimage seems to have yielded the writer no insights and no utterance truly his own. (Driver, 1964)

This lengthy criticism is cited to suggest that what in certain contexts might be negative, may in other contexts be positive. Students in counseling and in college discussion groups frequently are seeking to find vocabulary for private experience and for the social issues of their day. There is often in student discussion groups some floundering while the members gauge the climate of the group and find a mode of expression. That Miller's contemporary pilgrimage is a familiar one, expressed in conventional language, may be a strong commendation of the play for use as outside reading or as a shared group experience.

The developmental stage of college students has been described as one of transition from the rigid self-control of the post-adolescent to the flexible control of the young adult. "An element of perfectionism, of striving for purity of thought and action is characteristic of the freshman" (Sanford, 1964, p. 87). Miller (1963) in his introduction to the play states, "Through Quentin's agony in this play there runs the everlasting temptation of Innocence, that deep desire to return to when, it seems, he was in fact without blame." Paradoxically Miller writes, "Quentin's impulse to feel in some concrete way his own authorship of his life and his person extends to his taking on guilt even for what he did *not* do." (Miller, 1964). Such violently conflicting turmoil has similar reverberation among some college youth who are on the cutting edge of self-affirmation.

Miller is accused by the play's critics of attempting some kind of self-justification for his "real life" behavior with Marilyn Monroe. His reply has been that the *main point* of the play is that man cannot escape his own capacity for destruction. If, indeed, it should happen that Quentin, in attempting to accept responsibility for his life still succumbs to self-justification and excuse—is not this the point of the play? Does not the play perhaps approach here that distinction for which the author wished—that it would cease to be a play *about* guilt and be an *act* of life dealing with guilt?

Counselors may be stimulated by the possible similarity between lawyer Quentin's client, Felice, and some of their own clients. Felice is the girl who continually blesses him, who had plastic surgery on her nose after feeling affirmed as a person through encountering him. She is also the one for whom Quentin declares he can feel no sense of significant concern—yet she continues to flit through his introspection. Two or three questions may be generated by Quentin's introspection: To what extent is a helpful encounter complete in itself? To what extent is an encounter a helpful one when the helper does not perceive the relationship to involve him in as personal a way as does his relationship with family and friends? To what extent is it possible for a counselee to project characteristics upon the counselor (create a counselor image) and to be helped by interacting with the characteristics he himself has created? Hear Quentin attempting to "explain" Felice to the Listener.

> She meant nothing to me: it was a glancing blow, and yet it's not impossible I stand in her mind like some important corner she turned in her life. I feel like a mirror in which she somehow saw herself as glorious . . .
> I don't understand why that girl sticks in my mind . . . Yes! She did, she offered me some . . . love, I guess. And if I do not return it, or if it doesn't change me somehow, it—it's like owing for a gift you didn't ask for . . .
> That's why she sticks in my mind. She brings some darkness, some dreadful element of power . . . Well, that's power, isn't it? To influence a girl to change her nose, her life? . . . It does, yes, it frightens me, I wish to God she'd stopped blessing me. (He laughs uneasily, surprised at the force of his fear) . . . Well, I suppose because there is a fraud involved; I have no such power. (Miller, 1963)

Perpetually the pendulum swings as Quentin seeks to deny his power for destruction and then, alternately, acknowledges that each man possesses such power. How to live with that power or "What to Do About Evil" is a keystone of the play. Quentin is profoundly aware of his destructive potential; one is not certain, however, whether he is ever able to come to terms with it—whether he is able to feel that however "unacceptable" he is, he is still "acceptable" simply by virtue of being. Holga, whose proffered love has created the play's dilemma, once said to him:

> I know how terrible it is to owe what one can never pay. And for a long time after, I had the same dream each night—that I had a child; and even in the dream I saw that the child was my life; and it was an idiot. And I wept, and a hundred times I ran away, but each time I came back it had the same dreadful face. Until I thought, if I could kiss it, whatever in it was my own, perhaps I could rest. And I bent to its broken face, and it was horrible . . . But I kissed it. (Miller, 1963)

William Stringfellow (1964) in a recent and provocative little book *Free in Obedience* observes that every man is accompanied in life by an image; he is often controlled or destroyed by that image and invariably it survives him. The image is distinguishable from the person, lies beyond his control and is in conflict with the person until the person surrenders his life in one fashion or another to the image. "And when that surrender is made, the person in fact dies, though not yet physically."

After the Fall describes life as the process of choice-making, but a choice-maker is no longer innocent and no longer victim, and therefore the play's characters worry about such things as guilt and responsibility. *After the Fall* is a play about expectations—man's response to the expectations of other men. Miller would rather not have the play be described as "about" something but would describe it as something—as "a way of looking at man and at his human nature."

C. E. Kennedy, "After the Fall: One Man's Look at His Human Nature," *Journal of Counseling Psychology* 12 (Summer 1965), 2. Copyright 1965 by the American Psychological Association. Reprinted by permission.

Time Left to Live

As the middle adult begins to think in terms of "time-left-to-live" instead of "time-since-birth," there comes a realization that not all the dreams (or other, even less fully expressed, intuitions) will ever be realized.[22]

[22] B. L. Neugarten, "The Awareness of Middle Age," in *Middle Age and Aging,* ed. B. L. Neugarten (Chicago: University of Chicago Press, 1968), p. 97.

Middlescence begins with a sense of loss. This loss leads to self-evaluation that laments the hope that was not fully realized. With the recognition that time is fleeting comes a sense of relief. The relief comes from the awareness that necessity now dictates that I (and others too) must accept what I am. The obligation to be something I'm not goes by the board. With that comes new hope and new strength to proceed with life, integrating resources from the newly affirmed estate of middle age.

Many of the attributes of the middle-age crisis are similar to earlier crises—meaning of life, guilt, quality of relationships. There is also an age or time-related dimension that is distinctive: because I've lived longer, the sorting through of my experiences is more complex. Many of the factors, such as reality of death, have a more immediate meaning. Death, for example, is illuminated by a parent's death or by consideration of the length "of time left" for a friend with cancer.

A New Look at Intimacy

The middlescent must rework the intimacy conflict. This involves a rethinking of solutions he thought were made at the end of adolescence. During middlescence old loyalties lose their attraction (see Quentin in *After the Fall*). There is a new awareness that men and women seem to speak a different language.

Problems of Communication   Communication problems, present for several years, break out with special urgency during this period of reevaluation. Couples may have difficulty identifying that they have problems in their communication. The usual procedure is to either deny the feelings or project the problem onto changes in the other person. George and Martha in the play *Who's Afraid of Virginia Woolf?*[23] demonstrate some of the language symbolism and "contracts" that can grow up between husband and wife through twenty years of marriage. Separate autobiographical accounts by a husband and wife—singer Pat Boone and Shirley—recount how each saw an increasing emptiness in their marriage to be the result of changes in, and the fault of, the other (Example 9–3). Shirley's story offers a graphic account of how pressure and lack of

---

[23] E. Albee, *Who's Afraid of Virginia Woolf?* (New York: Atheneum, 1961).

Example 9–3.
Pat and Shirley
Boone—A
New Life Script

Seldom has there been a couple whom the country has cast more accurately as the All-American couple than Pat and Shirley Boone. They were naïvely trusting—trusting of people, of each other and of God. Romantically their married life began as newly eloped teen-ager's, closely knit together in their conservative faith, struggling to establish a home, get an education, and begin a career. By their mid-thirties they were well established in Pat's career, they had four school-age daughters—and their marriage was breaking up.

After fifteen years, the relationship that began so idyllic was losing its foundation. Their respect for each other was no longer present. They no longer shared the same value system.

The value change did not come suddenly. It was a gradual reorientation with Pat accommodating to the demands of his professional life. It was a gradual reorientation also in Shirley's life as she felt increasingly left out, critical of Pat's "double standards" and sorry for herself. Her frequent accusation was, "You're no longer the man I married—you've changed." Pat's reply was, "We've got to change. We can't always be naïve children."

Shirley recalls her pain: "To live in terror is to live in hell on earth, and such was my life for approximately seven years. I was afraid for the future of my marriage. I was afraid for the fate of Pat's soul and, toward the end of my ordeal, I was afraid that I was losing my mind and would lose my children."

Pat remembers thinking: "Other women think I'm witty; they think I'm attractive and I get a kick out of their flattering attention. At home with Shirley there's nothing but conflict."

At the same time Pat had the gnawing suspicion that a lot of the conflict came because he did not have answers to the contradictions in his life. He had begun going in one direction and Shirley had joined him in that journey when they were married. Now he was heading for another goal in business and new directions in the entertainment field. Even the Show Biz goal was beginning to have some troubles. Pat wasn't sure what his movie image was or what he wanted it to be.

About that time a former insurance salesman became his financial adviser. "Clint Davidson was a giant influence on me," Pat said. "I had made a number of different efforts to recapture my earlier successes, but they failed. I had blundered in both my professional career and in business. (With my family problems, as well as other trouble) I could have easily gone down the drain spiritually. But then Clint Davidson, in his joyful way, came along as plain proof of what great things God can do in the life of a totally committed man, no matter what his business."

Pat's mid-life transition began to move toward healing and integration as he experienced a freedom to examine his commitments—to write a new script. Eventually Shirley joined him in sharing the new script.

Abstract from P. Boone, *A New Song* (Carol Stream, Ill.: Creation House, 1970); and S. Boone, *One Woman's Liberation* (Carol Stream, Ill.: Creation House, 1972).

understanding from others prompts the middlescent to question sanity and purpose for living.

Falling in Love Again

Falling in love seems to be the cure-all that relieves the boredom and reaffirms self-worth. It blazes for an instant and then takes on the more subdued light and heat of previous long-term companionships.[24]

For some the experience may have enhanced awareness of self, developed new skills of communication, or brought about resolutions to untenable earlier life-styles. The impulsive acting out of the second intimacy crisis can have growth dimensions. However, because the middlescent is usually related to family, the business world and a value system, impetuous pursuit of new loves may be damaging to others as well as (through guilt and anxiety) to his own peace of mind and well-being.

The middle adult phase 2, looking back in evaluation and forward with planning, fluctuates from despair to hope and from self-hatred to bubbling joy. How an individual functions may have input from hormonal imbalance, from conscious and unconscious psychological systems, from social opportunities, and from life-style presently experienced. Emotions run the gamut; as love and fantasy are high, so are jealousy, hostility, and outbursts of anger. Caught between teen-age children and aging parents, the 40-year-old gets it coming and going. There is also a feeling of guilt—perhaps unexpressed by him—at taking over from his own parents the decision-making authority.

Themes running through the middlescent crisis include death and identity, intimacy and alienation, power and impotence. Indeed, the years immediately ahead, for which this growth crisis is preparing the middle adult, are the years of maturity when he will exercise a greater freedom and the most power of his life.

A New Look at Power

How an individual responds to dilemmas of power may indicate how he will handle other aspects of the middle-age crisis—that is, whether he will define his role toward more responsibility and grow to fulfill that role, or whether

---

[24] Fried observed at a small seaside colony that out of a dozen middle-aged couples one partner in eight of the marriages and both partners in six of the marriages were having extramarital affairs. *The Middle-Age Crisis*, p. 3.

he will play it safe and avoid opportunities for "moving on." For example, such challenges may appear for the mother who recognizes a new step in life beyond child rearing.[25]

Because power for most men and women is associated with work, the ambivalence toward power receives frequent nudges from new opportunities present in the world of work. Evaluating one's rate of success against one's projected calendar evokes periods of intense anxiety.

The fear of loss or risk may tempt the individual to "chicken out," with claims of boredom. Some may not yet have gained the "freedom to fail" that is basic to the "freedom to succeed." Illnesses may at times express defenses against the risk of committing oneself to roles of power.

Dick Diver,[26] at 38, began to change. His professional work as a psychologist and writer began to lose its creativeness and he took to drinking heavily. The jealousy of Nicole, his wife, put her in a mental hospital for a time. When she returned, Nicole and Dick agreed they had little in common. But the security of his wife's fortune was a temptation so great, it stood in the way of any constructive rebuilding for Dick. In time Nicole was able to be

---

[25] Ibid., p. 132.

[26] F. S. Fitzgerald, *Tender Is the Night* (New York: Scribner, 1934).

9–5 *Pat and Shirley Boone*

9–6 *New interests and careers often emerge as women look beyond the child-rearing years. (Kansas State University Student Publications photo)*

free of her traumatic early childhood memories and also of her dependence upon Dick. Dick continued to go downhill.

The issues with which the middle adult must deal in the developmental crises of phase 2 are also the issues with which our society is struggling at this period of our history. Rollo May has discussed these in the two books *Love and Will* and *Power and Innocence*.

> The striking thing about love and will in our day is that, whereas in the past they were always held up to us as the *answer* to life's predicaments, they have now themselves become the *problem*. It is always true that love and will become more difficult in a transitional age; and ours is an era of radical transition. The old myths and symbols by which we oriented ourselves are gone, anxiety is rampant; we cling to each other and try to persuade ourselves that what we feel is love; we do not will because we are afraid that if we choose one thing or one person we'll lose the other, and we are too insecure to take that chance . . .[27]

269

[27] R. May, *Love and Will* (New York: Dell, 1974), p. 13.

May points out the destructive consequences for the individual to his personality when he is unable to will or refuses to make responsible choices.

> The bottom then drops out of the conjunctive emotions and processes—of which love and will are the two foremost examples. The individual is forced to turn inward; he becomes obsessed with the new form of the problem of identity, namely, Even-if-I-know-who-I-am, I-have-no-significance. I am unable to influence others. The next step is apathy. And the step following that is violence. For no human being can stand the perpetually numbing experience of his own powerlessness.[28]

Our individual histories and our special inheritances shape the distinct threads of life that is each of us. However, the pattern they weave will follow the major designs characterizing the common fabric of developmental processes through the life-span in our society. For the middle adult during the thirties and entering the forties, this will involve a time of great investment of energies in work and rearing of family. As one moves through the forties, there is a coming to new awarenesses, some looking inward, and some reconciliation of unsettled dilemmas in preparation for the period of maturity. That will be a time when many come to have a new measure of self-acceptance and be able to accept the acceptance from those around them. It is to the period of maturity that we will turn our attention in the next chapter.

Summary

Middle adult phase 1 is a time of high productivity. Having fully committed himself to his present life course during the age-30 review near the end of young adulthood, the middle adult works day and night to "make a success of it." The more he works, the more work he has to do. Community organizations, family, and industry look to the middle adult to get things done.

Gradually the middle adult begins to recognize that he is accepted as fully adult, that he does not need to seek to please older models. In Levinson's phrase the middle adult begins to BOOM (becoming one's own man). This is part of the preparation for accomplishing the developmental stage of generativity versus stagnation, the capacity to care for other adults and social concerns.

In the late forties, phase 2 enters with a time of intense introspection along

---

[28] Ibid., p. 13.

with real and imagined physical changes. *Middlescence* is the term sometimes given to the "second adolescence." With family responsibilities lessening, work and economic pressures stabilized, the middle adult has the opportunity to reaffirm the meaning of life. Thinking now in terms of "time-left-to-live," he tries out vicariously the best way to use that time. Turbulent though the mid-forties are, the searching and the new commitments are preparing the way for a more serene period of maturity when clear-cut recognition of the fruits of his labor will be forthcoming.

The apt phrases of Gail Sheehy help to outline the developmental processes of the middle adult years. Following the life-review period of young adult phase 2, which she calls catch-30, comes a period of rooting and extending—buying houses, climbing the career ladder, caring for children. This merges with the deadline decade, 35 to 45, "my last chance to make it big." Renewal or resignation comes in the late forties. "If one has refused to budge through the mid-life transition, the sense of staleness will calcify into resignation . . . On the other hand . . . If we have confronted ourselves in the middle passage and found a renewal of purpose around which we are eager to build a more authentic life structure, these [next] years may well be the best."[29]

Suggested Activities and Further Reading

1. Prepare a time line for people now in phase 1 and another for people in phase 2 of middle adult years. Phase 1 people were born in the late 1930s or early 1940s; phase 2 people were born in the late 1920s to mid-1930s. Relate such events as the Depression, World War II, and Korea to the different places on their time line.

2. Have a panel of middle adult, college, and high school students discuss the process of communication between generations.

3. Have a panel of women who have recently begun to work outside the home discuss how they arrived at this decision and the processes of adjustment this new life-style has required.

4. Have a panel of young adults and middle adult parents discuss their parenting experiences. Some stimulus material may be found in two articles in *Journal of Marriage and Family* 38 (August 1976), 3:519–534, "Family Photographs and Transition into Parenthood" and "Intergenerational Solidarity Versus Progress for Women" (activity of mother in daughter's choice of mate).

5. In order to know something of the socializing experiences that persons now in middle adult years may have had, read and report on some novels and plays that

[29] G. Sheehy, *Passages: Predictable Crises of Adult Life* (New York: Dutton, 1976).

were written during the 1930s and 1940s and that the Middle Adult may have read while in high school and college (for example, *For Whom the Bell Tolls, Grapes of Wrath, Our Town, The Great Gatsby.*

6. The marriage of Diahann Carroll, 40, and Bob DeLeon, 24, is a feature article in *Ebony* (September 1976). Can you find other articles that discuss marriages of the middle adult persons with persons from another age range (for example, Jacqueline Kennedy and Aristotle Onassis)?

7. Compare the views of middlescence or mid-life transition presented by Daniel Levinson, Barbara Fried, Gail Sheehy, and Roger Gould.

8. Discuss the kinds of physiological concerns that may worry the middle adults. How do you see these influencing their social activities and their feelings about themselves?

chapter 10

Maturity

It is possible to think of the expanse of years from the early thirties to the early sixties as one period and to call it middle age—bound on one end by a young adult period and on the other by old age. However, it seems to me to more clearly reflect the things going on during these years if we break that period into two stages: middle adult and maturity. This will mean that in reading from other sources referring to middle age, you will want to note more closely whether it is the hard-driving period of early middle adult, the questioning and reaffirming period of late middle adult, or the period beginning in the fifties of more measured and secure maturity (Example 10–1).

A New Look at Generativity

In this chapter we will consider the years 50 to 65. I have titled the period maturity because this term reflects some of the qualities of Erikson's last two stages of ego development: *generativity* and *integrity*. You will remember from the previous chapter that generativity is the concern for establishing and guiding the next generation. It is, therefore, a central aspect of the middle adult years, especially phase 1, in the individual's investment of self: in family, in work, and in community affairs. As an outcome of phase 2's working through again some issues of identity and intimacy, generativity becomes a fuller experience. Thus, entering maturity, the individual will be able to express at a new level of vision the attributes of generativity.

10–1 *The years of maturity bring stature, poise, and a measure of peace. (D. Hoerman, photographer)*

Erikson points out that the concern of caring for and guiding the next generation does not focus just on one's own offspring, but also looks to "other forms of altruistic concern and creativity . . . The ability to lose oneself in the meeting of bodies and minds leads to a gradual expansion of

Example 10–1.
Mazel Tov!
You're
Middle-Aged

It is a time when we can still gain from our past mistakes, cast off new directions, face new challenges. It's a time when we can savor the rich joys of yesteryear without getting mired in the past. It is a time when we become the sturdy bridge of several generations. It's a time when we are truly free, free at last.

So don't knock it. Don't play it by ear. Don't be content with swinging it. Don't rush through it, briefcase akimbo, as if it were a commuter train. *Savor it.* Invest yourself in it. You have paid your dues. Middle Age can be a glorious payoff. In this blessed period arching between acne and leisure village, between sunrise and sunset, you are the Gary Cooper at the High Noon of your life, and middle age can give you more bang for a buck than any other of your several incarnations.

From A. Vorspan, *Mazel Tov! You're Middle-Aged* (Garden City, N.Y.: Doubleday, 1974), p. 15.

10–2 *Wisdom and artistic skills are shared with younger generations.* (Manhattan Mercury *photo*)

ego-interests and to a libidinal investment in that which is being generated."[1]

It is probably fair to say that the interests of generativity occupy most people during the years of maturity. There is, however, an anticipation and a beginning to be oriented toward integrity, the last of Erikson's stages, which is the crisis of ego development of old age.[2]

Neugarten has described this blending of the two psychodynamic stages in her observations: individuals in the fifties and sixties develop an increased

[1] E. H. Erikson, *Identity: Youth and Crisis* (New York: Norton, 1968), p. 138.
[2] Ibid., p. 139.

"interiority," simultaneously maintaining an active, effective instrumental dealing with life.[3] Although a relatively comfortable state, maturity is a period of much significant change. There is a consolidation of experiences and resources and a reorientation of interests and activities. This reorientation will proceed along different lines for men and women, generally toward increased satisfaction for both. Let us, then, briefly draw a thumbnail sketch of the characteristics of this stage.

Years of Distinction

Color maturity phase 1 with the "air of distinction." Whereas the mode of coping with earlier transition periods may lead some 50-year-olds toward comic or tragic roles (Example 10–2), for most the opening years of maturity have stature and poise and a measure of peace—perhaps smugness at

Example 10–2.
Two Types
Enter Maturity

> The chief virtue traditionally associated with middle age is experience, but that cuts two ways. The person who arrives at 50 having ignored the opportunities for reassessment in midlife passage may take the familiar, mulish stance of protector of the status quo. It is no mistake that such people are called "diehards." Another stock figure is the middle-aged kid who denies his age and therefore his experience: the producer with mutton-chop whiskers who will be 26 until the fast fade to 60, the Mrs. Louds who wear yarn bows and ask their hubbies for Toyotas to play with, the professor who suspends the healthy skepticism of experience to embrace the evangelism of the young and the life-style of a Latin American revolutionary.
>
> On the other hand, people who have seen, felt, and incorporated their private truths during midlife passage no longer expect the impossible dream, nor do they have to protect an inflexible position. Having experimented with many techniques for facing problems and change, they will have modified many of the assumptions and illusions of youth. They are practiced. They know what works. They can make decisions with a welcome economy of action. A great deal of behavioral red tape can be cut through once people have developed judgment enriched by both inner and outer experience.
>
> From G. Sheehy, *Passages: Predictable Crises of Adult Life* (New York: Dutton, 1976), pp. 342–343.

[3] B. L. Neugarten and associates, *Personality in Middle and Late Life* (New York: Atherton Press, 1964).

times. Self-analysis and anxious searching of middlescence is past. Pressures of earlier years of rearing families, proving merit on the job, making contacts in the community are remote, brought to mind only by observing sons and daughters or younger colleagues.

Inheritance and investments have perhaps added additional dimensions to the business or family estate. The senior positions in social and professional organizations belong to the adult of maturity. His voice has special weight in decision making. According to the age-status research of Neugarten, men expected to reach their top job somewhere between the ages of 45 to 50.[4] In maturity, then, they will be settled into a position of strength. The top-level positions in business are held by men in their mid-fifties.

Being grandparents may have for some arrived during the earlier turbulent days of middlescence and with less satisfaction. During maturity the role of grandparent is accepted and enjoyed.

The years of maturity are much more comfortable for both men and women than the preceding middle adult years (Example 10–3). Where men in their forties expressed considerable boredom and frustration with their

---

[4] B. L. Neugarten, J. W. Moore, and J. C. Lowe, "Age Norms, Age Constraints, and Adult Socialization," *American Journal of Sociology* 70 (May 1965), 6.

10–3 *The senior positions in industry often go to men in their mid-fifties, and the voices of maturity have a decisive influence on civic boards.* (Manhattan Mercury photo)

**Example
10–3.**
Renewed
Relationships

Roger Gould contrasts the personal relationships of people in their fifties with those of people in the forties as follows:

In the 50s there is a mellowing and warming up. The negative cast of the 40s diminishes in their relationships to themselves, their parents, their children, and their friends . . .

They value their own spouses more and look within themselves at their own feelings and emotions, although not with the critical 'time pressure' eye of the late 30s or with the infinite omnipotentiality of the early 30s, but with a more self-accepting attitude of continued learning from a position of general stability. The spouse is seen now as a valuable source of companionship in life and less like a parent or source of supplies. Criticisms of the previous years are realigned to take into account this central change.

From R. Gould, "The Phases of Adult Life: A Study in Developmental Psychology," *American Journal of Psychiatry* 129 (November 1972), 5:526.

work, men of maturity are much less preoccupied with financial concerns or advancement. Men in the preretirement group of the Lowenthal study of four stages of life scored highest of any age group in expressing the greatest sense of well-being. Not only men are more at ease with themselves and their place in life, but also women. Although experiencing some of the tensions of achievement orientations, women are much less hostile and depressed than in their frustrating years of middle life.[5] The woman's uncertainty immediately preceding the empty nest is replaced with self-affirmation as she experiences new opportunities with new freedom.

Maturity brings composure, including a lessening of extremes of emotional highs and lows. There is thus less exuberance as well as less depression. Persons in the years of maturity have a greater sense of being in control of their lives, and they are experiencing less need to defend or maintain that control.

Neugarten captures some of these feelings in her reports of interviews with persons in the maturity age span. The following interview excerpts reflect some of the flavor of those feelings:

There is a difference between wanting to *feel* young and wanting to *be* young. Of course it would be pleasant to maintain the vigor and appearance of

[5] M. F. Lowenthal, "Psychosocial Variations Across the Adult Life Course: Frontiers of Research and Policy," *The Gerontologist* 15 (February 1975, Part I), pp. 11–12.

youth; but I would not trade those for the authority or the autonomy I feel—no, nor the ease of interpersonal relationships nor the self-confidence that comes from experience.[6]

I know what will work in most situations, and what will not. I am well beyond the trial and error stage of youth. I now have a set of guidelines . . . And I am practical.[7]

I discovered these last few years that I was old enough to admit to myself the things I could do well and to start doing them. I didn't think like this before . . . It's a great new feeling.[8]

You always have younger people looking to you and asking questions . . . you don't want them to think you're a blubbering fool . . . You try to be an adequate model.[9]

In the four-stages-of-life study, Lowenthal[10] finds the following quotation from the Neugarten article as appropriate for the preretired men, who manifest a willingness to speak their minds and have a sense of control. Neugarten wrote, "Middle-agers recognize that they constitute the powerful age group vis-à-vis other age groups; that they are the norm bearers and the decision makers; and that they live in a society which, while it may be oriented toward youth, is controlled by the middle-aged."[11]

More Comfortable Men

Sex differences in developmental patterns emerging during the preretirement years of maturity proceed along the following lines.[12] There seem to be two patterns among men. For the larger group it is a mellowing pattern. Not only are they beginning to reap the harvest of the heavy work commitment of early and middle life, but they are also beginning to reorient their aspirations and achievement drives. They are beginning to accept their present

[6] B. L. Neugarten, "The Awareness of Middle Age," in *Middle Age and Aging,* ed. B. L. Neugarten (Chicago: University of Chicago Press, 1968), p. 97.

[7] Ibid., p. 97.

[8] Ibid., p. 96.

[9] Ibid., p. 95.

[10] M. F. Lowenthal and associates, *Four Stages of Life* (San Francisco: Jossey-Bass, 1975), p. 70.

[11] Neugarten, "The Awareness of Middle Age," p. 93.

[12] Lowenthal, "Psychosocial Variations Across the Adult Life Course," pp. 9–12.

10–4 *For most men of maturity the focus of interest begins to shift from the world of work to the family and to interpersonal relationships. (Kathleen Ward, photographer)*

place on the career and social ladder as "far enough." They are shifting their interest toward developing skills and resources for interpersonal relationships with friends and family. A second, much smaller, group of men are those who appear at each of the three earlier stages as hard-driving men with insatiable achievement needs; they continue this pressure into preretirement years. For example, a study of aspiration level showed a group of older "high achievers" (average age 56) reporting greater willingness to move their homes and accept other inconveniences if this move meant greater opportunity than a group of younger men (average age 36) who had also achieved success.[13]

[13] L. Reissman, "Levels of Aspiration and Social Class," *American Psychologist* 18 (1953), pp. 233–242.

Men of maturity begin to give a clearer expression of their affection for their wives and how they respect the important contribution wives have made to their families. Looking back on child rearing, they attribute much of the teaching and nurture to their wives, indicating that they themselves had been busy making the living. With financial obligations less, they indicate a need for the companionship of their wives. Women may experience some ambivalence about how much of their energies they wish to continue to pour into home affairs. The attraction of a wider stage beckons many who enter work or take up education and community projects. Some women, who at earlier periods have not had sufficient exposure to society outside the family, may more quickly develop strong nurturing tendencies with their husbands taking the place of the children who have "left the nest."

More Expressive Women

Women of maturity begin a clear movement toward modification in self-concept and behavior. Whereas younger women in the study describe themselves as vulnerable, dependent on husbands, and weighed down by heavy responsibilities of family life, women of maturity begin to express many of the dominant attitudes and aggressive/achievement behaviors of men in middle age. Women of maturity are more likely than other women to describe themselves as "boss" in family matters. Some begin to take on more leadership roles in their community; others direct their new expressiveness toward managing affairs of their family, including the lives of children and grandchildren.

Maturity is the period with the highest percentage of women employed other than during the pre-child-rearing stage. The following paragraph describes changes in roles and activities experienced by women five years into the maturity stage. The investigator had found many of these women frustrated and uncertain at the time their youngest child was about to leave home. From the interviews five years later, the investigator reported: "These happier women had made expansive changes in their lives which they themselves had initiated: new training, new jobs, new houses, new husbands or boy friends, or lengthy trips abroad. This finding lends some support to our original hypothesis that the anticipatory stage just prior to the postparental period constitutes a critical period for family-centered women, which for some presages further growth."[14]

---

[14] Lowenthal, "Psychosocial Variations Across the Adult Life Course," p. 12.

Heyday for Grandparents

Interpersonal relationships are, of course, not as compartmentalized as the above paragraph suggests. The earlier way of life continues as before into the decade of the fifties with the patterns slowly rising to the surface as opportunities and past life history permit.[15] The psychological freedom occasioned by increased time and relief from the burdens of child rearing allows for increased intimacy and personal sharing of couples in the period of maturity.

[15] I. Deutscher, "Quality of Post Parental Life," *Journal of Marriage and Family* 26 (February 1964), 1:52–59.

10–5 *More women are in the work force during maturity than at any time other than the young adult years.* (Manhattan Mercury *photo*)

Masters and Johnson report that "Many a woman develops renewed interest in her husband and in the maintenance of her own person, and has described a 'second honeymoon' during her early fifties."[16]

Family relationships are also enriched by in-laws and grandchildren. Interviews with 70 grandparents in the Chicago area showed an age range of early fifties to mid-sixties for grandmothers and mid-forties to late sixties for grandfathers. Grandparenthood as reflected in a variety of studies[17] seems to carry forward the theme of the maturity period: a time of reaping benefits from past investments. Most grandparents experience many of the pleasures and satisfactions of parenthood with little of the parental strains. They feel that their grandchildren help keep them young. Grandchildren provide an opportunity for emotional outlet and the experience of sharing, and afford grandparents a sense of vicarious accomplishment and personal extension. Young adult grandchildren view emotional gratification as an appropriate and expected behavior from grandparents.[18]

For some grandparents, the role creates problems with self-image, and in some instances grandchildren complicate already strained relationships with sons or daughters and their spouses.

Grandparents relate with different styles. Some maintain formal roles that make sure they do not infringe on the parents' rights and responsibilities. Others are described as fun seekers who indulge themselves and their grandchildren for the purposes of fun equally enjoyable to both. In some instances, necessity dictates the grandparent role to be that of surrogate parent if a daughter or daughter-in-law is ill or working.

Stith[19] has pointed out some of the problems that may occur when grandmothers and daughters live in the same house and share responsibilities for child care. The fact that there is not a socially prescribed role for the grandmother in that situation causes blurring of responsibilities and possible conflict.

In the past, research on grandparenting has been studied as part of the

[16] W. H. Masters and V. E. Johnson, *Human Sexual Response* (Boston: Little, Brown, 1966), p. 243; see also R. N. Butler and M. I. Lewis, *Sex After Sixty* (New York: Harper & Row, 1976), Chapter 10.

[17] B. L. Neugarten and K. Weinstein, "The Changing American Grandparent," *Journal of Marriage and the Family* 26 (May 1964), 2. N. Stinnett and J. Walters in *Relationships in Marriage and Family* (New York: Macmillan, 1977) pp. 349–353 review the positive influences and problems of grandparenthood.

[18] J. F. Robertson, "Significance of Grandparents: Perceptions of Young Adult Grandchildren," *The Gerontologist* 16 (April 1976), 2:137–140.

[19] M. Stith, "Child-Rearing Attitudes in Three-Generation Households," Ph.D. dissertation, Florida State University, 1961.

10–6 *Grandparenting provides opportunities for sharing oneself and seeing an extension of one's life in new generations. (Kathleen Ward, photographer)*

experiences of old age. But because the family life cycle of marriage, child rearing, and the empty nest is proceeding at an accelerated pace, future research may profitably examine the anticipation of becoming grandparents in middle life. Differences in grandparenting activities at different age levels and with different ages of grandchildren need also to be considered. Activity patterns and attitudes experienced by persons as grandparents and later as great-grandparents is a further topic to be examined. Such family-role relationships may reflect significant differences in periods of maturity and old age.

Interiority and Self-centeredness

During the fifties and early sixties there are changes going on in the organization of our deeper levels of personality dynamics. These changes do not have a strong influence on the work and social activities of the years of maturity; rather, they are preparatory for the post-retirement years of old age.

Neugarten describes the indications of these changes observed in the TAT tests and in in-depth interviews of the Kansas City studies of adult life. "There were measurable increases in inward orientation and measurable decreases in cathexes for outer-world events beginning in late 40s and 50s."[20]

The intrapsychic data indicate that around age 50 there is in the dynamic unconscious psychological processes a movement toward constricting of psychic energies. In both sexes older people seemed to move toward more egocentric positions and to attend increasingly to the control and satisfaction of personal needs. In the period of old age, during the late sixties and seventies, expression of these psychological changes will be noticed in a tendency toward withdrawal from some social involvements. This withdrawal and more self-focused life was found to contribute to a high degree of life satisfaction for some persons but not for others. It was these data that served as the basis for the building of the disengagement theory of Cumming and Henry. This theory will be discussed further in the next chapter.

Increased interiority is reflected more in changed predispositions than in major changes of life-style during maturity. Older men seemed more receptive than younger men to their affiliative, nurturant, and sensual promptings; older women were more receptive than younger women to aggressive and egocentric impulses. Men appeared to deal with the environment in increasingly abstract and cognitive terms; women dealt in increasingly affective and expressive terms.[21]

In the psychological preparation for coming years, there is considerable individual variation as to when changes begin, but somewhere between 40 and 60, the following shift is observed: 40-year-olds see the environment as one that rewards boldness and risk-taking; individuals in their late forties and early fifties, having moved through the ambiguities of middlescence, see themselves as possessing energy congruent with the opportunities presented; 60-year-olds see the environment as complex and dangerous, no longer as something they can shape to their wishes. They see themselves as conforming and adapting to the demands of the external world. This has been described as movement from active to passive mastery orientation with age.

Whereas the projective data seemed to suggest some shrinkage of psycho-

---

[20] B. L. Neugarten, "Personality Change in Late Life: A Developmental Perspective," in *The Psychology of Adult Development and Aging,* eds. C. Eisdorfer and M. P. Lawton (Washington, D.C.: American Psychological Association, 1973), p. 321.

[21] Ibid., pp. 320–322.

logical life space and some flattening of affect during this period, information about socioadaptive qualities suggest that adjustment and personal well-being are not directly age-related. The individual continues the patterns and resources formed early in life.

Preparation for Retirement

As the adult in maturity moves into his sixties, another and sometimes difficult period of transition is dawning. Retirement is in the offing and some planning needs to be done. More than that, making some adjustment to the idea of retirement is a significant first task. There has been much discussion about the effect of retirement on physical and emotional well-being. It is not the condition of retirement that brings trauma; it is the "coming to terms"

10–7 *Maturity is a period of mellowing for most men, a time to relax and begin planning for the years of retirement. (Kathleen Ward, photographer)*

with the idea. Those who are able to incorporate retirement into their world-and-life view experience phase 2 of maturity with much less stress. Those who see retirement as a threat to their active life struggle through the last months before retirement and usually find old age a burden.

We will consider various aspects of retirement in the next chapter. In ending our discussion of maturity, we need only to remind ourselves that in all stages of transition, there is a preparation within the personality at various levels of consciousness before the social circumstances and behaviors bring the new stages into the life-style of an individual.

How persons presently in maturity will handle retirement when it arrives will undoubtedly be different from how people today experience that phenomenon. When we recognize the importance of biological changes and the maturational development that reflect the interaction of biology and life history, we also need to remember that the specific historical context is a crucial factor in understanding life developments. By analogy we can refer to the question Neugarten raised in discussing young adults and apply the concept to other commitments at other life stages. Speaking of young adults she asked: "What is the relation of timing and commitment to social causes, and the relation of both to personality development? . . . Shall we re-examine our earlier views that extremism and idealism among the young are an accompaniment of underlying biological changes? Why was it the 20-year-old who was the activist in 1968, the 15-year-old in 1970, but neither in 1972? And what differences will it make to the particular individuals by the time they reach Middle Age?"[22]

In that same vein we may ask: "How will today's person of maturity be affected by the social impact of the increasing presence of older people, of pressures for change of the public image of old age, and of possible changes in legislation?"

ON LEAVING MATURITY.   We may experience something of the savoring of success, the acknowledging of failures, and the looking forward to old age in Charlie Citrine, Saul Bellow's somewhat autobiographical character in *Humboldt's Gift*.[23]

Speaking more directly in an interview at age 60, Bellow shared his view of the dangers that may await the artist as he enters old age.

---

[22] B. L. Neugarten and N. Datan, "Sociological Perspectives on the Life Cycle," in *Life-Span Developmental Psychology: Personality and Socialization,* eds. P. B. Baltes and K. W. Schaie (New York: Academic Press, 1973), p. 69.

[23] S. Bellow, *Humboldt's Gift* (New York: Viking Press, 1975).

Many American writers cross the bar in their 60s and 70s . . . and become Grand Old Men, gurus or bonzes of the Robert Frost variety. This is how society eases us out. Sees us off on the immortal train, with waving and cheering and nobody listening. Just as well, because there's nothing but bombast coming from the rear platform. If I last long enough, I assume this will happen to me too. And then there are two possibilities. Either you've run out of imagination, in which case you're ready to be puffed up, held down like a barrage balloon by the cables before you float off into eternity. Or your imagination keeps cooking, in which case you're lucky. You're among the blessed. No man knows which way he's gonna go. He can only hope.[24]

Summary

Maturity begins around age 50 as the middle adult has sorted through a major self-evaluation and has possibly experienced a considerable personality change. In maturity the sense of being established and of possessing power and responsibility is at last realized.

An acceptance of self along with the progressive freedom from illusions regarding the omnipotence of groups and customs encourages a mellowing, especially for men of maturity. Striving for achievement is highest when the outcome is in doubt, but most men of maturity have accepted or see within their grasp the marks of achievement with which they are able to be content. Many women, freed from family responsibilities (and some perhaps from the husband's domination), formulate new life goals. New forms of expression begin to emerge for women of maturity that will carry them to a position of increasing power. This power will manifest itself in their marital relationship and/or in more active social roles.

Phase 2 of maturity begins shortly after 60. It encompasses some anxieties concerned with uncertainties about retirement. There are the practical details and planning. More crucially, there is another transition experience, a redefining and projecting oneself into a new role and new life-style. We will consider further the various approaches to retirement as we take up the next chapter, old age.

---

[24] W. Clemons and J. Kroll, "America's Master Novelist," (September 1, 1975), p. 40.

Suggested Activities and Further Reading

1. Prepare a time line for people now in phase 1 and another for people in phase 2 of maturity. Phase 1 people were children during the "roaring twenties" and the Prohibition era. People in phase 2 were babies or young children during World War I.

2. Watch the schedule of late-night movies for Barbra Streisand and Robert Redford in *The Way We Were,* or read the novel by Arthur Laurents of what life was like for today's persons of maturity when they were young adults during the war years and saw the rise of Russia, the Spanish Civil War, Mussolini, and Hitler.

3. Examine information about the middle-aged group (around age 50) and the preretirement group (around age 60) in Lowenthal's "Psychosocial Variations Across the Adult Life Course," *The Gerontologist* 15 (February 1975, Part 1), pp. 6–12. Compare areas of well-being and areas of stress for the two groups. Refer to the book *Four Stages of Life* for further data and discussion.

4. Read one of the following books describing the period of the fifties and sixties and relate it to your observation of the attitudes and activities of people you know in this age range.

    B. Hunt and M. Hunt, *Prime Time* (New York: Stein and Day, 1975).

    E. Le Shan, *The Wonderful Crisis of Middle Age* (New York: David McKay, 1973). Do you think she is describing the experiences of the middle adult, phase 2?

    S. Blanton, *Now or Never: The Promise of Middle Years* (Englewood Cliffs, N.J.: Prentice-Hall, 1959). Since the author is 76, do you think his orientation is directed more toward the period of old age?

    J. Harris, *The Prime of Ms. America* (New York: Putnam, 1975).

5. Have a panel of grandparents discuss the ambiguities in the role of grandparent, its satisfactions and frustrations. Relate to C. W. Shedd, *Grandparents: Then God Created Grandparents and It Was Very Good* (Garden City, N.Y.: Doubleday, 1976).

6. Conduct a survey to discover the ages of the persons in top executive and supervisory positions in your community. What are the ages of people in power positions as represented in TV shows?

7. Interview a representative sample of women 50 to 65 years of age to discover the number working outside the home, the type of employment, their reasons for working, and their satisfaction.

8. Have a group of students role play a discussion among people aged 58 to 63 about preparation for retirement.

chapter 11

Old Age

What's in the Term

As I talked to individuals and groups about names for the sequence of developmental stages used in this book, the question was frequently asked: "Isn't there another term you can use rather than 'old age'?" The inference is that there is something negative about the term *old*. It is perhaps similar to the situation of ten years ago if I had referred to a group as "black." Then the inference was that society "knew" white was good and therefore black was bad. Is the embarrassment of the title *old age* a reflection that society "knows" young is good and old is bad?

Time Line for Old Age

The mythical chronology in Example 11–1 profiles the progress of a member of the Boston aristocracy through his life stages until his death at age 67. Many today would view 67 as an early death because the average life-span in America is over 70 years.

This chapter deals with a period of indeterminate length. I am suggesting that this period begin with age 65 (roughly approximating the advent of retirement), although this kind of delineation has problems, as we shall see later in the chapter. As with all prior stages, individuals enter the conditions of a stage at somewhat different chronological ages. Entry varies with the life history, health, and the present environmental opportunities of the individual. Some persons of 55 will be more like persons of

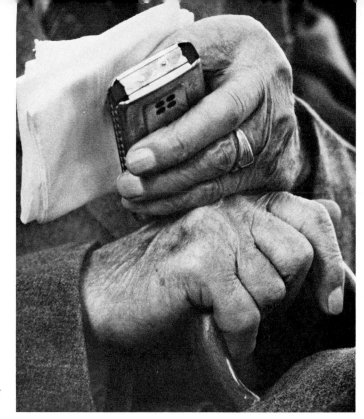

11–1 *Ready to serve.* (Manhattan Mercury *photo*)

old age discussed here, whereas some persons of 65 will be more like those discussed in the early aspects of maturity.

Neugarten has offered the concept of a period to be known as the "young-old." This may fittingly characterize the first phase of the period we are discussing in this chapter. An age range for the second phase is more difficult to conceptualize because time of death or the onset of senility varies so greatly. It is a temptation at this point to shift over and set the outline of that period on the basis of function rather than of years—to say the second phase of old age begins when the individual is no longer able to care for himself. However, our approach throughout the book has been to say, "What is going on with people who are in a particular age range? Although there are individual and subgroup variations, what are the prevailing trends and patterns of activity, health, and attitudes?" There really is no reason to depart from that approach at this point. So let us think of old age in terms of two phases: the first extending from approximately 65 to 75, and the second from 75 to death.

Example 11–1.
The Late
George Apley

For a detailed agenda of the pacing of an upper-class Bostonian through the stages of adulthood around the turn of the century, we have John P. Marquand's account of *The Late George Apley*. There had been an Apley each succeeding generation in Harvard since 1662. When George graduated from law school, a summer's experience in business showed him and his family that he would do better as a trustee rather than in rough-and-tumble business. He spent his professional career clipping coupons.

Following a brief—and quietly aborted—affair with Mary Monahan, a girl of lower social standing, at age 24 he married Catherine Bower from among his family's circle of friends. His son, John, and daughter, Eleanor, were born before George's father died, leaving a large fortune in trust for George to manage. His mother died a year or so later when George was 32. George's son graduated from Harvard, served in World War I, and married a girl of good connections. When George was 52, he became a grandfather and telegraphed Groton to have his grandson's name included among the entrance applicants. His daughter's marriage was less satisfactory to George because she did not induce her husband to take a position with the Apley firm and move near the family estate. George also noticed an increasing breakdown of social structure, with youth generally tending toward wildness and the Irish immigrants threatening to overrun Boston. Even George's old Uncle William, who successfully managed the mills and held out against the new labor, shocked the family by marrying his nurse when he was over 80.

George was out of the country in 1929, on a trip to Rome with his wife, when the stock market crash came. It did not seriously disrupt George's finances, but his health began to fail slightly and he began to plan his will and funeral. George Apley died three years later at the age of 67, leaving the family fortune and responsibilities in the capable hands of his son, John Apley.

Abstract from J. P. Marquand, *The Late George Apley* (Boston: Little, Brown, 1937).

Population and Socioeconomic Trends

One thousand Americans celebrated their 65th birthday today. There are 365,000 new 65-year-olds each year.[1] In 1900 there were only 3.1 million Americans over 65, about 4 per cent of the population. By 1975 there were

[1] R. N. Butler, *Why Survive? Being Old in America* (New York: Harper & Row, 1975), p. 16.

22 million people over 65 in the United States, 10.3 per cent of the total population.[2] In medieval society the average lifetime was 20 to 30 years; in the 1850s in America it was about 40 years; in the beginning of the twentieth century it was about 50 years; by 1975 the average life-span had increased to over 70 years.

Whereas the average lifetime has more than tripled from ancient times to the present day, the increase has come mostly in the improved statistics of childhood mortality, with some improvement in mortality rates during young and middle adult life. The smallest decline in the death rate among any age group is in the old-age group. The increasing number of people living to reach the period of Old Age is what accounts for the surging population growth of Old Age. Seventy per cent[3] of the people over 65 in 1970 had entered that age range since 1959. It should also be noted that the improved health care in earlier life and the available care to those of old age makes the quality of life during old age dramatically better than in earlier times.

More Time Left to Live

It is only recently that there has been a need to inquire about what happens in the forties and the years following.

In the past the last child left home usually near the end of the marriage, with one or both parents being near death. Today the point at which the last child leaves home marks about the midpoint in marriage. There are usually as many or more years ahead for the couple without their children as there were behind them with their children in the home.

With changes in economic conditions, the availability of alternatives in housing, and the mobility of our times, more people of old age maintain residences separate from their children. This rapid social transformation resulted in the formation of a new chapter in the life-span for which the script has not yet been written. There is a need for new ways of viewing this period. New guidelines and social roles are needed for persons during that additional twenty-five years. The new framework is needed for old people themselves and for others to know how to view and what to expect from this new sector of our society.

---

[2] W. P. Randel, "Certain Unalienable Rights," *American Issues Forum* (Washington, D.C.: The National Council on the Aging, November 1975.)

[3] Butler, *Why Survive?*, p. 16.

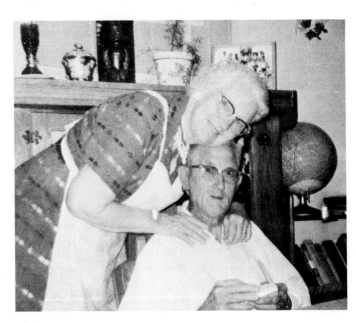

11–2 *Continuing good health means an extended period of companionship for couples into the retirement years.*

Need for New Socialization for Old Age

America is uncertain of how to relate to the new strengths of this group of its citizens. It struggles to maintain the high priority for the youth culture and finds it difficult to come up with a name for the over-65 group. The older people themselves know the terms they do not like; they are less sure of their preferences. "Mature American," "retired person," and "senior citizen" are preferred names; "old man" or "old woman," "aged person," "oldtimer," and "golden-ager" are the most disliked by persons over 65.[4]

An affirming term—connoting a picture of new interests, new freedom, new life-styles, and new contributions—has yet to be coined for the over-65 group (Example 11–2).

The person entering the period of old age now is unlike the person who became 65 thirty years ago. He feels and sees things differently because (1) he has been through a significantly different span of history with differing socializing influences and (2) the "social press," the climate of peers and community awareness, is different than in 1950.

How an individual approaches a life situation is greatly influenced by the social expectations prevailing in his culture. Currently in our society, there is

[4] L. Harris and associates, *The Myth and Reality of Aging in America* (Washington, D.C.: The National Council on the Aging, 1975), p. 228.

Example 11–2.
In the Name of
the Elder

> It is, perhaps, a revealing characteristic of the English language that, in its usage, there is no single, convenient noun commonly used to designate an old person . . . It should be noted that the dilemma is exclusive to our English tongue. Other languages have indeed definite and commonly used nouns for people of advanced age:
>
> | | | | | | |
> |---|---|---|---|---|---|
> | Greek: | Geron | German: | Der Greis | Spanish: | El veijo |
> | Latin: | Senex | French: | Le veillard | Danish: | Bamle |
> | Hindu: | Buddha | | | | |
>
> An intriguing thought is that in other cultures this may be indicative of their greater reverence for human aging with its precious increments of human qualities and, consequently, that it may mirror the status conception of their own elders.
>
> The noun ELDER which I have just used is hardly ever to be found in the vocabulary of the gerontologist . . . Any encyclopedia will show two meanings of the noun ELDER: It designates a person of advanced age. The fact that it also may happen to denote a church official gives the word ELDER a fortuitous added connotation of rank and perhaps of gentility. It stresses the improvement that comes with age. ELDER is a good English word. Like teacher and judge, it applies to man as well as woman. It deserves to be generally used in gerontology.
>
> Conclusion:
>
> To denote the rank of individuals of advanced age, the gerontologist should finally adopt the word ELDER as the word of choice. ELDER has a positive connotation of respect similar to those terms which are common in many another language. They are exemplified in the splendid Latin word senex from which derives the word senate, a council of elders.
>
> From E. F. Schmerl, "In the Name of the Elder—An Essay," *The Gerontologist* 15 (October 1975), 5:386.

great ambivalance and uncertainty concerning the effect of lengthened life. The book *Why Survive? Being Old in America*[5] won the Pulitzer Prize in 1976. It details the contradictory attitudes we have toward the old. We are not sure whether life should be open-ended. Is compulsory retirement a good thing? Is it a violation of individual rights? Does the concept of free schooling apply to all ages or just youth? Does the right to life also include the right to choose

[5] Butler, *Why Survive?*

not to live? Are there new ranges of human services that may be available if we can creatively conceptualize the continued contributions available from this segment of society?

Although such unstructured conditions create a greater freedom of movement and choice, Blau points out that without cultural guidelines the new freedom to choose is a burden, not an opportunity. She states: "This kind of cultural ambiguity helps explain why old age cannot be viewed merely as an economic, physical or psychological problem, or even as a combination of these, but must be understood as an existential problem for the older person and as a critical social problem for the larger society."[6]

What must come is the evolution of a new socialization toward a variety of roles and responsibilities for people in their sixties and seventies, even as there are social expectations for persons of other age groups. The age status in our society serves primarily the purposes of segregation. Thus far, our society has not experienced sufficient numbers of people living in good health with social, economic, and psychological well-being in the old age period so as to conceptualize their potential. As this group becomes larger and more expressive, it can be expected to influence nationally expressed policies and attitudes. This in turn will contribute to the clarification of role expectations within our culture. Experiences of women's groups and various minorities illustrate the place of legislative action in this regard.

Blau strongly states the importance of the social and political task.

> I do not deny the importance of the other problems that beset older people. Poverty, illness, inadequate and inappropriate housing are more widespread among the old than among any other age group—but they are not unique to old age . . . I question the wisdom of a society that allocates considerable resources and talent to prolonging human life but fails to provide meaningful social roles for older people. That, I submit, is the critical problem of aging in modern society.[7]

The Public Image

Society in general pictures those over 65 as nice old people with wisdom gained from years of living but not very effective now. They think the elderly lack energy and skill to deal with contemporary situations. However,

---

[6] Z. S. Blau, *Old Age in a Changing Society* (New York: Franklin Watts, 1973), pp. 2–3.

[7] Ibid., p. xi.

most people tend to think of *some* old persons they know personally as being different from *most* old people.[8] Those over 65 generally hold a similarly negative stereotype of old people but think of themselves and their situation as an exception.[9]

The point has been made repeatedly in this book that there is no uniform characteristic of old age or old people; however, society tends to lump those of an age group together and think of youth as all alike and old people as all alike. The Harris Poll's study of aging points out that the findings emphasize two things concerning the elderly: (1) the uniqueness of individuals, (2) there are other things—namely, poverty, education, and race—that distinguish people more than age. Social, economic, and psychological factors that affect individuals when they were younger often stay with them throughout their lives.[10]

Persons of all ages tend to see the advantages and disadvantages in old age. Leisure and freedom from responsibility are often cited as advantages of old age. The following comments illustrate how our view of old age is influenced by our own age and socioeconomic situation.

> An 18-year-old student in New Jersey explained what he feels are the best things about being over 65. "This is when you will have all your free time and, if you planned well, you will have enough money to live and travel."

> In the words of a 36-year-old housewife in New Hyde Park, New York: "You have a different attitude then. You don't beat around the bush. You have seen more, you have experienced more. People don't pick on you. There is more to enjoy."

> According to a 48-year-old Providence, Rhode Island, housewife: "The best thing is Social Security benefits. Also, if you meet the right people, you can enjoy life . . . You have more time to relax and enjoy the family."

> A 61-year-old black, unemployed operative in Hinston, North Carolina, replied: "Nowadays, they don't look their age. Some people over 65 are more

---

[8] L. D. Bekker and C. Taylor, "Attitudes Toward the Aged in a Multigenerational Sample," *Journal of Gerontology* 21 (1966), pp. 115–118. The article offers an interesting illustration of the effect of familiarity with individuals of different age ranges. They found that 20-year-olds with living great-grandparents saw their grandparents as less elderly than did 20-year-olds without living great-grandparents, although the grandparents in the study were about the same age in each group.

[9] Harris and associates, *The Myth and Reality of Aging*, pp. 48, 53.

[10] Ibid., p. 129.

active than some 55, like my sister. They usually have less worries, since their families are grown. They can draw Social Security."

To a 66-year-old housewife in Queens, New York, the best thing about being over 65 is "getting closer with my husband again. The children are grown up and I have more time to spend with my husband."

"Well, you take myself, for example," said a 68-year-old retired sales worker in Louisville, Kentucky. "My health is good and I don't have any worries of any kind. My retirement is fine, if you call it that. However, I'd like to have a part-time job where I could work two or three days a week."

A 74-year-old retired farmer in Elk Grove, California, explained, "You have, as a rule, more freedom to do what you wish. You are not tied down to a job. You have more freedom for leisure, to travel if you so choose. In a general category, you have more medical care provided for certain people. Medicare has certainly helped many people get the care they need."

In the words of an 88-year-old woman in Minneapolis, who is retired from her service job: "You don't have to worry so much. Your children are raised so you don't have to worry about their food and clothing. Your own wants are small. You don't care to go out much, and you don't eat much or buy many new clothes. These things aren's important anymore."[11]

The ideas of leisure and increased independence appeal more to the young than to those who have reached 65, and more to the affluent than to the poor. To the poor, Social Security and Medicare appear to rank high among the advantages of old age.

Society Sees Problems   It is an unfortunate fact of journalism that the "bad news" usually "makes news." Although some older persons do have financial and health problems and many are lonely and threatened by crime, the majority do not report more problems than younger people. This is quite in contrast with the public's impression of life in old age.

In one study, 60 per cent of the public listed "not having enough money to live on" as a problem for old people; only 15 per cent of people over 65 said

[11] C. Setlow, *Aging in America: Implications for Society* (Washington, D.C.: The National Council on Aging, 1976), pp. 3–4. *SOURCE: The Myth and Reality of Aging in America,* (c) 1975, a study prepared for The National Council on the Aging, Inc. (NCOA), Washington, D.C., by Louis Harris and Associates, Inc.

this was a problem for them. Sixty per cent of the public also said loneliness would be a problem for old people, whereas only 12 per cent of the elderly listed this. Half of the public thought poor health and fear of crime would be problems of old age, but less than a fourth of the elderly said this was a personal problem.

As with the young, so also with the elderly, the individual's income and educational level will influence the kinds of situations that become problems (Tables 11–1 and 11–2).

A professor of economics and family development has observed that largely as a result of stereotypes older persons constitute the largest deprived group in America. He advocates a Magna Carta for the aged through which

Table 11–1. "Very Serious" Problems of Public Personally (by Income)

	Total %	Total Public		
		18–54 %	55–64 %	65 and Over %
Not having enough money to live on				
Under $7,000	35	44	41	20
$7,000–$14,999	15	17	11	5
$15,000 and over	8	8	6	1
Fear of crime				
Under $7,000	25	27	24	24
$7,000–$14,999	15	14	18	21
$15,000 and over	9	9	9	17
Poor health				
Under $7,000	24	18	35	26
$7,000–$14,999	8	7	15	9
$15,000 and over	7	6	11	11
Poor housing				
Under $7,000	12	16	13	5
$7,000–$14,999	5	6	2	1
$15,000 and over	3	4	2	—
Not feeling needed				
Under $7,000	10	10	13	9
$7,000–$14,999	4	4	3	4
$15,000 and over	4	4	6	2

SOURCE: *The Myth and Reality of Aging in America,* © 1975, a study prepared for The National Council on the Aging, Inc. (NCOA), Washington, D.C., by Louis Harris and Associates, Inc. p. 132.

Table 11–2. "Very Serious" Problems of Public Personally (by Education)

	Total Public			
	Total %	18–54 %	55–64 %	65 and Over %
Not having enough money to live on				
Some high school or less	26	28	29	20
High school graduate, some college	15	17	12	8
College graduate	8	9	10	3
Fear of crime				
Some high school or less	21	18	25	25
High school graduate, some college	11	14	11	23
College graduate	9	8	15	10
Poor health				
Some high school or less	21	14	28	26
High school graduate, some college	9	8	14	14
College graduate	4	3	17	9
Not enough education				
Some high school or less	14	17	11	12
High school graduate, some college	4	5	2	2
College graduate	1	1	—	1
Loneliness				
Some high school or less	12	10	15	15
High school graduate, some college	6	6	9	9
College graduate	4	4	4	6
Poor housing				
Some high school or less	9	13	7	5
High school graduate, some college	6	6	5	2
College graduate	1	1	2	1
Not feeling needed				
Some high school or less	8	8	9	9
High school graduate, some college	5	4	7	5
College graduate	1	2	—	2

SOURCE: *The Myth and Reality of Aging in America,* © 1975, a study prepared for The National Council on the Aging, Inc. (NCOA), Washington, D.C., by Louis Harris and Associates, Inc. p. 139.

society would promote a new image showing older persons capable of further growth. The Magna Carta would encourage the nation to (1) examine retirement policies, (2) include courses on aging at all levels of education, (3) expand programs of adult education and adult conseling.[12]

[12] J. E. Montgomery, "Magna Carta of the Aged," *Journal of Home Economics* 65 (April 1973), pp. 12–13.

Elderly's Self-Image

The term *old age* is used to carry many messages; different groups use it positively or negatively to serve different causes. For those approaching 65, there is often confusion and anxiety because of this publicity and because of a lack of knowledge about the wide variety of life-styles and roles that characterize old age and post-retirement. Often the publicity is on the poverty, illness, and loneliness of people of old age. And we should not minimize it. Fifteen per cent of the people over 65 identify finances as a major problem for them.[13] However, this is not greatly different from the percentage of other age groups—youth and middle age—who also identify finances as a major problem. Poverty and the compounding effects of illness and social anomie are problems to be addressed as such, but the developmental stage of old age should not be associated with them exclusively.

Old age includes the whole spectrum of conditions from poverty to wealth, illness to health, ineptness to expertness, apathy to hope, lack of imagination to creativity, fear to courage. This variety makes it difficult for the elderly person who is attempting to relate to a single image of societal expectation. He needs to be encouraged to affirm his individuality.

SATISFACTION IN OLD AGE. Although the discrimination against elderly and the problems of poverty and illness of some tend to generate a negative stereotype, old people are as likely as people of any age level to say that this is the best period of their lives. About a third of all people say their present period of life is better than they expected it; a half say it is about the way they expected it. Income, education, and whether or not they are employed are more important influences on life satisfaction than age.

Activities of the Elderly

The public generally thinks of the elderly as sitting and thinking, watching television, or sleeping. The elderly report a much more active life. Socializing with friends, gardening, and other hobbies are high on their list.

Three fourths of the elderly (a similar proportion to the public at large) have indicated they would prefer to spend time with people of all different ages. Many of the elderly are active in helping members of their families. Most people in old age think of themselves as useful members of their community. In their view taking part in community activities and participating in government, fraternal, and religious organizations is important. Helping

---

[13] Harris and associates, *The Myth and Reality of Aging,* p. 129.

others and building up the neighborhood are characteristics of useful citizens.[14]

Family and Community Life

Role Exits   In understanding developmental processes it is helpful to study role exits[15] as we have utilized the study of role initiation in human experience. Role exits in earlier stages of life lead to new roles, for instance, from school to job, from singleness to parenthood. Widowhood and retirement do not naturally

[14] Ibid., pp. 62–63.

[15] Blau, *Old Age in a Changing Society,* see the chapter "Role Exit: A Theoretical Essay," pp. 210–245; see also J. J. Doud, "Aging as Exchange: A Preface to Theory," *Journal of Gerontology* 30 (September 1975), 5:584–594.

11–3 *At 52 the Dutch clock-repair woman, Corrie ten Boom—heroine of* The Hiding Place—*was put in a Nazi concentration camp. She survived, and at well past 80 years she was active as a public speaker, traveling to all parts of the world.* (The Hiding Place, *press photo*)

lead to valued new roles; rather, they remove the individual from significant roles in the two central institutions of his life—the nuclear family and the occupational structure. Studies of old age have frequently pointed to a decline in morale, with the observation that such lowered morale is not so much biologically related but comes from the obligation to give up social roles, such as work through retirement and marriage through widowhood. How individuals reengage society following the death of spouse reflects their location in the social system, previous patterns of coping with life, and the socioeconomic resources available to them.[16]

Retirement   Widespread retirement is a relatively new experience. In earlier years only the wealthy could retire. In 1900, two thirds of the men over 65 were working; in 1960 it had dropped to one third.[17]

We see the elderly among the leaders of our country at all periods of history. Simon Bradstreet was govenor of Massachusetts at 89. Ben Franklin was 70 when he helped draft the Declaration of Independence. Among many contemporary illustrations is Arthur Flemming, who at 70, after having served as professor, college president, and as Secretary of Health, Education and Welfare, was granted special permission by 62-year-old President Ford to continue as Commissioner on Aging.

Retirement has been viewed in recent years as an adjustment problem for men; however, as more women maintain active careers outside the home, retirement will increasingly become a consideration for them.

The arbitrariness of retirement appears to be the central issue. In earlier times when more people were self-employed in small businesses or rural activities, the individual could choose his own time and pace of retirement. Often he would move to part-time work before full retirement. Freedom of choice is still highly valued in all aspects of life.[18]

When older people see persons of old age in leadership positions—such as Senate and Supreme Court—they have mixed feelings. They think the model is good; however, if they have been required to retire, they may feel some injustice in their own circumstances.

---

[16] H. Z. Lopata, *Widowhood in an American City* (Cambridge, Mass.: Schenkman, 1973).

[17] M. W. Riley, A. Foner, and associates, *Aging and Society: Volume I, An Inventory of Research Findings* (New York: Russell Sage Foundation, 1968).

[18] P. Woodring, "Why 65? The Case Against Mandatory Retirement," *Saturday Review* 3 (August 7, 1976), 22:18–20.

11–4 *Seventy-year-old Arthur S. Flemming, Commissioner on Aging, had to receive special permission from President Ford to continue in that position. (OHD, DHEW photo)*

Whereas persons miss many things in retirement from their work—social relationships, a sense of meaning and contribution—the item mentioned first by most is the loss of income. At retirement many move from highest earnings to the lowest their income has ever been during their adult life.

Through trends in the labor force few persons have the choice of whether to continue working past 65. This prerogative is available primarily to the self-employed in small businesses and agriculture, groups whose population continues to reduce rapidly in the face of technological changes. Persons employed with large institutions, especially those with unions, usually have little option concerning retirement. Unions have encouraged lower retirement ages with pensions in order to improve the seniority status of younger workers and the availability of employment for young people waiting to enter the labor market. To what extent voluntary retirement would be an option for factory workers and persons in other careers is not clearly known at this point. The economic base of the potential retiree, his health, the availability of other options for meaningful activity, his earlier life-style, and the motivation of the work, all contribute to the attitude of persons toward retirement.[19]

[19] The economic needs of the young for employment in order to marry, buy a home, and rear a family is often contrasted with the situation of the older worker at the peak of his earning power, with children grown, the wife working, and most of the beginning expenses, such as equity for purchasing a house, already behind him.

11–5 *Self-employed older persons have more opportunity to continue working after age 65 than do those employed in industry.* (Manhattan Mercury *photos*)

In 1974, 61 per cent of all Americans worked for firms with a policy of fixed retirement age; 87 per cent of the personnel officers in the country agreed that most employers discriminate against older people.[20]

Some retired persons are glad to be retired, but others want to work. There are some who say they want to work but seem to avoid opportunities or fail to take the initiative to do so. Some of these nonworking persons cite poor health or old age as reason. However, it is possible that the problem for many older Americans is not that they themselves feel too old or too sick to work, but rather that they have been told they are. With frequent discouragement from working, disinterest in employment may have become a learned response for many older people who might otherwise prefer to work. In short, with over 4 million older unemployed or retired individuals who want to work, there exists a large untapped source of manpower.[21]

Contrary to some popular impressions, retirement does not automatically bring frustrations and poor health. Research tends to find more evidence of improved health following retirement than of health decrement.[22] For some older persons, retirement may result in major maladaptation; for others, the decreasing importance of economic achievement may free them to focus on interpersonal processes.

For many Americans, retirement is a time to travel, to hunt and fish, to return to a more rural setting, to devote time to a hobby or develop a new one. If work years have been pressed with busy schedules of employment and family, the retired person may be looking forward to quiet pursuits.

For some older persons, social isolation may be a problem. However, for people who have had isolation as a lifelong pattern, the isolation of old age may not pose a severe adjustment problem. On the other hand, the person whose lifelong pattern has been a series of marginal social relationships may find adjustments to later life extremely difficult.

These observations point out that an individual's earlier life pattern is a better measure, than reference to his age in understanding the kind of deprivation a particular situation will bring him. Lowenthal[23] has found that ad-

[20] Harris and associates *The Myth and Reality of Aging,* p. 213.

[21] Setlow, *Aging in America: Implications for Society,* p. 18.

[22] C. Eisdorfer, "Adaptation to Loss of Work," in *Retirement,* ed. F. Carp (New York: Behavioral Publications, 1972).

[23] M. F. Lowenthal and D. Chiriboga, "Social Stress and Adaptation: Toward a Life Course Perspective," in *The Psychology of Adult Development and Aging,* eds. C. Eisdorfer and M. P. Lawton (Washington, D.C.: American Psychological Association, 1973), pp. 304–305.

11–6 *This 84-year-old golfer urges his ball toward the hole in a tournament for men over 50.* (Manhattan Mercury *photo*)

justment appears to be more difficult for the complex, highly creative, achievement-motivated individuals. The interruption of their world causes considerable frustration and searching to find new ways to satisfy their need for personal expression. Other persons have looked forward to retirement for years as a time of leisure.

Family and Social Contacts Most of the elderly have considerable involvement with family. Three fourths of them have grandchildren and nearly half have great-grandchildren. Among the young-olds, three fourths of the men live with wives and nearly half of the women live with husbands. About a third of the young-old women live alone. We have mentioned in Chapter 3 the variety of services older persons provide for the younger families. Middle-aged children become increasingly supportive as their parents move into the later years of old age.

Loneliness is a problem for some older people as it is for some younger people, and is even more of a problem at certain times, such as during illness or holidays. However, older people do not identify loneliness as a problem much more frequently than other adults.[24]

Whereas the majority of those in old age are socially active, having frequent contacts with family and friends, we need to remind ourselves that there is a small percentage of old people (which in number of persons turns out to be millions) with greatly different lives, referred to as the "invisible elderly." They live in Single Room Occupancy (SRO) hotels in the inner city or are alone in nursing homes. The SRO elderly live alone in a single sleeping room virtually without access to resources for cooking, social and health services. Located in the midst of commercial inner city, they are nevertheless very much isolated. Some elderly, as is true of some children and

[24] Setlow, *Aging in America*, p. 9.

11–7 *A 107-year-old mother is surprised by her daughters with a birthday cake. Knitting projects help to keep this active lady occupied in her post-century years.* (Manhattan Mercury photo)

11–8 (*D. Hoerman, photographer*)

some homeless mothers, are transient, living and sleeping in the streets and parks.[25]

The schedules of many elderly and retired persons are as filled as they were in younger days. Nearly two out of ten men over 65 are working full or part time. Some have moved to be near family and friends or to be in retirement centers with special recreational facilities.

During old age, people continue to eat out, attend concerts, sports events, and church services, following interests characteristic of their earlier life-style. Such factors as education, finances, and transportation figure promi-

[25] Butler, *Why Survive?*, p. 23.

nently in their choice of activities.[26] Those who have belonged to country clubs, have been participants in music guilds, or frequent users of the library continue these activities in old age. Senior centers provide a resource for many. In 1974 about five million persons were participating in these programs. People most likely to use the centers were from low-income groups, although a tenth of persons with income over $15,000 were in attendance. Some programs are provided within the centers and some reach out into the community.

Older people are also involved in a variety of community volunteer endeavors, such as the Retired Senior Volunteer Program (RSVP), Foster Grandparents, and Gray Panthers, a political activism group. Other political and civic organizations claim a part of the time of older persons.

Church Attendance   Religion has always been thought to take on more importance as people enter old age. This appears to be true; however, the elderly express some drawing away from the organization of religion in favor of a more personal

---

[26] Setlow, *Aging in America,* p. 11.

11–9 *Social activity is encouraged through congregate eating centers that are a part of nutrition programs for the elderly.* (Manhattan Mercury *photo*)

11–10 *Older persons often participate as volunteers in programs serving other elderly.* (Manhattan Mercury *photo*)

experience. Older persons participate in church attendance about as much as adults of other age groups.[27]

Volunteer Work   Whereas the number of actual hours invested and the degree of efficiency of volunteer operations are often unclear, there is little doubt that a large share of human-service programs are carried on through volunteer labor. More than one third of all Americans participate in some form of volunteer work.

It is often suggested that volunteerism is a "coming field" for older persons. In 1974 the volunteer labor force was estimated to include four and a half million persons 65 and older, with the possibility that another two million could be recruited.[28]

Although older persons carry a fair share of the volunteer effort (28 per cent of 65 to 69 and 22 per cent of all over-65 are involved), they are no more

[27] Ibid., p. 28.
[28] Harris and associates, *The Myth and Reality of Aging,* pp. 94–103.

interested in working for free than are younger people. Most young and old agree that if a job is valuable, it sould be paid for.

Most older persons agree that volunteer work is a good way to invest their time and to help meet the community's needs, although about half feel that jobs given to volunteers are routine and boring. Young and old agree that older persons are good volunteers. We will discuss in Chapter 12 the possibility of changing attitudes about work and leisure.

The Elderly
Driver

The lack of public transportation together with many psychological reactions to loss of autonomy make driving important to older persons. Twelve per cent of the drivers on the road are over 60 years of age. Longitudinal studies of aging at the Duke University Center found older drivers to be careful and aware of their limitations. The percentage of accidents among older persons is relatively low. However, since they drive less miles than the average driver, their percentage of accidents per mile driven resembles that of adolescent drivers. As drivers become older, they tend to avoid routes of congested traffic and night driving.

Older persons who continue to drive express significantly greater life satisfaction than those who have given up driving. There is for many men a feeling of masculinity and self-worth associated with owning a car.[29] However, many older drivers indicate they would prefer to take public transportation if it were available rather than drive.

Intimacy in Old Age

We have noted that various developmental tasks need to be reexperienced at different periods in an individual's growth. Attitudes and skills in the expression of intimacy represent one such area. The task was similar—yet different—when experienced in adolescence, in young adulthood, in middlescence, and now in old age. In each previous situation there were uncertainties about what was going on within self and questions about what was going on in society. There were anxieties about meaning, commitments, and authenticity; and there were questions about expectations.

---

[29] D. T. Gianturco, D. Raum, and E. W. Erwin, "The Elderly Driver and the Ex-driver," in *Normal Aging II,* ed. E. Palmore (Durham: Duke University Press, 1975), pp. 173–179.

For people of old age, these uncertainties about self, others, and society norms exercise an important influence in personal development.

Society's
Taboo   One of the subtle taboos in our society that has served as a constraining and debilitating influence on development during older years has been the taboo of the discussion of "sex past 60." When Charlie Chaplin[30] became a father at 70, he was viewed as something of an oddity. There is embarrassment at the mental picture of sexual intimacy between older persons. We are more comfortable envisioning the couple on the front porch in their rocking chairs holding hands in nostalgia than we are envisioning them in the bedroom holding each other in ecstasy of climax. The taboo begins early, perhaps when the 40-year-old male first hears the whispered innuendo of "dirty old man" and the 40-year-old female sees what she perceives as pity and embarrassment in discussions of menopause.

Limited awareness and, therefore, limited acceptance of older persons' sexual needs and expression has resulted in little cultural support for older persons to acknowledge and enhance this part of their lives.

There is no physiological reason why sexual expression found satisfactory in younger life should not be continued into the period of older years as well.[31] Sexual activity is more prevalent among older persons than popular conceptions have suggested. There are people in old age who are uninterested in sexual activity for a variety of reasons, just as some are at other periods of life. For those who desire it, satisfactory sexual expression is an important contributor to health and well-being of older persons.[32]

One of the largest deterrents to healthy sexual experiences for older persons is the expectation and fear that sexual capacities will fail them at mid-life or shortly thereafter. This fear frequently inhibits their activity and causes them to develop rationalizations for avoiding risks. The most important factor in the maintainance of effective sexuality for the aging male or female is consistency of active sexual expression. The person who has had an active and satisfactory sex life in younger adult years will most likely continue to have one in later years.

As was indicated in our discussion of middlescence, better understanding of oneself and greater freedom from work and social constraints may result

---

[30] R. Manvill, *Chaplin* (Boston: Little, Brown, 1972), p. 215.
[31] R. N. Butler and M. I. Lewis, *Sex After Sixty* (New York: Harper & Row, 1976), p. 10.
[32] Ibid., p. 8.

in a new and more satisfying sexual expression after the years of child rearing are past.

There are many reasons why individuals may find some of their most fulfilling sexual experiences during old age. There are new freedoms from time constraints and from concerns of child bearing; there is the maturing awareness of life and self. Butler and Lewis sum up their study of sex after 60 with the following paragraph:

> Perhaps only in the later years can life with its various possibilities have the chance to shape itself into something approximating a human work of art. And perhaps only in later life, when personality reaches its final stages of development, can love-making and sex achieve the fullest possible growth. Sex does not merely exist after sixty; it holds the possibility of becoming greater than it ever was. It can be joyful and creative, healthy and health-giving. It unites human beings in an affirmation of love and is therefore also morally right and virtuous. Those older persons who have no partners and must experience sex alone need to know that this, too, is their right—a healthy giving to oneself that reflects a strong sense of self-esteem and worth. Those who informed us as we wrote this book have given every one of us a valuable gift—a realistic expectation of sex after sixty.[33]

Biology of Aging

Much of the literature about old age has been based on information from sick and institutionalized persons; its emphasis has been on decline in capabilities and functioning. When studies are made of healthy individuals living in comfortable homes and apartments, many of the grim stereotypes of old age are sifted as products of illness or unfortunate living conditions rather than age-related changes.

In a study of 47 volunteer men ranging in age from 65 to 91 with a mean of 71, selected for their good health and social competence, the human-aging project of the National Institute of Mental Health[34] found that they were vigorous, candid, interesting, and deeply involved in everyday living. In marked contrast to the usual stereotype of rigidity of the aged, these individuals generally demonstrated mental flexibility and alertness. They continued to be constructive, resourceful, and optimistic in their living.

[33] Ibid., pp. 144–145.

[34] J. E. Birren and associate, eds., *Human Aging I* and *Human Aging II* (Washington, D.C.: National Institute of Mental Health, 1971, DHEW Publications No. ADM-74-122, ADM-74-123.)

In contrast to the frequent suggestion that old age is accompanied by reduction in cerebral blood flow and decrease in oxygen consumption, no significant difference was found between these elderly men and a group of men with an average age of 21 years. Intellectual performance in the group of older men was superior to that of the group of 21-year-olds, although there were some signs of slowness among the elderly. Whether the slowness was associated with incipient or minimal states of disease, arteriosclerosis, or was a product of aging itself, was not known.

Memory   Most of us have lapses of memory for brief instants. For some older persons, failing memory is a major frustration. Until recently, science had not been able to account for the memory loss of amnesia victims or for the more gradual loss of memory of the aged. Early research that sought a section of the brain as the seat of memory has been abandoned in light of new understanding of the chemical functioning in cells.

Since the beginning of the 1970s there has been considerable optimism that we are on the verge of having available drugs to prevent memory loss and perhaps revive failing memory. In the summer of 1975 two New York hospitals began experiments with aged persons using a synthetic form of the pituitary hormone ACTH. Dr. David De Wied of the Netherlands[35] has found through animal research that this hormone apparently alerts the "memory machine" to the importance of a given event (no one really understands the process of memory). The result is that the brain fixes that event in its memory. Subsequent research studies in which the drug was used with amnesia victims that had had electroconvulsive therapy and with young, normal volunteers has proved encouraging.

What causes forgetfulness in the senile is still a mystery. It is possible that some wearing down of the pituitary or possibly the hypothalamus (whose secretion is also being studied in memory research) may result in limited or no production of the hormone. Shock treatment, head injuries, exceptional stress, and alcoholism may affect these organs temporarily in the same way senility does, resulting in the inability of the brain to file current events for future recall. It is also possible that diet or the metabolic processes of aging people may affect the functioning of the pituitary and memory.[36]

Researchers are extremely cautious in their present claims and predictions

---

[35] M. Pines, "The Riddle of Recall and Forgetfulness," *Saturday Review* 2 (August 9, 1975), p. 23.

[36] Ibid., p. 19.

in order not to excite false hopes; however, there is speculation that within a decade clinics may evaluate the level of the memory hormone in people and adjust it to optimum for learning and memory purposes. Such speculation engenders optimistic pictures of treatment also for retarded persons. However, caution is needed because such drugs put to wrong use might erase conscieces or fix memories to control people in certain ways. Even accidental alteration of the hormone level might cause the mind to so fill itself with minutia that it could not make meaningful distinctions.[37]

Intellectual Development

Research increasingly stresses that an understanding of the development of intelligence and its relation to aging must take into account the interaction of social class, ability level, period of history, as well as age. It is generally suggested that much of the difference presented in the stereotype of decrease in intellectual ability through aging is a reflection of social differences rather than age-related, maturational differences. Older individuals tend to have less formal education. They come from less-educated families and the interactive effect of this with differences in cultural stimulation result in different performances on intelligence tests. Individuals with severe economic or health problems also make lower intelligence scores.

A further compounding problem in interpreting research data has been the possible effect of a predeath drop. It appears that in the months immediately preceding death there is usually a marked drop in intellectual functioning —whatever the age of the individual. Cross-sectional research picks up the effects of this predeath drop and allows it to fallaciously influence the mean scores of different age groups. In an extensive review of the literature on adult development of intellectual performance, Baltes and Labouvie write, "The evidence accumulated is not sufficient to make precise statements about the nature of ontogenetic [individual] changes in intellectual performance, but it is certainly rich enough to seriously challenge the often stated stereotype of general performance decrement during late adulthood and old age."[38]

The American Psychological Association task force on aging makes the following statement:

---

[37] Ibid., p. 20.

[38] P. B. Baltes and G. J. Labouvie, "Adult Development of Intellectual Performance: Description, Explanation, and Modification," in *The Psychology of Adult Development and Aging,* eds. C. Eisdorfer and M. P. Lawton (Washington, D.C.: American Psychological Association, 1973), pp. 157–219.

Many studies are now showing that the intelligence of older persons as measured is typically underestimated. For the most part, the observed decline in intellectual functioning among the aged is attributable to poor health, social isolation, economic plight, limited education, lowered motivation, or other variables not intrinsically related to the aging process. Where intelligence scores do decline, such change is associated primarily with tasks where speed of response is critical.[39]

Age-grading causes the average environment for the elderly to be deficient in opportunity for educative and intellectual interchange and in stimulation to maintain intellectual effectiveness—that is, in our society there are few opportunities for older people to be involved in intellectual activities that keep their "wits sharpened." We need to view intelligence as a developmental factor requiring continuing exercise as much as other aspects of the physiological and psychosocial organism.[40] Much money and effort are invested in accelerating and facilitating the intellectual development of the young, with a minute amount for similar programs for older persons.

It would seem fair to conclude from the research that most of the differences in intellectual performance usually pictured as decline with old age are really differences associated with two factors: One is the difference reflected between persons reared in different generations; the other is the difference present in an individual in the few months immediately preceding death and usually associated with terminal illness. This would suggest that the intellectual performance of an individual changes rather little during the adult period through old age. Furthermore, it is suggested that intellectual development is highly alterable, even during old age, and that new national, social, and educational policies need to devote more efforts and resources for education throughout the life-span.

Is There an Aging Hormone?

Although it is well established that many of the changes we observe in older people are the product of disease and socioeconomic influences, the question still prevails as to whether there is also a specific mechanism of aging. The following paragraphs suggest some of the ideas being pursued by investigators.

[39] Eisdorfer and Lawton, *The Psychology of Adult Development and Aging,* p. ix.
[40] Baltes and Labouvie, "Adult Development of Intellectual Performance," p. 106.

TISSUE CHANGE AND DISEASE

> Some investigators view cellular change in an older person as age change, regardless of disease history, environment, or nutritional, or physical, or emotional condition. But other investigators define a true age change as one resulting only from factors intrinsic to the cell . . . Changes that come with age include alterations in the structure of cells, in their numbers, in the substances surrounding them, in the blood and the vessels that supply tissues and organs, in the organ systems and the regulating endocrine and nervous systems they depend on, and in the system of systems—the whole organism.[41]

Whereas it is usually disease, often heart disease, that results in the death of older persons, some argue that there must be some aging factor in the organism that increases a person's vulnerability to stresses and disease. Although different diseases bring mortality, they all kill large numbers of people in the later decades of life. This suggests that aging may be caused by one or more basic age-changes in the tissues. We discussed in Chapter 4 the changes in collagen as one possible factor contributing to aging. Collagen is the connective tissue that comprises one third of the total body protein. The toughening (or cross-linking) of collagen molecules increases with age. The change is most rapid between ages 30 and 50–perhaps setting the stage for vulnerabilities that take the toll during the next ten to twenty years.[42]

Ways to Lengthen Life   Since the days of Ponce de León and his search for the fountain of youth, people have asked, "Are there ways we can lengthen life?" Various research projects are investigating aspects of hypothesized agents such as mentioned in the last paragraph. Other work proceeds in areas related to the wider spectrum of problems of life at all ages such as economic, social, and psychological stress and various diseases. It has been estimated that a cure or preventive agent for heart disease would increase the average life by nearly 11 years. A similar prevention for cancer would increase life expectancy by 2.3 years.[43]

One of the problems in the research for increasing life is the length of time it takes to find the results. Havighurst is optimistic that helpful approaches to this problem are forthcoming. He states,

---

[41] DHEW, "Perspectives," in *Working with Older People: Biological, Sociological, Psychological Aspects of Aging* (Washington, D.C.: Public Health Service Publication), No. HSM-72-6006, p. 11.

[42] Ibid., p. iv.

[43] Butler, *Why Survive?*, p. 356.

It is necessary to find a more valid, more usable method of measuring the rate of aging, so that experiments could be completed within a few years. In this way, the effects of experimental treatments on the rate of aging, rather than on the death rate, could be observed. A battery of about 15 tests have already been developed that are painless, do not take much time, and can detect changes in the rate of aging within a period of 3 to 5 years.[44]

ENVIRONMENT AND LONGEVITY.   The immediate environment[45] of the older person influences his style of operation and thus the appearance of senility. Life-style and personality patterns of earlier years set the stage for the functioning of old age. Individuals with a life-style of conflict or perceived vulnerability will find the retirement years debilitating. Individuals experienced in a life-style of adaptation and effectiveness in problem solving and who have some choice in planning their later years will find retirement a more satisfying experience. They will continue to be involved in determining their mode of adaptation in old age.

Traumatic loss of environmental support through death of the spouse, being moved from familiar community and friends, or lack of income may have significant effect on morale, and the increased stress may result in physical illness. Thus the deteriorative functioning often associated with old age is not necessarily an age-related condition.

Longevity to some extent seems to be influenced by heredity. Parents who live longer have children who live longer.[46] Identical twins are more likely to live the same length of time than are fraternal twins or other siblings. Heredity may endow us with biological clocks and/or may create certain predispositions for disease.

People seem to live longer in cooler climates, but extermely cold climates create stress and shorten life. Less food intake prolongs life as does exercise and abstinence from smoking. There is also some suggestion that those experiencing high satisfaction with work live longer, as do persons of higher

[44] R. J. Havighurst, "Understanding the Elderly and the Aging Process," *Journal of Home Economics* 66 (April 1974), 4: 18. Havighurst also commented that "another possible way to prolong life—not as dramatic as reducing the rate of aging, but more practical—is to reduce the death rate by a constant factor. Appropriate health care, for example, could affect the death rate, which now doubles every 8 years after the age of 30, so that it would double only every 10 years."

[45] Alexander Leaf's reports of the hearty life-styles of the people living to be over 100 years of age, whom he studied in Russia, Kashmir, and Ecuador, present a rich and colorful challenge to some stereotypes of old age; see A. Leaf, "Every Day Is a Gift When You Are Over 100." *National Geographic* 143 (January 1973), pp. 93–119; A. Leaf, *Youth in Old Age* (New York: McGraw-Hill, 1975).

[46] J. Botwinick, *Aging and Behavior* (New York: Springer, 1973), p. 18.

socioeconomic levels. "The life expectancy of Mexican-Americans is estimated at 57 years, and for American Indians at 44 years. Blacks of all ages
make up 11 per cent of the total United States population, but they constitute
only 7.8 per cent of the elderly."[47]

Commenting on research data that indicate persons with high intelligence,
sound financial status, well-maintained health, and intact marriages live
longer, Botwinick suggested that improved educational opportunities,
greater financial help, better medical services, marriage counseling, and
organized opportunities for remarriage may contribute to improving the
length of life of many.[48]

Adaptability   The popular belief that old age brings conservatism and caution seems to be
supported by several laboratory tests. The caution or conservatism does not
seem to be a choosing between two alternatives of greater or lesser risk, but
rather, the older person seems to prefer not to make any changes. He more
frequently chooses the "no opinion" response on questionnaires. He may
not respond to faint sounds on a hearing test, although the sound registers
with him.

For example, in a study to test the "gambling" propensities of individuals,
a case situation is presented with several points of probability of success. The
individual was asked to indicate at what point he would advise someone to
risk investing. Older persons seemed to favor a more conservative approach.
However, further inspection of the data revealed a high proportion chose the
last alternative, which was "not to recommend investment under any circumstance." In a subsequent exercise, when the last choice was eliminated
and they were forced to recommend some risk, the differences between
young and old disappeared. It appears the tendency among the old is not to
become involved. There is some suggestion that the level of education and
conditions of personal security may be related to the tendency toward nonin-
volvement. With more education and more security there is less noninvolve-
ment.[49]

There is a slight decline in most physical functioning, beginning at the end
of adolescence and in early adult life; but significance of age-related decline is
very slight in old age. How the individual accommodates to life, his care of

---

[47] Butler, *Why Survive?*, p. 6.

[48] Botwinick, *Aging and Behavior*, p. 31.

[49] Ibid., p. 109.

his body, his style of life, his sense of purpose and value, and, unfortunately, how the environment provides for him by way of social and economic resources—these are the factors that influence many of the changes associated with aging. We most frequently confuse the effects of disease for the effects of aging. The poor have more health problems than those in moderate circumstances. The old-old have more health problems than the young-old; however, there is considerable overlap among persons of different chronological ages.

There is nothing in the biology of aging that says the problem-solving skills of a person of 68 need to be less than those of a person of 18, nor need his sociability or sexual enjoyment be less than that of a person of 28 or 38.

A recent report by Duke's Longitudinal Studies of Aging offers the following summary:

> The aged usually show more individual variability than the young . . . . Thus, even when there are significant mean differences between old and young, there is usually considerable overlap between the two distributions. This means that many older persons have better functioning and better scores than many younger persons . . . . It is impressive how many of the normal aged are able to compensate for their growing physical handicaps and maintain fairly stable levels of social and psychological functioning.[50]

Special Issues in Old Age

Old age touches on a wide spectrum of life processes that are present at all stages of life. Some of the processes take on special emphasis with old age because society is becoming aware that they impinge more acutely on this age group. Poverty, health and malnutrition, housing, transportation, and protection from crime are areas of concern in which the elderly have a special vulnerability. This vulnerability is usually a compounding one—that is, poverty makes it difficult for many elderly to find suitable housing; but more adequate housing, usually found in the suburbs, is inaccessible to transportation. Less expensive housing in the ghetto makes the elderly more vulnerable to muggings and other crimes. Fear of crime and lack of transportation causes many elderly to decline social events and the increased social isolation contributes to depression. This can lead to lack of hope and initiative to maintain or enhance the quality of life. Because these are issues that

---

[50] E. Palmore, ed., *Normal Aging II* (Durham: Duke University Press, 1974), p. 290.

affect individuals of all age levels, we will discuss them at greater length in Chapter 12.

There is another life experience with implications for all age levels. It may at times carry more traumatic adjustment difficulties when encountered at earlier life periods. It is, however, a more prevalent part of the ongoing events among the elderly. This is the experience of death.

Concerning   As I planned the outline for this book, I considered the topic of death for sev-
Death   eral of the earlier chapters—social processes, physiological processes, self-
processes, transpersonal processes. Each time it seemed that the topic would "fit in" better in the next chapter. And so it moved throughout the book until now in old age there is no further room for procrastination.

Persons teaching death education suggest that we relate to death as vitally as we relate to life. And yet, there seems to be no "convenient time" for death.

Relating to others intimately associated with death is a more familiar experience for old people than for persons of other age groups. As adults reach the early sixties, most will have experienced death among close friends and family; for persons in their seventies, death is an even more frequent event. However, many people in the helping professions are attempting to gain some background and perspective in order to be of more assistance to individuals throughout the life-span. Counselors, the clergy, and others are pointing out that we often desert the dying and the grieving because we do not know how to be of help; we are unfamiliar with the processes of death and grieving. There is an awareness of information to be considered and, for those of us who would be of assistance, there is a personal working through of our own emotional experiences in relation to this event. The following paragraphs simply offer an introduction to some of the issues, particularly as these relate to developmental tasks of adulthood. References at the end of the chapter will lead to further resources.

SOME PHYSIOLOGICAL CONSIDERATIONS

> She's gone forever! I know when one is dead and when one lives. She's dead as earth. Lend me a looking glass. If that her breath will mist or stain the stone, why, then she lives.
>
> Shakespeare, *King Lear*

How do we know when a person is really, irrevocably dead? Perhaps until recently the average person would have said, in agreement with King Lear, that a person is dead when he stops breathing. But even the general public is now less easily satisfied with that answer because technology is able to prolong breathing for increasing time periods. The controversial Karen Quinlan[51] case captured the headlines in 1975. The ambiguities of the criteria of death were dramatized throughout the nation as more and more experts (doctors, scientists, lawyers, ministers) expressed conflicting opinions.

In looking at opinions about definitions of death, one can find a subtle progression of changes within the past ten years with increasing disagreement over criteria as organ transplants occur more frequently. The majority of nonmedical persons is most comfortable with the guideline: "When the heart stops or breathing ceases." However, medical viewpoints are increasingly emphasizing "brain death"[52] as the significant criteria and insisting that the judgment must be a medical one. Others[53] point out that "brain death" is too broad a criteria. They suggest that death should be viewed as the termination of personal identity and that such identity resides in a more restricted portion of our brain, in the cerebrum. This merges with making judgments concerning the prospect for a meaningful life—that is, whether the brain has been so badly damaged as to prevent restoration of self-awareness and intelligent human functioning. The contradictory words "human vegetable" make us ask the definition of humanness—the question with which we began this book.

Some of the confounding legal reverberrations that can arise are illustrated by the case of Clarence Nicks and John Stuckwish.[54] Nicks was beaten in a barroom brawl so badly that his brain registered no electrical activity and he had no reflexes for hours. After a period the machine providing oxygen to his blood was turned off and his heart was transplanted to John Stuckwish. The following questions might be raised: If someone were to be charged with murder for Nicks' death, should it be his barroom assailant or the doctor who removed his heart? Or is Nicks still alive because his heart is beating in Stuckwish's body, but Stuckwish is dead because his heart has been removed?

A neurosurgeon has stated, "Every week in intensive-care units across our

[51] M. Clark, "A Right to Die," *Newsweek* 86 (November 3, 1975), pp. 58–69.

[52] Brain death has been described as "no reflexes, no spontaneous respiration, and no electroenchephalographic activity for twenty-four hours." Butler, *Why Survive?*, p. 376.

[53] J. Fletcher, "New Definitions of Death," *Prism* (January 1974).

[54] D. Hendin, *Death as a Fact of Life* (New York: Warner Paperback, 1973).

country we are pumping and medicating people who are dead."[55] The reconciliation of matters of death will probably be long in coming, involving continued input from social, legal, theological, and medical professions. In most instances the physician will continue to make the judgment, guided perhaps by broad legal statements.

SOME SOCIAL CONSIDERATIONS.   Until recently, death has been a taboo topic, reflecting our individual and corporate uneasiness at this phenomenon that would not lend itself to man's control.[56] Having become aware of some of the inhumanness with which we have dealt with persons in this experience, we are now actively involved in developing educative methods for "managing" this process. Perhaps in some instances we may perfect our technique to desensitize our awareness.

Medical techniques have often been the frustration of the individual in the lingering days of a terminal illness.[57] He is religiously given his medication, his X-ray treatments, and his vital signs are taken. But in the busyness no one has listened to his thoughts or recognized the decisions he is making about his life and its meaning; no one is administering to him a quarter hour of honest dialogue. We have often refused to recognize this transitional ego stage and, when confronted, too quickly shift to dealing with the body as though the transition were already completed and the person no longer existed.

AS WE APPROACH DEATH.   I am not sure there would have been a different meaning if the heading for this section had been "As Death Approaches." I think there might have been.

We have suggested that somewhere in the middle years there begins a shift from thinking about the number of years we have lived to time left to live. We are beginning to prepare for the integrative experiences of Erikson's eighth stage. Before the integration is completed, enabling us to accept our life script, there is the struggle to change life's circumstance. Our existential anxiety has to do with making choices through which our life will have meaning and significance. In later years we look back on the events of our life and impute meaning. Butler has suggested that early in late life there is a

[55] M. D. Heifetz, *The Right to Die* (Berkeley, Calif.: Berkeley, 1975).

[56] E. Becker, *The Denial of Death* (New York: Free Press, 1973).

[57] Butler, *Why Survive?* pp. 178–179. Butler discusses some of the ways the physicians' personal anxieties about death enter into their treatment procedures.

progressive return to consciousness of unresolved conflicts; working them out results in new significance and meaning of life for the individual and a greater serenity as he approaches death. Butler cites numerous literary works as examples of the life-review process: Ingmar Bergman's motion picture *Wild Strawberries*, Hemingway's *The Snows of Kilimanjaro*, Tolstoy's *The Death of Ivan Ilyich*, and the memoirs of Casanova, Clemenceau, Steffens, and others.[58]

With this reconciliation it is possibly easier for the elderly to accept death as a present part of life. Older persons tend to fear death less than do younger persons. When the elderly do experience strong emotional concern with death it is often associated with factors in living arrangements during latter days or with treatment for illness.[59]

There is an increasing amount of research data to suggest that the middle-age tendency toward an "increased interiority" advances markedly in the months just preceeding death.[60]

Elizabeth Kubler-Ross is a psychiatrist who has done much to cause our society to become conscious of the dying as a person. She has stressed the dying person's desire for candid encounter and the desire to participate responsibly in this last and very important step. She has suggested that making explicit the developmental pattern of dying may help us to acknowledge this as a life process.[61] She suggests the pattern contains six themes, of which one overarches the others: hope. The other themes or phases, fluctuating in the experience of the dying person, are denial, anger, bargaining, depression, and acceptance (Example 11–3).

It is almost an intuitive act of defense for people to reject what threatens them. Most persons move through the *denial* phase fairly rapidly, although they periodically need to pick up this defense to buffer them.

Next comes "why me" and *anger* at the injustice of having one's life interrupted. Part of the anger may be at the impersonal treatment and an appeal to others to recognize "I'm not dead yet." This is a difficult period for family and friends but it is important that the dying person and his anger be accepted and understood—not avoided.

Bargaining is a third phase; it may be with God or with those who care for

[58] Ibid., p. 413.

[59] Ibid., p. 413.

[60] M. A. Leherman and A. S. Caplan, "Distance from Death as a Variable in the Study of Aging," *Developmental Psychology* 2 (1969), 1:71–84.

[61] E. Kubler-Ross, *On Death and Dying* (New York: Macmillan, 1969).

Example 11–3.
Make Today
Count

When Orville Kelly discovered he had lymphoma, the gaiety went out of the family. Wanda and Orville did not refer to his illness. As a matter of fact, they almost stopped talking to each other at all. They took to sleeping in separate beds. The picnics with their children and evening rides for ice cream and ball games ceased.

When Wanda tried to talk to her friends about her situation, they said, "Don't think about it," and changed the subject. In time, their friends stopped visiting them. Theirs was a home where death had already taken over.

One day coming home from chemotherapy, Orville spoke aloud. "Wanda," he said, "You know I'm not dead yet." He pulled the car off the highway and parked. "Honey, I've got cancer. And I'll probably die of it. But I'm not dead yet. We've got to talk about it."

From that beginning of conversation flowed new life into the family. Their backyard barbeques with their children were reestablished that evening. A short while later Orville, a journalist, wrote an article for his local paper telling how it feels to be a person with terminal illness.

Hundreds of letters came in response to the article from families with similar problems. Orville and Wanda decided that perhaps people with life-threatening situations could help each other. They announced a meeting and eighteen people attended. They decided to call their group *Make Today Count*. There are now more than sixty MTC groups around the country and two years after the first meeting Orville was busy providing resources and guidance for the groups. His prognosis from the doctor was that he had from six months to three years to live. He has learned to live each day to its fullest.

Abstract from W. Kelly, "Until Tomorrow Comes," *Guideposts* (April 1976) pp. 2–6; see also O. Kelly, *Make Today Count*, (New York: Delacorte Press, 1976).

the dying person. It is a part of the process of coming to grips with the reality of the situation. It is the testing of all alternatives.

With recognition of bargaining's futility comes *depression*. Kubler-Ross suggests that we should recognize two kinds of depression. One is reactive depression—a reaction to loss. It is akin to what we experience in grieving for other losses: loss of personal appearance, position in retirement, loss of spouse in divorce or death. It must be expressed, followed by some encouragement from others that they are still supportive and that the individual is not forsaken as a result of his loss. The second kind is preparatory depression; it is "preparatory grief" as the individual anticipates the giving up of all he is and has on earth. A friend or helper's silent companionship of empathy in the hours of painful realization can assist the dying person toward the next step, acceptance.

Acceptance usually follows the working through of fear and denial, of anger, bargaining, and depression. It is the coming to terms with one's present situation. Free from disguise and defenses, the individual is able to be more open to the present without dread. Sometimes the quiet peace has the feeling of a time of rest before the long journey.

In this last phase, *hope,* which has afforded the individual strength to work through earlier periods, finds a new and more complete expression. It is now not a hope for a miraculous reversal but rather an affirmation of reconciliation of one's life with the whole of existence. It is a hope that the final communication with family will provide a sense of completeness so that their memories will look upon the fulfillment of this life and know that "it was good." Hope affords a tranquillity, a closeness with deeper meanings in one's existence and an acceptance of its goodness.

Communication rather than isolation and honesty rather than protectiveness are the needs of the dying person. Kubler-Ross stresses that they are also the needs of the grieving family. Too often, friends and organizations of goodwill have added to the pain and immobilization of grieving families. They have done this through the "cushioning treatment"—that is, they have wished to protect the privacy of the family and left them totally alone desiring not to cause the family pain by the discomfort of talking about their departed loved one.

Families need guidance and encouragement to enter freely with the dying person into the expression of his feelings and thoughts, accepting and sharing with him their own. Hospital staff or other helpers can provide important assistance to enable the bereaved and the dying to say farewell in the final days and weeks in an honest and personal way.

Such openness to the continuing realities of life is necessary for the family in the days and months of bereavement following death. Many persons experience severe emotional and physical problems during their bereavement. There is a higher-than-average death rate among surviving relatives. Drugs and psychological problems greatly impair work and social performance during the grieving period. Suicide is often a threat to self and a worry to friends of the grieving person.[62]

The grieving individual goes through some processes along with the

[62] C. M. Parkes, *Bereavement: Studies of Grief in Adult Life* (New York: International Universities Press, 1972).

dying individual; however, there is then a rather long period of catharsis, acceptance, and reorientation. The bereaved is often preoccupied with the loss and the thoughts of the person who has died. There is often numbness during the days up to the funeral. As the numbness begins to be replaced by the awareness of being left alone, anger at the situation and often at the person who is gone takes over. It is a reaction to a sense of injustice at the burden placed upon the bereaved.

Beginning to realize her aloneness and the new responsibilities upon her shoulders, the spouse may reach out rashly in desperate efforts to rearrange her life and to secure her economic and social circumstances. Lynn Caine recounts some of the absurd overtures she made to wealthy persons a few weeks after her husband's death. Her move from the city was both a social and financial blunder. She strongly recommends that a widow not make any decisions regarding major change in economic or career situations for several months. With equal fervor she stresses the importance of having continuing and as nearly normal contacts with friends and family.[63]

The aloneness experienced by widows is the most difficult aspect of bereavement. It is hard to know how much social isolation is at the base of the difficulty widows experience in accomplishing the necessary social and psychological reorganization of their lives. Left alone at first for the sake of privacy, and later because they do not fit the social patterning or because in desperation they talk about their problems, widows are in a social milieu that contributes to pathology rather than growth.

Bereavement involves first the expression of feelings associated with loss and then the rediscovery of the person they are and the resources they possess. Society affords some framework for marking the termination of life with funerals; it does very little about the passage of the bereaved into a positive new life status. The effect is often of the bereaved being shunted into a waiting pattern.

Family and persons in helping capacities can assist the bereaved toward positive action in role transition through continued active involvement with them. A working through of the grieving process may be aided if the bereaved has an opportunity to rehearse the final days of the loved one's life and to express feelings of anger, guilt, and confusion. Candid discussion of opportunities for new relationships may help the individual clarify her new social identity and to identify the many social roles and connections that should continue. Opportunity for such discussion with a close friend or fam-

---

[63] L. Caine, *Widow* (New York: Bantam Books, 1974).

ily member can provide the bereaved a "reality check." The feedback assists with new information and relieves anxieties and paranoia created by silence, misinformation, and distortion.

PHYSIOLOGICAL EFFECTS OF GRIEF AND BEREAVEMENT.   "On the whole, grief resembles a physical injury more closely than any other type of illness. The loss may be spoken of as a 'blow.' As in the case of physical injury the 'wound' gradually heals; at least, it usually does. But occasionally complications set in, healing is delayed, or a further injury reopens a healing wound. In such cases abnormal forms arise, which may even be complicated by the onset of other types of illness. Sometimes it seems that the outcome may be fatal."[64] Lynn Caine came down with viral pneumonia after the memorial service and was sick for three weeks. Fatigue plagued her for months.[65]

Interviews with grieving relatives show a remarkably uniform picture, including the following symptoms:

> Sensations of somatic distress occurring in waves, lasting from twenty minutes to an hour at a time, a feeling of tightness in the throat, choking with shortness of breath, need for sighing, and an empty feeling in the abdomen, lack of muscular power and an intense subjective distress described as tension or mental pain.[66]

Death is a highly significant aspect of life for the living as we approach it. The processes of bereavement require the assistance from helpers, family, and friends if there is not to be damage to health, to career, and to finances. Death and grieving are natural processes in the life of each of us. Their presence is only slightly more prominent among the elderly. Increasing study is helping us to better understand the influence of these events in the developmental tasks of adult life.

Developmental Processes of Aging

We have thus far in this chapter been occupied with descriptions of activities, attitudes, and characteristics of people in old age. What general framework or theory is available to provide integration and guide further research?

---

[64] Parkes, *Bereavement*.

[65] Caine, *Widow*.

[66] E. Lendemann, "Symptomatology and Management of Acute Grief," *American Journal of Psychiatry* 101 (1944–45), pp. 141–148; see also M. E. P. Seligman, *Helplessness: On Depression, Development, and Death* (New York: Freeman, 1975).

Differing points of view, perhaps reflecting differing value systems, have been put forth as the pattern for successful aging in post-retirement years. The "man-in-the-street" view, expressed by the activity and compensation theory, suggests that the older person desires to continue the activities and serve the same interests and values he had in earlier life. Confronted with physical and environmental limitations, he may adapt and compensate but essentially he attempts to maintain his earlier way of life with family ties and work or work substitutes.

Another theory that experienced considerable popularity for a while is the disengagement theory.[67] This suggests that a developmental characteristic of old age is for persons to withdraw from social involvements and to devote their psychological energies toward personal and introspective interests. The theory indicates that older persons wish to decrease their emotional investment in individuals and objects in their environment. Whereas the activity theory suggests that optimal behavior for the older person is to stay active and to keep social contacts, the disengagement theory suggests that the older person will have a greater sense of well-being if he develops psychological distance from others and maintains less involvement with events and problems of the world around him.

CONTINUITY OF PERSONALITY.   We have referred to these points of view in earlier chapters in discussions of the research in the Kansas City study,[68] the 40-year follow-up study of the Institute of Human Development,[69] and the study of the four stages of life.[70] The theme rising out of these studies is that the activity theory and the disengagement theory are presenting two of several possible modes of development in old age. Essentially the finding is that old age merely continues modes of behavior begun early in life. Except where severe economic, environmental, or health factors intervene, the person entering old age continues to express his own personality rather than being shaped by the fiat of social or biological factors.

The older person continues to maintain choice and to choose alternatives from his environment in accord with his long-established pattern of needs.

[67] E. Cumming and W. E. Henry, *Growing Old: The Process of Disengagement* (New York: Basic Books, 1961).

[68] B. L. Neugarten and associates, *Personality in Middle Age and Late Life* (New York: Atherton Press, 1964).

[69] H. S. Maas and J. A. Kuypers, *From Thirty to Seventy* (San Francisco: Jossey-Bass, 1974).

[70] M. F. Lowenthal, M. T. Thurnher, and D. Chiriboga, *Four Stages of Life* (San Francisco: Jossey-Bass, 1975).

In most instances there is no abrupt shift in personality with age, rather, the principle of integration promotes an increasing consistency. Those characteristics and interests that have been central in earlier life continue to orient the activity in later years.[71] In Example 11–4 note the active life-style and the interest in youth of Mr. Morgan in his young adult, young-old, and old-old stages.

There are considerable differences among individuals in old age. There are differences between men and women. There are also several different types of men and several different types of women. For example, the 40-year follow-up study noted four different life-styles among men and six different life-styles among women.[72] They reflect earlier differences that have continued for the individual life through the years.

Whereas continuity and pattern are prevailing in aging, it is possible to note factors that influence the alternatives available to old people that form the parameters within which the development moves. The social alliances and reference groups formed by the individual earlier in life constitute a part of his structure. Their support assists him to adapt and maintain psychosocial continuity and effectiveness that transcend many of the physical and intrapsychic losses he may encounter.[73]

A pressing desire for all people is to be needed. It is the sustained experience of being necessary to others that gives meaning and purpose to life and preserves its vitality. Opportunities to remain useful members of society are severely undermined by the required exits from adult social roles by those in old age. As community or individual changes influence the recognition of the elderly as worthy contributors to society, they begin to exchange their independence and creativity for more dependent life-styles.[74] Our task is to achieve new understanding of old age, to recognize the strengths of people in this period, and to help them continue to command recognition as contributing members of society.

Most people in old age are in reasonably good health. An analysis[75] of an annual record showed that more than four fifths of the people over 65 did not enter a hospital for even a brief stay during that year.

[71] R. J. Havighurst, B. L. Neugarten, and S. Tobin, "Disengagement and Patterns of Aging," in *Middle Age and Aging,* ed. B. L. Neugarten, pp. 161–172.

[72] Maas and Kuypers, *From Thirty to Seventy,* Chapters 2, 3.

[73] Neugarten and associates, *Personality in Middle and Late Life,* pp. 197–198.

[74] J. J. Doud, "Aging as Exchange: A Preface to Theory."

[75] Havighurst, "Understanding the Elderly and the Aging Process," p. 17.

**Example
11– 4.**
Mr. Morgan's
Wonderful
Constitution

(Excerpt from magazine account in 1954)*: Folks back in Smith County, Kansas, used to say, "Brad Morgan's not a halfway man." When Brad set out to clear a field or build a barn, he worked from daybreak 'til dark and wasn't to be stopped until the job was done.

That was 50 years ago, and today at 69 Brad Morgan—now the moving man of Manhattan, Kansas—is still a man who won't be stopped. It's everyday routine with him to pick up a refrigerator, adjust it lightly on his back, and start off up a flight or two of stairs with only a boy to "watch the corners."

The time Brad Morgan loves most is when he is bouncing along in his '38 Ford pickup with the blue sideboards. The little blue pickup is kept neat and trim and is so shiny that it almost glistens in the dark.

"Folks tell me she's an expense and that I should trade her in on a new one," Morgan says. "But I can't seem to take to the idea of parting with her. Besides all the kids know her."

In his business, Morgan naturally is one of the first to meet newcomers to the city. He quite naturally urges families to get lined up with a church. If there are children in the family, he usually manages to find an excuse to take them for a ride in his little blue pickup. And in many instances that pickup ride has been the deciding factor in where (and often whether) the children will attend Sunday School.

In many ways as he grew up, went to farming, and later entered the moving business, Brad Morgan increasingly championed the young people of the community. Somewhere along the line a respected friend told him. "To be a parent is a man's greatest privilege. The generation being reared today will shape the generations to come." This stuck with Brad. He became a father six times—two boys and four girls—and there was nothing good he wouldn't do for his family or other fellows and girls in the community. For instance, in 1921 the first 4-H Club in Smith County was organized with Brad as sponsor.

When time came for the oldest of the Morgan children to be graduated from high school, dust storms had swept the plains of Kansas bare. A move seemed logical. "I'm convinced that our children shall have a college education," Morgan said to his wife. When Morgan told his neighbors that he was going to put his farm up for sale and move to Manhattan so that his children could attend Kansas State, they thought he had departed from his senses.

Things were indeed rough for a few years after the Morgan family moved to Manhattan. Morgan went to work doing whatever he could with his truck. Mrs. Morgan kept rooms for college students. The children all found part-time jobs. The first of the six Morgan children to attend Kansas State College enrolled the fall that the family moved to Manhattan.

One of his customers watching 69-year-old Brad climb up near the van ceiling to adjust an unsteady piece after hours of back-breaking labor, exclaimed, "I don't see how you do it, Mr. Morgan!" Typically, he replied with a smile. "Well, lady, it just seems that the Lord has blessed me with a wonderful constitution."

In 1975, 20 years after I wrote this article, I sent the following letter to *Power*.

Back in August, 1954, we wrote a story for *Power* about Brad Morgan, the Moving Man. Last week I saw a picture in the Manhattan (Kansas) *Mercury* of a spry baldheaded gentleman sitting, surrounded by children in the middle of an elementary school recreation room. That's what prompted this 20-year up-date of his story. That "wonderful constitution" of Mr. Morgan's is still going strong. Now over 90 years of age, the Moving Man has shifted careers but not his focus on children and Christian service.

One of the first to volunteer for the RSVP program when it began last year was Brad Morgan. "I've always liked music," he told the RSVP coordinator. "Used to sing top tenor in a male quartet but my tenor's slipped quite a little these last few years. Still play my harmonica though. Been playing ever since I learned "Home on the Range" out in my home territory of Smith County where Doctor Higley wrote it. Harmonica's a mighty useful instrument. You can always carry one along in your pocket with you—gives you a lot of comfort and some pretty lively tunes—whichever you've a mind for."

Now every Thursday afternoon, there is a third person in the team that goes to College Hill Nursing Center to lead the "Weekly Sing time." There's the pianist, the song leader, and there's Mr. Morgan with his harmonica.

It's the RSVP assignment to help in the elementary schools' music program that nearly causes Brad to burst his buttons in anticipation every week. Working together with one of the music teachers, Mr. Morgan explains and demonstrates the harmonica. Along with that explanation goes a generous measure of recollected Kansas history, and Morgan philosophy of health habits, humor, and Christian living, topped off by a few lively numbers by way of concert.

★ C. E. Kennedy, "He Hauls Furniture—and Kids!" *Power Magazine* 12 (August 22, 1954), 3:1–3.

We may anticipate the future and recognize the place that continuing education may have in mobilizing the energies of people in old age. For example, people over 65 with a college education represent an elderly elite. They participate more in political and civic activity, do more reading and studying, are more involved as volunteers, acknowledge fewer problems, and express greater life satisfaction. However, we should remember that most of this group also have higher incomes from prior earnings and invest-

11–11 *When the president of the university presented Mr. Morgan's son with the Distinguished Service to Agriculture award, Mr. Morgan was a proud witness. (Kansas State University Student Publications photo)*

11–12 *Mr. Morgan plays his harmonica in an elementary school music class. (Manhattan Mercury photo)*

ments than those with less education. This makes it possible to be more active and more satisfied.

We can expect the college-educated portion of older Americans to triple, from 7 per cent to 20 per cent, by the 1990s.[76] It will take in a larger proportion of persons from lower social classes. How they will respond to the challenges of old age may be significantly influenced by programs of continuing education, which would better prepare them to hold and advance informed and constructive attitudes toward social policy relating to conditions affecting older persons.

Erikson's Eighth Stage: Ego Integrity

Given adequate economic resources, provisions for health care, and social opportunities, individuals during old age will continue to develop in accord with the personality patterns and life-style uniquely their own. As they move through their later years, there is among men a tendency toward mellowing and among women a tendency toward greater expressiveness. These changes will be part of the bringing together of their life experience that Erikson[77] describes as achieving a sense of integrity, of recognizing patterns and affirming the meaning of life experience.[78]

Erikson has suggested that only in the older person who through the years has been involved with the creation and preservation of things and ideas does the fruit of seven earlier stages gradually ripen. Wisdom, Erikson says, is the expression of successful process in the integrity stage of human development. It is this component, the wisdom of old age, that each society needs for balance and perspective.

Summary

It is easy to be extreme about old age—to see either its contributions or its deficiencies. It is important that we keep both in mind. However, in order to

[76] R. J. Havighurst, *Aging in America: Implications for Education* (Washington, D.C.: The National Council on the Aging, 1976), p. 16.

[77] E. H. Erikson, *Insight and Responsibility* (New York: Norton, 1964), p. 133.

[78] Butler points to the danger that too much emphasis on maintenance of identity may stifle growth and cause people to feel locked into earlier life-styles, thus become passive. R. Butler, *Why Survive?*, pp. 400–401.

work toward a new national image of old age and to correct an imbalance in popular thought, we will need to deliberately stress the positive potential of this period.

The prevailing popular picture of weakness and lack of creativity lumps all old people (except our one or two close friends) into a common stereotype. The study of old age presents a different picture. There is greater diversity among the elderly than among any age group. This period poses crucial developmental tasks; the solution comes from the combination of resources from earlier life-styles, from the availability of social, psychological, and economic resources in the community, and from the individual's health and physical energies.

In the earlier phase of old age, individuals deal with the transition of retirement. The time when that event actually occurs varies. However, society has established 65 as a mythical landmark and most persons beyond that age cope with retirement as part of their present experience. They recognize the impressions of their families and fellow workers that they are "old" and "ready for retirement". Retirement involves conceptualizing new roles. Some older people have looked forward to this with anticipation, some have repressed the idea. The relatively good health and availability of millions of persons in retirement establishes them as a large untapped manpower pool.

Death is a fact of life, especially in old age. Although in the first phase of old age the majority are living with spouses, widowhood increases during this period. This poses further challenges of adjustment in life-style, including work and living arrangements. In this period individuals are integrating the meaning of their lives with the total context of life, death, and human purpose. There is thus some change in personality and in the values ascribed to different events.

There are some decrements in physical functioning as people move through old age. However, one of the most important corrections we need to make in our thinking concerns the physical aspects of aging. A large proportion of the "symptoms" we associate with old age are the symptoms of disease, poverty, and inadequate community resources. Persons in old age who are well educated, have good income, meaningful work experience, continuing marriages with close family relationships, respect and approbation from the community and their peers are generally intellectually alert and in good physical health. Indeed, old age offers a notable demonstration of the adaptability of the human organism and how we are able to compensate with new social and psychological skills for many of the physical limitations we accrue through time.

In research theories older people have been viewed as a subculture separated from other aspects of society by their negative stereotype and the negative responses given to them. They have been seen to have the attributes of a minority group with their people experiencing the second-class status effects of ageism, prejudices, and the handicaps of low income, low social status, and low self-image. However, the major formulations of theory have been concerned with activity versus disengagement views of old age. Neither perspective appears to describe all elderly.

A more inclusive perspective comes from the developmental framework that indicates adaptation to aging will go forward along the lines of the individual's past life. Personality patterns and life-styles formed earlier will cause some to disengage, whereas others' earlier life-style encourages continued activity. If we have been successful in earlier life the chances are good we will be successful in old age.

For all of us there appear to be some developmental changes within our inner life, beginning in our forties. As we enter old age, there is some deepening of our inner life and less strong attachments to some social and environmental events. Whereas inner reorganization may signal some freedom for disengagement, the social needs of the individual continue strongly. Most older people want the choice of making continued contributions to their society. Where there is marked withdrawal, it is usually as a result of some lack in the way that the environment has provided opportunity for the individual to participate.

Suggested Activities and Further Reading

1. Prepare a time line for people now in phase 1 and another for people in phase 2 of old age. Phase 1 people were born during the first decade of the twentieth century. People in phase 2 were born in the last years of the nineteenth century. The popular novel *Ragtime,* by E. L. Doctorow (New York: Random House, 1975), has its setting during the time the people of old age were children and youth. Note how the position of events on the time lines of young and middle adults (such as the first man in space) has shifted considerably on the time line of old age.

2. For a useful overview of the major concepts of aging with an applied perspective, read J. D. Manney, Jr., *Aging in American Society* (Ann Arbor, Mich.: The Institute of Gerontology, University of Michigan, 1975). This is a resource book prepared for use in training workshops for administration on aging staff. The institute also has published a number of helpful Occasional Papers; note especially number 11, *No. Longer Young: The Older Woman in America.*

3. On the occasion of the tenth International Congress of Gerontology, *The Gerontologist* published an international issue (vol. 15, no. 3, June 1975) that contains reports from a number of countries in Europe, the Far East, and North and South America. The quarterly information bulletin *Ageing International* (International Federation on Aging, 1909 K Street, N.W., Washington, D.C., 20049) provides research briefs and information on international activities in gerontology.

4. For a model of an approach to the study of the elderly in one community, see *The Gerontologist* (vol. 16, no. 1, February 1976). Part 2 is devoted to a case study of Chicago.

5. Discuss ways in which the attitudes and activities of people in old age are influenced by their earlier life experiences. For different types of stimulus material, see two articles in *Journal of Gerontology* (July 1976)—T. H. Brubaker and E. A. Powers, "The Stereotype of 'Old': A Review and Alternative Approach," and A. R. Rowe, "Retired Academics and Research." Also bring to the discussion illustrations from your own observation of people who are successful in old age.

6. Monitor one of the regular weekly television programs for one week, keeping a record of the roles given to persons in old age.

7. Find out if there is a death-education course offered in your community and ask the instructor to discuss the developmental aspects of death; see R. Kastenbaum, "Is Death a Life Crisis?" in *Normative Life Crises,* eds. N. Datan and L. N. Ginsberg (New York: Academic Press, 1975).

8. Discuss the thoughts and pictures that come to your mind as you read the following excerpt from R. Coles, *The Old Ones of New Mexico* (Albuquerque: University of New Mexico Press, 1973), pp. 20–21.

> *Domingo Garcia is 83 years old and his wife, Dolores, is also 83. They are Spanish-speaking Americans living on a small farm in the New Mexico hills where Garcia families have had small cattle herds for more than two hundred years. Physician and writer Robert Coles tells of having breakfast with Mrs. Garcia.*

"Domingo and I have been having this same breakfast for over fifty years. We are soon to be married fifty-five years, God willing. We were married a month after the Great War ended; it was a week before Christmas, 1918. The priest said he hoped our children would always have enough food and never fight in a war. I haven't had a great variety of food to give my family, but they have not minded. I used to serve the children eggs in the morning, but Domingo and I have stayed with hot bread and coffee. My fingers would die if they didn't have the dough to work over. I will never give up my oven for a new one. It has been here forty years, and is an old friend. I would stop baking bread if it gave out. My sons once offered to buy me an electric range, they called it, and I broke down. It was a terrible thing to do. The boys felt bad. My husband said I should be more considerate. I meant no harm, though. I didn't deliberately say to myself: Dolores Garcia, you have been hurt, so now go and cry. The tears came and I was helpless before them. Later my husband said they all agreed I was in the right; the stove has been so good to us, and there is nothing wrong—the bread is as tasty as ever, I believe. It is a sickness, you know: being always dissatisfied with what you have, and eager for a change."

She stops here and looks lovingly around the room. She is attached to every piece of furniture. Her husband made them: a round table, eight chairs, with four more in their bedroom, the beds there, the bureau there. She begins to tell how good Domingo is at carving wood: "That is what I would like to say about Domingo: he plants, builds, and harvests, he tries to keep us alive and comfortable with his hands. We sit on what he has made, eat what he has grown, sleep on what he has put together . . . Buying, that is the sickness. I have gone to the city and watched people. I don't ask people to live on farms and make chairs and tables; but when I see them buying things they don't need, or even want—except to make a purchase, to get something—then I say there is a sickness."

Part THREE

LOOKING AHEAD

chapter 12

Facilitating Adult Development: Issues and Resources

In **Part Two** we were thinking about being an adult at different age levels. We have looked at some of the developmental tasks that adults deal with at different stages. In this chapter we will step back and, keeping the various stages in mind, consider some of the services and public policy needed to assist individuals toward optimal growth through the adult years. As we start this chapter, we want to ask questions such as, "What are the special health, educational, counseling, recreational, and spiritual resources adults may need at different life stages?" "What are the industrial and legislative policies influencing concerns such as retirement, transportation, and housing?" "What are some of the present concerns regarding special services such as television, nursing homes, communitiy centers, family counseling?" This is, indeed like opening Pandora's Box. We can touch on only a few of the issues and offer some observations that may help in exploring further the areas of special interest to you.

Much of the present writing and activity have been directed toward special needs of people in old age. Here we would like to begin by considering resources for development throughout the life-span.

Issues and Resources

The Factor of Time

When we think of adult development, time is a frequent point of reference: how many years we have lived; how many years we have yet to live. With improved health, our expected length of life has increased. Time becomes a factor as individuals live longer periods after child rearing and fol-

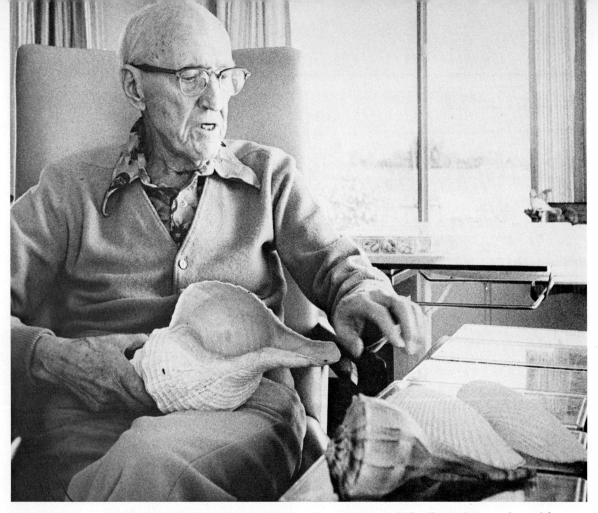

12–1 *An 88-year-old nursing home resident organizes a shell collection begun earlier in life.* (Manhattan Mercury *photo*)

lowing retirement. The effect of technology on the world of work has caused the designated workweek to shrink. With an increase in leisure hours many Americans question what to do with this time.

Time is associated with identity. How I use time is a reflection of my purpose and meaning; it also shapes how I feel about myself. My sense of well-being, of optimism, of initiative, and of creativity are influenced. The opportunities available for work, play, social relationships, education, worship, creative endeavors, and human service influence significantly how I use my time. It is also influenced by the social expectations and values a community places on different uses of time.

Leisure   Our increasing productivity in the work force is creating an expanding period of leisure for most individuals, and present society is unsure how to handle this phenomenon. We can either continue our national product at about the same level, or with our increased efficiency we can keep persons employed at approximately the same level and increase our per capita gross national product. If we maintain present limits on our national product, we will soon move to half-day or half-week work schedules, or begin retiring many people before the age of 40.[1]

Already we are faced with important social questions: "What does leisure mean to the average American?" "How does leisure relate to work in our present value system?" There are many ways to use leisure time: games, watching TV, socializing with friends, art, crafts and hobbies, education, community service. To which of these, if any, does society assign positive values equal to work?

Most people indicate that they prefer to have more time for work and less time for leisure.[2] We are a work-oriented society. The more education, the higher the individual places work in his value system.

The term *leisure time* is ambiguous because nonwork hours may often be designated to preparation for work (the teacher reading journal articles as background for class discussion) or in recuperation from the fatigue of work so that the time is not "free" for another activity. Community activities that grow out of one's employment situation may take up part of the nonwork time.[3] Participation on mental-health committees is one example.

Social policy toward leisure has important implications for workers in middle years as they guage the number of years before retirement. Shortening workdays or increasing vacation time will have an impact on adults throughout the life-span.

Seen from a larger perspective, an assessment of potential leisure time could suggest a national policy of continuing adult education, with some concept of sabbatical renewal and educational leave. It could raise the possibility of tremendous manpower resources that could be directed in volunteer or "compulsory" (legal or social/psychological) Vista-type human-service

[1] J. M. Kreps, "The Allocation of Leisure in Retirement," in *The Retirement Process,* ed. F. M. Carp (Washington, D.C.: U.S. Government Printing Office, 1966).

[2] E. Pfeiffer and G. C. Davis, "The Use of Leisure in Middle Life," *The Gerontologist* 11 (1971, Part 1), 3:187–195.

[3] J. R. Kelly, "Work and Leisure: A Simplified Paradigm," *Journal of Leisure Research* 4 (1972), 1:50–62.

12–2 *Many ages and types of activity are involved in leisure. (a, University for Man, Manhattan, Kansas, photo; b, Kansas State University Student Publications photo; c, University for Man, Manhattan, Kansas, photo; d, RSVP, Manhattan, Kansas, photo)*

b.

a.

c.

d.

programs. At present the attitudes toward volunteer service are something less than positive. It is reflected in the generally ineffective way in which volunteers are used: there is little selection, training, supervision, or recognition of volunteers as responsible workers. Many more responsible roles could be assumed by volunteers with better planning. However, the prevailing implicit feeling, that worthwhile work must be recognized by remuneration prevents both the potential volunteer and community agencies from entering wholeheartedly into a team relationship.

Increased nonwork time will have an effect on adults' involvement in family and work. Consider these examples: the wife of a retired worker lamenting about how difficult it is to have her husband underfoot all day; the factory worker, already moonlighting with an evening job, taking on a third job for the long weekend as his factory goes to a four-day week. Kimmel suggests that Freud's answer to the question of what a normal person should be able to do may need to be rewritten: the marks of the mature person are the ability to love, to work, and to *leisure*.[4]

Increasing attention in research is given to the use of senior centers as two different points of view develop.[5] One view, the social agency model, conceptualizes senior centers as programs designed to meet the needs of the elderly, which will be most likely used by the poor and the disengaged. The other view, the voluntary organization model, conceptualizes that participants in senior centers will also be active in other community activities. Research is pointing to the need for a variety of centers to serve the needs of different subgroups.

The needed varitey of resources for creative leisure will reflect not only age levels but also ethnic, educational, and religious backgrounds. For example, there is an indication[6] that blacks 65 and older participate more actively in voluntary organizations than do comparable groups of whites. It is possible that part of this difference is due to the greater participation of aged blacks in church-related groups. Educational resources will be a primary consideration in planning for leisure and adult development throughout the life-span.

---

[4] D. C. Kimmel, *Adulthood and Aging* (New York: Wiley, 1975), p. 271.

[5] P. Taietz, "Two Conceptual Models of the Senior Center," *Journal of Gerontology* 31 (March 1976), 2:219–222.

[6] F. Clemente, P. A. Rexroad, and C. Hirsch, "The Participation of the Black Aged in Voluntary Associations," *Journal of Gerontology* 30 (July 1975), 4:460–472.

Education   As we come to have more time available, many of us will look to some form of education. Some will seek new skills for new careers; some will seek an opportunity to clarify and plan for the next steps and new aspects of life; others will pursue ideas and learning for their pure delight.

Every year nearly a third of the adults in this country who are not full-time students engage in some form of continuing education.[7] Study programs are sponsored by universities, churches, labor unions, employers, public schools, libraries, and community centers. The more education an individual has, the more likely he will be to participate in it. Only 10 per cent of persons with grade school education are involved in adult education, whereas 57 per cent of college graduates participate in it. By the 1990s we can expect the average education of people over 65 to reach that of high school graduation. As the national level of education increases, so will participation in adult education.[8]

The impact of the increasing time and educational interest of adults is changing the thrust of higher education. It is adapting itself toward a philosophy of lifelong learning. More classes are offered at hours and places con-

12–3 *Nearly a third of the adults in this country engage in some form of continuing education.* (*photo University for Man, Manhattan, Kansas*)

[7] R. J. Havighurst. *Aging in America: Implications for Education* (Washington, D.C.: The National Council on the Aging, 1976), p. 1.

[8] Ibid., p. 2.

venient for working adults. Continuing-education programs and community colleges are growing. Some universities are creating a top-level administrative position as Dean of Lifelong Learning to direct the varied resources of the university to include the adult learner as an important participant (Example 12–1).

Special programs such as women's centers, education for the elderly, preparation for retirement, and life-planning workshops are being established. Resources for counseling and guidance become increasingly important as

Example 12–1.
Mondale on
Lifetime
Learning

We now have zero population growth at one end of the spectrum . . . and a rapidly increasing number of older adults at the other end. This demands that our perception of the whole cycle of human life undergo a radical change. Bernice Neugarten has coined a useful phrase—the "young-old–—to describe what is really a new population group which deserves our attention. These are the people between 55 and 75 years old. As a group, they are getting healthier, and more educated. Many of them are technically retired. But they will increasingly demand more options for personal growth and community service. We have an obligation to provide opportunities to make the existence of Americans of every age meaningful.

I am personally excited and encouraged by a new movement which seems to address many of these needs we are discussing . . . the movement toward "lifetime learning." This is the idea that all of us . . .regardless of age . . . encounter throughout our lives a series of changing demands . . . and that we must shape education in its broadest sense to help us meet these needs.

At one stage of life, the need may be for retraining for a new job; at another stage we may require civic education—how to do our taxes, how to influence the political process. And at another time we may require education for what one distinguished educator has called "the free self"—that part of us and of our time which is not beholden to a job or to other requirements of subsistence.

I hope that somewhere in our massive educational establishment in Washington we can start to develop the capability of working toward this goal. We have incredible resources in HEW, in the Administration on Aging, in the National Institute of Education . . . the concept would be to introduce a "Lifetime Learning Act" which could become a part of the extension of major higher education and vocational education legislation.

From W. S. Mondale, "The Lifetime Learning Act: Proposed Legislation," *The Counseling Psychologist* 6 (1976), 1:67. Excerpts from remarks that Mondale delivered as senator at the Center for Research in Human Aging, Hunter College, New York, April 16, 1975.

more adults have occasion to make choices at the transition stages of life and as the concept of continued development becomes a part of the adult frame of reference.

ADULT COUNSELING.   The inevitability of role transformations occurring for men and women at different times throughout their lives provides the rationale for increasing resources in adult counseling.[9] There is also need for information to help adults in career changes and to help individuals to locate special services or to make life-planning decisions.[10]

Whereas professionals from many backgrounds may be involved in adult counseling, a case can be made for the manpower resource for counseling older people by older people themselves.[11] Peer group counseling has been found effective for certain kinds of situations.[12] Training programs for professionals and paraprofessionals[13] working with older adults must help the counselor to bring together an understanding of the helping relationship, an understanding of the processes of adult development, and an understanding of the counselor's own biases concerning aging.[14]

There are many kinds of education and counseling resources for facilitating adult development. They include formal academic classes, strength groups, continuing education, and family-life education. Note the intermingling of educational and personal support aspects in Example 12–2.

Family Life Education   An increasingly active form of adult education, known as family-life education, is being offered through a variety of community organizations. It is based on the premise that each new stage in the family life cycle requires new skills and new understandings.[15] Family-life education is usually offered in

[9] N. Schlossberg, "The Case for Counseling Adults," *The Counseling Psychologist* 6 (1976), 1:33–36.

[10] L. D. Schmidt, "Issues in Counseling Older People," *Educational Gerontology* 1 (April–June 1976), 2:187–192.

[11] S. L. Pressey, "Age Counseling: Crises, Services, Potentials," *Journal of Counseling Psychology* 20 (1973), 4:356–360; S. L. Pressey and A. D. Pressey, "Major Neglected Need Opportunity: Old Age Counseling," *Journal of Counseling Psychology* 19 (1972), 5:362–366.

[12] E. Waters, S. Fink, and B. White, "Peer Group Counseling for Older People," *Educational Gerontology* 1 (April–June 1976), 2:157–170.

[13] One half of the counselors in a study were considered "age-biased." L. Troll and N. Schlossberg, "How 'age-biased' Are College Counselors?" *Industrial Gerontology* (Summer 1971), pp. 14–20.

[14] J. Hartwig, "A Competency-based Approach to Adult Counseling and Guidance," *Counselor Education and Supervision* (September 1975), pp. 12–20.

[15] Report of the National Commission on Family Life Education, "Family Life Education Programs: Principles, Plans, Procedures," *The Family Coordinator* (July 1968), pp. 211–214.

Example 12–2.
Continuing
Education for
Women

To summarize briefly the highlights of our empirical findings so far: Women who participate in continuing education programs are an exceedingly diverse group that does not fit the stereotype of the bored housewife dabbling in a little culture. These women are serious, determined, and very frequently pragmatic in their goals. Those women who enter continuing education with a strong career orientation differ in many respects from the other participants: they express less traditional views about the role of women, are more supportive of the women's movement, and have more self-confidence. Although they are also more likely to be dissatisfied at home, their children and husbands are generally supportive of their work and educational activities. Practically all the women see their continuing education as being highly beneficial both personally and professionally. Many report profound changes in their self-concepts. Although only a minority of these women could be labeled activists, they are uniformly supportive of the women's movement and see it as a positive force in their lives.

Whereas the women's movement has given women the freedom to "be," continuing education has provided the support and training that adult women need to develop their talents and to acquire skills that enable them to enter or reenter the labor market. The same might be said about other campus efforts, such as women's studies, women's centers, and programmatic research.

The very existence of these programs provides a psychological boost to a woman considering venturing from her home. The programs are proof that she is not alone and that she will be meeting and attending classes with women in similar positions with similar concerns. The programs indicate that, as an adult, she can go to college or begin a career; others like her have done it successfully.

The programs offered by continuing education are strongly based on the job market and organized to develop skills for competent performance. Most provide skill-oriented courses, as well as liberal arts curricula, to meet the diverse needs and interests expressed by their clients. Counseling and career guidance play key roles in the educational process.

From H. S. Astin, "Continuing Education and the Development of Adult Women," *The Counseling Psychologist* 6 (1976), 1:59–60.

workshops or a short series of meetings directed toward aspects of family life. Concepts derived from research in family life and behavioral science form the basis of the experiential-type classes.

Family-life education may be offered through church groups, PTA groups, extension and continuing-education classes, mental health and family service centers, public health departments, and some pediatric and medical centers. The classes follow the stages and developmental tasks of adult life. Community agencies are beginning to work together to develop community-wide programs.[16,17] The following are illustrative of topics in such programs.

Preparation for Marriage Classes provide an orientation to the roles and responsibilities of marriage. Such courses usually include information on family planning, genetic counseling, budgeting, as well as skill experiences in communication.

Parent-Child Relationship Classes may begin in prenatal days, preparing expectant parents for infant care. They provide parents an opportunity to consider the adjustments required by a third person in their life. The sequences of parenting classes will consider characteristics of children at different age levels. Classes will focus on skills required for assisting children with different tasks. Discipline and creativity are illustrative of the topics considered for parents of school-age children. Drugs and sex education are illustrative of discussion with parents of adolescents.

Marital Enrichment Classes are increasingly popular offerings that provide husbands and wives opportunities to review the quality of their marriage and to develop new skills and goals.

Singles groups focus on different areas including the adjustments of divorced persons, widows, and single parents.

Family Strength Groups may either focus on helping families look at roles, responsibilities, goals, and ways of communicating; or they may be groups that bring together eight to fifteen persons from two or more living units who form a family-type relationship.

Life Planning Groups deal with new roles and ways of self-expression for men as well as women. They help people prepare for retirement, for second careers, for new forms of leisure.

Life Stages Groups may consider roles of grandparents and roles of middle-aged persons with parents in old age; they may consider characteristics of aging; some may consider alternative forms of living for the elderly. Not only do the elderly need the opportunity to consider their experiences, but also their families need the opportunity to consider what effect the older person's aging will have in their lives.

[16] C. E. Kennedy and J. Southwick, "Inservice Program for Family Life Educators: Cooperative Program with Mental Health Centers and University" *The Family Coordinator* (January 1975), 1:75–79.

[17] R. H. Jewson, executive director of the National Council on Family Relations, reviewed a number of cooperative community programs in "Trends and Resources for Community Family Life Education Programs," a paper presented to the annual meeting of the American Home Economics Association, 1976, Minneapolis.

Death Education. This is an area that has moved rapidly in recent years to form its own discipline. There is at least one professional organization of death educators. The *Omega* is a journal publishing literature dealing with the art of death education. The goals of death education are to help individuals give expression to the many kinds of emotions and attitudes they experience in relation to the death of a family member or another loved one. This also involves the individual's clarifying the meaning of his own life and eventual death. Helping parents and teachers to know how to assist children to deal with death is also a goal of these programs. Death education is usually a part of the preparation curriculum for persons working in nursing homes and caring for the terminally ill.

Housing   Where we live and the security of our living space is vital to our freedom to grow. More than two thirds of all older Americans, however extensive or limited their other assets, own their own homes. Many older persons and others on fixed or limited incomes face the prospect of losing their homes as property taxes increase. Alternative approaches are being considered to deal with this problem. Some states provide refunds on property taxes that exceed a fixed percentage of income. Other approaches suggest that the Federal government reimburse states up to half the tax refunded on the basis of income. There are also plans to provide tax refunds to owners of rental property so that the elderly and persons on limited income can find suitable housing.

Communities and nonpublic ventures through churches, unions, and business firms are sponsoring various approaches to housing for adults with special needs as alternatives to the congregating of the elderly poor in run-down inner-city hotels. The Housing and Community Development Act provides for direct Federal loans to groups sponsoring housing for the elderly and the handicapped. It provides that units be rented at a maximum of 25 per cent of the income of the eligible tenants.

Adequate housing stands first among the needs of the elderly, and is basic to whatever each older person may choose to do in the pursuit of happiness. There is great variety among the arrangements.[18] Many continue to live in their own homes. Some have need for handyman assistance with yard work or minor home repairs. Some need a housekeeper to come in periodically to

---

[18] F. M. Carp, "User Evaluation of Housing for the Elderly," *The Gerontologist* 16 (April 1976), 2:102–111; R. Newcomer et al., "Assessing the Need for Semi-Dependent Housing for the Elderly," *The Gerontologist* 16 (April 1976), 2: 112–117.

help with cleaning and home management. Both types of assistance are difficult to obtain. Programs are being developed through combined efforts of labor, health, social rehabilitation, and aging departments to make this form of home-care service available within the financial limits of the elderly. In some instances the young-old retired persons can find meaningful opportunities to continue their usefulness through part-time employment in these programs.

Some persons have the financial resources and personal interests to move into retirement villages. These may be communities of mobile homes or any number of variations of apartment and small-home arrangements. Services vary also within the community from minimal grounds maintenance to complete food and health care.

Nursing Homes

A form of housing for the elderly that has received a disproportionate amount of publicity has been nursing homes. Whereas only 5 per cent of the elderly are in nursing homes at any one time, 20 to 25 per cent will spend some time in a nursing home (Example 12–3).

It is easy to be confused as to the different types of care provided in institutions identified as long-term-care facilities. There are three types: Extended

Example 12–3.
The Nursing
Home
Population

The Moss Senate Subcommittee report in 1974 showed the average age of the one million residents of nursing homes to be 82. Only 10 per cent are married; 50 per cent have no living relatives or no direct relationship with a distant relative.

Seventy per cent of the residents are women; 96 per cent are white. Sixty to 80 per cent are poor, although they may not have been when they entered old age, and have been on public assistance or the Federal Supplemental Security Income Program. About 85 per cent of those persons who enter nursing homes die there, and the average length of stay is 1.1 years. One third of all residents admitted die within the first year, another third live up to three years. The lack of counseling preparation and orientation for admission into a nursing home contributes to the high mortality rate.

Adapted from F. Moss, "Nursing Home Care in the United States: Failure in Public Policy," Subcommittee Report on Long-term Care of the Aged. (Washington, D.C.: U.S. Government Printing Office, 1975), p. xii; and from R. N. Butler, *Why Survive? Being Old in America* (New York: Harper & Row, 1975), p. 267.

Care Facility (ECF), Skilled Nursing Home (SNH), Intermediate Care Facility (ICF). The ECF is in reality an arm of the hospital. It provides a continuation of the nursing care the patient received in the hospital. There is a limit to the length of time the patient can remain in the ECF. SNH also provides considerable nursing care. There is no time limit on the length of stay and a patient may come into the SNH without first having been in a hospital.

Persons living in an ICF are referred to as residents. They do not need extensive nursing care but do need more care than their family or other community arrangements can provide. Personal care, simple nursing care, and intermittent nursing care are the services under the jurisdiction of ICFs. It is ICFs that most people have in mind when thinking of nursing homes.[19]

There are many problems associated with the development of nursing home services (see Example 12–4). A large part is that it is expensive to provide these services and most persons receiving the services are poor. Confu-

Example 12–4.
Administering a
Nursing Home

There are frequently many regulatory bodies which set standards and regulations for nursing home care. These include departments of health, departments of welfare, and often departments of education as they are associated with staff training. In most states there are also nursing home associations which promote standards and philosophy of treatment. The complexity of the situation in which nursing homes find themselves contributes to a variety of problems in regard to: staffing, meeting regulatory standards, and providing training for nursing home personnel. In the midst of all this there is a danger that the personal, social, psychological, as well as physical needs of the elderly residents themselves may be lost in the storm of concern over administrative issues and the desires to upgrade medical care.

There is a major problem of turnover of nursing home staff. In 1973 there was a 71 per cent turnover rate among registered nurses and a 75 per cent turnover rate of aides and orderlies.

Efforts to correct medical and safety deficiencies in nursing homes has resulted in a hospital-like atmosphere in many homes. Efforts are now being directed toward improving the quality of personal life. In most states activities directors are a required part of the staff to develop programs aimed at restoring and/or maintaining social abilities of residents.

Adapted from R. N. Butler, *Why Survive? Being Old in America* (New York: Harper & Row, 1975), Chapter 9.

[19] R. N. Butler, *Why Survive? Being Old in America* (New York: Harper & Row, 1975), pp. 269–270.

sion also exists concerning placement in and regulation of the homes. A study conducted by Brandeis University's Levinson Gerontological Policy Institute found that among 100 persons in Massachusetts nursing homes

37 needed full-time nursing care;
26 needed minimal supervised "living";
23 could get along at home with periodic home visits by nurses;
14 needed nothing.[20]

Many persons are in nursing homes lacking alternatives or lacking clarity in planning for their care. When we project our thinking in terms of what would be the ideal form of care for old people, we have to think of two issues: "How could the present nursing home facilities be better," and "How can our communities provide better alternatives than nursing homes for some of the elderly."

Robert Butler has suggested some of the qualities he would like to see in an "ideal" nursing home. Some of his suggestions are as follows:

The nursing home should avoid the hospital or motel atmosphere and create a homelike atmosphere with many ties into the community. Providing a sanctuary when rest is needed, it should have the physical and staff means to assist the resident to maintain an active life in the community. Counselors and other educational staff would help residents to continue creative, business, human-service, and educational activities.

The nursing home would be a base of operation, not a place of confinement. The focus of the nursing home's activities should be toward the community outside and not solely toward "inpatient care." Services such as physical therapy and other health-care resources could be provided by the nursing home for the elderly living in their own homes or in "supervised" apartments housing several elderly persons.

The nursing home should be part of an integrated human-service complex that would provide outreach services into the community for older residents. It would also be actively involved in health maintenance of those living in the home and would have ready access to hospital resources as these become necessary.[21]

---

[20] Prepared by Levinson Gerontological Policy Institute, Brandeis University, *Alternatives to Nursing Home Care: A proposal,* U.S. Senate Special Committee on Aging (Washington, D.C.: U.S. Government Printing Office, 1971).

[21] Butler, *Why Survive?,* Chapter 9.

12–4 (*photo University for Man, Manhattan, Kansas*)

SPECIAL PERSONNEL.   In order to help the elderly maintain as nearly a normal life as possible, special kinds of human-service personnel have been suggested. One proposal[22] has been a National Personal Care Corps of case aides, homemakers, home-health aids, and visiting nurses to provide services that will help individuals remain in their own homes. It is interesting to compare our present resources for home care and services with those in Scandinavia where the emphasis is on staying at home rather than going to an institution. Denmark has one home aid for every 87 old people, Norway one for every 176, Sweden one for every 320, and the United States one for every 4,766.[23]

Alternative Forms of Housing

Many factors contribute to the congregating of individuals in neighborhoods according to age levels, among them, socioeconomic conditions, ethnic identities, and a sense of rootedness in home communities.[24]

There are individuals who avoid close involvement with many persons,

[22] Ibid., pp. 297–298.

[23] W. P. Randel, "America in the World," *American Issues Forum* (Washington, D.C.: The National Council on the Aging, 1976).

[24] B. W. Smith and J. Hiltner, "Intraurban Location of the Elderly," *Journal of Gerontology* 30 (July 1975), 4:473–478.

particularly with persons differing in age from themselves; however, most people prefer to have the opportunity to interact with persons of several age levels. True, youth tend to congregate with youth, older people with older people, and young families with young families. The common interests and similar life-sytles attract this grouping.[25] The problem comes when groupings are formed in such ways that interaction among them is difficult—and here housing has an influence.

The task is to formulate modes of community living in which some separate congregating of age groups is possible and at the same time interaction among them is encouraged—perhaps necessitated. Shared facilities are one way. Community planning and programing that builds on the exchange of services and needs that each age group offers will, of course, be a crucial factor. This will require some modification of popular attitudes about work and leisure, and about education and age.

There has been a tendency to think of education, work, and leisure as occurring in sequence and that the sequence is education in youth, work in middle life, and leisure in old age. This must be changed if we are to develop successful programs involving older persons providing services for the younger, and the younger providing services for older people.

NEW COMMUNITIES.   Experiments with "new communities" are attempting to develop the physical and social arrangements for improved communication among people. Such experiments need to extend our concept of work to include a wider array of human services. We must discover ways to include among the human-service manpower many of the people we have heretofore excluded from the labor force—the young and the old. We must utilize different levels of competence, such as the handicapped, and different periods of service, such as part-time work and short-term assignments.

Our communities need to provide the physical arrangements that encourage participation of intergenerational groups in shared recreational and health activities, such as folk dancing, hiking, bicycling, lawn games, and gardening. The tendency toward forced age segregation needs to be alleviated. It is no more constructive than is segregation according to race, religion, or social class.[26] Ours is a pluralistic society. The richness of our heri-

---

[25] J. Jacobs, *Fun City: An Ethnographic Study of a Retirement Community* (New York: Holt, Rinehart and Winston, 1974). Jacobs raises significant questions about the rationale used in planning separate communities for retired persons.

[26] Butler, *Why Survive?,* p. 404.

a.

12–5 *Many persons enjoy participating in activities with individuals from other age groups. (a, Kansas State University Student Publications photo; b, Kathleen Ward, photographer)*

b.

tage lies in our heterogenity. We grow as we contribute to one another's lives, as we learn from one another. Younger generations need the models of the lives of their elders. Their sense of identity comes from these roots; their sense of hope and affirmation of life come from knowing experientially what people are like in older years and how they deal with those years.

Older parents, after they move into retirement communities, usually continue to interact with younger family members. The amount of help and friendship networks that are established seems to vary considerably in different retirement communities. However, the number of friendship ties in the community does not seem to influence the involvement older persons have with other family members.[27]

Public Relations   An analysis of the elderly in adolescent fiction found them to be unimportant people—bit players. They were neither good nor bad, but rather, people who inhabited the fringes of the plot.[28]

The prejudice of ageism has come about through a variety of factors, including lack of adequate information concerning the experiences and characteristics of old people. Inadequate information contributes to prevailing negative stereotypes. Changing the public image about aging is an issue that can be addressed directly through improved public relations and through education of persons of all ages.

At present, ageism with its discrimination and stereotyping has placed the elderly in the status of a minority group. It is important to help the elderly avoid the negative attributes of defensiveness and despair that are natural in such situations. It is important also to emphasize the heterogenity of the elderly. However, having recognized the dangers, we then acknowledge the value of the coming movement among the elderly toward distinguishing themselves as a group. There is value in helping society to recognize their potential as new consumers and new voters.

NEW CONSUMERS.   Thus far, industry has not begun to recognize the vast new market present among the elderly, who are experiencing the most rapid growth of any segment of society. There is considerable reciprocal benefit

---

[27] S. R. Sherman, "Mutual Assistance and Support in Retirement Housing," *Journal of Gerontology* 30 (July 1975), 4:479–483.

[28] D. A. Peterson and E. L. Karnes, "Older People in Adolescent Literature," *The Gerontologist* 16 (June 1976), 3:225–231; C. Aronoff, "Old Age in Prime Time," *Journal of Communication* 24 (1974), 4.

for the elderly and for industry to recognize this untapped pool of purchasers. As industry begins to study the needs and ways to develop saleable products for this new consumer group, the industry will also begin to identify and promote its positive aspects. Older persons will be needed for consultation and for sales and promotion work. Among the more than 20 million elderly there are, to be sure, victims of poverty and illness. But there are also millions financially sound and able to purchase items they consider worthwhile. The stereotype of the aging as helpless, incapable of good judgment, and poor credit risks can be broken. It is proposed that not only would old people benefit from new products, but also new jobs would be created, helping to diminish resentment toward the old. This is but one illustration of the mutual benefit of incorporating the elderly into society. Similar observations concerning the "industry" of education could be made in the recognition of the elderly as potential students.

NEW VOTERS.   The more than 20 million people over 65 represent a substantial group of voters. The elderly also can expect to find support for their cause among younger people. In 1974, eight out of ten younger persons and seven out of ten older persons said there was need for concerted action to improve conditions for people over 65. About a fifth of both old and young said they would surely join such a group for action on issues affecting the elderly, another fifth said they probably would, and half said that even though they would not be joiners they would support the goals of such a group.[29] This sort of interest can have significant impact on public policy.

Public Policy and Aging[30]   "Equality of rights under the law shall not be denied or abridged by the United States or by any State on account of *age*." This is not a part of the Constitution at the time of this writing. Except for the last word, it is identical to the 27th Ammendment affording equality of the sexes. It is an issue being promoted by many persons concerned with facilitating the continued development of adults throughout the entire spectrum of life. Changes in at-

---

[29] L. Harris and associates, *The Myth and Reality of Aging in America* (Washington, D.C.: The National Council on the Aging, 1975), pp. 230–231.

[30] Some of the material for this section was drawn from papers prepared for the American Issues Forum by Professor W. R. Randel under the auspices of The National Council on the Aging. Nine articles prepared by Randel were distributed to 2,000 newspapers across the country to facilitate dialogue. They are available from The National Council on the Aging, Washington, D.C.

titudes, behaviors, and resources come about through involvement in local activities and study of local situations, and through legislative programs.

Congress has expressed its awareness of some of the disadvantages experienced by the elderly and has moved toward making some correction of those situations. Medicare, the medical insurance program, was added to Social Security in 1965. In that same year the Older Americans Act established within the Department of Health, Education and Welfare an Administration on Aging that makes grants for special services. In 1972 an amendment to this act provided for meals for the needy aged. Other important congressional measures have included the addition of a cost-of-living adjustment to Social Security, establishment of Federal minimums for old-age assistance, protection for individuals in private pension plans, and authorization of Federal loans for housing for the elderly.

Legislation involving aging has suffered from the lack of adequate information and the tendency to operate in response to crisis rather than in terms of developmental planning. Lawmakers have debated the issue of whether to deal with the aged on a categorical basis—singling them out for special consideration—or whether to plan for them as part of a larger generic population. There has also been a tendency to deal with specific aspects of the life of the aged—for example, health care or income—rather than plan for the total life of an individual. Often the practicalities of a political situation or of a social era have dictated such dichotomies. One analysis of our nation's approach to public policy offered the following summary:

> We are suggesting that given the resultant stalemates of the dilemmas created by categorical versus generic approaches, holistic versus segmented programming, current political context versus future planning designs, and crisis versus rational planning, aging legislation has been caught in a morass of conflicting and competing interests and issues. The result of these fragmented approaches is that in most cases involving major aging legislation, policy makers have abdicated moral responsibility by passing laws based on flimsy and often inaccurate data. At the same time, researchers in the field of gerontology have all but ceased to provide any current data useful for drafting legislation. They have often despaired over being able to influence the policy process.[31]

Work toward a national policy on aging and closer involvement of researchers in the field of gerontology will help to create more effective planning. The continued interest and political involvement of all persons con-

---

[31] P. A. Kerschner and I. S. Hirschfield, "Public Policy and Aging: Analytic Approaches," in *Aging,* eds. D. S. Woodruff and J. E. Birren (New York: Van Nostrand, 1975), p. 357.

cerned with aging are necessary to stimulate the kind of public awareness that is needed for effective public policy.

A Look at the Future

The Public   We have thus far in this chapter been discussing some of the issues to be dealt with by society to facilitate effective adult development. Let us now consider briefly some of the possible directions social and professional changes may take in the coming years.

One optimistic prediction regarding the field of aging is that in the next 25 years there will be (1) a shift of political philosophy (as great as that from Hoover to Roosevelt) that will allow aging and the aged an equitable share in national resources; (2) the enunciation of a clear national policy for the field of aging; (3) a voting block of individuals who consider themselves to be old that will support legislation for persons in the later stages of life; and (4) a declaration by the Supreme Court stating that compulsory retirement at a fixed age is unconstitutional.[32] Although the editor of the journal that published the prediction took issue with the conclusions, he strongly encouraged gerontologists to project their sights into the future.[33]

As we look into the future, we can anticipate an increasing proportion of our population to be older adults (by 2020 the over-65 group will have doubled the twenty million of 1970), who will have a greater awareness and be much more active. The fact that increasing numbers of older persons will be planning on pensions supported by an increasingly smaller work force—according to present arrangement—means that this impending "crunch" is heading for some serious political consideration.[34]

Whereas we can anticipate aging to be a featured topic on the political agenda, to what extent can we expect the elderly to exercise an influence? Studies[35,36] indicate that older persons are very interested in politics. Where there is a lack of participation, it has usually been associated with low socio-

[32] D. A. Peterson, C. Powell, and L. Robertson, "Aging in America: Toward the Year 2000," *The Gerontologist* 16 (June 1976), 3:264.

[33] Ibid., "Editor's Note," p. 270.

[34] N. E. Cutler and J. R. Schmidhauser, "Age and Political Behavior," in *Aging,* eds. Woodruff and Birren, p. 399.

[35] S. Verba and N. H. Nie, *Participation in America* (New York: Harper & Row, 1972).

[36] N. D. Glenn and M. Grimes, "Aging, Voting and Political Interest," *American Sociological Review* 33 (1968), pp. 563–575.

economic status. Level of education[37] is also an important factor in political participation. In 1950 the ratio of over-65 persons with a high school education was one to four; in the year 2000 this ratio will be reversed. These same persons, who will become 65 in the year 2000, as youth will have been involved in, and supportive of, political activity. The increasing number and vitality of organizations such as the National Caucus of the Black Aged, National Council of Senior Citizens, Gray Panthers, and American Association of Retired Persons serve to stimulate an age consciousness and subjective age identity,[38] we therefore can anticipate an active influence from older adults in the future political deliberations on aging.

The Profession

We have observed that our nation's population profile is changing toward greater proportions of persons in the adult years. Accompanying this population change is an increased interest in study of the aging process. Some professional groups have developed position papers with recommendations for social policy, program development, and career training for increasing numbers of persons whose clientele will be individuals moving through different stages of adult life.

Significant research in adult development and aging is being carried forward in such disciplines as anthropology, architecture, developmental psychology, economics, health-care services, home economics, population research sociology, town planning, and in a variety of educational, medical research, and family service settings.[39] Aging is being recognized as an important area of social concern both nationally and internationally.

In an address to the tenth International Congress on Gerontology, Ethel Shanas observed, "Just as the 1960s saw the emergence and legitimation of research on family planning, the environment, and women, the 1970s have seen the emergence of social research on aging as a legitimate and even necessary topic for investigation. There has been a general recognition that middle age and old age have unique features which must be studied and understood for themselves just as adolescence and childhood are studied for themselves . . . The General Assembly of the United Nations, reflecting the

[37] L. W. Milbrath, *Political Participation* (Chicago: Rand McNally, 1965).

[38] V. L. Bengtson and N. E. Cutler, "Generations and Inter-generational Relations in Contemporary Society," in *Handbook of Aging and the Social Sciences,* eds. E. Shanas and R. Binstock. (New York: Van Nostrand, 1976), p. 155.

[39] E. Shanas, "Gerontology and the Social and Behavioral Sciences: Where Do We Go From Here?" *The Gerontologist* 15 (December 1975), 6:499–502.

concern of both the developed and developing countries, [has] requested the Secretary-General to prepare a report on the conditions and needs of the elderly."[40]

The establishment in 1974 of a National Institute of Aging within the National Institutes of Health pointed to a mark of national recognition for the special concerns of the middle-aged and older sectors of our society. One of the members of the American Psychological Association's Task Force on Aging commented on the future of the study of aging as follows:

> As one views the year 2000 with reference to the problems of the aged, it becomes quite clear that a larger and larger proportion of voters, consumers, and men of leisure as well as workers will be drawn from the age group beyond 65. What can one say that has not already been said regarding the changes this shift in population will bring? It will be as great if not greater than the shift from rural to urban centers, and its impact on education, industry, health, and business can only be guessed. How to prepare to serve such a tremendous population is a crucial issue.[41]

High on the list of priorities recommended by the APA Task Force was the development of a wide range of adult education programs. Needed in such programs of lifelong learning are retraining for second careers, opportunities for enrichment, and keeping up with recent advances and leisure skills. Some adults want training to raise their career goals or to maintain their present occupational status.[42]

As there is increased awareness of needs for services for adults throughout the life-span, there will also be an increased need for persons with an understanding of the processes of adult development and aging. There are different approaches to the training. Some gerontology programs are based in one department or discipline, such as psychology, sociology, or home economics. Some programs are interdisciplinary, preparing students from a wide range of disciplines—architecture, public administration, and nursing, for example—to have a gerontological orientation.

The variety of "urgent topics" for research by future gerontologists is staggering. The list could include study of roles for the retired, the widowed,

---

[40] Ibid., p. 499.

[41] J. Zubin, "Foundations of Gerontology: History, Training, and Methodology," in *The Psychology of Adult Development and Aging,* eds. C. Eisdorfer and M. P. Lawton (Washington D.C.: American Psychological Association, 1973), p. 10.

[42] C. Eisdorfer and M. P. Lawton, "Recommendations to the White House Conference on Aging: APA Task Force on Aging," in *The Psychology of Adult Development and Aging,* p. ix.

and the dying person, and study of roles for the four-generation family and the sequential family. The effects of new health and educational techniques such as biofeedback and mediation are another area of study, as is the evaluation of approaches to counseling for second careers and counseling to protect citizens against fraud and confidence games. We will need to understand more about differences in the aging of men and women and about differences among ethnic groups. More basically, we must proceed toward the clarification of the theory of adult development and aging.

It is encouraging to note that research scientists are located both in centers for the study of aging and in a wide range of campuses and agencies throughout the nation. Leadership reflects both male and female influence. (Example 12–5). As we noted earlier, an analysis of articles appearing in *The*

Example 12–5.
Women and Socio-gerontology

An overview of the social and behavioral science disciplines within the broad area of aging indicates that women have played a significant role in the emergence of the field and in the development of a body of knowledge within that field. The reasons for this are varied—perhaps because the area of aging is a relatively new one and hence more open to members of minority categories, or perhaps because it is a socially appropriate one for women to enter because it has affective caring implications. Women have had opportunities to enter into and become prominent in this field more than in the traditional ones. In fact, it would appear that women may be given more recognition among professionals in the social and behavioral areas of gerontology than within their own home institutions. As we examine the development of the Gerontological Society, we find that women have served as presidents of the Society, as chairpersons, spokeswomen, presidents of sections, or as other important officials of the organization. Their occupancy of such positions was rarely, if ever, as "Tokes," but rather as the result of well-deserved acknowledgement and recognition of their commitments to the general interdisciplinary area of gerontology. Two were winners of the Kleemeir Award and all are ovinal thinkers. They are, if not by age, then certainly by virtue of their contributions, our foremothers.

. . . Their contributions have been . . . with reference to pure research, applied aspects, and political implications. They have called attention to a broad picture of aging as well as some of the specific differences between men and women in patterns of aging . . .

From M. M. Seltzer, "Women and Sociogerontology," *The Gerontologist* 15 (December 1975), 6:483–484.

Gerontologist showed one third of the material coming from the twenty leading institutional sources; two thirds came from other sources with considerable input from young professionals working in gerontology.[43]

The prevalence of undergraduate courses[44] in adult development and aging will be increased to provide better general education, thus correcting negative images and erroneous information concerning aging. Undergraduate courses and possible courses in high school will be opportunities for recruiting young people into the career field of gerontology. Courses in gerontology will also form an important part of the training programs of paraprofessional personnel in community programs of health, recreation, and social services (Example 12–6).

In the applied field there will be need for gerontology teachers at all levels—from elementary and high school to vocational and community college to university and graduate centers. Professionals trained in gerontology

Example 12–6.
Training in
Gerontology

> Within this period [the past two years] the acceptance of gerontology as a teaching subject by universities and other higher education institutions has multiplied. Within this time frame the importance of transmitting gerontological knowledge to a growing body of interested undergraduate and graduate students as well as the active clinician has increasingly become recognized.
>
> Because the fundamental purpose of post-secondary education institutions (universities, four-year colleges and two-year institutions) is the development and transmission of knowledge, every opportunity should be made available for the transmission of this knowledge to current and forthcoming practitioners to learn about the processes of aging. These kinds of knowledge are basic to planning and practice and their evaluation. Such education programs should be available on at least three levels: (a) long-term education, (b) short-term training, (c) continuing education . . . To help make this possible, it is suggested that each state be covered by an umbrella of higher education institutions capable of providing both care knowledge and skill expertise in aging.
>
> From J. Kaplan, "The New Age of Old Age," *The Gerontologist* 15 (December 1975), 6:485.

[43] J. D. Rasch, "Institutional Origins of Articles in *The Gerontologist: 1961–1975*," The *Gerontologist* 16 (June 1976), 3:276–279.

[44] For a helpful description of such a program, see I. M. Hulicka and J. B. Morganti, "An Undergraduate Concentration in the Psychology of Aging: Approach, Program and Evaluation," *Educational Gerontology* 1 (April–June 1976), 2:107–118.

will be needed in educational and career counseling as well as in family service and mental health centers. Nursing homes and medical centers will require that their nutrition, recreation, and activity personnel have backgrounds in adult development and aging.

Summary

Our increasing appreciation of the factors influencing adult development is having exciting implications in all sectors of society. We are formulating considerations about the meaning of time as we have longer lives and shorter work periods. Because our use of time is associated with our identity, the legislation and community attitudes affecting work and leisure are vital to the morale. The meaning of leisure relates to development of programs of lifelong learning and to the rethinking of the significance of volunteer and paid employment.

Continuing education will have an important impact on the form of higher education. Also, we can anticipate that programs of family-life education will increase as continuing growth and development come to be an *expected* experience throughout adult life. More time for volunteer work and second careers and the relating of life goals to the total range of human relationships will necessitate development of additional resources for adult counseling and guidance.

Arrangements for housing influence our ability to render services and relate to members of different generational groups. Alternative and experimental approaches to housing are being developed. Individuals with handicapping conditions require special arrangements and the enterprise of nursing homes or other care-giving institutions can be expected to receive new planning in the years ahead. Only 5 per cent of the elderly live in nursing homes, and their situation requires improvement. However, some older persons in nursing homes could live elsewhere, and many presently at home could have their quality of life significantly improved with development of more services arranged for their needs.

The increasing size and activity of an older population will make aging an important topic in political considerations, possibly leading to the development of a national policy on aging. Industry and other segments of society can also be expected to recognize consumer potential among the older adult sector.

The study of adult development and aging is one of the newer and most rapidly growing professions. Future training can be expected for the development of professional gerontologists, for the development of gerontological emphasis within other professions, and for the development of paraprofessionals and volunteers in a wide range of human services. An understanding of adult development can become also an important part of general and public school education.

Suggested Activities and Further Reading

1. Find out from the admissions offices of schools in your community the percentage of students in middle adult, maturity, and old age. Make a calendar of continuing-education activities, workshops, short courses, and conferences scheduled for the coming month.

2. Interviews with women students over 30 indicated that homemaking and college study are satisfying multiple goals for many women. (R. Hoeflin, E. Pickett, and L. Folland, "College: the Dual-Role Testing Ground," College of Home Economics, Agricultural Experiment Station Research, paper 2-J-76, Kansas State University, Manhattan, Kansas, 66506). Have a panel of older women students discuss their expectations, satisfactions, and special needs as college students.

3. The section "Symposium—Educational Intervention and Gerontology," in *The Gerontologist* 15 (October 1975, Part 1, 5:423–451), contains papers relating continuing education to the developmental needs of middle and later adult life, suggesting that the adult learner will force new modes of instruction and new goals upon higher education. For a discussion of *andragogy,* see M. S. Knowles, *The Modern Practice of Adult Education, Andragogy Versus Pedagogy* (New York: Association Press, 1970).

4. Have a panel discussion on retirement and leisure, presenting different aspects of the meaning of leisure and the pros and cons of retirement. For background, see A. H. Olmstead, *Threshold: The First Days of Retirement* (New York: Harper & Row, 1975); and R. C. Atchley, *The Social Factors in Later Life* (Belmont, Calif.: Wadsworth, 1972), Chapters 9, 10.

5. Observe in the different community centers serving older people—for example, senior centers, congregate eating programs, Retired Senior Volunteer Program, transportation programs, nursing homes—and share your observations with the class.

6. Bring in resource people from the community to dissuss alternative approaches to institutional care for the elderly. See several articles in *The Gerontologist* 14 (February 1974), 1, for ideas; see also Shura Saul's *Aging: An Album of People Growing Old* (New York: Wiley, 1974), for perceptive vignettes of aging persons.

7. Have people who cope successfully with different stress situations share with the class their approach and perspective. Have class members bring accounts from literature and observation, for example, J. R. Phillips, "How I Cope with Sickle Cell Anemia," *Ebony* 31 (February 1976), 4:104–112; E. G. Valens, *The Other Side of the Mountain* (New York: Warner Paperback, 1975); C. L. Sanders, "Quincy Jones Talks About Life and Death," *Ebony* 31 (March 1976), 5:133–138; J. Eareckson and J. Musser, *Joni* (Grand Rapids; Zondervan, 1976).

8. Assemble a resource file of information on further training and career opportunities in gerontology: (1) interview persons in community with gerontological training; (2) collect or prepare job descriptions for different occupations with gerontological background; (3) write for brochures of gerontological curriculums and other training opportunities; (4) develop a file of gerontological related organizations and agencies; (5) find out about student membership in the Gerontological Society, the American Psychological Association—Division 20, the American Home Economics Association, the American Personnel and Guidance Association, and so on.

Bibliography

Adorno, T. W., E. Frenkel-Brunswik, D. J. Levinson, and R. N. Sanford. *The Authoritarian Personality.* New York: Harper & Row, 1950.

Agee, J. *Letters of James Agee to Father Flye.* New York: George Braziller, 1962.

Albee, E. *Who's Afraid of Virginia Woolf?* New York: Atheneum, 1961.

Allport, G. W. "Functional Autonomy of Motives." In *The Person in Psychology.* Boston: Beacon Press, 1968.

Alsop, S. *Newsweek* 83 (March 11, 1974), p. 92.

Alter, M. "Multiple Sclerosis and Climate." *World Neurology* 1 (1960), pp. 55–70.

Aronoff, C. "Old Age in Prime Time." *Journal of Communication* 24 (1974) 4.

Ashton-Warner, S. *Spinster.* New York: Simon and Schuster, 1960.

Astin, H. S. "Continuing Education and the Development of Adult Women." *The Counseling Psychologist* 6 (1976), 1:59–60.

Auerbach, C. *The Science of Genetics.* New York: Harper & Row, 1961.

Baltes, P. B., and G. J. Labouvie. "Adult Development of Intellectual Performance: Description, Explanation, and Modification." In *The Psychology of Adult Development and Aging,* eds. C. Eisdorfer and M. P. Lawton. Washington, D.C.: American Psychological Association, 1973.

Baltes, P. B., and K. W. Shaie, eds. *Life-Span Developmental Psychology: Personality and Socialization.* New York: Academic Press, 1973.

Becker, E. *The Denial of Death.* New York: Free Press, 1973.

Becker, H. S., and A. L. Strauss. "Careers, Personality and Adult Socialization." *Journal of American Sociology* 62 (1956), 3.

Bekker, L. D., and C. Taylor. "Attitudes Toward the Aged in A Multi-generational Sample." *Journal of Gerontology* 21 (1966), pp. 115–118.

Bellow, S. *Humboldt's Gift.* New York: Viking Press, 1975.

Bellucci, G., and W. J. Hoyer. "Feedback Effects on the Performance and Self-Reinforcing Behavior of Elderly and Young Adult Women." *Journal of Gerontology* 30 (July 1974), 4:456–460.

Benedict, R. *Patterns of Culture.* New York: Mentor Books, 1934.

Bengtson, V. L. "Generation and Family Effects in Value Socialization." *American Sociological Review* 40 (June 1975), pp. 358–371.

Bengtson, V. L., and N. E. Cutler. "Generations and Inter-generational Relations in Contemporary Society." In *Handbook of Aging and the Social Sciences,* eds. E. Shanas and R. Binstock. New York: Van Nostrand, 1976.

Bengtson, V. L., and D. Haber. "Sociological Approaches to Aging." In *Aging,* eds. D. S. Woodruff and J. E. Birren. New York: Van Nostrand, 1975.

Bengtson, V. L., P. L. Kasschau, and P. K. Ragen. "The Impact of Social Structure and Aging Individuals." In *Handbook of the Psychology of Aging,* eds. J. E. Birren and K. W. Schaie. New York: Van Nostrand, 1977.

Bennett, D. J. *Nine O'Clock in the Morning.* Plainfield, N.J.: Logos International, 1970.

Bennett, D. J., and R. Bennett. *The Holy Spirit and You.* Plainfield, N.J.: Logos International, 1971.

Bernardo, F. M. "Survivorship and Social Isolation: The Case of the Aging Widower." *The Family Coordinator* 18 (1970), pp. 11–25.

Bird, C. *Everything a Woman Needs to Know to Get Paid What She's Worth.* New York: David McKay, 1973.

Birren, J. E. *The Psychology of Aging.* Englewood Cliffs, N.J.: Prentice Hall, 1964.

Birren, J. E., and associates, eds. *Human Aging I* and *Human Aging II.* Washington, D.C.: National Institute of Mental Health, 1971. DHEW Publications No. ADM- 74-122, ADM-74-123.

Bischof, L. J. *Adult Psychology.* New York: Harper & Row, 1969.

Blau, Z. S. *Old Age in a Changing Society.* New York: Franklin Watts, 1973.

———. "Structural Constraints on Friendships in Old Age." *American Sociological Review* 21 (1961), pp. 429–439.

Bloom, E., and C. E. Kennedy. "The Student and His Parents." *National Association of Women Deans and Counselors* 33 (1970), 3:98–105.

Boggan, E. C., et al. *The Rights of Gay People: An American Civil Liberties Union Handbook.* New York: Dutton, 1975.

Boone, P. *A New Song.* Carol Stream, Ill.: Creation House, 1970.

Boone, S. *One Woman's Liberation.* Carol Stream, Ill.: Creation House, 1972.

Botwinick, J. *Aging and Behavior.* New York: Springer, 1973.

Boylin, W., S. K. Gordon, and M. F. Nehrke. "Reminiscing and Ego Integrity in Institutionalized Elderly Males." *The Gerontologist* 16 (April 1976), 2:118–124.

Braaton, L. J. "The Movement from Non-Self to Self in Psychotherapy." *Journal of Counseling Psychology* 8 (1961), 1:20–24.

Brayfield, A. H., and C. E. Kennedy. "Social Status of Industries." *Journal of Applied Psychology* 38 (1954), 4.

Brody, S. J. "Policy Issues of Women in Transition." *The Gerontologist* 16 (April 1976), 2:181–183.

Bromley, D. B. *The Psychology of Human Ageing.* Baltimore: Penguin Books, 1974.

Brown, B. *New Mind, New Body-Biofeedback: New Directions for the Mind.* New York: Harper & Row, 1974.

Bush, I. E., and V. B. Mahesh. "Hirsuitism and Emotional Tension." *Journal of Endocrinology* 18 (1959), 1.

Butler, R. N. "Guest Editorial: Early Directions for the National Institute on Aging." *The Gerontologist* 16 (August 1976), 4:293–294.

_____. *Why Survive? Being Old in America.* New York: Harper & Row, 1975.

Butler, R. N., and M. I. Lewis. *Sex After Sixty.* New York: Harper & Row, 1976.

Caine, L. *Widow.* New York: Bantam Books, 1974.

Campbell, A. *Seven States of Consciousness.* New York: Harper & Row, 1974.

Carp, F. M. "Ego-Defense or Cognitive Consistency Effects on Environmental Evaluations." *Journal of Gerontology* 30 (November 1975), 11:707–711.

_____. "User Evaluation of Housing for the Elderly." *The Gerontologist* 16 (April 1976), 2:102–111.

Carter, H., and P. C. Glick. *Marriage and Divorce: A Social and Economic Study.* Cambridge, Mass.: Harvard University Press, 1970.

Castaneda, C. *The Teachings of Don Juan: A Yaqui Way of Knowledge.* University of California Press, 1968.

_____. *A Separate Reality.* New York: Simon and Schuster, 1971.

_____. *Journey to Ixtlan.* New York: Simon and Schuster, 1972.

_____. *Tales of Power.* New York: Simon and Schuster, 1974.

Chance, P. "Telepathy Could Be Real." *Psychology Today* 9 (February 1976), p. 40.

Chickering, A. W. "The Developmental and Educational Needs of Adults." Paper presented to annual meeting of the American Personnel and Guidance Association, April 1975, New Orleans.

Chilman, C. S. "Families in Development at Mid-Stage of the Family Life Cycle." *The Family Coordinator* 17 (October 1968), pp. 297–312.

Clark, B. W., and M. Trowe. "The Organizational Context." In *College Peer Groups: Problems and Prospects for Research,* eds. T. M. Newcomb and E. K. Wilson. Chicago: Aldine, 1966.

Clark, M. "A Right to Die," *Newsweek* 86 (November 3, 1975) pp. 58–69.

Clemente, F., P. A. Rexroad, and C. Hirsch. "The Participation of the Black Aged in Voluntary Associations." *Journal of Gerontology* 30 (July 1975), 4:460–472.

Clemons, W., and J. Kroll. "America's Master Novelist." *Newsweek* (September 1, 1975), p. 40.

Cleveland, W. P., and D. T. Gianturco. "Remarriage Probability After Widowhood: A Retrospective Method." *Journal of Gerontology* 31 (January 1975), 1:99–103.

Coleman, R., and B. Neugarten. *Social Status in the City.* San Francisco: Jossey-Bass, 1971.

Coles, R. *Uprooted Children.* New York: Harper & Row, 1970.

Colson, C. W. *Born Again.* Old Tappan, N.J.: Revell, 1976.

Conklin, F. "Should Retired Women Live Together?" *NRTA Journal* 25 (1974), pp. 19–20.

Covan, R. S. "Speculations on Innovations to Conventional Marriage in Old Age." *The Gerontologist* 13 (1973), 4:409–411.

Cumming, E., and W. E. Henry. *Growing Old: The Process of Disengagement.* New York: Basic Books, 1971.

Cutler, N. E., and R. A. Harootyan. "Demography of the Aged." In *Aging,* eds. D. S. Woodruff and J. E. Birren. New York: Van Nostrand, 1975.

Cutler, N. E., and J. R. Schmidhauser. "Age and Political Behavior." In *Aging,* eds. D. S. Woodruff and J. E. Birren. New York: Van Nostrand, 1975.

Danskin, D., and E. D. Walters. "Biofeedback and Voluntary Self-regulation: Counseling and Education." *Personnel and Guidance Journal* 51 (1973), 9:633–638.

Darby, W. J. "Nutrition." In *Family Medical Guide,* ed. D. G. Cooley. Des Moines: Meredith, 1974.

Day, C. *Life with Father.* New York: Knopf, 1935.

Deutscher, I. "The Quality of Post Parental Life." *Journal of Marriage and Family* 26 (February 1964), 1:52–59.

DHEW. "Perspectives." In *Working with Older People: Biological, Sociological, Psychological Aspects of Aging.* Washington, D.C.: Public Health Service Publication. No. HSM-72-6006.

Dollard, J., and N. E. Miller. *Personality and Psychotherapy.* New York: McGraw-Hill, 1950.

Doud, J. J. "Aging as Exchange: A Preface to Theory." *Journal of Gerontology* 30 (September 1975), 5:584–594.

Drevenstedt, J. "Perceptions of Young Adulthood, Middle Age, and Old Age." *Journal of Gerontology* 31 (January 1976), 1:53–57.

Driver, T. F. "Arthur Miller's Pilgrimage." *The Reporter,* (February 27, 1964).

Du Bois, C. *In the Company of Man,* ed. J. B. Casagrande. New York: Harper & Row, 1960.

Duvall, E. M. *Family Development.* Philadelphia: Lippincott, 1967.

Eisdorfer, C. "Adaptation to Loss of Work." In *Retirement,* ed. F. Carp. New York: Behavioral Publications, 1972.

Eisdorfer, C., and M. P. Lawton, eds. *The Psychology of Adult Development and Aging.* Washington, D.C.: American Psychological Association, 1973.

––––––. "Recommendations to the White House Conference on Aging: APA Task Force on Aging." In *The Psychology of Adult Development and Aging.* Washington, D.C.: American Psychological Association, 1973.

Erickson, V. L. "Deliberate Psychological Education for Women: From Iphigenia to Antigone." *Counselor Education and Supervision* 14 (June 1975), pp. 297–309.

Erikson, E. H. *Childhood and Society.* New York: Norton, 1950.

––––––. *Identity: Youth and Crisis.* New York: Norton, 1968.

––––––. *Insight and Responsibility.* New York: Norton, 1964.

Fasteau, M. F. *The Male Machine.* New York: McGraw-Hill, 1974.

Fitzgerald, F. S. *Tender Is the Night.* New York: Scribner, 1934.

Fletcher, J. "New Definitions of Death." *Prism* (January 1974).

Fortune, Great American Scientists. Englewood, N.J.: Prentice-Hall, 1961.

French, J. D. "The Reticular Formation." *Scientific American* (May 1957).

Frenkel-Brunswik, E. "Adjustments and Reorientation in the Course of the Life Span." In *Middle Age and Aging,* ed. B. L. Neugarten. Chicago: University of Chicago Press, 1968.

Fried, B. *The Middle-Age Crisis.* New York: Harper & Row, 1957.

Friedman, M., and R. H. Rosenman. *Type A Behavior and Your Heart.* Greenwich, Conn.: Fawcett Crest, 1975.

Gendlin, E. T. *Experiencing and the Creation of Meaning.* New York: Free Press of Glencoe, 1962.

Gerard, R. W. "What Is Memory?" *Scientific American* (September 1953).

Gerber, I., et al. "Anticipatory Grief and Aged Widows and Widowers." *Journal of Gerontology* 30 (March 1975), 2:225–229.

Gianturco, D. T., D. Raum, and E. W. Erwin. "The Elderly Driver and the Ex-driver." In *Normal Aging II,* ed. E. Palmore. Durham: Duke University Press, 1975.

Glamser, F. D., and G. F. DeJong. "The Efficacy of Preretirement Preparation Programs for Industrial Workers." *Journal of Gerontology* 30 (September 1975), 5:595–600.

Glenn, N. D., and M. Grimes. "Aging, Voting and Political Interest." *American Sociological Review* 33 (1968), pp. 563–575.

Goldschmidt, W. Foreword to *The Teachings of Don Juan: A Yaqui Way of Knowledge,* by C. Castaneda. New York: Ballantine Books, 1969.

Goudy, W. J., E. A. Powers, and P. Keith. "Work and Retirement: A Test of Attitudinal Relationships. *Journal of Gerontology* 30 (March 1975), 2: 193–198.

Gould, R. "Adult Life Stages: Growth Toward Self-Tolerance." *Psychology Today* 8 (February 1975), 1:78.

———. "The Phases of Adult Life: A Study in Developmental Psychology." *American Journal of Psychiatry* 129 (November 1972), 5:521–531.

Goulet, L. R., and P. B. Baltes, eds. *Life-Span Developmental Psychology: Research and Theory.* New York: Academic Press, 1970.

Green, E., and A. Green. "The Ins and Outs of Mind-Body Energy." *Science Year, the World Book Science Annual.* Chicago: Field Enterprises, 1973.

Guhl, A. M. "Pecking Order of Hens." *Scientific American* (October 1954).

Haley, A. *Roots.* New York: Doubleday, 1976.

Harris, L., and associates. *The Myth and Reality of Aging in America.* Washington, D.C.: The National Council on the Aging, 1975.

Hartwig, J. "A Competency-based Approach to Adult Counseling and Guidance." *Counselor Education and Supervision* (September 1975), pp. 12–20.

Hatfield, M. O. *Conflict and Conscience.* Waco, Texas: Word Books, 1971.

Havener, L. "Living Together." *Wheaton Alumni.* Wheaton, Ill: June 1976.

Havighurst, R. J. *Aging in America: Implications for Education.* Washington, D.C.: The National Council on the the Aging, 1976.

———. "History of Developmental Psychology: Socialization and Personality Development Through the Life-Span." In *Life-Span Developmental Psychology: Personality and Socialization,* eds. B. P. Baltes and K. W. Schaie. New York: Academic Press, 1973.

———. *Human Development and Education.* New York: Longmans, Green, 1957.

———. "Understanding the Elderly and the Aging Process." *Journal of Home Economics* 66 (April 1974), 4:17–20.

Havighurst, R. J., B. L. Neugarten, and S. Tobin. "Disengagement and Patterns of Aging." In *Middle Age and Aging,* ed. B. L. Neugarten. Chicago: University of Chicago Press, 1968.

Hayes, M. P., and N. Stinnett. "Life Satisfaction of Middle-Aged Husbands and Wives." *Journal of Home Economics* 63 (1971), pp. 669–674.

Heath, S. R. "The Reasonable Adventurer and Others." *Journal of Counseling Psychology* 6 (1959) 1:3–14.

Hebb, D. O. *The Organization of Behavior.* New York: John Wiley, Inc., 1949.

Heifetz, M. D. *The Right to Die.* Berkeley, Calif.: Berkeley, 1975.

Heisenberg, W. *Physics and Beyond.* New York: Harper Torchbook, 1971.

Hembrough, B. L. "A Two-fold Educational Challenge: The Student Wife and the Mature

Woman Student." *Journal of National Association of Women Deans and Counselors* 20 (1966), 163.

Hemingway, E. *The Old Man and the Sea.* New York: Scribner 1952.

Hendin, D. *Death as a Fact of Life.* New York: Warner Paperback, 1973.

Hendrickson, N. J., D. Perkins, S. White, and T. Buck. "Parent-Daughter Relationships in Fiction." *The Family Coordinator* 24 (July 1975), 3:257–262.

Hershenson, D. B. "Life-Stage Vocational Development System." *Journal of Counseling Psychology* 15 (January 1968), 1:23–30.

Hewes, H. "Quentin's Quest" *Saturday Review* (February 5, 1964).

Heyman, D. K., and D. T. Gianturco. "Long-term Adaptation by the Elderly to Bereavement." *Journal of Gerontology* 28 (1973), 3:359–362.

Hill, R. B. *The Strengths of Black Families.* New York: Emerson Hall, 1972.

Hoffer, E. *The True Believer.* New York: Mentor Books, 1951.

Hoffman, L. W. *The Employed Mother in America.* Chicago: Rand McNally, 1963.

Horney, K. *Our Inner Conflicts: A Constructive Theory of Neurosis.* New York: Norton 1945.

Houston, J. "Putting the First Man on Earth." *Saturday Review* 2 (February 22, 1975), 11:28–32.

Howe, I. *World of Our Fathers: The Journey of the East European Jews to America and the Life They Found and Made.* New York: Harcourt Brace Jovanovich, 1976.

Hoyt, D. P. "Rationality and the Grading Process," *Educational Record* 51 (1970), pp. 305–309.

Hoyt, D. P., and C. E. Kennedy. "Interest and Personality Correlates of Career-Motivated and Homemaking-Motivated College Women." *Journal of Counseling Psychology* 5 (1958), 1:44–49.

Hulicka, I. M., and J. B. Morganti. "An Undergraduate Concentration in the Psychology of Aging: Approach, Program and Evaluation." *Educational Gerontology* 1 (April–June 1976), 2:107–118.

Huxley, A. *Brave New World.* New York: Bantam Books, 1932.

Jackson, D. and N. *Living Together in a World Falling Apart.* Carol Stream, Ill: Creation House, 1974.

Jacobs, J. *Fun City: An Ethnographic Study of a Retirement Community.* New York: Holt, Rinehart and Winston, 1974.

James, W. *Varieties of Religious Experience.* New York: Mentor Books, 1952.

Jewson, R. H. "Trends and Resources for Community Family Life Education Programs." Paper presented to annual meeting of the American Home Economics Association, 1976, Minneapolis.

Jones, J. *From Here to Eternity.* New York: Signet Books, 1953.

Jung, C. *The Undiscovered Self.* New York: Mentor Books, 1959.

Kahl, J. A., and J. M. Goering. "Stable Workers, Black and White." *Social Problems* (Winter 1971), pp. 306–318.

Kaplan, J. "The Family in Aging." *The Gerontologist* 15 (October 1975), 5:385.

———. "The New Age of Old Age." *The Gerontologist* 15 (December 1975), 6:485.

Kardiner, A. *Psychological Frontiers of Society.* New York: Columbia University Press, 1945.

Katz, M. M. "What This Country Needs Is a Safe Five-Cent Intoxicant." *Psychology Today* 4 (February 1971), 9:28–30.

Kazin, A. Quoted in I. Howe, *World of Our Fathers.* New York: Harcourt Brace Jovanovich, 1976.

Keen, S. "The Cosmic Versus the Rational." *Psychology Today* 8 (July 1974), 2:56.

Kelly, J. R. "Work and Leisure: A Simplified Paradigm." *Journal of Leisure Research* 4 (1972), 1:50–62.

Kelly, O. *Make Today Count.* New York: Delacorte Press, 1976.

Kelly, W. "Until Tomorrow Comes." *Guideposts* (April 1976) pp. 2–6.

Kelsey, M. *Encounter with God.* Minneapolis: Bethany Fellowship, 1972.

Keniston, K. *The Uncommitted: Alienated Youth in American Society.* New York: Harcourt Brace Jovanovich, 1965.

———. *Young Radicals: Notes on Committed Youth.* New York: Harcourt Brace Jovanovich, 1968.

———. "Youth: A 'New' Stage of Life." *American Scholar.* (Autumn 1970), pp. 631–654.

Kennedy, C. E. "After the Fall: One Man's Look at His Human Nature." *Journal of Counseling Psychology* 12 (Summer 1965), 2.

———. "He Hauls Furniture—and Kids" *Power Magazine* 12 (August 22, 1954) 3:1–3.

———. "Patterns of Parent-Student Communication," *Journal of Home Economics* 63 (1971), 7:513–520.

Kennedy, C. E., and J. Southwick. "Inservice Program for Family Life Educators: Cooperative Program with Mental Health Centers and University." *The Family Coordinator,* 24 (Jan. 1975), 1:75–79.

Kerschner, P. A., and I. S. Hirschfield. "Public Policy and Aging: Analytic Approaches." In *Aging,* eds. D. S. Woodruff and J. E. Birren. New York: Van Nostrand 1975.

Kimmel, D. C. *Adulthood and Aging.* New York: Wiley, 1975.

Kinsey, A. C., and associates. *Sexual Behavior in the Human Female.* Philadelphia: Saunders, 1953.

Kohlberg, L., and R. Kramer. "Continuities and Discontinuities in Childhood and Adult Moral Development." *Human Development* 12 (1969), pp. 93–120.

Kosberg, J. I., and J. F. Gorman. "Perceptions Toward the Rehabilitation Potential of Institutionalized Aged." *The Gerontologist* 15 (October 1975, Part I), 5:398–403.

Kreps, J. M. "The Allocation of Leisure in Retirement." In *The Retirement Process,* ed. F. M. Carp. Washington, D.C.: U.S. Government Printing Office, 1966.

Krishna, G. *The Awakening of Kundalini.* New York: Dutton, 1975.

Kubler-Ross, E. *On Death and Dying.* New York: Macmillan, 1969.

———. "When Face to Face with Death." *Readers Digest* 109 (August 1976), 652:81–84.

Lask, J. P. *Eleanor and Franklin.* New York: Norton, 1971.

Leaf, A. "Every Day Is a Gift When You Are Over 100." *National Geographic* 143 (January 1973), pp. 93–119.

———. *Youth in Old Age.* New York: McGraw-Hill, 1975.

Lecky, P. *Self Consistency.* New York: Island Press, 1945.

Leherman, M. A., and A. S. Caplan. "Distance from Death as a Variable in the Study of Aging." *Developmental Psychology* 2 (1969), 1:71–84.

Lendemann, E. "Symptomatology and Management of Acute Grief." *American Journal of Psychiatry* 101 (1944–45), pp. 141–148.

LeMasters, E. E. *Parents in Modern America.* Homewood, Ill: The Dorsey Press, 1970.

LeShan L. "The Case for Meditation." *Saturday Review* 2 (February 22, 1975), 11:26–27.

_____. "Physicists and Mystics: Similarities in World View," in *The Medium, the Mystic and the Physicist*, ed. L. LeShan. New York: Viking Press, 1974.

Levi, L. *Stress.* New York: Liveright, 1967.

Levin, R. J., and A. Levin. "Sexual Pleasure: The Surprising Preferences of 100,000 Women." *Redbook* Magazine (September 1975), pp. 51–58.

Levinson, D., et al. "Periods in the Adult Development of Men: Ages 18–45." *The Counseling Psychologist* 6 (1976), 1:21–25.

_____. "The Psychosocial Development of Men in Early Adulthood and the Mid-Life Transition." In *Life History Research in Psychopathology*, vol. 3, eds, D. F. Ricks, A. Thomas, and M. Roff. Minneapolis: University of Minnesota Press, 1974.

Levinson Gerontological Policy Institute, Brandeis University. *Alternatives to Nursing Home Care: A Proposal.* U.S. Senate Special Committee on Aging. Washington, D.C.: U.S. Government Printing Office, 1971.

Lewis, S. *Arrowsmith.* New York: Harcourt Brace Jovanovich, 1925.

_____. *Babbitt.* New York: Harcourt Brace Jovanovich, 1922.

_____. *Cas Timberlane.* New York: Random House, 1945.

_____. *Dodsworth.* New York: Harcourt Brace Jovanovich, 1929.

_____. *Main Street.* New York: Harcourt Brace Jovanovich, 1920.

Lilly, J. *Center of the Cyclone.* New York: Julian Press, 1972.

Loevinger, J., and R. Wessler. *Measuring Ego Development.* San Francisco: Jossey-Bass, 1970.

Lopata, H. Z. *Widowhood in an American City.* Cambridge, Mass.: Schenkman, 1973.

Lowenthal, M. F. "Psychosocial Variations Across the Adult Life Course: Frontiers for Research and Policy." *The Gerontologist* 15 (February 1975, Part 1), 1:6–12.

Lowenthal, M. F., and D. Chiriboga. "Social Stress and Adaptation: Toward a Life Course Perspective." In *The Psychology of Adult Development and Aging*, eds. C. Eisdorfer and M. P. Lawton. Washington, D.C.: American Psychological Association, 1973.

Lowenthal, M. F., M. T. Thurnher, and D. Chiriboga. *Four Stages of Life.* San Francisco: Jossey-Bass, 1975.

Luce, G. G. "Biological Rhythms." In *The Nature of Human Consciousness,* ed. R. E. Ornstein. San Francisco: Freeman, 1973.

_____. *Body Time.* New York: Random House, 1971.

Maas, H. S., and J. A. Kuypers. *From Thirty to Seventy.* San Francisco: Jossey- Bass, 1974.

Maddox, G. L. "Retirement as a Social Event in the United States." In *Middle Age and Aging,* ed. B. L. Neugarten. Chicago: University of Chicago Press, 1968.

Maloney, G. A. *The Breath of the Mystic.* Denville, N.J.: Dimension Books, 1974.

Manvill, R. *Chaplin.* Boston: Little, Brown, 1972.

Marquand, J. P. *The Late George Apley.* Boston: Little, Brown, 1937.

Marshall, C. *Something More.* New York: McGraw-Hill, 1974.

Maslow, A. H. *Motivation and Personality.* New York: Harper & Row 1970.

_____. *The Farther Reaches of Human Nature.* New York: Viking Press, 1971.

Masters, W. H., and V. E. Johnson. *Human Sexual Response.* Boston: Little, Brown, 1966.

_____. *The Pleasure Bond.* Boston: Little, Brown, 1975.

Maugham, W. S. *Of Human Bondage.* Garden City, N.Y.: Doubleday, 1915.

May, R. "Existential Psychiatry: An Evaluation." *Journal of Religion and Health* 1 (1961), 1.
———. *Love and Will.* New York: Dell, 1974.

McClelland, D. C. "The Power of Positive Drinking." *Psychology Today* 4 (January 1971), 8:40.
———. *Roots of Consciousness.* Princeton, N. J.: Van Nostrand, 1964.

McLuhan, M., and Q. Fiore. *The Medium Is the Massage.* New York: Bantam Books, 1967.

McQuade, W., and A. Aikman. *Stress.* New York: Bantam Books, 1974.

Mead, G. H. *Mind, Self and Society.* Chicago: University of Chicago Press, 1934.

Mead, M. *An Anthropologist at Work.* Boston: Houghton Mifflin, 1959.

Melzack, R. *The Puzzle of Pain.* New York: Basic Books, 1973.

Meyer, R. and Meyer, N. "Setting the Stage for Lincoln Center." *Theatre Arts* (January 1964).

Milbrath, L. W. *Political Participation.* Chicago: Rand McNally, 1965.

Miller, A. *After the Fall.* New York: Viking Press, 1963.
———. *Death of a Salesman.* New York: Viking Press, 1949.
———. "With Respect for her Agony—But with Love." *Life* (February 7, 1964).

Mitchell, E. D. "Outer Space to Inner Space: An Astronaut's Odyssey." *Saturday Review* 2 (February 22, 1975), 11:20–21.

Mondale, W. S. "The Lifetime Learning Act: Proposed Legislation." *The Counseling Psychologist* 6 (1976), 1:67.

Monroe, R. *Journeys Out of the Body.* Garden City, N.Y.: Doubleday, 1971.

Montgomery, J. E. "Magna Carta of the Aged," *Journal of Home Economics* 65 (April 1973), pp. 12–13.

Mortimer, J. "Occupational Values Socialization in Business and Professional Families." *Sociology of Work and Occupations* 2 (February 1975), 1:29.

Moss, F. "Nursing Home Care in the United States: Failure in Public Policy." Subcommittee Report on Long-term Care of the Aged. Washington, D.C.: U.S. Government Printing Office, 1975. p. xii.

Mowrer, O. H. *Kentucky Symposium: Learning Theory and Clinical Research.* New York: John Wiley 1954.
———. *Psychotherapy: Theory and Research.* New York: Ronald Press, 1953.

Murray, H. A. *Explorations in Personality: A Clinical and Experimental Study of Fifty Men of College Age.* New York: Science Editions, 1938, 2nd printing, 1965.

National Commission on Family life Education. "Family life Education Programs: Principles, Plans, Procedures." *The Family Coordinator* (July 1968), pp. 211–214.

Nesselroade, J. R., and H. Y. Reese, eds. *Life-Span Developmental Psychology: Methodological Issues.* New York: Academic Press, 1973.

Neugarten, B. L. "Adult Personality: Toward a Psychology of the Life Cycle." In *Middle Age and Aging,* ed. B. L. Neugarten. Chicago: University of Chicago Press, 1968.
———. "Age Groups in American Society and the Rise of the Young-Old." *Annals of the American Academy of Political and Social Science* (Sept. 1974), pp. 187–198.
———. "The Awareness of Middle Age." In *Middle Age and Aging,* ed. B. L. Neugarten. Chicago: University of Chicago Press, 1968.
———. "The Future and the Young-Old." *The Gerontologist* 15 (February 1975, Part II), 1:4–9.

_____. "Personality Change in Late Life: A Developmental Perspective." In *The Psychology of Adult Development and Aging,* eds. C. Eisdorfer and M. P. Lawton. Washington, D.C.: American Psychological Association, 1973.

Neugarten, B. L., and associates. *Personality in Middle and Late Life.* New York: Atherton Press, 1964.

Neugarten, B. L., and N. Datan. "Sociological Perspectives on the Life Cycle." In *Life-Span Developmental Psychology: Personality and Socialization,* eds. P. B. Baltes and K. W. Schaie, New York: Academic Press, 1973.

Neugarten, B. L., R. J. Havighurst, and S. Tobin. "Personality and Patterns of Aging." In *Middle Age and Aging,* ed. B. L. Neugarten. Chicago: University of Chicago Press, 1968.

Neugarten, B. L., and J. W. Moore. "The Changing Age-Status System." In *Middle Age and Aging,* ed. B. L. Neugarten. Chicago: University of Chicago Press, 1968.

Neugarten, B. L., J. W. Moore, and J. C. Lowe. "Age Norms, Age Constraints, and Adult Socialization." *American Journal of Sociology* 70 (May 1965), 6.

Neugarten, B. L., and K. Weinstein. "The Changing American Grandparent." *Journal of Marriage and the Family* 26 (May 1964), 2.

Newcomer, R., et al. "Assessing the Need for Semi-Dependent Housing for the Elderly." *The Gerontologist* 16 (April 1976), 2:112–117.

Newman, F. "A Preview of the Second Newman Report." *Change* (May 1972), pp. 28–37.

_____. *Report on Higher Education.* Washington, D. C.: HEW U.S. Government Printing Office, 1971.

Niebuhr, R. *The Nature and Destiny of Man.* New York: Scribner, 1943.

Noyes, R., and R. Kletti. *Psychiatry* 39 (1976), pp. 19–27.

Nye, F. I., and F. M. Bernardo. *Emerging Conceptual Frameworks in Family Analysis.* New York: Macmillan, 1967.

Ornstein, R. E. *The Psychology of Consciousness.* San Francisco: Freeman, 1972.

Orwell, G. *Animal Farm.* New York: Harcourt Brace Jovanovich, 1946.

Palmore, E. *The Honorable Elders: A Cross-Cultural Analysis of Aging in Japan.* Durham: Duke University Press, 1975.

_____, ed. *Normal Aging II.* Durham: Duke University Press, 1974.

_____. "Predicting Longevity: A New Method." In *Normal Aging II,* ed. E. Palmore. Durham: Duke University Press, 1974.

_____. "The Status and Integration of the Aged in Japanese Society." *Journal of Gerontology* 30 (March 1975), 2:199–208.

Palmore, E., and K. Manton. "Agism Compared to Racism and Sexism." *Journal of Gerontology* 28 (July 1973), 3:363–369.

Palmore, E., G. L. Stanley, and R. H. Cormier. "Widows with Children Under Social Security. U.S. Department of HEW. Washington, D.C.: Government Printing Office, 1966.

Parkes, C. M. *Bereavement: Studies of Grief in Adult Life.* New York: International Universities Press, 1972.

Perkins, H. V. *Human Development.* Belmont, Calif.: Wadsworth, 1975.

Peters, G., and C. E. Kennedy. "Close Friendships in the College Community," *Journal of College Student Personnel* 11 (November 1970), 6:449–456.

Peterson, D. A., and E. L. Karnes. "Older People in Adolescent Literature." *The Gerontologist* 16 (June 1976), 3:225–231.

Peterson, D. A., C. Powell, and L. Robertson. "Aging in America: Toward the Year 2000." *The Gerontologist* 16 (June 1976), 3:264.

Pfeiffer, E., and G. C. Davis. "The Use of Leisure in Middle Life." *The Gerontologist* 11 (1971, Part 1), 3:187–195.

Pineo, P. C. "Disenchantment in the Later Years of Marriage." *Marriage and Family Living* 23 (1961), pp. 3–11.

Pines, M. "The Riddle of Recall and Forgetfulness." *Saturday Review* 2 (August 9, 1975), p. 23.

Ponti, C. *Supersenses.* New York: Quadrangle, New York Times Book, 1974.

Pressey, S. L. "Age Counseling: Crises, Services, Potentials." *Journal of Counseling Psychology* 20 (1973), 4:356–360.

Pressey, S. L., and A. D. Pressey. "Major Neglected Need Opportunity: Old Age Counseling." *Journal of Counseling Psychology* 19 (1972), 5:362–366.

Randel, W. P. "America in the World." *American Issues Forum.* Washington, D.C.: The National Council on the Aging, 1976.

————. "Certain Unalienable Rights." *American Issues Forum.* Washington, D.C.: The National Council on the Aging, November 1975.

Rasch, J. D. "Institutional Origins of Articles in *The Gerontologist* 1961–1975." *The Gerontologist* 16 (June 1976), 3:276–279.

Raushenbush, E. *The Student and His Studies.* Middletown, Conn.: Wesleyan University Press, 1964.

Reissman, L. "Levels of Aspiration and Social Class." *American Psychologist* 18 (1953), pp. 233–242.

Richardson, D. *Peace Child.* Glendale, Calif.: Regal Books, 1974.

Richardson, M. S. "Self Concepts and Role Concepts in the Career Orientation of College Women." *Journal of Counseling Psychology* 22 (1975), pp. 122–126.

Richardson, M. S., and J. L. Alpert. "Role Perceptions of Educated Adult Women: An Exploratory Study." *Educational Gerontology* 1 (April–June 1976), 2:171–185.

Riley, M. W., A. Foner, and associates. *Aging and Society: Volume I, An Inventory of Research Findings.* New York: Russell Sage Foundation, 1968.

Ring, K. "A Transpersonal View of Consciousness: A Mapping of Farther Reaches of Inner Space." *The Journal of Transpersonal Psychology* 6 (1974), 2:125–155.

Ringwald, B., et al. "Conflict and Style in the Classroom." *Psychology Today,* (February 1971).

Roberts, T. B. *Four Psychologies Applied to Education.* New York: Schenkman, 1975.

Robertson, J. F. "Significance of Grandparents: Perceptions of Young Adult Grandchildren." *The Gerontologist* 16 (April 1976), 2:137–140.

Rodgers, R. H. *Family Interaction and Transaction.* Englewood Cliffs, N.J.: Prentice-Hall, 1973.

Roe, A. *The Making of a Scientist.* New York: Dodd, Mead, 1953.

Rogers, C. R. "Empathic: An Unappreciated Way of Being." *The Counseling Psychologist* 5 (1975), 2:2–10.

————. *On Becoming a Person.* Boston: Houghton Mifflin, 1961.

Rooney, J. F. "Friendship and Disaffiliation Among the Skid Row Population." *Journal of Gerontology* 31 (January 1976), 1:82–88.

Rosen, B. C. "The Achievement Syndrome: A Psychocultural Dimension of Social Stratification." *American Sociological Review* 21 (1956), pp. 203–211.

Rosow, J. M. *The Worker and the Job.* Englewood Cliffs, N.J.: Prentice-Hall, 1974.

Rubin, K. H., and I. D. R. Brown. "A Life-Span Look at Person Perception and Its Relationship to Communications Interaction." *Journal of Gerontology* 30 (July 1975), 4:461–468.

Sanford, N. *College and Character.* New York: Wiley, 1964, p. 87.

———. *The American College.* New York: Wiley, 1962.

Sargent, J. D., E. E. Green, and E. D. Walters. "Preliminary Report on the Use of Autogenic Feedback Training in the Treatment of Migraine and Tension Headaches." *Psychosomatic Medicine* 35 (1973), pp. 129–135.

Sargent, J. D., E. D. Walters, and E. E. Green. "Psychosomatic Self-regulation of Migraine Headaches." *Seminars in Psychiatry* 5 (November 1973), pp. 415–428.

Schlossberg, N. "The Case for Counseling Adults." *The Counseling Psychologist* 6 (1976), 1:33–36.

Schmerl, E. F. "In the Name of the Elder—An Essay." *The Gerontologist* 15 (October 1975), 5:386.

Schmidt, L. D. "Issues in Counseling Older People." *Educational Gerontology* 1 (April–June 1976), 2:187–192.

Seeley, J. R., R. A. Sim, and E. W. Loosley. *Crestwood Heights.* New York: Wiley, 1956.

Seidenberg, R. *Corporate Wives—Corporate Casualties?* New York: Anchor Books, 1975.

Seligman, M. E. P. *Helplessness: On Depression, Development, and Death.* New York: Freeman, 1975.

Seltzer, M. M. "Women and Sociogerontology." *The Gerontologist* 15 (December 1975), 6:483–484.

Selye, H. *Stress of Life.* New York: McGraw-Hill, 1956.

———. *Stress Without Distress.* Philadelphia: Lippincott, 1974.

Setlow, C. *Aging in America: Implications for Society.* Washington, D.C.: The National Council on the Aging, 1976.

Shanas, E. "Gerontology and the Social and Behavioral Sciences: Where Do We Go From Here?" *The Gerontologist* 15 (December 1975), 6:499–502.

Shanas, E., and associates. *Old People in Three Industrial Societies.* New York: Atherton Press, 1968.

Sheehy, G. *Passages: Predictable Crises of Adult Life.* New York: Dutton, 1976.

Sherman, S. R. "Mutual Assistance and Support in Retirement Housing." *Journal of Gerontology* 30 (July 1975), 4:479–483.

Shoben, E. J. "Work, Love and Maturity." *Personnel and Guidance Journal* (February 1956), pp. 326–332.

Simpson, R. "Review Symposium on Work in America." *Sociology of Work and Occupations* 2 (May 1975), 2:182–187.

Sistrunk, J. "Community Attitudes Affect Post High School Plans," *Student Development Series.* Manhattan, Kansas: Department of Family and Child Development, Kansas State University, 1972.

Sistrunk (McNeil), J., A. Fretwell, and C. E. Kennedy. *Windows into Student Life: Growth and Change During College Years.* Manhattan, Kansas: Kansas State University, 1972.

Skolnick, A., and J. H. Skolnick. *Family in Transition.* Boston: Little, Brown, 1971.

Smith, A. *Powers of the Mind.* New York: Random House, 1975.

Smith, B. W., and J. Hiltner. "Intraurban Location of the Elderly." *Journal of Gerontology* 30 (July 1975), 4:473–478.

Snyder, S. H. "Amphetamine—A Sketch." *Psychology Today,* 5 (January 1972) 8:45.

Sperry, R. W. "Left-Brain, Right-Brain." *Saturday Review* 2 (August 9, 1975) 20:30–33.

Spitz, R. "Hospitalism: An Inquiry into the Genesis of Psychiatric Conditions in Early Childhood." *The Psychoanalytic Study of the Child* 1. 1 (1945) pp. 53–74, 1945.

Stapleton, R. C. *The Gift of Inner Healing.* Waco, Texas: Word Books, 1976.

Stephenson, R. R. "Occupational Choice as a Crystalized Self Concept." *Journal of Counseling Psychology* 8 (1961), 3.

Stinnett, N. and J. Walters. *Relationships in Marriage and Family.* New York: Macmillan, 1977.

Stith, M. "Child-Rearing Attitudes in Three-Generation Households." Ph.D. dissertation. Florida State University, 1961.

Stringfellow, W. *Free in Obedience.* New York: Seabury Press, 1964.

Strong, E. K., Jr. "Permanence of Interest Scores Over 22 Years." *Journal of Applied Psychology* 35 (1951), pp. 89–91.

Super, D. E. *Psychology of Careers.* New York: Harper & Row, 1957.

Sussman, M. S., and L. Burchinal. "Kin Family Network: Unheralded Structure in Current Conceptualizations of Family Functioning." *Marriage and Family Living* 24 (August 1962) 3.

Sutich, A. J. "The Emergence of the Transpersonal Orientation: A Personal Account." *Journal of Transpersonal Psychology* 8 (1976), pp. 5–19.

Taietz, P. "Two Conceptual Models of the Senior Center." *Journal of Gerontology* 31 (March 1976), 2:219–222.

Tart, C. T. "The Basic Nature of Altered States of Consciousness: A Systems Approach." *Journal of Transpersonal Psychology* 8 (1976), 1:45–64.

————. "States of Consciousness and State-Specific Sciences." *Science* 176 (June 16, 1972), pp. 1203–1210.

Taylor, J. "The Relationship of Life Satisfaction and the Determinants Associated with the Fourth Decade of Life." Ph.D. dissertation, Kansas State University, 1975.

Teitz, J. *What's a Nice Girl Like You Doing in a Place Like This?* New York: Coward-McCann & Geoghegan, 1972.

Terkel, S. *Working.* New York: Avon Books. 1974.

Thurnher, M. T. "Family Confluence, Conflict and Affect." In *Four Stages of Life,* ed. M. F. Lowenthal et al. San Francisco: Jossey-Bass, 1975.

Tournier, P. *The Meaning of Persons.* New York: Harper & Row, 1957.

Townsend, P. "The Emergence of the Four-Generation Family in Industrial Society." In *Middle Age and Aging,* ed. B. L. Neugarten. Chicago: University of Chicago Press, 1968.

Treas, J., and A. Van Hilst. "Marriage and Remarriage Rates Among Older Americans." *The Gerontologist* 16 (April 1976), 2:132–136.

Trent, J. W., and L. L. Medsker. *Beyond High School.* San Francisco: Jossey-Bass, 1968.

Troll, L., and N. Schlossberg. "How 'Age-biased' Are College Counselors?" *Industrial Gerontology* (Summer 1971), pp. 14–20.

Verba, S., and N. H. Nie. *Participation in America.* New York: Harper & Row, 1972.

Vorspan, A. *Mazel Tov! You're Middle-Aged.* Garden City, N. Y.: Doubleday, 1974.

Walker III, S. "Blood Sugar and Emotional Storms: Sugar Doctors Push Hypoglycemia." *Psychology Today* 9 (July 1975), 2:69–74.

Wallace, R. R., and H. Benson. "The Physiology of Mediation." *Scientific American* 226 (February 1972), pp. 85–90.

Warner, W. L., R. J. Havighurst, and M. B. Loeb. *Who Shall Be Educated?* New York: Harper & Row, 1944.

Waters, E., S. Fink, and B. White. "Peer Group Counseling for Older People." *Educational Gerontology* 1 (April–June 1976), 2:157–170.

Watson, G. *Nutrition and Your Mind: The Psychochemical Response.* New York: Harper & Row, 1972.

Watthana-Kasetr, S., and P. S. Spiers. "Geographic Mortality Rates and Rates of Aging—A Possible Relationship?" *Journal of Gerontology* 28 (July 1973) 3:374–379.

Wead, R. D. *Catholic Charismatics.* Carol Stream, Ill.: Creation House, 1973.

Weg, R. B. "Women and Biogerontology," *The Gerontologist* 15 (December 1975), 6:483.

Weil, A. *The Natural Mind.* Boston: Houghton-Mifflin, 1972.

Weinbergen, L. E., and J. Milham. "A Multi-Dimensional, Multiple Method Analysis of Attitudes Toward the Elderly." *Journal of Gerontology* 30 (May 1975), 3:343–348.

Weiss, R. S. *Marital Separation.* New York: Basic Books, 1975.

White, R. W. *The Enterprise of Living* New York: Holt, Rinehart and Winston, 1972.

———. "The Healthy Personality." *The Counseling Psychologist* 4 (1973), 2:7–8.

———. *Lives in Progress: A Study of the Natural Growth of Personality.* New York: Holt, Rinehart and Winston, 1966.

———. "Motivation Reconsidered: The Concept of Competance." *Psychological Review* 66 (1959), pp. 297–333.

———. ed., *Study of Lives.* New York: Atherton Press, 1963.

Widick, C., L. L. Knefelkamp, and C. A. Parker. "The Counselor as a Developmental Instructor." *Counselor Education and Supervision* 14 (June 1975), pp. 286–296.

Wilensky, H. L. "Orderly Careers and Social Participation: The Impact of Work History on Social Integration in the Middle Mass." *American Sociological Review* 26 (August 1961), 4.

Williams, J. W., and M. Stith. *Middle Childhood: Behavior and Development.* New York: Macmillan, 1974.

Wolfe, T. *You Can't Go Home Again.* New York: Harper & Row, 1940.

Woodring, P. "Why 65? The Case Against Mandatory Retirement." *Saturday Review* 3 (August 7, 1976), 22:18–20.

Woodruff, D. S. "Introduction: Multidisciplinary Perspectives of Aging." In *Aging,* eds. D. S. Woodruff and J. E. Birren. New York: Van Nostrand, 1975.

Woodruff, D. S. and J. E. Birren, eds. *Aging: Scientific Perspectives and Social Issues.* New York: Van Nostrand, 1975.

Wyly, M. V., and I. M. Hulicka. "Problems and Compensations of Widowhood: A Comparison of Age Groups." Paper presented to annual meeting of the American Psychological Association, 1975. Department of Psychology, State University College at Buffalo, New York.

Yankelovich, D. "The Meaning of Work." In *The Worker and the Job,* ed. J. M. Rosow. Englewood Cliffs, N. J.: Prentice-Hall, 1974.

———. *The New Morality: A Profile of American Youth in the 70s.* New York: McGraw-Hill, 1974.

Zubin, J. "Foundations of Gerontology: History, Training, and Methodology." In *The Psychology of Adult Development and Aging,* eds. C. Eisdorfer and M. P. Lawton. Washington, D.C.: American Psychological Association, 1973.

Name Index

A

Adorno, T. W., 146
Agee, J., 45, 207
Aikman, A., 126, 127, 252
Albee, E., 265
Albrecht, G. L., 45
Allport, G. W., 41, 209
Alpert, J. L., 105
Alsop, S., 176
Alter, M., 26
Aronoff, C., 360
Ashton-Warner, S., 254
Astin, H. S., 351
Atchley, R. C., 208, 369
Auerbach, C., 25

B

Baltes, P. B., 187, 189, 287, 316, 317
Beauvoir, S. de, 157
Becker, E., 324
Becker, H. S., 100
Bekker, L. D., 297
Bellamy, E., 93
Bellow, S., 287
Bellucci, G., 22
Benedek, J., 245

Benedict, R., 30, 103, 104
Benet, S. V., 45
Bengtson, V. L., 19, 30, 45, 113, 203, 364
Bennett, D. J., 177, 179
Bennett, R., 177
Benson, H., 175
Bernardo, F. M., 49, 86
Best, C. H., 130
Binstock, R., 364
Bird, C., 107
Birren, J. E., 10, 16, 19, 30, 82, 122, 130, 202, 205, 314, 362, 363
Bischof, L. J., 89
Blanton, S., 289
Blatty, W. P., 183
Blau, Z. S., 87, 296, 302
Blazer, D., 184
Bloom, E., 228
Boggan, E. C., 67
Boone, P., 265, 266, 268
Boone, S., 265, 266, 268
Botwinick, J., 319, 320
Boylin, W., 149
Braaton, L. J., 151
Bradstreet, S., 303
Brayfield, A. H., 97
Brody, S. J., 107
Bromley, D. B., 121, 123, 130

M

Maas, H. S., 50, 199, 200, 201, 330, 331
McClelland, D. C., 98, 169
McLuhan, M., 29
McQuade, W., 126, 127, 252
Maddox, B., 113
Maddox, G. L., 103
Mahesh, V. B., 26
Maloney, G. A., 176
Manney, J. D., 337
Manton, K., 27
Manvill, R., 313
Marquand, J. P., 292
Marshall, C., 91, 177
Maslow, A. H., 24, 141, 162
Masters, W. H., 78, 283
Maugham, W. S., 239
May, R., 269–70
Mead, G. H., 138
Mead, M., 103, 104, 105
Medsker, L. L., 221, 222
Melzack, R., 124
Menninger, R., 176
Meyerhoff, B. G., 209
Milbrath, L. W., 364
Milham, J., 31
Miller, A., 93, 260
Miller, N. E., 151
Mitchell, E. D., 181
Mondale, W. S., 349
Monroe, R., 162
Montgomery, J. E., 300
Moore, J. W., 34, 37, 73, 89, 211, 236, 251, 277
Morgan, G. B., 331, 332–33, 334
Morganti, J. B., 367
Moss, F., 354
Moustakas, C., 157
Mowrer, O. H., 141, 146
Murray, H. A., 138, 152, 205, 209
Musser, J., 370

N

Nehrke, M. F., 149
Nesselroade, J. R., 187
Neugarten, B. L., 14, 34, 37, 50, 51, 73, 89, 103, 188, 191, 192, 193, 194, 195, 211, 236, 251, 264, 276, 277, 279, 283, 285, 287, 331
Newcomb, T. M., 223, 245
Newman, F., 212, 222
Nie, N. H., 363
Niebuhr, R., 179
Noyes, R., 160
Nye, F. I., 49

O

Ogg, W., 227
Olmstead, A. H., 369
Ornstein, R. E., 125, 178
Orwell, G., 27
Ostrander, S., 183
Otto, H. A., 112

P

Palm, J. D., 130
Palmore, E., 9, 27, 29, 88, 184, 201, 202, 312, 321
Parker, C. A., 229
Parkes, C. M., 327, 329
Perkins, D., 207
Perkins, H. V., 42, 119, 155
Peters, G., 228
Peterson, D. A., 360, 363
Pfeiffer, E., 345
Phillips, J. R., 370
Pickett, E., 369
Pineo, P. C., 77
Pines, M., 315
Ponti, C., 171
Porter, L. W., 16
Potok, C., 245
Powell, C., 363
Powell, J., 157
Powers, E. A., 111, 338

Subject Index